Advanced Financial Accounting

Second Edition

Advanced Financial Accounting

Second Edition

John Samuels
Colin Rickwood
Andrew Piper

McGRAW-HILL Book Company (UK) Limited

London • New York • St Louis • San Francisco • Auckland • Bogotá • Guatemala
Hamburg • Lisbon • Madrid • Mexico • Montreal • New Delhi • Panama • Paris
San Juan • São Paulo • Singapore • Sydney • Tokyo • Toronto

Published by

McGRAW-HILL Book Company (UK) Limited

MAIDENHEAD • BERKSHIRE • ENGLAND

British Library Cataloguing in Publication Data
Samuels, John 1938–
  Advanced financial accounting.—2nd ed
  1. Financial accounting
  I. Title   II. Rickwood, Colin 1947–
  III. Piper, A. G. (Andrew George), 1929–
  657'.48
  ISBN 0-07-084182-9

Library of Congress Cataloging-in-Publication Data
Samuels, J. M. (John Malcolm), 1938–
  Advanced financial accounting.

  Includes bibliographical references and index.
  1. Accounting.   I. Rickwood, Colin.   II. Piper, Andrew.   III. Title.
  HF5635.S19   1989   657'.046   88—28006
  ISBN 0-07-084182-9

1234IL 8909

Typeset, printed and bound
by Interprint Limited, Malta.

Contents

CONTENTS

Preface

In 1981 the first edition of this book described accounting as fast changing. The output of pronouncements provides evidence to support such a description. During the past seven years the UK Accounting Standards Committee has produced 14 exposure drafts, issued 6 new standards and revised 4 others; the number of international standards has doubled from 13 to 26; the 1981 Companies Bill has become an Act consolidated in the Companies Act, 1985.

Just as in periods before 1981, the development of accounting since that period has not been simply an expansion into new areas. Chapter 1 discusses the lack of an agreed set of principles, the lack of an agreed conceptual framework. As a result, unique solutions to accounting problems are not available. Instead alternatives can be generated, and the selection of a standard will depend partly on the conditions existing at the time of selection. Progress involves reviewing past practice in the light of change, and turning attention to areas that present problems of particular importance currently. Solutions are never final.

Although the changes since the first edition have meant that there was a considerable need for revision and expansion, the underlying foundations and structure remain.

Standard setters have placed more emphasis on leases and pensions and this is reflected in this book by the devotion of whole chapters to these topics. A new chapter has been added to examine the needs of special purpose transactions, and, in an expanded volume, all chapters have been updated and revised to respond to the developments in accounting theory and company law.

The book is complemented by the publication of a workbook which provides further illustrations of practical, worked examples and more problems for self-examination.

We are grateful to many for their help and in particular would like to thank Guy Loveday of Chart Tutors, for making available some questions he has devised; the Institute of Chartered Accountants in England and Wales, and the Chartered Association of Certified Accountants for permission to reproduce certain of their examination questions, and Karen Hanson, Frances Landreth, Maureen Leveson and Sue Urquhart for their valuable assistance in preparing a readable typescript of the book.

J.M.S.
C.P.R.
A.G.P.

1. Theoretical foundations

A theory is 'a system of rules, procedures and assumptions used to produce a result'.[1] One result—a very important result of the financial accounting exercise undertaken within a company—is the annual production of a balance sheet and a profit and loss account. What is the nature and purpose of these corporate financial reports? What are they designed to achieve? What is the financial accounting theory that underlies the production of such statements?

These questions are not easy to answer. The American Accounting Association (AAA) concluded in 1977 that 'a single universally accepted basic accounting theory does not exist at the present time'.[2] It still does not. Much effort has been devoted to the development of a theory of accounting that is logical, with a consistent system of rules, procedures and assumptions. This chapter will consider the literature that deals with this objective. Accounting has developed as a practical subject, with decisions being made as to which alternative accounting treatment should be followed, but it is based unfortunately on an inconsistent set of rules and assumptions.

Without a theory to settle the question of which accounting practices ought to be employed, either the law or the pronouncements of an accounting standards body have been used to achieve some degree of uniformity. While this may give the impression that financial accounting practice is dominated by compulsion and restriction, the lack of a universal theory offers an opportunity for initiative. Accountancy has developed and continues to develop; new practices may be worth considering; practice must respond to change; specific instances and methods of treatment will require understanding and interpretation.

The work of an accountant cannot be delegated to a pre-programmed automaton. Although theory at the moment does not tell us which methods are right, its role is in identifying general implications, interpreting and integrating practice, and exploring possible new approaches to accounting. There is no 'best' way of accounting, but an arbitrary selection should be avoided. In establishing a standard practice, theory can play a vital role in clarifying the issues to be settled. Even the assumed need for uniformity should be assessed on the basis of theory.

Accounting is concerned with the measurement and communication of useful financial information and, as such, exists for its practical merits. It follows that theory needs to consider its practical relevance; in our examination of theory, the objectives of accounting receive an extended study before we go on to consider the major theoretical contributions to the understanding of income and the balance sheet. Attention is given to the environmental considerations and to the historical cost basis, the traditional basis on which accounting reports are produced.

It should not be particularly surprising that it has not been possible to supply one theory that is appropriate for all situations, that meets all the different needs. There are so many uses of accounting data, so many different ways of applying the information. A single approach to providing asset values and profit figures is unlikely to be optimal to all users. Some users of accounting statements are interested in stewardship, in ensuring that funds have been used properly and that their investment in the company is secure. Other users are interested in the profit performance in the last period. Still others are interested in information that can be used for prediction purposes. It is doubtful that one set of measurement rules can provide information that will satisfy the differing needs of all the users of financial statements. Any choice of accounting method will depend on which class of user(s) the statement is aimed at, and with what objectives.

1.1   Objectives of financial reports

'The fundamental objective of corporate reports is to communicate economic measurements of and information about the resources and performance of the reporting entity useful to those having reasonable rights to such information.' This is the objective as seen by the authors of 'The Corporate Report', a discussion paper published in the UK by the Accounting Standards Committee (ASC) in 1975.[3] It is similar to the conclusion reached by a study group in the USA: 'The basic objective of financial statements is to provide information useful for making economic decisions.'[4] This basic objective is general in nature, but it was supported by details of 11 more specific objectives. The emphasis in these objectives is on assisting users of financial reports to make economic decisions. Many of the objectives are concerned with providing users with information to enable them to predict, compare and evaluate the enterprise's earning power and its potential cash flows.

Two of the other objectives of financial standards included in this US study (known as the Trueblood Report) are of particular interest. One is 'to serve primarily those users who have limited authority, ability, or resources to obtain information and who rely on financial statements as their principal source of information about an enterprise's economic activities'. This emphasizes that the statements should be designed primarily to meet the needs of the non-specialist user, rather than those of the financial community. Another interesting objective is 'to report on those activities of the enterprise affecting society which can be determined and described or measured and which are important to the role of the enterprise in its social environment'. This points to a wider role for financial statements, a topic that will be discussed further later in the chapter. The Trueblood Report had an important influence on the Financial Accounting Standards Board's concepts statement.[5]

There is another aspect to financial reporting in addition to that of assisting users of reports with their economic decision-making. This aspect is brought out in a statement by the Accounting Standards Committee (ASC), which distinguishes between 'users' objectives, which are legally orientated, and in which certainty of calculation is the main aim, and those needs that are orientated towards economic factors in which judgement may be more important than certainty'.[6] The importance of this distinction will be appreciated when we consider the users of financial reports. In the 'Corporate Report', the following groups are identified 'as having a reasonable right to information and whose information needs should be recognized':[7]

(a) the equity investor group, including existing and potential shareholders and holders of convertible securities, options or warrants;
(b) the loan creditor group, including existing and potential holders of debentures and loan stock, and providers of short-term secured and unsecured loans and finance;
(c) the employee group, including existing, potential and past employees;
(d) the analyst–adviser group, including financial analysts and journalists, economists, statisticians, researchers, trade unions, stockbrokers and other providers of advisory services such as credit rating agencies;
(e) the business contact group, including customers, trade creditors and suppliers and, in a different sense, competitors, business rivals and those interested in mergers, amalgamations and takeovers;
(f) the government, including tax authorities, departments and agencies concerned with the supervision of commerce and industry, and local authorities;
(g) the public, including taxpayers, ratepayers, consumers and other community and special interest groups such as political parties, consumer and environmental protection societies and regional pressure groups.

Certain of these groups, for example the loan creditor group and the government, will at times be more interested in the certainty they can attach to the figures in the reports than in using the figures to evaluate the future earning power of the company. At times where tax, fraud or the legality of dividend payments are involved, the less subjective the figures are, the better.

The objective of financial reporting is seen in these two reports published by accounting bodies as satisfying the needs of the users of the reports. In the UK and USA, the accounting reporting systems have traditionally placed greater emphasis on satisfying the needs of the investor, loan creditor and business contact groups than those of the other groups. The arguments for and against a particular accounting principle are usually seen in terms of their impact on these three groups, in particular on the welfare of the investor group. This overemphasis on the interests of a few groups can be criticized.[8] It is true that the 'Corporate Report' lists the public as one of the groups having a reasonable right to information, but the public's interests have traditionally not had an impact on accounting principles and reports.

Accounting reports have an impact on individuals other than those who are the direct users of the reports. Almost all members of society, as either consumers, taxpayers or employees, can be seen as being affected in some way by financial reports. Undoubtedly, the form of such reports and the principles and practices of accounting affect management decisions. Pricing policies, investment policies, employment decisions and decisions on foreign currency exposure are all influenced by the way in which profit is measured, the methods used for the calculation of depreciation and the way in which foreign currencies are translated. Similarly, financial reports can influence governments in their fiscal and monetary decision-making. Financial reports can, therefore, influence nearly all members of society. If this argument is accepted, then it follows that the objective of financial reports is to communicate information to enable decisions on social welfare to be made. The objectives should be seen perhaps in terms of being useful from a social welfare point of view, rather than being useful for the personal economic decisions of a number of user groups. The interests of third parties need to be taken into account. This might seem to many accountants to be a somewhat grandiose objective, and there are certainly practical problems when it comes to deciding how financial reports can best satisfy human and social needs, but this approach does focus attention on the wider responsibilities of financial reporting.

1.2   Accounting theory

If the objective of financial reports is to communicate economic measurement of, and information about, the resources and performance of the business, what rules should be applied to measure the resources currently being employed and the past performance? Is a consistent and comprehensive set of rules and procedures really needed to guide practice? Do we need to bother with theories of accounting?

Watts and Zimmerman[9] argue that accounting theories serve a number of overlapping functions. One is the need to be able to describe existing practice, to be able to rationalize what we at present do. A second is the need to meet the demand of those who require financial information for prediction purposes. A third is what is referred to as the 'justification demand'. This is the need to have a theory to support the measurement practices that a particular interest group wants adopted because such practices will benefit them at the expense of another group. A fourth is to meet the demand of governments and regulatory bodies who are concerned with the role that financial statements play in wealth transfers and in discussions on the efficiency of enterprises and on the public interest.

Clearly, therefore, there are reasons why we need to be able to define the nature and purpose of corporate financial reports, and to be able to justify the rules, procedures and assumptions that are employed in producing these reports. And clearly, such a theory would be valuable.

Theory can be normative or positive. A normative approach examines the world as it *should* be;

a normative theory tries to provide rules as to what *should* happen. (For example, it would be concerned with what is the best method of accounting for changing price levels.) To do this, it is of course necessary to have a clear idea of the precise objectives, in our case of financial statements.

A positive approach to theory is concerned with the world as it *is*, with how accountants and investors actually do behave as opposed to how they should behave. Friedman[10] describes a positive science as 'a body of systematic knowledge concerning what is'. In accounting it would be concerned with, for example, why firms choose historic cost accounting rather than current cost accounting, with why accounting standard bodies choose one method of foreign currency translation rather than another.

Watts and Zimmerman believe that much of the normative work on accounting theory is a waste of time. They refer to much 'normative' work as attempts to 'supply excuses which satisfy the demand created by the political process'. They point out that it is generally concluded that 'financial accounting theory has had little substantive direct impact on accounting practice or policy formulation'. They see accounting theory as an economic good. The demand for theories arises partly because accounting procedures are a means of achieving wealth transfers. Because one interest group may wish to achieve a wealth distribution different from that of another, it needs a theory, an accounting theory, to help justify the wealth transfer. Therefore, 'a variety of accounting theories is demanded on any one issue'.

Watts and Zimmerman argue that it is the diversity of interests that has prevented a general agreement on accounting theory. Other writers have made similar points, but do not necessarily come to the same conclusion with regard to the supremacy of 'positive' over 'normative' theory. Horngren,[11] for example, sees the setting of accounting standards as being as much the product of political action as of flawless logic or empirical findings.

We shall return to the setting of accounting standards in the next chapter. First, however, we shall consider the various approaches to accounting theory that have been adopted by writers on this topic. Whittington,[12] in tracing the historical development of accounting theory, identifies three stages, which he classifies as the empirical inductive approach, the deductive approach and the new empiricist approach.

1.3 The descriptive/inductive approach

The early literature on financial accounting theory was descriptive. It did not try to explain what should happen, or analyse the consequences of what did happen: it merely analysed practices that were being followed. The reasons why certain rules were followed were deduced, and an attempt was made to generalize, to find what principles, 'if any', the procedures being followed had in common. This was an attempt to rationalize current practice, to analyse, compare and draw conclusions. It was not an attempt to argue that one principle or accounting technique was better than another.

This approach can be useful if common principles can be found; it offers some guidance to standard-setters as they are faced with many problems. It might not lead to the 'right' solution to new problems, but it would lead to consistency. It gives the impression that there is some underlying logic to the accounting techniques.

A major problem with this approach, however, is the fact that it does not result in a theory that can give guidance when new situations arise or in situations that require fundamental change. For example, the problem faced by the standard-setters in giving guidance on accounting for changing price levels arose in part because the principles that were being followed in existing practice were based on a stable unit of measurement. Another difficulty with the empirical inductive approach to theory is that there are problem areas that are not new, where it is unclear what practice should be followed—for example, accounting for mergers. Current practice is itself unclear and subject to change.

1.4 The normative/deductive approach

This is the pure theory approach, which attempts to develop theories that will provide a basis for selecting from alternative accounting techniques. It attempts to provide an approach that will allow us to decide which technique is 'best'.

Whittington traces three stages of this deductive approach: the true income approach, the user needs approach, and the information economics approach.

1.4.1 The true income approach

From an economic point of view, the problem, at least in theory, is simple. The objectives of financial accounting should be to measure 'true income'. The profit and loss account should show the true income of a business over a period; the balance sheet should show its 'true value' as at a certain date. Early writers on normative financial accounting theory followed this path. Profit, or income, as it is usually referred to in academic literature, is a term that is in almost continuous use in the business world. There is a wide feeling that the meaning of the term *is* understood, at least approximately. Despite the difficulty of its measurement, this general understanding may not be much in disagreement with the theoretical concept. The classic definition on the concept of income was supplied by Hicks[13] in terms of the maximum amount an individual can consume in a period and still expect to be as well off at the end of the period as at the beginning. Once 'well-offness' has been maintained, the excess is profit.

The meaning of 'well-offness' is a source of difficulty. While one can conceive of the measure that represents how much can be spent (or paid out in dividends) without reducing the opening resources, quantifying it is a different matter. Hicks was ready to point this out. In his examination of dynamic economic concepts, he deliberately postponed the introduction of the concept of income because he felt it was not suitable for logical precision. He asserts it is not a logical category but 'a rough approximation used by the businessmen ... a rough practical precept'. To attempt to quantify Hicks's definition, some unrealistic assumptions are necessary. Assume that it is known that prices of all goods and services including interest rates will remain constant. Consider the position of a trader who is about to commit £100 to a short-term venture which should result in his receiving £110 at the end of the venture. Provided he faces no other benefits or costs from the venture, the profit over its life is £10, since he can spend this at the end leaving his £100 intact. Prices must remain constant to ensure that £100 is worth the same at the beginning and end of the period, given any set of tastes for different goods.

The necessity of introducing interest rates and a short time period warrants further explanation. The concept of profit put forward by Hicks is forward-looking (or *ex ante*). He is concerned to identify profit at the start of the project, which can be done only if the outcome is certain. The need to assume certainty removes us further from reality but is compatible with the techniques of discounted cash flow (as used in investment appraisal techniques). 'Well-offness' is equivalent to present value under the assumptions made above. Where the value at the end of a given period represents a series of future benefits instead of a cash sum, it is evaluated by finding its present value discounted at the going rate of interest. Under certainty, the opening value is the discounted future benefits, comprising the end value and the profit element. The symmetry of this situation turns out to mean that profit is the interest that would be earned at the known rate on the opening value.[14] This concept of income is described as 'pure economic income'.[15] If the rate of interest changes at any future period, this result will not hold; the difference caused by the interest change will no longer permit unique quantification, as there is theoretical support both for the difference to be included in profit and for the difference to be excluded from profit.

When considering accountability, measurement of profit is required after the event (*ex post*) rather than in anticipation of it. However, this does not remove the problems of quantification. Since profit measurement is required for ongoing businesses, values always involve consideration of future benefits. *Ex post* measurement introduces further complexity.

The forward-looking *ex ante* approach perceived profit as the creation of value throughout the period, having the nature of a flow produced by the stock of value. This stock, requiring measurement at the start and end of the period, is described as 'capital'.

The stock and flow classification is applied in theoretical analysis of *ex post* profit. While value created as the flow expected from the capital stock is accepted as profit, gains in the value of that stock caused not by operating activities but by external changes are not flows. The different nature of these gains leads many writers to recommend separating them from profit. They arise unexpectedly in *ex post* measurement since forward-looking measures would have already anticipated them and 'internalized' their value. Their unexpected nature leads to the description 'windfall gains', and their association with holding the assets rather than operating them produces the term 'holding gains'.

In measuring profit in the accounts of businesses, there are two alternative approaches. The first follows directly from the theoretical definition. Profit is the increase in the capital value of the business adjusted for any net distributions; the adjustment would recognize that dividends are the equivalent of spending or consumption by the business owners and are therefore additions to profit. The corollary of this is that new capital subscribed would equate to negative consumption. The requirement is for measurement of the beginning- and end-of-period capital values in order to find the increase. This requirement is met in accounting by the opening and closing balance sheets of a business. The balance sheet is being regarded as the prime account, with the profit and loss account becoming a residual.

The alternative is a more dynamic approach, which attempts to record increases and decreases in capital values throughout the period. This is the basis followed by the familiar double-entry bookkeeping method. Occurrences leading to increases in value are recognized as revenue items. The costs of achieving the resulting revenue are deducted from that revenue to produce the profit and loss account as the prime account. The double-entry mechanism produces a debit entry equal to every credit entry. This profit measurement approach allocates those debit or credit entries relating to the current period's income flows to the profit and loss account, leaving the unallocated debit and credit balances to form the balance sheet. In this approach, termed the 'net production method', the balance sheet becomes the residual.

The net production method provides the advantage of being able to indicate the activities that have produced the profit. It offers a partial solution to the problem of deciding whether holding gains are to be included in profit as it permits the presentation of a profit, excluding the holding gains identified, while an all-inclusive measure can be included to produce a balance sheet reflecting both types of value change.

The two approaches will not always produce the same results, and where it is desired to achieve a particular interpretation in both the profit and loss account and the balance sheet, some adjustment procedures may be necessary. This will be illustrated when the backlog depreciation problem is discussed as part of the consideration of accounting for price change in Chapter 13. In that chapter the history of the inflation accounting debate is traced. The economic concept of income enables the different views to be clarified. Differences can be seen in the approaches to asset measurement in valuing the capital of the business; some writers support current selling price, others replacement costs and others current costs; some prefer applying a general index to historical costs. Disagreement on a 'best' approach cannot be unquestionably resolved by reference to theory. In the event, the standard on the subject was withdrawn.

The economic concept of value obtained by discounting future cash flows is much in evidence in the leasing standard (see Chapter 5). In the exposure draft of 1988 on 'special financial transaction', considered in Chapter 16, assets to be recorded are identified if they provide the probability of future economic benefits to the business.

1.4.2 The user needs approach

Instead of attempting to frame the concept of a unique 'true income' by theoretical development, this approach commences by acknowledging that financial accounts serve a number of different user groups. It is argued that the 'best' accounting measures for each user group can be found by identifying each group and ascertaining the information they need and the purposes for which they need it. The view put forward by the standard-makers in the USA and the UK that financial statements are produced for the benefit of the users in making their decisions is widely accepted and has already been discussed. However, this description of purpose is far too vague to assist in identifying what should be incorporated in accounting reports.

For some time, the efforts of academics and standard-setters were influenced by a consideration of what decisions were made using a company's published accounts. It was commonly assumed that the dominant use was in the buying and selling decisions involving shares of the company. If accounts were to meet these reqirements, then, ideally, they should supply the data that users sought in their investment decision process. This data requirement could not be identified. The decision processes vary between users and over time for a particular user; further, users are unlikely to reveal how they make decisions (both because they are unable to describe their own processes and because they would not wish to sacrifice any perceived competitive advantage their process offers).

An alternative to identifying specific users' decision requirements was to consider more general decision models and data requirements. The predictive properties of reports were considered a desirable feature.

This approach to identify the needs of financial accounts conflicts to some extent with the theoretical understanding of the operation of the markets involved. The impact of the efficient market hypothesis[16] will be considered in Section 1.5; one implication of it is that, since buyers and sellers of shares react quickly to all available information, reliable predictions of share price change are rapidly reflected in actual share prices. If a rise in value could be predicted, the enthusiasm to try to take advantage of this rise would cause the price to rise until no such advantage remained. (A predicted fall would encourage selling and lead to a drop in price.) The very large gains to be made have attracted considerable expertise and effort in producing such predictions, and the ease and speed of trade in the stock markets means that price changes in response to new information occur almost immediately. Statistical studies of stock markets have confirmed that such change occurs in much less than 24 hours. On this time scale, the production of published accounts involves enormous delays. Most of the information contained in accounts has been predicted and absorbed before their publication.

Further evidence can be found which conflicts with the idea that the prediction of share values constitutes the major use of accounts. While the issue of preliminary results can lead to market reactions, the publication of the more elaborately presented final accounts appears to provide little or no new information for share-dealing purposes. With preliminary information available, the final accounts rarely provide any surprises. However, companies put considerable effort into their final accounts, including new and additional information often above and beyond that required to satisfy the legal or standard requirements. In terms of share price effects, the benefits to companies would appear small compared with the effort involved. A rise in share price does not provide a company with any more share capital, unless it is about to make a new issue, in which case there would be ample opportunity to provide any further information considered beneficial.[17] If we believe successful companies would not regularly act against their own interests, then the publication of additional accounting information should be explicable. A number of writers[18] have suggested that the publication of audited accounts is a mechanism employed to bring the activities of company management into greater conformity with the goals of the suppliers of capital. A survey revealed that the professional qualified accountants included in the sample considered this stewardship objective to be the most important.[19]

The Trueblood Report suggested that stewardship may be to restrictive a description: 'Accountability extends beyond the element of stewardship involved in the safe-keeping of assets entrusted to custody. It encompasses the use and conversion of those assets as well as decisions not to use them.' The requirement to account each year to the financial community and to shareholders in particular will act as a control on management. Managers are prepared to accept this accountability so that they can use the capital provided by their financiers without regular interference. Accountability is seen as a vital element in an economic system where capital is acquired and owned by individuals who need not carry out the management and operation of resources. Stamp emphasized the importance of accountability:[20]

> The word that best describes the relationship between a company and its management on the one hand and the external users of the company's published financial reports on the other hand is 'accountability'. A company reports to outsiders because it feels it is accountable.... The whole notion of financial reporting by a public company implies accountability to those outsiders.

While the share value approach concentrates on shareholders, Stamp took a broad view of what is meant by 'outsiders'. Creditors, particularly long-term lenders to a company, will often establish rights to receive accounts and may go further, specifying certain safeguards in terms of the reported accounting value. For example, a debenture issue may limit the permitted gearing ratio.

In fulfilling this accountability requirement, two related reports have emerged as dominant, namely, the profit and loss account and the balance sheet. Considerable conceptual difficulties make these reports less than ideal for this purpose, mainly because there is no unique measurable concept of profit and loss. Nevertheless, the practical value attributed to these two reports is indicated by their continued survival and extensive use, not only throughout and beyond the world of capital-market-financed companies, but also in organizations of varying size and structure whether or not there is a regulatory requirement for them.

These measures do embody the broader requirements of accountability perceived by the Trueblood Report, which are then expanded upon. 'An objective of financial statements is to supply information useful in judging management's ability to utilise enterprise resources effectively.'

The ability of management to generate income while enhancing the resouces available to the company is the property to which the profit and loss account and balance sheet address themselves. The reports form yardsticks of the elements of progress that are of primary concern. It is on the basis of profitable activity and possession of suitable resources that the compay's abilities can be judged to pay dividends and interest, to settle obligations to creditors and lenders, to maintain and expand operations, to justify the continued support of suppliers of finance.

Meeting accountability objectives does not mean that financial reports are completely divorced from decision-making. In addition to the influence that their future publication has on managerial decisions, users must decide to continue to support the existing management, to exercise their legal rights against the directors, or to withdraw their support. Accountability is an important consideration when it is decided to commit further capital to the company; the investor or lender can assess whether sufficient accounting controls exist to protect his investment against the possibly conflicting wishes of management by recognizing what reports of management action he can demand.

The credibility of these reports will be a crucial factor in determining their value in fulfilling the accountability criterion. Given the discretionary nature of the measurements used in profit and loss and balance sheet reporting the importance of an audit is obvious. The auditor acts as an independent accountant who attests to the validity of the view of the company's progress indicated by the accounts, a satisfactory audit enabling the auditor to report that in his opinion the financial statements 'give a true and fair view of the state of affairs and income' of the company. The need to state that this is an opinion is a further result of the elusive nature of the accounting measures reported.

One approach to identifying the general properties of accounting information required to meet users' needs is to view users as receivers of information. Explicit recognition may be given to the limitations of users in their ability to handle large quantities of data from many sources by the following six properties.

● *Materiality and relevance* The task of the preparer of financial statements is to present information that has a bearing on the purposes of the users. Information is relevant if it might influence the decisions of those entitled to receive it. However, the capacity to handle data is limited. If too much information is presented, it may obscure the significance of the relevant data in the report. Financial reporting requires a summary of information to enable the meaning of the report to be understood by the typical user; it requires a selection of the significant. A parallel consideration should be the cost of the reporting. There is no justification for reporting information of minor importance at an expense in excess of its maximum value.

● *Timeliness* This is a further aspect of relevance, and once again the desirability of having information that is current must be tempered by the costs of its production.

● *Comparability* All economic decisions involve a comparison of alternatives; this will be aided by supplying data that can be readily compared. Two properties support this aim: consistency and uniformity. Any changes in the methods of determining data need justification, as the resulting loss of comparability reduces the value of those data. Uniformity may be desirable, but only to the extent that it provides comparability. There is considerable opposition to uniformity as a goal in itself. Different organizations have different problems, different control needs, so that the importance of particular information varies. With costs of reporting varying also, what is worthwhile reporting for one business may not be for another. Further, since accounting is not an exact science, it is held that accountants should be given the scope to portray the reports in the way they consider most informative.[21] Fixing a uniform practice may inhibit progress and response to economic forces for change.

In addition to the need to consider the cost of measurement, under uncertainty the following properties are desirable in a method of measurement.

● *Objectivity and verifiability* Objectivity is a term with many meanings, but in this context it refers to measures that are impersonal or lack a personal bias. This feature is supported by verifiability, the ability of a measure to be confirmed by an alternative expert.

● *Reliability* This is the statistical property of limited dispersion of results of independent measurements. The results obtained by separate attempts to measure the same event or value will vary less with a more reliable method of measurement. Clearly, lack of reliability makes verification difficult.

● *Freedom from bias* This is not a repetition of limited subjectivity but a distinct statistical term. It refers to the need for a method to produce measures near to the 'true' value of what is being measured. An incorrectly set weigh-bridge may produce results that fit the above definitions of reliability, objectivity and verifiability; however, false results would be produced if it consistently reported weights of, say, only 90 per cent of those that would have been reported if it had been correctly set.

1.4.3   Information economics

This approach is based on a relatively new branch of economic theory. Information can be seen as an economic good. If people want information they will pay for it, and the more useful the information, the more they will pay. It is the accountant's job to supply that information, but there is a cost. In an unregulated market, if the expected overall benefits exceed the cost, the information will be supplied by the company to those willing to pay.

There is a cost to a company in making information available, and if this exceeds any benefits the company might perceive for itself, it would only supply the information in an unregulated market if it charged for that information. In an unregulated market, if individuals perceive the benefits from possessing the information to be greater than the price being charged for it, they will be willing to pay the price.

In a regulated market, it is the regulators who decide what information should be made available to all users. The information is made available whether the user wants it or not. This has been an issue in the inflation accounting debate. The ASC, a regulator, has required companies to produce inflation-adjusted accounts. There is a cost to the company in producing this information. The question to be asked is whether the additional benefits to users of the adjusted accounts warrant the cost. The user has the information available at zero price, as the company carries the cost. Some have argued that the current cost information was not being used by investors, so why should companies incur the cost?

One of the main objectives of company financial reports is seen to be the provision of information to investors to enable them to make decisions. Existing shareholders have a legal right to such information as they are the owners of the company, but why should regulators require that the information be made publicly available? Why should this information be a 'public good'? One argument is that it would be costly to exclude non-purchasers or non-shareholders from the information. Another, stronger, argument is that information has a social value, that it enables capital markets to function more effectively. Its availability enables funds to be allocated to the companies that can show the possibility of achieving the greatest future returns. Capital markets are thereby referred to as being 'allocationally efficient'. Making information publicly available also makes the markets 'a fair game'. This means that all players have an equal chance to make or lose money. The reason regulators are so worried about 'inside information' and 'insider dealing' is that these enable one group of investors to get rich at someone else's expense through what is regarded as unfair means. Not all would agree; some would argue that, if one group (through their 'wits', or ability to 'buy' non-publicly available information) can benefit, then the best of luck to them!

The regulators are trying to achieve an information system that has a social value, by which is meant that it should be possible for an individual to increase his/her expected utility without a reduction in the expected utility of any other individual. In order to bring this about, of course, it is necessary for the regulators (in our case, accounting regulators) to understand the impact on the market of the information that would be released. How do the different measurement methods and the items disclosed affect users' decisions? There is a considerable literature on whether or not the major stock exchanges of the world are efficient, i.e. whether the quoted share prices reflect all publicly available information. Part of such information consists of the financial reports of companies. There has been much research into the impact of accounting information on share prices. The way in which the market reacts to changes in accounting measurement techniques and to the release of new information could be one of the factors taken into account in the decision-making processes of standard-setters. Indeed, standard-setting is itself one way of regulating the information that flows to the market. One justification for standard-setting is that without it the market would be less efficient. Beaver makes the point that 'financial statement information is inherently a social commodity'. Standard-setting itself involves issues of social choice, with the standard-setters deciding which information should be disclosed and which should not. There will be a return to this point in the next chapter.

Financial accounting reports have a number of economic consequences, of which some are foreseen by the issuing company and some are not. The effect on share prices has already been mentioned; in addition, the way in which transactions are reported can affect the financial decisions of companies. For example, the treatment of gains and losses in foreign currency conversion and translation can affect decisions on foreign exchange management. The accounting rule to be used in deciding whether a particular lease is a finance lease or an operating lease can influence the terms of the leasing agreement. Many empirical studies have been undertaken to determine the economic consequences of these and other accounting policies.

This leads to the third stage of accounting theory: the positive approach, involving, empirical studies to ascertain how individuals and markets do in fact behave.

1.5 Positive/empiricist approach

The most recent mode of literature on financial accounting theory is that described by Whittington as 'new empiricism'. Enthusiastic advocates of this approach believe that 'the objective of accounting theory is to explain and predict'. They see theory as being useful only if it offers an explanation of what is happening now and a prediction of what will happen in the future. This is in sharp contrast to the more traditional 'normative' approach to accounting theory, which is concerned with what accounting practice ought to be.

It can be argued that there is room in the subject for both approaches; the subject is far from perfect, and all research should be welcomed. Unfortunately, as in many areas of academic research, the advocates of one method become so convinced of its virtues that they denigrate all others.

The access to large amounts of data and to computers has resulted in an abundance of empirical research. This approach to accounting theory attempts to determine the predictive ability of the various methods of alternative measurement. According to this approach, the measure 'with the greatest predictive power with respect to a given event is considered to be the best method for that particular purpose'. Accounting reports are used for many purposes, including attempts to predict future profits, to predict bankruptcy, to predict default on loans and to predict being the target of a takeover bid. It could be that one accounting measurement method is better than another for a particular purpose. For example, current cost profits might be a better prediction of future profits than historic cost profits; cash flow data might be a better predictor of company failure than accrual accounting data; quarterly earning figures might be a 'good' predictor of annual profits. These and many other hypotheses have been tested.

If it is found that one accounting method is better than another for prediction purposes, then it is argued by supporters of this approach that this is the method standard-setters should support.

Some of the studies have made a contribution to our knowledge of how the markets work, and of how users respond to accounting reports, for example how accounting reports affect share prices. One problem with this approach is how far it is possible to generalize about the results.

The positive research can be divided into that which asks 'what'-type questions and that which asks 'why'-type questions. Examples of the 'what' type of question include the work of Ball and Brown,[22] who examined the information content of annual earnings figures, analysing the market reaction to earnings figures. Ball and Brown, and others, examined the time-series properties of annual earnings; they were trying to ascertain whether earnings follow a random walk. Kaplan and

Roll[23] tested the stock market reaction to changes in accounting measurement techniques. In the UK there has been considerable research into the stock market reaction to current cost accounting information, the main study being that by Carsberg and Page.[24]

The 'why' type of question attempts to ascertain why accounting standard-setters support one form of accounting technique rather than another, and why, given a choice firms adopt one technique rather than another. The two 'why' questions are related in that standards are the result of political pressures within the standard-setting bodies and some of the pressure comes from business firms, so one can attempt to ascertain why firms press for the adoption of a particular technique.

An example of a why question is, 'Why did the ASC choose to recommend the current cost method of inflation accounting rather than the current purchasing power method?' One method can give a different impression of a firm's performance to another.

The research is based on what is known in economics as 'agency theory'. There are many groups that have an interest in the financial reports of a company. The income or wealth of the groups can depend on the reported results. One interest group may benefit from one set of figures, and another from a different set. The role of one group, 'corporate management', in external financial reporting has been examined by Kelly and others.[25] Watts and Zimmerman identify the relevant costs and benefits of alternative accounting methods. They were interested in why managers lobby standard-setting boards on proposed standards. They attempt to identify how the standard might affect the firms' cash flow and hence shareholders' wealth.

This is the type of positive research now being undertaken into accounting theory. Attempts are made to ascertain what actually happens, and then to find a theory that provides reasons for what has been observed. If we knew how individuals behaved, if we knew how the market reacted to accounting numbers, this knowledge could be used by accounting standard-setters.

There are however problems with this approach. How far is it possible to generalize the results? If, for example, it is found in one company that management would benefit from the adoption of one approach, and they lobby to achieve this, does it mean that the same conclusions could be drawn with respect to the behaviour of agents of another company?

The empirical research that measures *what* has happened is not too difficult; however, it is not easy to develop a positive theory that explains *why* this has happened. The overemphasis on a positive approach has been strongly criticized by Christenson and others.[26] All the approaches to the development of an accounting theory that have been mentioned above have their uses. Even the attempt to rationalize existing practice, referred to above as the indicative approach, can be useful in that it can lead to insights into the way the market does behave, and existing practice is certainly one of the influences on new standards.

The literature on accounting theory is rich. Unfortunately, until recently it does not seem to have had much impact on accounting practice.

1.6 Fundamental accounting concepts

Periodically, the accounting regulators turn to accounting theory to justify a particular practice they wish to have adopted. In the past, theory does not seem to have had much of an impact on practice, but debates at a professional level on such issues as accounting for changing prices, and accounting for special-purpose transactions, indicate an increasing awareness of the accounting theory literature.

Financial accounting has existed for many centuries, even with no agreement on theory and objectives. We shall now consider what are sometimes called the 'principles', 'rules', 'concepts' or 'conventions' that underlie the accounting reports that are actually produced. In SSAP 2 on

Disclosure of Accounting Policies[27] there is an attempt to clarify the position; it tries to explain the general principles that are being employed to cope with the practical problems faced every day in producing financial reports.

The statement begins by explaining that it is not attempting to develop a basic theory of accounting, but is mainly concerned with ensuring that companies disclose in their financial reports the accounting policies followed. It seeks to clarify what is meant by the word 'policies'. It differentiates between

(a) fundamental accounting concepts
(b) accounting bases
(c) accounting policies.

We will return to accounting bases and policies later in this chapter (see Sections 1.8 and 1.9 below).

Fundamental concepts, it is explained, are 'working assumptions having general acceptance' at a point in time. They underlie the financial accounts produced by a business enterprise at a point in time. In no way are accounting concepts the same as accounting theory: they are just broad assumptions. They are practical rules which are adopted generally but can be varied and possibly changed over time.

The ASC singles out four particular concepts for special mention: the going concern concept, the consistency concept, the prudence concept and the accruals concept. The standard requires that 'any material differences from the four fundamental concepts as well as the critical accounting policies must be disclosed and suitably explained. If financial reports are to be valuable as communicators of information, these disclosures are important, clarifying which, of a spectrum of available methods, have been utilised.'

The four concepts mentioned in the standard are as follows:

● *Going concern*   This postulate, sometimes referred to as 'continuity', is introduced to cope with the problem of periodic reporting for an entity having a life extending beyond the current period. It represents the assumption that, provided there is no significant evidence to the contrary, the entity will be assumed to continue in existence long enough to carry out its commitments, sell its stock in trade in an orderly manner and derive the use from its assets not purchased for resale. A machine held to provide production capacity will be valued for the use that can be made by operating it rather that what it would fetch in the open market. If continuity is not expected, a different approach to valuation and reporting must be taken.

● *Consistency*   Reflecting the user need of comparability, this principle requires the accounting treatment to be consistent both within a particular period and between different periods. Where changes occur, there is a need to provide information to help the user understand the effects, possibly by quantifying the change and/or adjusting results already reported. Chapter 6 examines a particular aspect of such change in considering prior-year items which have been the subject of standardization (SSAP 6).

● *Prudence*   It is often recommended that, in accounting, pessimism should be adopted in preference to optimism, given the uncertainty that necessarily exists in the reporting of financial results. This conservative approach implies that revenue and profit should not be anticipated, but provision should be made for any expected liabilities; assets should be valued at the lowest of several possible values, while liabilities and expenses should be valued at their highest. This approach is justified by assuming that overstatement is more dangerous than understatement, and that a businessman's optimism needs to be tempered with the accountant's pessimism. However, it is a defective method of dealing with uncertainty, as it is not free from bias. Understatement can lead to poor decisions just as overstatement can; it supports the concealing and distortion of data considered 'optimistic' and can have indirect effects that run totally counter to its main objective. The understatement of asset values may result in an overstatement of profit owing to the reduction in the associated depreciation charge.

● *Accruals*   When considering the accounting entity (see below), the need to produce reports for particular periods needs to be considered. From an economic point of view, the income measurement adopted in accounting concentrates on recording events leading to increases or decreases in capital values, rather than on comparing opening and closing values. For this, a means must be given for matching events to periods. The nature of income is such that the revenues of a period are not always the receipts of that period and the expenses are not always the outlays. Sales are recognized in the period in which they are invoiced; payments made in one period that produce benefits in another are treated as expenses of the period in which the benefits are derived. Although this may not represent the legal or physical position, substance over form (see below) is invoked and the financial reality is represented by tracing events to the appropriate period. This approach is known as an 'accruals approach' and involves the process known as 'matching'.

Before examining matching, it is of note to mention a feature of income reporting that stems from the accruals approach but is not always explicitly recognized. This is *income smoothing*. If future changes in value are anticipated fully, as suggested by the *ex ante* economic concept of income, the effects of such changes will be spread over a number of periods and the resulting income figures will show a smoother trend than without that anticipation. To the extent that accrual allows the reporting of receipts and outlays to be spread or allocated to 'appropriate' periods, it permits smoothing. Some would argue that this is desirable if it produces an income figure that projects the general trend of progress, rather than fluctuations caused by uneven cash flows, while highlighting any major deviation from this trend as a cause for special concern. Smoothing is given effect in many accounting practices; depreciation and amortization spread expenditure of a capital or unusually 'lumpy' nature; the treatment of taxation involves smoothing (see 'Deferred taxation', Chapter 8); extraordinary and exceptional items are separated in an attempt to remove distortions from the smooth recurring trend of reported income (see Chapter 7).

Although the standard recognizes these four concepts, two of importance which it does not include are the accounting entity, and substance over form.

● *The accounting entity*   This is the organization identified as having a distinct existence of its own for accounting purposes. A definition of the accounting entity determines the boundaries of the subject to be reported upon, aiding in the selection of what is relevant, and what should be included in reports. In order to overcome the problems of reporting for an entity whose life stretches into the unforeseeable future, it is also usual to divide the life into periods of time. In effect, boundaries are set for the entity in terms of time as well as economic activity or interest group. Accounts are produced to show the results relating to a particular period (typically a year), and the effects relating to the entity for that year are of prime relevance.

● *Substance over form*   This supports reporting to reflect financial reality in preference to the legal position. There are many examples of this, including the reporting of assets acquired on a long-term lease as if they were, in fact, owned (see Chapter 5), and the treatment of associated companies (see Chapter 9) where the group's share of the earnings of the associate are reflected in group accounts and not merely the dividends to which there is a legal right.

1.7 The matching process

The matching process, the approach by which traditional accounting has achieved periodic income measurement, is conceptually simple. It is the recognition of revenue when it is 'realized' and the subsequent deduction of costs that can be related (or 'matched') to the creation of that revenue.

1.7.1   Revenue recognition

The desire to meet the concepts of accruals and prudence has been embodied in the realization criteria for recognizing revenue, as can be seen in the following statement made by the AAA: 'The essential meaning of realization is that a change in an asset or liability has become sufficiently definite and objective to warrant recognition in the accounts.'[28]

The criterion for establishing whether realization has taken place is normally the occurrence of a critical event, typically a sale. The evidence and trigger for recognizing a sale and recording the revenue is often the issuing of an invoice, but there are exceptions. The critical event for a hire purchase or leasing revenue may be the receipt of cash; with long-term contracts, it may be appropriate to recognize the revenue in relation to the progress of that contract, accruing part of the total income from the contract in all or many of the periods during which the contract is carried out (see Chapter 3).

Increases in value that have not been 'verified' by the critical event criteria are often referred to as 'unrealized'. Further, because they generally arise through the holding of assets rather than trading or operating activities, they tend to be labelled 'unrealized gains' and are separated from other income. This realization approach is compatible with the postulates and conventions introduced earlier.

1.7.2   Matching of expenses

Matching would be unnecessary if income were measured by identifying net increases in value continuously. This is not the case. The recording of revenue, reported on the basis of realization, is separated from that of expenses. Since the acquisition and payment for the services and other inputs that produce the revenues do not coincide with the realization of revenues, some attempt to relate revenues and expenses is required. The accruals approach is satisfied by tracing expenses to the period in which the associated revenue is realized and reported. This is the matching process.

Associations between revenues and expenses are not always obvious, so procedures have been established to expedite matching. Costs are classified into two categories, product costs and period costs, to permit either *product matching* or *period matching*. Of these two forms, only the former is fully suited to being described as matching. When there is direct association of costs with specific output, and hence specific revenue, these costs can be readily identified for matching to take place. Another significant problem exists, namely, the measurement of those costs. A solution is offered by the historical cost basis, which is dealt with later in this chapter; alternative solutions are discussed in Chapter 13 when price change is considered explicitly. Direct association for the purpose of matching is achieved in current accounting practice when costs can be traced to particular products. This generally applies to items known as direct costs including raw materials, direct labour and subcontract costs.

An association with output is achieved for many indirect costs using allocation or apportionment methods and overhead absorption procedures. Both direct and indirect costs that have been associated with products are linked with those products and treated as expenses when revenue from the product is recognized or carried forward to future periods.

When costs are carried forward, or inventoried as assets, this must be in anticipation of future matching. Indirect costs are also carried forward at times when future matching is anticipated, even if the association with products has not been established. Costs are capitalized (or treated as assets) in this way to be linked with products that may not exist at the time of capitalization. However, prudence is a major limitation, requiring a reasonable expectation that the future revenues against which matching is anticipated will exceed the costs capitalized.

There is some controversy among academics, if not among practitioners, concerning the carrying forward of fixed costs. With varying volumes of output, this promotes smoothing. It is argued that the fixed cost incurred while producing products in an earlier period avoids the need to use capacity in the later period in which the product is sold. The opposite view is that, since the costs are fixed, no additional costs are incurred with the intention of benefiting other periods, and therefore no cost should be carried forward. This latter view is not generally adopted in practice.

Period matching does not involve carrying forward costs for future matching and is not strictly an accruals approach, but is actually an exception to product matching. It arises when there is insufficient basis for establishing any association between cost and product, and when the opportunities for future matching either are no longer considered to exist (as in the case of obsolete stock) or are considered insufficient in size or certainty for carrying forward to be prudent.

In these cases, the costs of goods and services are 'matched' to the period in which the goods and services are used or the expenditure incurred. In addition, it is occasionally argued that, where costs are incurred on a recurring basis at a relatively constant level, there is no material distortion of the income of any period by period matching instead of product matching, and that the additional costs of achieving product matching would not be worth the effort.

1.8   Accounting bases

In providing a distinction from accounting concepts, SSAP 2 gives an explanation of accounting bases. These are the 'methods which have been developed for expressing or applying fundamental accounting concepts to financial transactions and items'.

By their nature, accounting bases are more diverse and numerous that fundamental concepts, since they have evolved in response to the variety and complexity of types of business and business transactions, and for this reason there may justifiably exist more than one recognised accounting basis for dealing with particular items.

In the course of practice there have developed a variety of accounting bases designed to provide consistent, fair and as nearly as possible objective solutions to these problems in particular circumstances; for instance bases for calculating such items as depreciation, the amounts at which stocks and work in progress are to be stated, and deferred taxation.

Accounting bases provide an orderly and consistent framework for periodic reporting of a concern's results and financial position, but they do not, and are not intended to, substitute for the exercise of commercial judgement in the preparation of financial reports. Where a choice of acceptable accounting bases is available judgement must be exercised in choosing those which are appropriate to the circumstances and are best suited to present fairly the concern's results and financial position; the bases thus adopted then become the concern's accounting policies. The significance of accounting bases is that they provide limits to the area subject to the exercise of judgement, and a check against arbitrary, excessive or unjustifiable adjustments where no other objective yardstick is available. By definition it is not possible to develop generalised rules for the exercise of judgement, though practical working rules may be evolved on a pragmatic basis for limited use in particular circumstances. Broadly, the longer a concern's normal business cycle—the period between initiation of business transactions and their completion—the greater the area subject to judgement and its effect on periodic financial accounts, and the less its susceptibility to close regulation by accounting bases. These limitations to the regulating powers of accounting bases must be recognised.

1.9   Accounting policies

According to SSAP 2, accounting policies are 'the specific accounting bases selected and consistently followed by a business enterprise as being, in the opinion of the management, appropriate to its circumstances and best suited to present fairly its results and financial position'.

The importance of the standard, which requires clear explanations of the accounting policies followed by a reporting entity, is readily asserted:

> In circumstances where more than one accounting basis is acceptable in principle, the accounting policy followed can significantly affect a concern's reported results and financial position and the view presented can be properly appreciated only if the policies followed in dealing with material items are also explained. For this reason, adequate disclosure of the accounting policies is essential to the fair presentation of financial accounts. As accounting standards become established through publication of statements of standard accounting practice, the choice of accounting bases regarded as generally available will diminish, but it has to be recognised that the complexity and diversity of business renders total and rigid uniformity of bases impracticable.
>
> The items with which this statement is mainly concerned are those which are subject to the exercise of judgement as to how far they should be dealt with in the profit and loss account for the period under review, or how far all or part should be carried forward in the balance sheet as attributable to the operations of future periods. The determination of the anual profit or loss of nearly every business substantially depends on a systematic approach to a few material items of this type. For the better appreciation of the view they give, annual accounts should include a clear explanation of the accounting policies followed for dealing with these few key items. The intention and spirit of this statement are that management should identify those items of the type described which are judged material or critical for the purpose of determining and fully appreciating the company's profit or loss and its financial position, and should make clear the accounting policies followed for dealing with them.

1.10 Three basic dimensions

Although SSAP 2 makes no reference to the basic dimensions, the ASC has recognized that 'any system of accounting is dependent on the basis selected for stating assets, the capital maintenance concept adopted and the unit of measurement used'.[29] Whether the approach concentrates on balance sheet valuation or on measurement of changes in capital values, the same basic problems face the accountant. As prices change, a choice arises not only in the valuation of the assets that make up the capital value, but also in the comparability of the opening and closing valuations; and there are even alternatives for the units in which the valuations are expressed.

As a result, any system of accounting for profit must adopt a policy on three basic dimensions: 'the units of measurement', 'the valuation model' and 'the concept of capital maintenance'. Each of these deserves attention. These may be combined in a number of ways.

In the present-day economy, money plays a major role as a common medium of exchange. It is appropriate, therefore, in any aggregation of economic values, to adopt money as a common *unit of measurement*. However, prices change, which means not only that the value of particular goods change in relation to money, but also that the value of money changes in relation both to particular goods and to collections of goods; money is not a stable unit of value.

In tackling another of these dimensions, the *valuation model*, there is a need to consider the fact that values change over time (requiring the selection of a point or points of time at which the value is current), and also that more than one value exists at a given time. A current market value may differ depending on whether the viewpoint of a buyer or a seller is taken, and there could be an array of anticipated future values for different owners depending on their perceptions of the future and the uses to which they are variously able to put the particular asset.

Measuring profit for a business in terms of the maximum distribution that could be made before the capital value is reduced has been re-expressed as the maximum distribution while maintaining capital intact. In applying this to businesses in times of changing values, the questions 'Which capital?' and 'In what terms is it maintained?' become relevant; the answers are to be supplied by the adoption of a *concept of capital maintenance*.[30]

To answer the first of these questions, the extent of the capital of the business must be established. Among suitable definitions are the shareholders' capital or, alternatively, all long-term investment by shareholders and lenders. The second question addresses itself to the manner in which the capital is considered to be maintained. Debate has centred on two major concepts, physical capital and economic capital. An extreme interpretation of the former would recognize profit only after ensuring that the same physical assets could be provided from capital allowing for them to be in the same condition as at the beginning of the period. This interpretation views the business capital as a stagnant entity, particularly when physical assets are rapidly becoming obsolete and anachronistic in a world of technological change. A modified interpretation of the physical capital maintenance concept, which is more consistent with such change, can be described as operating capital maintenance. Here, the capital base from which profit is measured is that which enables the same output to be achieved.

Even this operating concept fails to reflect the full dynamism of economic change, since not only are methods of manufacture modified over time, but the nature, range and desirability of the products themselves are always likely to undergo major changes. Maintaining the capacity to produce a volume of gas lamps would probably not be regarded as a full response to the changes that have occurred in the economy. The economic capital maintenance concept seeks a full response to change, requiring capital to be measured in terms of its current real value, maintaining its purchasing power.

The idea of maintaining capital intact has been given considerable importance, but it must be qualified. Economics provides no absolute justification for maintaining capital intact; it is not necessarily unethical to fail to maintain capital. Capital maintenance has been employed as a theoretical construct, a point of reference from which measurement can take place. Legal rules regarding dividends have been drawn up (see Chapter 7) in terms of profit, which may offer some protection for creditors, although it must be recognized that the rules take on the imprecision associated with profit measurement.

1.11 Historical cost accounting rules

The Companies Act 1985 indicates that companies should normally determine the amounts included in their financial statements in accordance with the historical cost accounting rules (4 sch. 16). Before considering specific standard practices, it is useful to consider how the basic dimensions apply to historical cost accounting.

The suggestion that historical cost accounting is what was used in the past while current cost accounting is what is used at present is clearly an example of an examination blunder. However, it is true that, from its origins, accounting adopted an historical cost basis. Early accounting practice was to record transactions and accumulate such records; it was a later development to consider the usefulness of the balance sheet (or list of balances), and, subsequently, the account to which balances no longer representing assets or liabilities were written off (the embryonic profit and loss account). Early accounting practice can be justified if the transaction records it provided gave cost-effective information for operating a business and for the purposes of control and accountability.

The essential feature of historical cost is that the major source of measurement of value is provided by the monetary sum representing the exchange value of transactions. Sales are recorded at the contracted sales value, as is the effect on the debtor's account for the credit sale. The initial value placed on each item purchased is the agreed amount to be paid for its acquisition.

If the matching process is considered, the historical cost basis involves, first, the accumulation of all direct expenditures on a particular product plus allocations of other expenditures that can be traced to the particular product. The value of a product is obtained in a manner that treats the expenditures incurred directly or indirectly on its production as if they are attached to the product. Thirlby described the method in these terms in a lecture given in 1945:

> He [the accountant] assumes ... that the things acquired carry the money with them and that bits of the things flowing into different departments or products of the business ... or bits of the assumed life period of the things acquired carry bits of the money with them.[31]

In this manner, original expenditures may be included in stock values (or inventories). When the products are sold, the accumulation of expenditures (or 'bits of money') attached to the product expire, no longer representing value. This expiration transforms the expenditure into expenses of the period producing totals that would include 'cost of goods sold'. Here is the realization process in action. With period matching, expenditures for which no product matching is achievable or anticipated are aggregated with other similar items, and expire immediately.

As the above quote indicates, for these assets a life is assumed and the original expenditure (historical cost) is expired over this life, a process more familiarly known as 'depreciation'. Expiry and realization are spread over the life of the asset by means of the depreciation charges. As a result, the historical cost basis matches current revenues with costs of goods sold, measured by expenditures made in the original acquisition of the input. Where inputs are drawn from a pool of resources purchased at different prices, there is a need to attach values to the particular issues from the pool, and the usual approach is arbitrarily to assume a flow pattern of additions and issues (e.g. FIFO—first-in–first-out). It is interesting to observe that the historical cost depreciation figure may have been derived from an expenditure some years before the revenue is recognized, and the depreciation charge is included in the profit and loss account.

In the historical cost balance sheet, assets consist of the unexpired expenditure balances; a stock figure may result from the flow pattern assumed for a pool of similar items; fixed assets will be valued at the original expenditure less amounts written off for depreciation.

Even when adhering to historic cost accounting rules according to SSAP 2, 'it has to be recognised that the complexity and diversity of business renders total and rigid uniformity of bases impracticable'; but, 'as accounting standards become established through publication of statements of standard accounting practice, the choice of accounting bases regarded as generally available will diminish.' The process by which such standards are set is the subject of the next chapter.

Notes

1. *Collin's English Dictionary*, 1987.
2. American Accounting Association, Committee on Concept and Standards for External Reports, 'Statement on Accounting Theory and Theory Acceptance', AAA, 1977.
3. Accounting Standards Committee, 'The Corporate Report', ASC, 1975, p. 28.
4. Report of the study group on 'Objectives of Financial Statements', AICPA, 1973.
5. Financial Accounting Standards Board, *Statement of Financial Accounting Concepts*, no. 1. 'Objectives of financial reporting by business enterprises', FASB, 1978.
6. Accounting Standards Committee, 'Setting Accounting Standards: A Consultative Document', ASC, 1978, p. 27.
7. 'Corporate Report', p. 17.
8. W. Beaver and J. Demski, 'The nature of financial accounting objectives: a summary and synthesis', Studies on Financial Accounting Objectives, supplement to *Journal of Accounting Research*, **12**, 170–187, 1974; J. Demski, 'Choice among financial reporting alternatives',

Accounting Review, **49**, 2, 221–232, April 1974; R. G. May and G. L. Sundem, 'Research for accounting policy: an overview', *Accounting Review*, **51**, 4, 747, October 1976; J. Ohlson and G. Buckman, 'Toward a theory of financial accounting', *Journal of Finance*, **35**, 2, 537–547, May 1980; D. Cooper and M. Sherer, 'The value of corporate accounting reports: Arguments for a political economy of accounting', *Accounting, Organisations and Society*, Vol. 9, 63/4, 1984.

9. R. L. Watts and J. L. Zimmerman, 'Towards a positive theory of the determination of accounting standards', *Accounting Review*, January 1978.
10. M. Friedman, 'The methodology of positive economics', *Essays in Positive Economics*, Chicago, University Press, 1953.
11. C. T. Horngren, 'The marketing of accounting standards', *Journal of Accounting*, October 1973.
12. G. Whittington, 'Financial accounting theory: an overview', *British Accounting Review*, Autumn 1986.
13. J. R. Hicks, *Value and Capital*, 2nd edn, Clarendon Press, Oxford, 1946.
14. This can be shown as follows. Let the rate of interest be a constant and the future benefits be A_1, $A_2, \ldots, A_n, \ldots, A_t$ for each period 1 to t:

$$\text{Opening value} = I_0 = \frac{A_1}{1+r} + \frac{A_2}{(1+r)^2} + \cdots + \frac{A_n}{(1+r)^n} + \cdots + \frac{A_t}{(1+r)^t}$$

$$\text{Closing value including profit} = I_1 = A_1 + \frac{A_2}{1+r} + \cdots + \frac{A_n}{(1+r)^{n-1}} + \cdots + \frac{A_t}{(1+r)^{t-1}}$$

$$= I_0(1+r)$$

$$\text{Profit} = I_1 - I_0 = I_0(1+r) - I_0$$

$$= rI.$$

15. S. S. Alexander, 'Income measurement in a dynamic economy' (revised by D. Solomons), in W. T. Baxter and S. Davidson (eds), *Studies in Accounting*, 3rd edn, ICAEW, 1977.
16. R. Ball and R. Brown, 'An empirical evaluation of accounting income numbers', *Journal of Accounting Research*, Autumn 1968; M. Firth, *The Valuation of Shares and the Efficient Markets Theory*, Macmillan, London, 1977; S. Keane, 'The efficient market hypothesis: the implications for financial reporting', Gee, ICAS, 1980; B. Lev, *Financial Statement Analysis: A New Approach*, Prentice-Hall, Englewood Cliffs, NJ, 1974.
17. Greenball suggests that accounting reports cannot predict and were never intended to predict: M. N. Greenball, 'The predictive ability criterion: its relevance in evaluating accounting data', *Abacus*, June 1971.
18. Including M. C. Jensen and W. H. C. Meckling, 'Theory of the firm: managerial behaviour, agency costs and ownership structure', *Journal of Financial Economics*, October 1976, and R. L. Watts, 'Corporate financial statements, a product of the market and political processes', *Austrian Journal of Management*, April 1977.
19. B. V. Carsberg, A. Hope and R. W. Scapens, 'The objectives of published accounting reports', *Accounting and Business Research*, Summer 1979.
20. E. Stamp, 'Corporate reporting: its future evaluation—A Research Study', CICA, 1980.
21. See A. M. C. Morison, 'The role of the reporting accountant today', *The Accountants Magazine*, September 1970.
22. Ball and Brown, 'Empirical evaluation'.
23. R. S. Kaplan and R. Roll, 'Investor evaluation of accounting information: some empirical evidence', *Journal of Business*, April 1972.

24. B. V. Carsberg and M. Page (eds), *Current Cost Accounting: The Benefits and the Costs*, ICAEW, 1984.
25. L. Kelly, 'The development of a positive theory of corporate management's role in external financial reporting', *Journal of Accounting Literature*, Spring 1983.
26. C. Christenson, 'The Methodology of Positive Accounting', *Accounting Review*, January 1983.
27. SSAP 2 *Disclosure of Accounting Policies*, ASC, 1972.
28. Committee on Accounting Concepts and Standards, 'Accounting and Reporting Standards for Corporate Financial Statements and Preceding Statement and Supplement', AAA, 1957.
29. Accounting Standards Committee, *Accounting for the Effects of Changing Prices: a Handbook*, ASC, 1986.
30. Specific attention is given to these questions in D. P. Tweedie and G. Whittington, *Capital Maintenance Concepts: The Choice*, ASC, 1985.
31. G. F. Thirlby, 'The subjective theory of value and accounting "cost"', *Economica*, February 1946.

Further reading

Baxter, W. T. and S. Davidson (eds), *Studies in Accounting*, 3rd edn, ICAEW, 1977.

Bird, P., *Accountability: Standards in Financial Reporting*, Haymarket, London, 1973.

Hendriksen, E. S., *Accounting Theory*, Irwin, Homewood, Ill., 1970.

Lee, T. A., *Company Financial Reporting—Issues and Analysis*, Nelson, London, 1976.

Most, K. S., *Accounting Theory*, Grid, Columbus, Ohio, 1977.

Parker, R. H. and G. C. Harcourt (eds), *Readings in the Concept and Measurement of Income*, Cambridge University Press, 1969.

Watts, R. L. and J. L. Zimmerman, 'Towards a positive theory of the determination of accounting standards', *Accounting Review*, January 1978, pp. 112–134.

Watts, R. L. and J. L. Zimmerman, 'The demand for and supply of accounting theories: the market for excuses', *Accounting Review*, April 1979, pp. 273–305.

Watts, R. L. and J. L. Zimmerman, *Positive Accounting Theory*, Prentice-Hall, Englewood Cliffs, NJ, 1986.

Zeff, S. A., *Forging Accounting Principles in Five Countries: A History and an Analysis of Trends*, Stipes, Champaign, Ill., 1971.

Zeff, S. A., 'The rise of economic consequences', *Journal of Accountancy*, December 1978.

Questions

1 '... we ought to define a man's income as the maximum value which he can consume during a week, and still expect to be as well off at the end of the week as he was at the beginning.' This quotation is what Hicks referred to as the 'central meaning' and is at the heart of the economic value model in financial accounting theory. However, it is of course defined in terms of an individual. How well does the model stand up when applied to the context of modern business?

2 (a) Describe briefly the theory underlying Hicks's economic model of income and capital. What are its practical limitations? (10 marks)

   (b) Spock purchased a space invader entertainment machine at the beginning of year 1 for £1,000. He expects to receive at annual intervals the following receipts; at the end of year 1, £400; end of year 2, £500; end of year 3, £600. At the end of year 3 he expects to sell the machine for £400.

   Spock could receive a return of 10% in the next best investment.

   The present value of £1 receivable at the end of a period discounted at 10% is as follows:

End of year 1	0.909
End of year 2	0.826
End of year 3	0.751

Required:

Calculate the ideal economic income, ignoring taxation and working to the nearest whole pound.

Your answer should show that Spock's capital is maintained throughout the period and that his income is constant.   (10 marks)

(20 marks)
ACCA, 2.8, RFA, December 1985

3   (a) What do you understand by the term 'revenue recognition'?   (10 marks)
    (b) Briefly outline a policy on revenue recognition for each of the following:
         (i)   magazine subscriptions received by a publisher;   (3 marks)
         (ii) the sale of cars on credit terms;   (3 marks)
         (iii) work-in-progress on a long term contract.   (4 marks)

(20 marks)
ACCA, 2.8, RFA, December 1987

4   You are required to briefly explain the following five accounting concepts AND to discuss for each the implications for financial statements if that concept was abandoned:
    (a) the entity concept;
    (b) the money measurement concept;
    (c) the time interval concept;
    (d) the stable monetary unit concept;
    (e) the substance over form concept.   (20 marks)
ACCA, 2.8, RFA, June 1987

5   The economic income model has three forms: ideal income, *ex ante* income and *ex post* income.
    (i)   Describe each of these three models of income measurement.
    (ii) Say which of these models you consider to be most relevant to the practice of accounting. Give the reasons for your choice.

(20 marks)
ACCA, 2.8, RFA, December 1987

6   Considerable importance has been attached to the need for 'objectivity' or 'verifiability' in accounting reports.
    (a) Compare this need with other user and measurement needs.
    (b) To what extent would you agree that the 'matching principle' helps to achieve objectivity?

7   'Value is added continuously ... the practical problems of revenue recognition have in turn produced the realization and matching principles.'
    (a) Explain how traditional accounting approaches carry out the process of 'revenue recognition'.
    (b) Examine the profit measure that results from 'the realization and matching principles' by considering the user and measurement needs of accounting information.

8   The International Accounting Standard no. 1, 'Disclosure of Accounting Policies', which became operative in 1975, states:

Three considerations should govern the selection of and application by management of the appropriate accounting policies and the preparation of financial statements:
    (i)   *Prudence*
          Uncertainties inevitably surround many transactions. This should be recognised by exercising prudence in preparing financial statements. Prudence does not however, justify the creation of secret or hidden reserves.
    (ii) *Substance over form*
          Transactions and other events should be accounted for and presented in accordance with their substance and financial reality and not merely with their legal forms.
    (iii) *Materiality*
          Financial statements should disclose all items which are material enough to affect evaluations or decisions.

Required:

    (a) Explain how these provisions differ from the Statement of Standard Accounting Practice no. 2, 'Disclosure of Accounting Policies', which was adopted in the United Kingdom in 1972.
                                                                                         (6 marks)

(b) Discuss the extent to which you think that the United Kingdom Standard no. 2 requires revision as a result of the different provisions of the International Accounting Standard no. 1 or as a result of accounting practices permitted under later United Kingdom Statements of Standard Accounting Practice.   (12 marks)

(c) Discuss the benefits of making international standards directly applicable in all countries in which financial statements are published.   (7 marks)

(25 marks)
ACCA, 3.1, AFA, December 1987

2. The place and development of accounting standards

The accounting standard-setting bodies see their objectives as providing reports to satisfy user groups. Whether or not this is the reality of the standard-setting situation is another matter. Watts and Zimmerman refer to the attempts by these bodies to justify their approach to standard-setting as the market for excuses, as an attempt to rationalize their actions.[1] They argue that the standards in fact reflect the needs of particular parties, not users, who lobby for a certain approach to be adopted in a standard. The standard is sold to user groups in terms of the public interest, but this, it is argued, is in fact not the case. We will return to this argument later in the chapter.

2.1 The need for standards

In the previous chapter we considered the objectives of financial reports, both in terms of satisfying the needs of users, and in terms of their effects on other interest groups. The next question to consider is what information should be disclosed in these reports.[2] The Companies Act 1985 lays down minimum statutory requirements for the preparation of company accounts. This Act consolidated the greater part of the Companies Acts from 1948 through to 1983, although certain provisions are contained in separate Acts, for example those relating to insider dealing and business names.

An important influence on the Companies Acts in the UK in recent years has been developments in the EEC. The Community has a long-term goal of harmonizing company legislation in member countries. Part of this involves harmonizing financial disclosure and asset and profit measurement practices in the different countries. The EEC produces directives which over time have to be incorporated into the legislation of the member countries. The directives usually allow for more than one treatment of any controversial item. One reason why the UK needed to introduce a new Companies Act in the 1980s was to incorporate the provisions of the EEC 4th Directive on the format of company accounts.

Another set of regulations that influence the disclosure requirements in accounting statements concerns those that need to be followed by listed companies. In the UK these are the regulations of the Stock Exchange in London, which are given in the *Admission of Securities to Listing*, known as the Yellow Book. For companies whose shares are traded on the Unlisted Securities Market (USM), there are also additional disclosure requirements.

The law sets minimum standards of disclosure, but it will usually follow behind new ideas and developments, and will not always cover technical aspects of accounting reporting. Companies and their accountants, in their reporting practices, not only need to meet the requirements of law, but, in order to satisfy the statutory auditors, need to follow generally accepted accounting principles. It is at this point that the need for accounting standards may arise. Are generally accepted accounting principles sufficiently clear and precise to make the accounts useful to the user?

'If corporate reports are to be useful and to fulfil their fundamental objective, we believe they must possess the following characteristics. They must be (a) relevant, (b) understandable, (c) reliable, (d) complete, (e) objective, (f) timely and (g) comparable.'[3] Unfortunately, financial reports have not always met, and do not always meet, these requirements for usefulness. The accounting profession has, at various times, been criticized for not producing relevant, reliable, objective and comparable financial reports. The profession, wishing to keep its own house in order, has therefore, over time, taken an increasing responsibility towards ensuring that financial reports are useful.

In an attempt to reduce the range of choice of accepted accounting principles, to increase confidence in the figures, and to make accounting reports more understandable, it may be necessary to introduce standards. Of course, there are many groups of users, all of whom have slightly different needs, and so the problem referred to earlier can be seen: which groups of users' needs are considered to be the most important?

In the early 1940s, the Institute of Chartered Accountants in England and Wales (ICAEW) produced guidance statements for members on the best practice to follow in preparing accounts. These were recommendations on accounting principles, an attempt to narrow the range of possible reporting practices. The recommendations did not escape criticism. As early as 1953, Baxter was concerned (but not surprised) at the lack of theoretical foundation for these recommendations, 'Is it wise for any group of men to say what is true or right in matters of theory'?[4] Baxter argued that it was not possible to support any particular practice on the grounds of theory alone. Despite the fact that recommendations were being produced, accounting reporting practices did not escape further criticism in the 1960s. Stamp, among others, argued that there was a need for the recommendations, the guidance statements, to be more firmly based on the objectives of accounting.[5] He argued that pronouncements should be based on the theoretical concepts of accounting.

In addition to this academic criticism, there was criticism from the users of the financial statements.[6] A 'credibility gap' had developed. The users of financial statements often did not know how to interpret the accounts that were being produced. In preparing their accounts, some companies were choosing, from the range of accepted practices, those that made the profit position of the company appear in the best possible light. The companies that used this imaginative form of accounting were often run by people whom the Americans would refer to as 'financial gunslingers', following practices described in the UK as 'creative accounting'. Other companies were preparing accounts based on the traditional accounting principles of 'conservatism' and 'prudence'. Hence the credibility gap: a reader of a set of accounts could not always tell whether it had been prepared on the basis of a conservative set of principles or on the basis of the highest possible profit.

There is, of course, no such thing as a (true) correct profit or loss figure to reflect a year's activities. There is a range of possible profit or loss figures that can be produced on the assumptions that are made. At one end of the range is what some would regard as the 'exaggerated' profit figure, and at the other end is what others would regard as the excessively cautious profit figure. The fact that there is a possible range of profit figures (even with standards), and not a unique figure, should not come as a surprise to anybody who knows something about accounting. The profit and loss account reports the performance over a period of time, but the business does not usually come to an end at the close of that period: contracts may be only half completed; goods may have been produced but not sold; equipment that has been purchased is still usable; and not all customers have paid for goods and services received. Accounting reporting does not just involve measuring what has happened in the past; it also, of necessity, involves making assumptions about certain aspects of what will happen in the future.

These problems, combined with questions such as how to allow for inflation, how to record the transactions accompanying a merger or takeover, and whether the accounting treatment for owning 20 per cent of the equity of a company is different from the treatment for owning 40 per cent of the equity, mean that there can be a whole range of possibilities for anyone wishing to indulge in creative accounting.

The credibility gap was important, because one of the factors that influence investors, bankers and others in their decision-making is how they interpret the financial statements presented to them. The investors' decisions are important, for not only do they affect the demand for a company's shares, but at times of mergers and takeovers they can affect the survival of a company in its existing form. The reputations of some businessmen were built up on the basis of their use of creative accounting. Even conservative executives sometimes had to abandon their more prudent assumptions when preparing accounts, or run the risk of seeing their companies taken over because they were not producing the performance of what were though to be the more dynamic companies. There was clearly a need for accountants to tidy up reporting practices.

The English Institute responded to the criticisms from the users of reports. A 'Statement of Intent on Accounting Standards' was issued in 1969.[7] The Accounting Standards Steering Committee (later the name was changed to the Accounting Standards Committee (ASC)) commenced in 1970. It was initially formed by the English Institute, and almost immediately was joined by the Scottish and Irish Institutes. The Chartered Association of Certified Accountants (ACCA) and the Chartered Institute of Management Accountants (CIMA) joined in 1971, and the Chartered Institute of Public Finance and Accountancy (CIPFA) in 1976.

The ASC was clear in its own mind about the need for and nature of standards. In a consultative document published in 1978, it stated:

(a) Accounting standards are necessary and will continue to be necessary. One of their main aims should be to narrow the choice of accounting treatment so as to make financial statements reasonably comparable one with another.
(b) Statements of Standard Accounting Practice (SSAPs) should continue to be used as definitive principles in financial statements and not merely as a benchmark against which deviations can be measured.
(c) A material departure from an SSAP should continue to be allowed only in those exceptional circumstances where to adhere would fail to give 'a true and fair view' in a particular case, or because to follow the SSAP would be demonstrably inappropriate.[8]

The history of standard-setting in the USA is in fact more involved and goes back further than that of the UK.[9] The users of accounts in the USA became very critical in the 1920s of the levels of corporate disclosure. It was in fact in the early 1930s in the USA where the now familiar terms, 'accounting principles' and 'accepted principles of accounting', first appeared. The Securities Exchange Commission was created in 1934, and it was given authority to determine what accounting and auditing procedures were needed. The Commission was critical of the accounting methods of the time. An outstanding intellectual contribution to the subject was made by Paton and Littleton.[10]

Following much discussion on the subject of accounting principles and standards, the American Institute of Certified Public Accountants (AICPA) established the Accounting Principles Board (APB) in 1959. The Board published 31 opinions before it was dissolved in 1973. An opinion prescribed specific accounting principles and procedures that were to be followed. It should be remembered that the first standard, the first requirement relating to accounting principles and procedures, did not appear in the UK until 1971. The USA was therefore ahead of the UK in the standard-setting process. Because it was ahead, the arguments against the setting of standards by the accounting profession itself were first heard in the USA. The complaints criticized the APB for the lack of participation by organizations other than the professional accounting body. In 1973 came the formation of the present accounting standard-setting body, the Financial Accounting Standards Board (FASB), which allowed for membership by individuals who, although experienced in the field of finance, were not necessarily professional accountants.

Many other countries, including developing countries, have set up accounting standard-setting boards. In 1973 an International Accounting Standards Committee (IASC) was formed by the professional bodies of nine countries. This body has grown, and by 1987 it had representatives from about 70 countries. The Committee produces what are referred to as 'International Accounting Standards'. The application of these standards depends on the willingness of the professional bodies in the different countries to promote them and on the importance of the particular professional bodies in their own countries. The IASC has had an influence on the development of standards within many countries. In the UK the accounting bodies support the work of IASC, although they do not subordinate their authority for standard-setting to this international body.

2.2 The setting of standards

During the 1970s, all the members of the ASC were qualified accountants, members of the governing professional accounting bodies. In 1980 it was suggested that membership should be widened to bring in members who represented *users* of financial statements. This suggestion was in response to criticism that wider interests than just those of the professional bodies should be represented in standard-setting.

Accounting regulation requires value judgements by society.[11] This means that, if there is to be any chance of a standard being considered 'acceptable' to a wider community, it is necessary to have representatives of interest groups other than accountants. The ASC reviewed its standard-setting process in 1983 and revised the composition of its membership to incorporate users of accounting reports.

The composition of the ASC as at the end of 1987 allowed for up to 20 members, up to five of whom were to be representatives of users of financial statements. In addition, the constitution allows for two additional non-voting representatives of the government to be co-opted to the Committee.

The normal procedure for developing a standard has evolved over the life of the Committee. The ASC decides on a programme of subjects that need a standard. For each subject, a subcommittee is formed of representatives of accountants in public practice, in industry, in commerce and in specialist and non-specialist interests. The first stage in the preparation of the standard is the commission of research studies on the topic under consideration. When the studies have been prepared, the second stage is the discussion and eventual preparation of a preliminary draft of a standard by the relevant working party. The third stage is one of early consultation. Copies of the preliminary draft are made available to the technical committees of the constituent accounting bodies, and these are discussed by these committees and at regional meetings of the accounting bodies. The ASC may also hold meetings with organizations that are likely to be significantly affected by the proposals.

The fourth stage is the preparation by the subcommittee of the exposure drafts, the subcommittee having taken into account the comments received at the previous stage. These drafts are mailed to major organizations and companies and are reprinted in the professional accounting journals. Comments are invited on the drafts, and the period open to receive comments is usually six months. The fifth stage is the receipt and consideration of these comments by a panel of the ASC. Further consultation now takes place with representatives of bodies whose comments indicate problems with the proposed standard. An innovation following FASB practice has been the holding of open meetings at which any interested parties are welcome to attend and express their opinions on the proposal. The sixth stage is the preparation of the proposed SSAP incorporating any amendments to the exposure draft in the light of the comments received and the consultations that have taken place. The seventh stage is the approval of the proposed standard by the councils of the six accounting bodies who comprise the Consultative Committee of Accounting Bodies (CCAB). The ASC is a joint committee of the six accounting bodies, who act together on the

CCAB. Each of the six bodies needs to approve the standard before it is published as an accepted standard. The publication of the SSAP is the eighth stage.

2.2.1   Nature of standards

It must not be thought that, as a result of all the research, discussion and consultation that goes into a statement, the principles expounded in the statement and the practices that it advocates are necessarily right, and that all other approaches to the problem are wrong. Right and wrong imply that it is possible to choose logically between alternatives. We do not know which accounting practices are right and which are wrong, as we have no objective standards by which to compare the alternatives. There is no agreed theory of accounting; there is no model that enables us to decide that, in order to achieve some objective, one accounting practice is better than another. There is no universal acceptance of a meaning, for measurement purposes, of many relevant terms, including 'profit'.

There are a number of theories of accounting, and these were considered in the previous chapter. Watts and Zimmerman express the view, however, that no one theory of accounting will ever be able to explain or justify the accounting standards that we have, owing to the nature and diversity of the effective demand for standards.[12]

This argument leads to an alternative approach to measurement and disclosure. Many authors point to the myriad uses of accounting data, and to the large number of decision models in use, in practice and in theory, and maintain that it is impossible to produce a set of income and asset numbers that are optimal to a wide range of users.[13] This means either that different reports are produced for different user groups, or that accountants concentrate on disclosing disaggregated data, or that general-purpose statements are produced.

The accounting standards that we have, and those that will be produced in the future, are pragmatic. They are each the result of the interplay of three forces: political pressure, existing accounting practice, and accounting theory, which might have a small amount of influence. The process of arriving at a standard means that it is a compromise. A committee prepares the standards after consultation with many people and a number of relevant interest groups. With so much consultation, and so many organizations and pressure groups having an influence on the final standard, there is bound to be a fair amount of give and take. It must not even be thought that the practice that eventually becomes the accepted standard has received unanimous approval at all stages of its development. It could well have passed any particular stage only by a vote, say, with an outcome of ten in favour and eight against.

This point is being emphasized not in any way to discredit a statement of standard practice, but to show why the approved practice is not 'right' and all other possibilities 'wrong'. It is the practice accepted by the balance of a particular group of people and interest groups as being the best at a particular point of time. A different group of people involved in the various stages of the development of the standard, or the same people consulting at a different time, could well have produced a different standard. A further point is that an alternative possible practice, one that was not recommended by the Standards Committee, but which received minority support, might be almost as acceptable as the one that is recommended. It is not a matter of deciding upon the right practice, but of deciding upon the practice that is the most acceptable one out of a number of possibilities, all of which have something to be said for them.

The accounting standard-setting procedure in the UK and the USA is a bargaining process.[14] In the USA, however, the powerful government agency, the Securities and Exchange Commission, oversees the work of the FASB. There is not such a watching body in the UK, although with the changes being introduced through the SIB it is possible that the position could alter. The UK system is based on the principle of self-regulation except where this can be shown not to work; the

US system does not trust self-regulation. The accounting standard-setting process in the UK is based on achieving compromise solutions to issues, based on a consideration of the interests of the groups concerned with the standard-setting process.

Despite the criticism of academics, the exposure drafts and statements hardly even use theoretical concepts to support the proposals. The ASC does regard the research stage as the first step in the preparation of any standards. But often the research is carried out in professional offices, in order to ascertain the existing range of practices and the arguments for and against each approach: it is not research into the general problem of the conceptual framework of accounting, or an attempt to ascertain the social choice process to be used to determine any particular accounting standard.

A conceptual framework consists of a collection of agreed objectives.[15] For accountants, such a framework would allow accounting policy-makers to decide on controversial standards, without making judgements that can be seen to be in favour of one interest group at the expense of another. In the USA much research has been undertaken into the conceptual framework of accounting, but the results have not yet led to an agreed framework. The ASC has long been conscious of the lack of a conceptual framework in the UK. It has answered critics by pointing out that this criticism is

broadly equivalent to the compliant that the ASC has failed to define the meaning of 'profit', the purpose of the 'balance sheet' and the implications of 'capital maintenance'. The critics argue that, once these are clearly explained, it will be possible to construct an edifice of accounting standards with such soundly based foundations that the resulting SSAPs could be seen to have a clear logical development. The ASC believes, however, that while such a foundation would be a great advantage, it is unavailable at present.

The users of financial statements have different objectives, and in the absence of unanimity it is not possible to develop an acceptable foundation based on definitions of 'profit', the 'balance sheet', or 'capital maintenance' which would be universally accepted. This partly arises because accounting is in a transitional stage between historical cost accounting and accounting based on current values. It also arises because there is a partial conflict between the prudence concept of accounting (which seeks not to anticipate profits) and the accruals concept (which seeks to match, so far as possible, revenues and costs attributable to the same accounting period). In any event, in the absence of agreed definitions, progress must be made on a pragmatic basis, step by step.[16]

It is true that there are no universally accepted ideas on how to measure profit and what values should go into a balance sheet. Not all would agree, however, that this is because accounting is at a transitional stage, or because there is conflict between the prudence concept and the accruals concept. Many would argue that the lack of an agreed theory is much more fundamental.

In spite of the research efforts of academic accountants, an 'agreed conceptual framework' has not and may never be produced. Perhaps, therefore, the ASC is wise in not waiting for such an agreement to emerge. There are those who favour the present approach, and those who are worried about it. Edey supports accounting standards as produced at present, because they speed up, and improve, the process of communication.[17] This justification is based on standards having only a limited role; it is necessary for the standard to be accepted and understood by users, but it is not necessary for it to be optimal.

Cushing has argued that it does not matter that those who participate in the standard-setting process cannot agree on the principles that should govern all standards and so cannot agree on an optimal set of standards.[18] It does not matter because, although they cannot agree on the overall position, they can agree on the treatment of particular items that appear in financial statements. Cushing would argue that it is better to proceed step by step with what can be agreed upon—a sequential approach—than to be bogged down looking for a overall framework.

Bromwich has also answered in support of the sequential approach. He argues that the utility function of the user of financial statements has a number of components. If the components are independent of each other, then a financial statement will be seen by the user to be beneficial if it satisfies some of these components; it will be beneficial even if it does not give the user all that he would like.[19]

Morison, on the other hand, believes that, without an agreed conceptual framework, any selection of a standard is arbitrary.[20] Enforcing the adoption of the standard by companies is likely to cause mindless uniformity. This is similar to Baxter's argument that to lay down 'principles' leads to rigidity, which may inhibit new approaches to the problems.[21] Baxter and Morison would favour recommendations on accounting practice, but not enforced standards.

Earlier in this chapter, seven characteristics that corporate reports must possess in order to be useful to users were mentioned. Accounting standards can be justified on the grounds that they are trying to improve the usefulness of financial statements. Let us see which of the seven characteristics have been improved by the introduction of standards.

Relevance means that the financial statements must meet users' needs. In that some users, such as investment analysts and financial institutions, make effective comments during the preparation of a standard, presumably the introduction of standards does meet their needs. There are other user groups, however, who would not seem to benefit from the standards, and there are those who argue that standards such as SSAP 16 make reports less relevant. On balance, however, a plus for standards is that they make financial reports more understandable, even if only because they increase disclosure on accounting policies. Moving to another required characteristic, there is no reason to believe that standards on balance improve reliability. The information was verified by auditors as being 'true and fair' before the introduction of standards as well as after. Standards have, however, helped to make financial reports more complete, calling for the production of such figures as those in a sources and application of funds statement.

It can be argued that standards are not objective, because we have no agreed theory of accounting, no conceptual framework. The accounts are not, as far as we know, biased in favour of one interest group, but we are not sure, because we still do not have an agreed measure of profit or capital maintenance. Standards have not improved the timeliness of accounts, but they have definitely improved comparability; there is now greater consistency in the application of accounting concepts and policies.

Against the above-mentioned good points about standards must be weighed the criticisms that they are arbitrary, lead to rigidity, and inhibit new accounting approaches.[22]

As has already been mentioned, the influences that come together to shape an accounting standard are existing practice, theoretical ideas and political pressures. Many writers have argued that standard-setting is a political process. Hope points out that the ASC is more likely to find its standards considered politically acceptable by the community if the changes proposed are only incremental to existing practice and existing standards, rather than if they are a radical departure from them.[23]

2.2.2 Recommended practice or enforced standards

In general, the SSAPs are intended to apply to all financial accounts which purport to give a 'true and fair view' of the financial position of a business and its profit and loss. Certain of the standards that have been issued, however, are relevant only to large enterprises. Small companies tend not to undertake research and development, to engage in foreign currency transactions or to hold investment properties.

The question of whether the standards, if relevant, should apply to all companies irrespective of size is controversial. Small companies often argue that for them to comply with accounting standards is an unnecessary and expensive burden. An alternative view is that those who refer to the account of small companies, for example bank managers, need to be confident that they understand the meaning of the published figures. In fact, the research undertaken by Carsberg and

Page on the burden of accounting standards found that there was no evidence to suggest that in general small companies find compliance with standards burdensome.[24] The ASC in 1987 set up a working party which concluded that standards should normally apply to all companies irrespective of size.

Views differ as to whether a standard should be enforced or whether it should just be a recommendation of what is considered to be best practice. At present, the position is that 'Significant departures in financial accounts from applicable accounting standards should be disclosed and explained. The financial effects should be estimated and disclosed unless this would be impracticable or misleading in the context of giving a true and fair view. If the financial effects of the departure from standards are not disclosed, the reasons should be stated.[25] The professional bodies make clear that there is an obligation on its members to observe accounting standards or justify departures. Where the members act in their capacity as directors or officers of a company, they should use their best endeavours to ensure that accounting standards are observed in the accounts of the company. Where the members are acting as auditors, not only do they need to ensure that any significant departures from standards are disclosed, but also, if they concur with the departure, either explicitly or implicitly, they need to justify why they do so.

The question of whether or not an accounting standards body should approve the use of just a single accounting procedure to deal with a problem area, or whether it should approve a list of acceptable alternatives, is one that has been the subject of much debate. As previously explained, a recommended best procedure may be only marginally superior to the second-best. The argument in favour of a single approved procedure rests on the assumption that this minimizes confusion and misunderstanding by the users of accounting information. Confusion is bad in that it can lead to incorrect decisions, for example the misallocation of resources in the capital markets. Investors may be misled as to the true performance of a company over a period of time, as they sometimes were before standards were introduced. An argument against unique standards is that to recommend a single procedure will be unfair on certain companies. This in itself can lead to incorrect decisions, for example (again) to the misallocation of funds in the capital markets. The companies being forced to follow an inappropriate procedure could well finish up with a share price that does not reflect true value.

It is because there is no generally accepted theory to guide us in selecting between the alternative possibilities that some people argue that recommendations on reporting practice are acceptable, but not enforceable, standards. Supporters of recommendations would argue that if a company wishes to depart from the recommended practice it should be free to do so, but it should show in its accounts, by way of a note, the financial effect of departing from the recommendation, and its reasons for adopting an alternative approach. This is, in fact, the practice at the present time. Accounting standards are not meant to be rigid rules. Departures from standards are allowed, but the departure needs to be disclosed and explained. It must be remembered that the overriding consideration in preparing accounts is to give a true and fair view.

In fact, the ASC, recognizing the difficulties of attempting to introduce standardization in certain issues and faced with increasing levels of non-compliance, introduced in 1986 its Statements of Recommended Practice (SORPs)

> The primary aims in issuing SORPs are to narrow the areas of difference and variety in the accounting treatment of the matters with which they deal and to enhance the usefulness of published accounting information. SORPs are issued on subjects on which it is not considered appropriate to issue an accounting standard at the time.

The object of these statements is to set out current best practice. SORPs always take into account the principle laid down in accounting standards. It is recognized that it would be impracticable for accounting standards to cater for all situations. In applying a modified or alternative treatment, it is important to have regard to the spirit of, and reasoning behind, any relevant accounting standards. The recommendations contained in SORPs will always have regard to this spirit and reasoning. They may, therefore, be indicative of the treatment that should be adopted in a situation not specifically catered for by accounting standards.

Unlike accounting standards, SORPs are not mandatory on members of the governing bodies of the ASC. It follows that entities that do not follow a SORP are not obliged by the ASC or, normally, its governing bodies to disclose the fact or the nature of any departure.

SORPs may be developed and issued by the Accounting Standards Committee. Alternatively, they may be developed and, after approval and franking by the ASC, issued by an 'industry' group which is representative of the industry concerned for the purpose of developing SORPs specific to that industry and is recognized as such by the ASC. Such SORPs are referred to as 'franked SORPs'.

2.3   Where are we now?

If there were an agreed theory of accounting and agreed objectives, it would be possible to choose between alternative accounting principles and practices on a rational basis. There is no agreed theory, and there are disagreements on objectives. In 1977 the AAA set up a committee to survey the literature on accounting theory and to report on the state of the art at that time.[26] This survey was 'intended to provide the foundation necessary for our subsequent examination of the reasons that the profession has been unable to achieve concensus on a "general" theory of external reporting'. The divergent theories of external reporting were seen to arise as a result of differences in specifications of users' needs. The multiplicity of theories that exist was seen as mutually exclusive, precluding therefore a synergistic combination.

Among the obstacles it saw to the acceptance of a universal theory were: (1) the problem of relating theory to practice, (2) the allocation problem, (3) the difficulty with normative standards, (4) difficulties in interpreting security price-behaviour research, (5) the problem of cost–benefit considerations in accounting theories and (6) limitations of data.

The committee concluded that it was not possible to dictate that one theory should be accepted to the exclusion of all others; that all theories have some flaw; and that 'external reporting theory has a wider scope than that which has generally been perceived'. Not surprisingly, in view of all the obstacles it mentioned, it does not see the role of accounting theories as any more than a partial aid to policy decisions at the present time. Returning to the point made at the beginning of the chapter, and also by the committee, namely that external reporting has a wider scope than generally perceived, one approach to the problem of choosing between alternative reporting practices is to measure the impact of accounting reports and changes in accounting practices on stock market prices. This has been the subject of much research.[27] The rationale for this approach is that shareholders and investors are important users of accounting reports and it is worthwhile observing how they use the information provided, and using the reactions of this group to decide on which accounting practice is best. This is, of course, only a partial analysis.

The approach can be criticized in that it ignores the externalities. Shareholders make decisions on the basis of financial information; their decisions effect many people, and if we are concerned with setting a standard that needs to maximize general welfare rather than shareholders' welfare, then we need to be concerned with the wider impact of the accounting reports.

A vast volume of research has in fact been concerned with the impact of accounting reports on stock exchange prices. The stock market is said to be 'efficient' if the prices fully reflect all available financial information. This is sometimes seen as a way of enabling choices to be made between alternative accounting practices. Indeed, one way in which the current cost accounting standard, SSAP 16, was assessed was by monitoring its impact on share prices.[28] There are those, however, who do not believe that efficient market tests provide a logical basis for making choices between accounting policies. They are worried about (among other things) free riders, those who do not pay for the financial reports but nevertheless use them for gain.

Studying the partial impact of accounting standards is relatively easy; it is very much harder to measure the wider impact. However, the fact that it is harder does not mean that the idea should be ignored. It can be argued that one should choose between alternative accounting possibilities by measuring their respective contributions towards social welfare. Of course, social welfare is almost impossible to measure, but this does not mean that one can retreat into measuring the impact of accounting reporting on just certain user groups, for example the effect on share prices. As Zeff argues, any change in reporting practices must be assessed in terms of its impact on the 'decision-making behaviour of business, governments, unions, investors and creditors'.[29] A change in a standard can have an impact on very many more people than those who are usually considered part of the 'user groups'.

Accounting standard-setters should, as far as is possible, take into account the economic consequences of their actions. Undoubtedly, the way in which certain items can be reported in the financial accounts affects certain decisions that are made. As one example of this, the dividing line used in the accounting standard on whether or not a lease transaction should be capitalized affected the management decision on whether to lease or purchase an asset, and on the terms that would be incorporated into the document recording any leasing transaction.

Of course, it is extremely difficult, if not impossible, for accounting policy-makers to be able to assess all the direct and indirect results of the policies they decide upon. On the leasing question, for example, were accounting policy-makers, in determining whether a transaction was to be classed as a finance lease or an operating lease, expected to take into account the possible employment consequences of a company deciding, because of the approved accounting treatment, not to go ahead with a decision to use an asset, because it could not be classed as a finance lease?

The fact that secondary and redistributional effects of decisions are hard to calculate does not mean that they should be ignored. They are additional factors that a socially aware accounting standard-setting body needs to consider.

Accounting standard-setting is one attempt to improve the reporting system. It is, however, not the end of the story, and within five to ten years it is reasonable to assume that we will be trying other methods to improve communication between businesses, shareholders, potential investors, employees, the government and all other users of accounts. We will also be concerned with the impact of accounts on third parties as well as the user groups.

In the 1970s the business world, the financial community and the accounting profession had high expectations from accounting standards. By the mid-1980s, considerable disillusionment had set in. In the UK, the level of non-compliance was increasing. Regrettably, the Accounting Standards Committee was not even monitoring the level of non-compliance. In 1987 attempts were being made (in the UK) to improve the credibility of accounting standards and the standard-setting process. A working party under the chairmanship of a respected businessman was set up to see if improvements could be introduced.

There are at least two areas of major concern. One is that, on many important issues, the accounting standard-setting bodies either cannot agree on the appropriate treatments or else take too long to come to a recommendation. Accounting at the time of changing prices is an example of the first problem; off-balance-sheet financing is an example of delay.

In the USA there was concern that, on many of the major issues that were emerging in the fields of finance and accounting, there were no standards or recommendations with regard to the appropriate accounting treatment. It was taking a considerable time for the FASB to produce a standard, and during this period the preparers of accounts could do as they liked, to the confusion of the users. The FASB, in an attempt to overcome this problem, set up an 'Emerging Issues Task Force'. In the UK there is also a considerable lag between the time when an accounting issue emerges and the time when, if at all, a standard or statement is produced.

The other area of major concern is that the accounting treatment that is being recommended, both in the UK and the USA, is designed more to satisfy the interests of the preparers of accounts than those of the users. A political process is involved in reaching a concensus agreement. For various reasons, such as having to look after the interests of their client groups or because some actually are selected to represent the preparers of accounts, members of the standard-setting bodies are not always concerned primarily with the needs of users.

This is unfortunate, because preparers of accounts are often concerned with ensuring that there is as little change as possible to their existing way of doing things. Understandably, they want to minimize costs. They also tend to prefer accounting practices that are inclined to smooth changes in income and earnings, rather than those that give the impression of greater volatility.

It is intended that the information disclosed, and the financial statements produced, will give a 'true and fair' view of the state of affairs of the company. Perhaps our expectation of the outcome of the accounting standard-setting process is too high. Existing knowledge is such that standards cannot be produced that will command universal support, that will not be seen to favour one interest group at the expense of another. As Bromwich points out, many of the problems are not amenable to logical analysis.[30] Their solutions await development in a wide range of disciplines. Yet the subject of accounting standards is important and should not be swept under the carpet. The credibility of financial accounts is what justifies the accounting profession. If the public and/or the government feel that the accounting profession is no longer to be trusted, if it is felt that it is not acting responsibly, then changes will be introduced.

Notes

1. R. L. Watts and J. L. Zimmerman, 'The demand for and supply of accounting theories: the market for excuses', *Accounting Review*, April 1979.
2. P. Taylor and S. Turley, *The Regulation of Accounts*, Basil Blackwell, Oxford, 1986.
3. Accounting Standards Committee, 'The Corporate Report', ASC, 1975, p. 28.
4. W. T. Baxter, 'Recommendations on accounting theory', *The Accountant*, October 1953; reprinted in W. T. Baxter and S. Davidson (eds), *Studies in Accounting Theory*, Sweet & Maxwell, London, 1962.
5. E. Stamp, 'The public accountant and the public interest', *Journal of Finance*, Spring 1969.
6. E. Stamp and C. Marley, *Accounting and the City Code*, Butterworth, London, 1970.
7. Institute of Chartered Accountants in England and Wales, 'Statement of Intent on Accounting Standards in the 1970s', ICAEW, 1979.
8. Accounting Standards Committee, 'Setting Accounting Standards: A Consultative Document', ASC, 1978.
9. S. A. Zeff, *Forging Accounting Principles in Five Countries*, Stipes, Champaign, Ill., 1972.
10. W. A. Paton and A. C. Littleton, *An Introduction to Corporate Accounting Standards*, AAA Monograph no. 3, 1940.
11. M. Bromwich, *The Economics of Accounting Standard Setting*, Prentice-Hall, Englewood Cliffs, NJ, 1985.
12. R. L. Watts and J. L. Zimmerman, 'Demand for . . . accounting theories'.
13. K. V. Peasnell, 'The function of a conceptual framework for corporate financial reporting', *Accounting and Business Research*, Autumn 1982.

14. R. Macve, 'A Conceptual Framework for Financial Accounting and Reporting', ICAEW, 1981.
15. Peasnell, 'Function of a conceptual framework'.
16. A.S.C., 'Setting Accounting Standards', p. 27.
17. H. C. Edey, 'Accounting standards in the British Isles', in W. T. Baxter and S. Davidson (eds), *Studies in Accounting*, ICAEW, 1977.
18. B. Cushing, 'On the possibility of optimal accounting principles', *Accounting Review*, April 1977.
19. M. Bromwich, 'The possibility of partial accounting standards', *Accounting Review*, April 1980; M. Bromwich, 'The setting of accounting standards', in M. Bromwich and A. G. Hopwood (eds), *Essays in British Accounting Research*, Pitman, London, 1981.
20. A. M. C. Morison, 'The role of the reporting accountant today', *The Accountants Magazine*, January/February 1970; reprinted in Baxter and Davidson (eds), *Studies in Accounting Theory*.
21. Baxter, 'Recommendations'.
22. Edey, 'Accounting standards'.
23. A. Hope, 'Accounting policy: theory or pragmatism or both', Submission on the Accounting Standards Committee's Document, *Setting Accounting Standards*, Vol. 11, ASC, 1979.
24. B. Carsberg and M. Page, *Current Cost Accounting: Benefits and Costs*, ICAEW, 1984.
25. Institute of Chartered Accountants in England and Wales, *Accounting Standards 1980*, ICAEW, 1980.
26. American Accounting Association, Committee on Concepts and Standards for External Financial Reports, 'Statement on Accounting Theory and Theory Acceptance', AAA, 1977.
27. R. Ball and R. Brown, 'An empirical evaluation of accounting income numbers', *Journal of Accounting Research*, Autumn 1968; M. Firth, *The Valuation of Shares and the Efficient Markets Theory*, Macmillan, London, 1977; S. Keane, 'The efficient market hypothesis: the implications for financial reporting', *Gee*, ICAS, 1980; B. Lev, *Financial Statement Analysis: A New Approach*, Prentice-Hall, Englewood Cliffs, NJ, 1974.
28. Carsberg and Page, *Current Cost Accounting*.
29. S. A. Zeff, 'The age of economic consequences', *Journal of Accounting*, December 1978.
30. Bromwich, *Economics of Accounting Standard Setting*.

Further reading

Beaver, W. H., *Financial Reporting: An Accounting Revaluation*, Prentice-Hall, Englewood Cliffs, NJ, 1981.
Blake, J., *Accounting Standards*, 2nd ed, Pitman, London, 1988.
Bloom, R. and P. T. Elgers, *Accounting Theory and Policy*, 2nd edn, Harcourt Brace, Jovanovich, New York, 1987.
Carsberg, B. and T. Hope (eds), *Current Issues in Accounting*, 2nd edn, Philip Allan, Oxford 1984.
Harvey, M. and F. Keen, *Financial Accounting: Theory and Standards*, 2nd edn, Prentice-Hall, Englewood Cliffs, NJ, 1983.
Morris, R. D., 'Signalling, agency theory and accounting policy choice', *Accounting and Business Research*, Winter 1987.
Rutherford, B. A., 'The true and fair view doctrine: a search for explication', *Journal of Business Finance & Accounting*, Winter 1985.
Taylor, P. and S. Turley, 'Applying economic consequences analysis in accounting standard setting: a tax incidence approach', *Journal of Business Finance and Accounting*, Winter 1986.
Walker, M., 'The information economics approach to financial reporting', *Accounting and Business Research*, Spring 1988.

Whittington, G., 'Positive accounting theory: a review article', *Accounting and Business Research*, Autumn 1987.

Questions

1. The Accounting Standards Committee has frequently been criticized for its failure to develop a 'conceptual framework'.

   Required:
   (a) What is generally understood by the term 'conceptual framework'?   (4 marks)
   (b) What advantage(s) might arise from using a 'conceptual framework'?   (8 marks)
   (c) What do you consider would be the difficulties in trying to develop a conceptual framework in the UK?   (8 marks)
                                                                                              (20 marks)
                                                                          ACCA, 2.8, RFA, December 1985

2. Examine the concept of a 'true and fair' view in the context of financial reporting in the UK and briefly discuss its implications in relation to accounting standards.   (20 marks)
                                                                          ACCA, 2.8, RFA, December 1985

3. Accounting standards can be categorized as follows:
   Type 1 description of accounting practice;
   Type 2 presentation;
   Type 3 disclosure;
   Type 4 valuation and profit measurement.

   (a) Give ONE example of an SSAP that belongs to each category and briefly justify your categorization of it.   (8 marks)
   (b) What do you consider is the essential problem that each category seeks to overcome? Only brief comments are required.   (6 marks)
   (c) How successful have each of these categories of standard been and why?   (6 marks)
                                                                                              (20 marks)
                                                                          ACCA, 2.8, RFA, December 1986,

4. Schedule 4 of the Companies Act 1985 states that amounts to be included in respect of all items shown in a company's accounts shall be determined in accordance with 'accounting principles'.

   Describe each of these accounting principles.   (20 marks)
                                                                          ACCA, 2.8, RFA, December 1986

3. Tangible assets

In the first chapter, the role played by asset valuation was explained in theoretical terms. In particular, when using the historical cost basis, assets represent unrealized expenditure, stored in anticipation of inclusion in future profit and loss statements as expenses through the matching process. Tangibility was considered an advantageous property for accounting purposes. This property is generally associated with physical form, although the classification is not always consistent. 'Debtors', which are rights to future receipts, provide a source of conflict. They are not usually considered to be intangibles, but they do not possess the physical form of a tangible. The view adopted in the previous chapter would consider all assets to be more dependent on future receipts than on physical form. The identification of tangible assets may rely mainly on the strength of evidence that verifies the existence of the asset. Physical form offers strong evidence.

The desire for prudence, objectivity and verifiability means that tangible assets predominate other balance sheet assets. As a result, the accounting treatment of these assets will be particularly significant. Physical form is important not only for accounting purposes, but in the business environment as well. It is the physical form of a machine that actually creates output. Physical possession is an important indicator of ownership, certainly in terms of substance, if not in terms of legal form also.

Nevertheless, accounting for tangible assets has its problem areas: valuation is a major problem, even when an historical basis is employed; write-downs of recorded asset values are required to reflect obsolescence, deterioration and the value changes that arise from changes in tastes and needs; methods must be found to deal with pools of physical assets; prudence creates additional difficulties, particularly when it conflicts with other conventions. This chapter examines the accounting treatment of those tangible items with physical form, namely, stock and work in progress, giving particular attention to long-term contracts and fixed assets (the long-term operational assets). This last group includes depreciable assets, and an examination of depreciation forms a significant part of this chapter.

3.1 Stocks and work in progress

This section considers stocks and that work in progress which is normally turned over within an accounting period (a year).

Normal business activity continually transforms raw materials into partly completed goods and subsequently into finished goods before they are sold. 'Stocks and work in progress' includes raw materials, consumable stores and other assets purchased for resale or for incorporation into products to be sold, products and services in intermediate stages of completion, and finished goods. The problem of pools of resources applies particularly here, since prices of inputs tend to fluctuate; attention must be given to the establishment of a cost valuation ensuring that this does not produce a valuation that is greater than that which can be matched against future revenue. The effects of the approach on reported profit and loss must be considered. No area of accounting has produced wider differences in practice than the computation of the amount at which stocks and work in progress are stated in financial accounts. This statement prefaced the related standard, SSAP 9, issued in May 1975.[1] It provides an assessment of the task of the Accounting Standards Committee.

Although the exposure draft ED 6 had been issued in May 1972, the three years between this and the standard were occupied more by discussion with the Inland Revenue about the taxation implications than by debate in relation to its adoption in accounting practice.

The essential requirement of the standard is that:

> The amount at which stocks and work in progress, other than long-term contract work in progress, is stated in periodic financial statements should be the total of the lower of cost and net realizable value of the separate items of stock and work in progress or of groups of similar items.[2]

By way of amplification, costs are explained as follows:

> In order to match costs and revenue, 'costs' of stocks and work in progress should comprise that expenditure which has been incurred in the normal course of business in bringing the product or service to its present location and condition. Such costs will include all related production overheads, even though these may accrue on a time basis.[3]

These general principles are now part of the Companies Act 1985, and the implementation of these requirements can be examined.

3.1.1   Treatment of resource pools

There are a number of techniques addressed to the problem of relating to specific units of stocks and work in progress the expenditure that arises where numbers of identical items are purchased, made and used at different times. The standard recognizes that the selection of job, batch or process costing will depend on the production methods employed in particular situations. However, it gives clear guidance in an appendix[4] to the suitability of the assumed flow of stock items. As will be explained, this guidance is concerned more with balance sheet values than with the values entering the profit and loss account.

A target is set for the fairest practicable approximation to 'actual cost', referring to historical cost. LIFO (last-in–first-out) and base stock methods produce stock valuations that relate to a remote past purchase, although the cost of goods sold is normally more recent. The appendix to the standard considers these methods to be rarely suitable, showing concern for the balance sheet. Similarly, the use of the most recent or current input price is rejected because of its incompatibility with the historic cost basis.

The specific tracing of expenditure direct to units obviously fulfils the requirement of an 'actual' or historic cost most closely. Where direct tracing is not available two common methods remain and are quoted as suitable examples in the appendix. These are average unit cost and FIFO. The disadvantage of the latter has been implied above; it produces charges in the profit and loss account based on events further in time from the realization date. However, these methods are relatively simple to operate, particularly when compared with the complex LIFO procedures allowed and employed in the USA.

Two bases other than the use of past costs are given attention. Standard costs, provided they are regularly reviewed and updated, can bear a sufficient relationship to 'actual' costs to meet the needs of the pronouncement. The use of selling price as a method of arriving at cost is acceptable only in limited circumstances. It is useful in establishing a value for minor by-products. The costing of joint products and by-products is recognized as a particularly arbitrary exercise,[5] so the establishment of the value of a by-product in terms of its sales value net of subsequent costs will satisfy a need. The actual cost of the main product(s) should be calculated by deducting the net realizable value of by-products produced from the total cost of main products and by-products. In other cases, selling price should be used as a basis for establishing cost only when no suitable costing system exists. A reasonable approximation to cost must be given, usually by deducting a gross profit margin from the full selling price. Critics would argue that this is artificially building in a profit margin in a future period, while to not make the deduction anticipates the profit that has not yet met the requirements for realization. The net realizable value approach is examined later in this section.

3.1.2 Cost and the inclusion of overhead

Following the requirement to include in cost all expenditure incurred in bringing the product to its present location, all production overheads are to be included with direct costs. Some consideration was given in Chapter 1 as to whether or not indirect costs should be included and carried forward to future periods. This reflects an opinion on whether or not there was a benefit to the future period from the earlier overhead expenditure. The standard appears to accept that there is,[6] even when considering time apportioned overhead. The exceptions are items that are clearly not linked with production, or those not incurred in the normal course of business.

In particular, overhead costs of general management, as distinct from functional management, should be excluded along with abnormal items such as exceptional spoilage or unusual idle time. It is appropriate to add in selling overhead only when valuing stock for which firm sales contracts exist. Financing charges including interest would not normally be included, although an exception is the property industry, where for development properties this is more like a normal production cost. Storage costs would be excluded in most cases since they are a part of the cost not of bringing a product to its present location and condition, but merely of keeping it there. This would not be the case when storage was part of the production process, such as for the maturing of alcoholic spirits, particularly whisky.

It is clear that depreciation of production facilities should be part of the relevant overhead. However, the resulting cost will be affected by how recently the assets were purchased. If prices have been rising, the company with older assets will have lower depreciation charges and lower stock values. A greater problem would arise for a company that had revalued its assets under these circumstances. Strict adherence to SSAP 9 requires that only expenditure actually incurred must be included in inventory values. The revaluation is not such an expenditure, and apparently the depreciation on the revaluation would have to be excluded from the overhead included in stock. Stock values would remain at the low value that would have arisen without asset revaluation; all the depreciation on the revaluation would have to be written off to the profit and loss account, reducing current profit. A more flexible interpretation of the standard, including the full depreciation charge in the overhead to be allocated to stock value, would achieve better comparability between companies and less distortion.

The method of overhead allocation is also given attention. Adhering to the requirement that stock should include costs incurred in the normal course of business, allocation should be based on the normal level of activity. In establishing a normal level, three considerations are suggested; the normal physical capacity of the facilities, budget information, and recent achieved levels. Care must be used in the use of budgets, as they are often prepared not as the plan of expected achievement, but as a target offering desired motivational effects. The difference between the target and expectations is a distortion that must be eliminated for costing purposes. Coats Paton's policy appears to have little problems in establishing volume: 'Costs are established on the basis of existing levels of production.' This does not specifically recognize the need to establish a normal level, but considers only the actual level.

3.1.3   Net realizable value and stock write downs

During periods of rising prices, 'actual' cost is more likely to understate than overstate stock values. However, obsolescence, deterioration and a change in market conditions can all lead to a decline in value below cost. Prudence and the matching approach indicate that values carried forward must be in anticipation of future matching. The standard recognizes the possibility of such a decline by requiring valuation to be at the lower of cost and net realizable value.[7]

Net realizable value is the current selling price less the costs of completing and selling the product. This does pose measurement problems in establishing both the selling price and the deduction to be made, particularly for a product that has only begun to be manufactured. The figure to be deducted from selling price will be relatively large, introducing plenty of scope for error. An alternative market valuation is supplied by the current buying price of the inputs, i.e. the *replacement cost*. Although this may be used as an *estimate* of the realizable value, and has obvious advantages for goods far from completion, it should not be adopted as an *alternative* to the net realizable value, particularly if it is used to increase the write-down from cost.

Some companies attempt to recognize the possibility of a decline in value by carrying out a systematic write-down of slow-moving stock items. A formula is applied taking account of the age of the stock. This approach is consistent and easy to verify, but it cannot be applied without considering whether circumstances have changed, which would warrant a modification of the formula, or even the abandonment of the formula approach in favour of direct measurement of the net realizable value.

The standard makes it very clear that the 'lower of cost and net realizable value' should be applied to separate items or groups rather than total stock.[8] This can produce differences, as illustrated in the following example:

Stock item	Cost	NRV	Lower of cost and NRV	Unrealized loss	Unrealized gain
	£	£	£	£	£
A	300	270	270	30	—
B	500	510	500	—	10
C	250	220	220	30	—
D	450	490	450	—	40
	1,500	1,490	1,440	60	50

Application of the standard would result in a stock valuation of £1,440. If aggregates had been compared, the value of £1,490 would have been selected. The difference arises because unrealized gains of £50 have been included in the aggregate result, offsetting the unrealized losses. Products B and D are effectively being valued at £510 and £490 respectively, i.e. at *above* cost.

The immediate write-down from cost to net realizable value is the recognition of a holding loss. In identifying the need to make a write-down, events occurring after the balance sheet, but before publication of the accounts, will provide valuable information. However, a decline in replacement cost should not produce any write-down so long as the net realizable value continues to exceed cost.

3.1.4   Disclosure

The standard requires disclosure of the accounting policies employed in establishing the cost and net realizable value.[9] There is also a requirement for stocks and work in progress to be suitably analysed, either in the balance sheet or in associated notes, to indicate the amounts of stock held of each major type.

3.2 Long-term contract work in progress

In addition to stocks and work in progress of items normally turned over in the short term, SSAP 9 deals with long-term contract work in progress ('long-term work in progress'), defining this as follows:

> A contract entered into for manufacture or building of a single substantial entity or the provision of a service where the time taken to manufacture, build or provide is such that a substantial proportion of all such contract work will extend for a period exceeding one year.[10]

ED 40 has proposed a slightly different definition: 'where the time taken to manufacture, build or provide is such that the contract activity falls into different accounting periods and normally is expected to extend for a period exceeding one year'. However, the specific duration of peformance may not be the sole distinguishing feature of such a contract, and where the reporting entity is substantially engaged in contracts that extend for more than one year, it may not be appropriate to adopt a separate accounting policy for shorter-term contracts.

3.2.1 Special considerations

The major features of long-term work in progress are first that the production or construction cycle extends over several accounting periods, and second that in many cases they do not represent standard products so that experience of past costs cannot help forecast the future. Finally, because they represent 'single substantial entities', there is not the opportunity for the cancelling out of minor errors that can arise even when an unbiased measurement approach is applied with reasonable care. On the other hand, the size and often the on-site location of this type of work in progress increases the proportion of expenditure that is directly traced to the stock item. Stock-flow problems are generally less significant. Overhead considerations closely resemble those that are relevant to other stock and work in progress: the same standard requirements apply. Special mention is made of interest in the standard. Interest is normally to be excluded from overhead, although the standard does permit its inclusion if the financing can be specifically identified with the contract.

Owing to the length of time taken to complete long-term contracts, there is much support for taking credit for profit while contracts are in progress. If profits were recognized only when contracts are completed, the trend of profit would be erratic. Whenever a contract is successfully completed, profit will show a surge; in other years, despite the business activity that may have been carried out with due efficacy, there would be no profit to report relating to the long-term work in progress. This would be unsatisfactory for a number of reasons. Results would not reflect the overall progress of the business; any desire to smooth the trend of profit would be frustrated; there is rejection of the interpretation of the matching concept as a method to achieve recognition of benefits and costs in the period in which they arise. Taking credit for profit before completion may be a solution to these difficulties, but it does not accord with the prudence convention. Prudence conflicts with realism.

ED 40 was issued in November 1986 as there was a conflict between the valuation requirement of SSAP 9 to include 'any attributable profit' and the requirement of the Companies Act 1985 (Schedule 4) to state current assets 'at purchase price or production cost'. At the time of going to press, ED 40 has not been incorporated into a standard.

3.2.2 Standard requirements

SSAP 9 comes down in favour of recognition of profit before projects are completed, although some acknowledgement of prudence is included in the statement:

> The amount at which long-term contract work in progress is stated in periodic financial statements should be cost plus any attributable profit, less any foreseeable losses and progress payments received and receivable; such excesses should be shown separately as provisions.[11]

Cost has been discussed above, but the establishment of attributable profit and foreseeable loss, plus presentation requirements including that of progress payments, remain to be dealt with.

3.2.3 Attributable profit

The basic approach to the calculation of attributable profit is to take a fraction of the total expected profit, that fraction representing the work completed as a proportion of the total contract work. This approach is adapted partly to suit particular circumstances and partly to comply with the prudence considerations indicated in the appendix to the standard.

The appendix to the standard first includes an example of the former.[12] Where a contract can be seen to comprise a number of parts, with prices determined and invoiced for each part, it is clearly a suitable approach to recognize profit on each part, treating each such part as a separable element of the whole. This is qualified with prudence in mind, by requiring recognition of any foreseeable loss on the whole contract as soon as it is foreseen. Consider the following illustration:

	Value of work certified £'000s	Costs incurred £'000s	Progress payments Received £'000s	Due £'000s
Incurred	300 (Stage 1)	230 (Stage 1)	250	50
	—	40 (Stage 2)		
		270		
To completion (estimates)	1,200	1,190		
	1,500	1,460		

Treating stage 1 as a separate part of the contract, the profit attributable to this part is £70,000 (£300,000 less £230,000). However, on the balance of the project a loss of 30,000 can be foreseen, the value of the subsequent stages of the contract being £1,200,000, while costs incurred and estimated for this part are £1,230,000. Valuing that part of the subsequent stages of the contract already carried out at cost, the balance sheet would include:

	£	£
Long-term WIP	340,000	
less Forseeable losses	30,000	
		310,000
less Progress payments received and receivable		300,000
		10,000
Contract debtor		50,000

Attributable profit recognized will be £40,000 (i.e., profit on the first stage less foreseeable losses). This is reflected in the valuation of long-term work in progress at cost of £270,000 plus the profit giving £310,000. Had the contract not been divided into stages the calculation would differ. The basic data would appear as follows:

	Value of work certified £'000s	Costs incurred £'000s	Progress payments Received £'000s	Due £'000s
Incurred	300	270	250	50
To completion	1,200	1,190		
	1,500	1,460		

The percentage of completion is commonly based on the certified proportion. With £300,000 certified out of a total of £1,500,000, one-fifth of total expected profits might be recognized. Since total expected profits are £40,000 (£1,500,000 less £1,460,000), attributable profit is £8,000 and the value of long-term work in progress would be £278,000. The division into stages reflected the success of stage 1 better than this latter approach.

If the costs to completion had been £800,000 instead of £1,190,000, there would have been no foreseeable loss and the first approach would have reported long-term work in progress at £340,000 before deducting progress payments, including attributable profit of £70,000; no profit element is added in respect of the work costing £40,000 as no part of this stage has been certified. Under the second method, since total expected profits are now £430,000, one-fifth of that figure, or £86,000, will be included in the stock valuation. This higher figure is more of a reflection of the profit on the final stages of the contract than that from stage 1 alone.

The rest of the appendix to the standard is concerned almost exclusively with prudence. No attributable profit should be included unless the outcome can be *reasonably* foreseen.[13] If it is impossible to make a reasonable estimate of costs to completion, no profit can be taken. The word *'reasonably'* can be interpreted only subjectively, but since the standard sets out to recognize some profit where not imprudent to do so, it would go against the spirit of the standard to interpret 'reasonably foreseen' in terms of very high levels of certainty. This would permit prudence to override the attempt at matching, so attention must be given to establishing what is the earliest point at which profits can be taken with acceptable confidence.

In the illustration, work certified was used to establish the fraction of the contract completed. Any such prudent approach is acceptable, cash received being used in instances where certification of work completed is not available. However, reducing this fraction by a constant amount in pursuit of prudence would appear totally inappropriate. A traditional view was to apply two-thirds of the proportion of work completed to profit. This will create erratic profit fluctuations, the remaining one-third of profit suddenly being reported at the completion of a project. If care is taken not to underestimate costs to completion and to estimate total sales value conservatively by considering possible rectification and guarantee costs and any penalty clauses, a prudent treatment is already adopted and any further formula adjustment introduces unnecessary distortion. The standard adopts an approach consistent with this view.

This does not mean that all companies included attributable profit in their accounts. No doubt they considered the situation for each contract, or part thereof, with prudence and were unable to satisfy themselves that the inclusion of profit was appropriate.

3.2.4 Foreseeable losses

The calculation of foreseeable losses has been illustrated, but the standard draws attention to areas that need to be considered in ensuring that such losses are identified. With inflation in mind, the appendix to the standard directs attention to the effects of price change on the future costs of materials, wages and salaries, and overhead.[14] In quantifying the foreseeable loss, overheads must be given full consideration, extending to administrative overhead when a contract whose future costs are expected to exceed future income will probably occupy a material part of the administrative capacity.

3.2.5 Presentation

Long-term work in progress does not produce many problems for record-keeping. Expenditure, invoicing or billing and cash collections are straightforwad transactions. Attributable profit (and a foreseeable loss) is not recorded in direct response to a transaction but is a calculated accounting adjustment. The required double entry is a debit to the long-term work in progress account to increase the value of the asset, and a credit to the profit and loss account.

Disclosure requirements for long-term work in progress are given in SSAP 9.[15] It requires a separate statement, in the balance sheet or attached notes, of the amount of work in progress at cost plus attributable profit less foreseeable losses, and of the cash received and receivable as progress payments. This treatment was shown in the earlier illustration. As with other stock and work in progress, a statement of the accounting policy is required, and it is clear that a number of policy areas exist here, including the recognition of work completed and the stage at which profits can be foreseen.

Before the Companies Act 1985, the disclosure requirements in SSAP 9 were considered satisfactory, although in retrospect it is possible that the 'turnover' amount in the profit and loss account was not clearly related to the balance sheet amounts of stock and work in progress and debtors. The major problems arose as the law emphasized that profit should not be included in the amount shown for stocks, and that only realized profits should be included in the profit and loss account. However, the use of the generally accepted accounting principles as prescribed in SSAP 9 and the requirement to present a true and fair view solved the problem. As the annual survey reports,[16] many companies have ignored the statutory requiremens and have reported in the same way as previously, sometimes adding a note that there was a departure from the statutory valuation rules so that a true and fair view can be presented.

Using the figures from the earlier illustration, it should be clear that the amount of £310,000 includes profit and should not appear as part of the stocks amount shown in the balance sheet. ED 40 proposes that long-term contracts should be disclosed in the balance sheet as follows:

(a) the amount of long-term contracts, at costs incurred, net of amounts transferred to cost of sales, after deducting foreseeable losses and applicable payments on account, should be classified as 'long-term contract balances' and separately disclosed within stocks. The balance sheet note should disclose separately the balances of:
   (i)   net cost less foreseeable losses; and
   (ii) applicable payments on account;
(b) the balance of payments on account (in excess of amounts recorded as turnover and off-set against long-term contracts) should be classified as 'payments on account' and separately disclosed within creditors;
(c) the amount by which recorded turnover is in excess of payments on account should be classified as 'amounts recoverable on contracts' and separately disclosed within debtors;
(d) the amount by which the provision or accrual for foreseeable losses exceeds the costs incurred (after transfers to cost of sales) should be disclosed within either provisions for liabilities and charges or creditors as appropriate. The amount need not be separately disclosed unless material to the financial statements.[17]

Appendix 3 of ED 40 gives further consideration to the presentation of long-term contracts in financial statements, reflecting the basic principle that 'amounts recoverable on contracts' will be classified as part of Debtors. The £10,000 balance would be described as 'amount recoverable on contract' and included in Debtors rather than in Stocks.

As with other stocks and work in progress, treating long-term work in progress in accordance with SSAP 9 and ED 40 is considered to ensure material compliance with the international standard IAS 11.

3.3   Fixed assets

The elements of this category may be more descriptively termed the 'long-term operating assets' and include land, buildings, plant and machinery.[18] A discussion of the accounting for these assets is incomplete without giving some consideration to depreciation, which is considered later in this chapter. However, attention in this section is directed to other matters, primarily those aspects of accounting relevant when using an historical cost basis; current value considerations are dealt with in Chapter 13, which is concerned directly with the effects of price change.

When the historical cost basis is being used, asset accounting commences with a classification of outlays as *capital expenditure* rather than revenue expenditure. Capital expenditures are debited to an asset account, and the expenditure is said to be 'capitalized'. Capitalization takes place when the benefits of the expenditure are expected to extend over period(s) beyond the one in which the expenditure arises; however, materiality considerations would indicate that if the expenditure or the benefits are not of a significant size, no capitalization should take place, the expenditure being written off as an expense of the current period. This procedure is an application of the accruals and matching conventions, carrying forward capital expenditures to the future for subsequent matching during the periods when the benefits anticipated in asset acquisitions expire.

3.3.1   Requirements and recommendations

Although no UK standard has been issued specifically directed at this topic, the FASB has made pronouncements in the USA, and in January 1981 the IASC issued an exposure draft E18, which formed the basis for IAS16, 'Accounting for Property, Plant and Equipment', published in March 1982. In addition, the ICAEW issued an Accounting Recommendation (2.205(s. 20)) in February 1974. This is concerned with the valuations of property produced by professional valuers (i.e. assets shown at a valuation), rather than with the use of the historical cost basis, and is more relevant in the later discussion of revaluation. The recommendation gives approval to only two bases of valuation: existing use valuation and, where appropriate, depreciated replacement cost. This latter base is applicable to property usually of a specialist nature, which is rarely traded. An explanation of this basis is given when asset valuation is considered in Chapter 13.

The major requirements for the reporting of fixed assets are found in the Companies Act 1985, Schedule 4.

3.3.2   Establishing acquisition cost

Adherence to the historical cost basis requires that assets should initially be recorded at their cost of acquisition. One of the tasks of an accounting standard would be to indicate what costs to include in the acquisition cost. The going concern assumption offers some guidance. Asset values, measured at cost, are not required to reflect the amount for which the asset can be sold. Under this assumption, the value should show how much it has cost to provide the asset, subject to the limitaton that this must not exceed expected future benefits against which it can be matched. It follows that acquisition cost includes locating the asset and preparing it for its intended productive use, where these costs are met by the acquirer.

This supports the inclusion of transport costs, including insurance, during transit. Duties and taxes are included, although the convention is not to deduct the savings that are made when capital allowances are used to reduce corporation tax.[19] This treatment of capital allowances requires recognition in accounting for deferred taxation, which is considered in Chapter 8. Under SSAP 4, a grant aiding the purchase of a fixed asset can be treated either as a deduction from cost or as a deferred credit. Practice varies, with about equal numbers of companies surveyed following each practice. Installation costs are an element of acquisition costs. Often a standard asset is purchased and converted for the special use to which it is to be applied. The costs of conversion are also an acquisition cost.

When it has been recognized that these costs of location and preparation are to be included, the basic acquisition price to which they are added can be considered. The majority of assets are acquired as a result of a purchase transaction for cash or on the usual business credit terms. The cash price or invoice price will normally be the basic acquisition cost; the only exception is when the purchase is not an arm's-length transaction, in which case the purchase price must be corrected.

Three major sources of arm's-length prices exist, the objective being to establish the price that would have been paid in the market at the time of acquisition. List prices may be a source but care must be used with this source since it may be that this does not represent the price of typical transactions; it is very possible that all customers are given substantial discounts. A second source is the prices that are being paid in current transactions for the same type of asset. Alternatively, use can be made of the prices paid for similar assets which can be adjusted to establish the desired price. If representative and reliable information is available giving current agreed prices, then this will provide the basis for calculating an arm's-length price. However, information meeting these requirements is not available in many cases and the final major source, the professional valuation, may be the only suitable source.

An arm's-length price will be required when assets are acquired in exchange for other assets formerly owned by the business. An additional source of acquisition cost is available in this case, namely the value, in the accounts of the business, of the assets given in exchange for those assets acquired. However, use of this source will hide any gain or loss made on the disposal of the assets given. Disclosure is more complete if an arm's-length price is used and the gain or loss on disposal revealed.

A further difficulty in establishing acquisition costs arises when a number of assets are purchased for a single sum. In this case the price paid must be apportioned among the assets. Arm's-length prices, if available, offer a reasonable basis for such apportionment. This identification of separate asset values may be of significant importance, particularly when the assets are depreciated on a different basis and, consequently, have differing impact on revenue results. If buildings are to be depreciated while there is no depreciation of land, separation of the land and building assets acquired in a single transaction provides a means of implementing these depreciation policies.[20]

When some assets are acquired, the purchase consideration is not settled within a short period but comprises a series of payments possibly over a number of years. In capitalizing the purchase consideration, the present value of the series of payments must be established. Discounting techniques, using a realistic current interest rate, will enable an acquisition cost to be established. This approach to determining a capital value from a series of future payments is similar to that employed in accounting for instalment and hire purchase sales and is dealt with in another chapter.

One further situation in which the acquisition cost must be calculated is when assets are constructed by a business for its own use. Like long-term contract work in progress, the calculation is normally required for a single substantial item so that the proportion of direct costs traced to the construction is usually high. The calculation of appropriate overhead poses an interesting question: Should the regular overhead rate be applied to this contract? The major relevant consideration is the level at which the facilities are employed at the time of the construction. If the business is operating near capacity, then the construction work can be considered to displace activity creating products for external sales. Since the construction is displacing such opportunities, there is an opportunity cost. Charging the full overhead is only allocating to the assets costs that would have been allocated to the products for external sales not made because of the construction. If this is the case, a consistent approach would give the same treatment to overhead for the construction of assets for own use as that for long-term work in progress, discussed earlier in this chapter.

When a business is operating at well below its capacity, it is less appropriate to charge the full overhead, particularly overhead that would be incurred whether or not the asset is made. Low utilization of capacity may encourage a business to make an asset for its own use even though other businesses are better equipped to make such an asset. Full overhead apportionment might result in a cost greater than the current market price of the asset. The external market price should impose an upper limit on the asset value.

A similar result can arise if unexpected costs are incurred in constructing an asset. Again, total actual cost might exceed the external price and the same upper limit would be appropriate in this case.

For self-constructed assets, the financing costs involved with the construction before the asset is completed may become material. A strong case for their inclusion in acquisition cost can be made, as they are a part of getting the asset ready for use.[21]

3.3.3 Subsequent additions to acquisition cost

Apart from the depreciation of assets, which is discussed in the next section, other circumstances may lead to changes being made to the asset value subsequent to its acquisition.

Repairs and overhauls are carried out with the intention of improving the value of a used asset. The recurrent nature of most repairs makes it inappropriate to capitalize them. The expenditure must be repeated at a similar level in future periods, so the existence of a benefit to be carried forward is doubtful. The recurrence also means that charging such repairs as an expense of the period in which they occur may produce results materially the same as capitalizing them and spreading the expense over a number of years.

However, major overhauls are not of a recurrent nature, and there is some justification for recognizing the resulting increase in value from the expenditure. Two alternative accounting treatments are available: either the asset account can be increased, or the depreciation account can be decreased. In the latter case the depreciation account is being treated in part as a provision for major overhauls. In either case it is necessary to adjust future depreciation in order to write off the addition to the asset value arising from the overhaul over the periods that it benefits.

3.3.4 Revaluation and market value

The writing up of acquisition values as a result of a revaluation is a departure from the historical cost basis. The significant parts of the Companies Act 1985, indicated earlier, require disclosures in the year of incorporation in the accounts of dates and separate values plus details of the valuers and the basis they adopted. The Accounting Recommendation (s.(20)) set out the acceptable bases and indicated that regular valuations (every three to five years) are advisable when the potential difference between a proposed valuation and the amount at which it is currently shown is material. Directors are required to report significant changes in the fixed assets and particularly to indicate the existence of substantial differences between the market values and the book values of land. No guidance is given on whether or not it is appropriate to incorporate revaluations into accounts. However, SSAP 19 requires that an annual revaluation on the basis of open market value should be incorporated in accounts for *investment properties* as opposed to long-term operating assets.

The title of SSAP 6 indicates that it deals with extraordinary items. These are examined and explained in Chapter 7, and it will be seen that several transactions or economic events give rise to charges or credits which are reflected in reserves without passing through the profit and loss account.

The treatment of surpluses arising from revaluations is governed by SSAP 6, para. 13, which states: 'unrealized surpluses on revaluation of fixed assets ... should be credited direct to reserves'. Since it is unrealized, it is not available for distribution purposes and should be included among non-distributable reserves, a revaluation surplus account being appropriate. A proposed supplement to SSAP 6, ED 16, considered the treatment of unrealized deficits, suggesting that a suitable treatment would be to write off the deficit against any revaluation surplus arising from the same asset if it existed; to the extent that the surplus was insufficient or did not exist, the deficit should be charged to the current year's profit and loss account. These did not appear in the revised standard adopted in August 1986.

ED 16 also considered the disposal of revalued assets. At the time of the sale, any revaluation surplus arising from the asset sold becomes a realized gain and should be transferred from the revaluation surplus account to revenue reserves without passing through the profit and loss account.

When a revaluation is incorporated in accounts, attention must be given to the implications for depreciation and deferred tax (see Section 3.4.2 and Chapter 8, respectively).

3.4 Depreciation

Depreciation is an integral part of accounting for assets with finite lives. Costs are capitalized with a view to future matching, and this matching is achieved when depreciation charges are made. SSAP 12 includes the following definition in an explanatory note:

> Depreciation is a measure of the wearing out, consumption or other reduction in the useful economic life of a fixed asset, whether arising from use effluxion of time or obsolescence through technological or market changes.
>   Depreciation should be allocated so as to charge a fair proportion of cost or valuation of the asset to each accounting period expected to benefit from its use.[22]

It is particularly interesting to compare the two sentences that constitute the above definition. The first is concerned with the loss of value and is directed at balance sheet accounting. The second puts emphasis on charges made to accounting periods turning attention to profit and loss accounting. The two roles played by depreciation are identified. Ideally, the charge in the profit and loss accounts, the debit entry, reflects the benefit made available for use in the period, while the increase in the provision for depreciation in the balance sheet, the credit entry, measures the decline in value over the period. This ideal cannot be fully achieved because the size of the charge and loss of value may not coincide, and because perfect measures of these amounts are not available.

SSAP 12 (originally issued in 1977) was reviewed during 1981, but the only major change was to recognize a separate category of fixed assets; investment properties. This led to the issue of SSAP 19 in November 1981 at the same time as the revised SSAP 12. Investment properties are defined as an interest in land and/or buildings held for its/their investment potential. They should be carried in the balance sheet at open market value. There is a conflict between Companies Act 1985 (Sch. 4s. 18 and 32), which requires any fixed asset with a limited useful economic life, including revalued properties, to be depreciated, and SSAP 19, which states that no depreciation should be provided in respect of freehold investment properties. In December 1982 'A Review of SSAP 12' was published; this led to ED 37 in March 1985 and to another revised SSAP 12 issued in January 1987.

Depreciation can be considered in terms of its contribution to the application of a concept of capital maintenance. If, for example, physical capital maintenance is adopted, depreciation provisions should be calculated to provide a fund to enable the asset to be replaced at the end of its life. This is a consideration relevant to depreciation accounting when allowance is made for price change, and it is considered in Chapter 13. The historical cost basis requires the acquisition cost of the asset, less its estimated residual value, to be allocated over the life of the asset in a manner that achieves suitable matching of depreciation charges to revenue in each period of its life.

Even the use of the historical cost basis does not enable depreciation charges to be calculated objectively. The calculation will utilize a number of measures, as follows:

● *Acquisition cost or valuation*
● *Useful life*   This may be measured in terms of time or the units of output of the asset. The useful life of an asset may be determined either by its physical attributes or through obsolescence. Physical deterioration may mean that the costs involved in continuing to use an old asset, including repairs and loss of service, are greater than those involved with a new asset; the asset might become beyond repair. This deterioration may arise principally through the passage of time or through use, so that the appropriate measure of useful life is time or output, respectively. Obsolescence arises through economic change. If the demand for the output declines sufficiently, it may no longer be worthwhile operating the asset. Alternatively, technological change might result in the availability of a new asset that carries out the function of an existing asset so much better, or at such lower cost, that it is advantageous to replace the existing asset by the new version. In the case of both the demand decline and availability of a new asset, the existing asset becomes obsolete and its useful economic life has come to an end. Estimates of useful life will involve considerable uncertainty.
● *Residual value*   The total depreciation to be charged over the useful life will be the difference between acquisition cost and residual value at the end of the asset's useful life. Again, there will be considerable uncertainty in estimating this value.
● *Method of allocation*   A choice must be made from the different methods available (see Section 3.4.2).
● *Interest*   Some depreciation methods involve the use of an interest rate.

3.4.1   Disclosure requirements

Schedule 4 of the Companies Act 1985 requires disclosure of the following:

(a) the cumulative amount of provisions for depreciation at the beginning and end of the year;
(b) the amount provided in respect of the year;
(c) adjustments made in consequence of the disposal of any asset, or for any other reason.

SSAP 12 requires that, for each major class of depreciable asset, disclosure is made of:

(a) depreciation methods used;
(b) useful economic lives or depreciation rates used;
(c) total depreciation charged for the period;
(d) gross amount of depreciable assets and the related accumulated depreciation.[23]

3.4.2   Methods of calculating depreciation

Apart from measuring depreciation by carrying out annual revaluations, many methods are available for calculating depreciation over a life measured in terms of time. They can be classified into three types: the straight-line method, accelerated methods, and methods recognizing interest costs. The first two are discussed in introductory accounting texts. The *annuity method* includes an interest rate in its calculation of depreciation in order to make allowance for the cost of financing the asset. It takes into account the view that, when it is reasonable to assume that the *operating benefits* are equal in all periods of the useful life of the asset, the *net benefits* increase over that life since the financing costs decline. At the start of the useful life of the asset, all the benefits are yet to be realized and the asset has not been able to repay any of the finance invested in it. Realization can be viewed as repayments, even though no actual repayment need take place. The outstanding capital invested in the asset can be considered to decline over the useful life, and the financial cost (imputed interest) can decline similarly.

The results achieved when using the annuity method of depreciation show that, if the present value of the earnings is equal to the asset cost, the return on the opening asset value is the required cost of capital. Of the methods available, the annuity method produces results that are the closest equivalent to the pure economic income measure introduced in Chapter 1, which utilizes discounting. It gives explicit consideration to the cost of capital tied up in assets. However, where operating benefits are not expected to arise equally in each year, the annuity method would need to be adapted. An interest-adjusted output approach is appropriate.

Despite its theoretical advantages, the annuity method is rarely used in external reporting. It is more complex and requires extra information: the interest rate. If a zero rate of interest is used, the results become identical to those obtained using the straight-line method. No particular method is required by the relevant standard.

3.4.3   Which assets should be depreciated?

The ASC makes it very clear that SSAP 12 requires that all assets that have a finite useful life must be depreciated. Paragraph 10 begins 'It is not appropriate to omit charging depeciation of a fixed asset on the grounds that its market value is greater than its net book value.' To omit depreciation on these grounds is to allow two accounting events of entirely different economic nature to cancel out. The increase in value is a holding gain, whereas the depreciation is an operating charge.

Buildings are not an exception to this requirement. Paragraph 12 states: 'Buildings have a limited life which may be materially affected by technological and environmental changes, and they should be depreciated having regard to the same criteria as in the case of other fixed assets.' The international standard IAS 4 adopts the same strict view.

The only exception explicitly mentioned in SSAP 12 is freehold land, which will not normally require a provision for depreciation since its life is extended indefinitely. Even in this case, circumstances may arise which do require depreciation. Changes in the 'desirability' of land because of its access to inputs or markets or for social reasons may result in a decline in value and a need for the book value to be written down. Land is also subject to depletion, when natural resources it contains are extracted.

It is appropriate to remind readers of the discussion earlier in this chapter and the particular rules relating to investment properties.

3.4.4   Revisions and changes in depreciation

The standard identifies four cases in which the depreciation charges may change from those envisaged when the asset was first acquired.[24]

The first case requires an asset to be written down if future revenue in excess of the book value is no longer expected. If the net book value of the asset is not considered to be recoverable in full, it must be written down immediately to the estimated recoverable amount. Depreciation should then write off this revised value over the remaining useful life of the asset.

Another example arises when assets are revalued upwards. The standard requires depreciation to be calculated using the revalued amount and a current estimate of the remaining useful life. Disclosure of any material effect on depreciaton is required in the year of the revaluation. No adjustment is recommended to be made for depreciation charged in prior years. There have been some companies who revalued the assets upwards and continued to charge depreciation to the profit and loss account based on the old, lower, value. Paragraph 16 requires the depreciation charge in the profit and loss account to be based on the carrying amount of the asset in the balance sheet, whether historical cost or revalued amount. The whole of the depreciation charge should be reflected in the profit and loss account. No part should be set directly against reserves.

Revisions in depreciation charges will also take place if the method is changed. The standard again indicates that the unamortized asset value at the time of the change should be written down over the remaining useful life using the new method. Material effects of the change should be disclosed in the year of change, but again, no prior-year adjustments are required. The need to revise the method indicates a strong possibility that the net book value based on the rejected method is not considered correct. It follows that future depreciation provisions may not relate to an acceptable value of the asset. However, adding the prior year's adjustments to those resulting from the change relating to the current year will further complicate the reporting of the current results, and it may be this consideration that has led to the treatment required by the standard.

The final revision considered, resulting from a change in the estimated useful life, is treated similarly. When the useful life estimate is revised, the cost not yet depreciated should be charged over the revised remaining useful life. Once again, the rejection of the original estimate calls into question the depreciation before the revision, giving support for prior-year adjustments, although this is not the treatment recommended in the standard.

3.4.5   Investment properties

Investment properties can be distinguished from operating, tangible assets. While an operating asset is acquired to provide an integral part of the productive capacity of the business, investment properties are acquired either with the intention of refurbishing them in order to gain from the enhancement of their value, or with the intention of getting capital growth from the increase in the rent income and eventual sale value. It resembles an investment in work in progress or in financial securities more closely than an operating asset.

Standard SSAP 19 identifies an investment property by the characteristic that it can be disposed of without interfering with the company's trade. If a substantial part of the property (more than one-third) is occupied by the company, including subsidiaries, for its own purposes, or is occupied by an associated company, it should not be treated as an investment property.

The standard proposed that investment properties should not be subject to periodic charges for depreciation, but should be revalued annually at their open market value. The revaluation should be incorporated into the balance sheet, with the changes in value disclosed as a movement on a revaluation reserve passing through the profit and loss account only if the existing total revaluation reserve is insufficient to cover a deficit. The revaluation reserve should be prominently disclosed in financial statements. The disclosure requirements of SSAP 12 concerning the names and qualifications of valuers should apply to investment properties. SSAP 19 recognizes that an employee or officer of a company can legitimately carry out the annual valuation of an investment property, but if an employee does act at the valuer, it should be disclosed.

3.4.6   Depreciation on freehold buildings

During the exposure period preceding the revised and additional standard, some concern was expressed with respect to the necessity to provide depreciation when market value was in excess of book value.

The annual survey for 1985–86 concludes that 'listed companies are showing an increasing tendency to not depreciate their freehold buildings or long leasehold property'.[25] The usual reasons include:

(a) depreciation is not material;
(b) buildings are frequently revalued;
(c) market value exceeds book value;
(d) buildings are maintained to high standard so depreciation charge is not necessary.

An example is provided by Grand Metropolitan plc in their annual report for the year ended 30 September 1986. They disclose that it is the group's policy to maintain all its public houses and hotels to a high standard in order to protect their trade. Because of this, such properties maintain residual disposal values in the aggregate at least equal to their book values, and accordingly no provision for depreciation is made.

Notes

1. SSAP 9, 'Stocks and Work in Progress', ASC, 1975.
2. Ibid., para. 26.
3. Ibid., para. 3. SSAP 9 corresponds sufficiently closely to the International Accounting Standard 2 (IAS 2) to enable the Accounting Standards Committee to state that compliance with SSAP 9 will ensure compliance with the IAS 2 'Valuation and presentation of inventories in the context of the historical cost system'. IAS 2, which was issued soon after SSAP 9 in October 1975, is the less restrictive, permitting LIFO in certain circumstances in addition to the methods permitted under SSAP 9.
4. SSAP 9, Appendix paras. 11–13.
5. Ibid., Appendix para. 15.
6. Ibid., para. 3.
7. Ibid., para. 26.
8. Ibid., para. 26.
9. Ibid., paras. 28, 29.
10. Ibid., para. 22.
11. Ibid., para. 27.
12. Ibid., Appendix para. 22.
13. Ibid., Appendix para. 23.
14. Ibid., Appendix para. 24.
15. Ibid., para. 30.
16. L. C. L. Skerratt (ed.), *Financial Reporting 1985–86, A Survey of UK Published Accounts*, ICAEW, 1986, p. 112.
17. Accounting Standards Committee ED 40, ICAEW, 1986, para. 29. See also G. Loveday, 'ED 40—What about the balancing figure?' *Accountancy*, June 1987, p. 27; Companies prefer SSAP 9 to ED 40.
18. Some definitions of fixed assets extend to the inclusion of intangibles and long-term investments in securities. A more restricted definition is adopted here; intangible assets are dealt with in Chapter 4, and trade investments in Chapter 9.
19. L. C. L. Skerratt (ed.), *Financial Reporting 1979–80: A Survey of UK Published Accounts*, ICAEW, 1980.
20. In this case, since no depreciation is charged for land, other methods can achieve the desired result. This would not be true where two different finite lives were chosen for assets purchased in this joint manner. See W. T. Baxter, 'Depreciation and property companies', *The Accountant's Magazine*, May 1980.

21. C. P. Rickwood, *Accounting Treatment of Capitalized Interest*, Certified Accountant Publications, London 1983.
22. SSAP 12, 'Accounting for Depreciation', 1987, ASC, para. 3.
23. Ibid., para. 22.
24. SSAP 9, paras. 19, 22, 21 and 18, respectively.
25. Skerratt; *Financial Reporting 1985–86*.

Further reading

Allen, D., 'Flexible answer to a stock problem', *Accounts Weekly*, 14 October 1977.

Baxter, W. T., *Depreciation*, Sweet and Maxwell, London, 1971.

Baxter, W. T., 'Depreciation and property companies', *The Accountant's Magazine*, May 1980.

Carty, J., 'ED 37 feedback', *Certified Accountant*, June 1986.

Edwards, J. R., 'Depreciation and fixed asset valuation in Railway Company Accounts to 1911', *Accounting and Business Research*, Summer 1986.

Loveday, G., 'Ed 40—what about the balancing figure?' *Accountancy*, June 1987.

Loveday, G., *Accountant's Digest 201. 'A guide to accounting standards–SSAP 12 (Revised) "Accounting for Depreciation"'*, ICEAW, 1987.

Morris, R. D., 'Lee *v* Neuchatel Asphalte Company (1889) and depreciation accounting: two empirical studies', *Accounting and Business Research*, Winter 1986.

Naim, A., 'Valuing publishers' stocks: the accounting problems', *Accountancy*, March 1979.

Paterson, R., 'Stock valuation since SSAP 9', *Accountancy*, April 1979.

Questions

1. The stock records of Kingston Keys Ltd showed the following:

Product	Units	Cost per unit £	NRV per unit £
A	100	2.00	2.10
B	300	1.00	.90
C	150	1.60	1.80
D	200	3.00	2.80

   You are required to:
   (a) Determine the value of stock assuming the lower-of-cost-or-market rule is applied (i) to each product individually; (ii) to the total stock.
   (b) Show the entries required to record any necessary write-down of stock value from cost to the value calculated in (i) above.
   (c) Outline the arguments for and against the adoption of valuing stock under the LIFO method.
   (12 marks)

2. You are required to answer the following in accordance with SSAP 9, *Stocks and work in progress*:
   (a) SSAP 9 requires stock to be valued at the lower of the two following amounts: cost or net realisable value. How would you arrive at the 'cost' of finished goods stock in a manufacturing company?
   (14 marks)
   (b) The following information relates to Unipoly plc, a manufacturer of can openers, for the year ended 31 May 1987.

   You are required to calculate the cost of finished goods stock in accordance with SSAP 9.

	£
Direct materials cost of can opener per unit	1
Direct labour cost of can opener per unit	1
Direct expenses cost of can opener per unit	1
Production overheads per year	600,000
Administrative overheads per year	200,000
Selling overheads per year	300,000
Interest payments per year	100,000

There were 250,000 units in finished goods stock at the year end. You may assume that there was no finished goods stock at the start of the year and that there was no work in progress.

The normal annual level of production is 750,000 can openers, but in the year ended 31 May 1987 only 450,000 were produced because of a labour dispute.   (6 marks)
(20 marks)
ACCA, 2.8, RFA, December 1987

3. ED 37: *Accounting for depreciation* (1985) makes proposals for changes in SSAP 12 (1977, revised 1981), similarly titled.

    Required:
    (a) Summarise the principal changes that ED 37 proposes to make in SSAP 12.   (10 marks)
    (b) Give your views on the necessity of a revision of SSAP 12 at this time.   (7 marks)
    (c) Examine the principles on which the useful economic lives of fixed assets should be determined for the purposes of depreciation accounting.   (8 marks)
    (25 marks)

4. In February 19X5, Keighley Construction Ltd commenced work on building a new shopping centre under a contract with Ashton Developments plc. The work is comprised of two elements, the construction of shop premises and the provision of a multi-storey car park. At 31 December 19X5, Keighley's records showed:

	Work certified £'000s	Costs incurred £'000s	Costs to completion £'000s	Contract price £'000s
Shops	4,900	4,350	450	5,600
Car park	500	600	1,900	2,400

Invoices in respect of this contract amounting to £4.2m had been sent to Ashton Developments and as a result £3.4m had been paid by them to Keighley at the end of 19X5.

You are required to:
(a) Indicate what according to SSAP 9 should be included in Keighley's profit and loss account for 19X5 and in the balance sheet at the end of that year as a result of the above contract.   (11 marks)
(b) Discuss the recommendations of SSAP 9 (stocks and work in progress) for stock valuation in respect of:
    (i)   the inclusion of overhead in cost;
    (ii) the use of standard costs; and
    (iii) market values   (16 marks)
    (27 marks)

4. Intangible assets

The word 'tangible' can have two meanings. Either it can mean that something is capable of being touched or felt, that it has a physical substance, or it can mean 'capable of being clearly grasped by the mind'. In the previous chapter the physical form of assets was discussed. Using the first meaning of the word, intangible assets would be those assets which, although of some value to the business, do not have physical form, do not have physical substance.

It is, however, not completely satisfactory to base a definition of intangibles solely on physical form. As was mentioned in the previous chapter, the strength of the evidence that the asset will produce future receipts has also to be considered. This is employing the second definition: 'capable of being grasped by the mind'. The stronger the evidence, the greater the tendency to consider the asset as tangible. The weaker the evidence, the greater the tendency to ignore the asset altogether, not even regarding it as intangible.

The following classes of assets, which do usually appear in financial statements, could be considered by one or the other definition of the word to be intangible:

(a) some current assets, such as debtors, and prepaid insurance: although neither of these assets has physical form, there is usually strong evidence of the existence of the asset, and the evidence as to the future receipts or benefits is usually so strong that these items are classed as tangible;

(b) goodwill, patents, copyrights, trademarks and franchises: these operational assets are clearly intangible; they do not have physical form, and there may not be strong evidence that they will produce future receipts;

(c) deferred charges, such as capitalized research and development expenditure or advertising expenditure: again, these are clearly intangible, possessing no physical form and little or no clear evidence that they will lead to future receipts.

An intangible asset therefore has no physical substance; it is expected to confer some benefit to the business beyond the current accounting period, but the evidence is not strong. There are other 'assets' of a business that would meet these criteria, but are not disclosed in financial statements: for example, an education and training programme of a business, or a particularly skilled labour force. These types of asset are intangible because the business does not own them. There have been suggestions that such human assets should be reported, but support for the idea is not strong, the main criticism being that there is no guarantee that the business will continue to benefit from the services of these 'assets'; the individuals involved could easily leave the business. The evidence as to the future benefits of these assets is therefore weaker than that for the intangible assets that are usually included in accounts.

This chapter will concentrate on categories (b) and (c) above.

4.1 Accounting for intangible assets

Accounting for intangibles is almost identical to accounting for tangibles. First, there is the acquisition when the cost of the asset has to be ascertained and recorded. In Chapters 9 and 10, the way in which one intangible, 'goodwill, arising on consolidation', is measured and recorded is explained. Similarly, with other intangibles, whether patents or research and development expenditure, the cost—the value—needs to be ascertained. Second, during the period of use, the asset has to be amortized. The amount of the value that has been consumed during the period has to be ascertained. Measuring amortization can be a particularly controversial problem with intangible assets. Finally, consideration must be given to disposal at the end of the useful economic life of the asset.

There is no accounting standard in the UK dealing with intangible assets collectively. There is a statement in SSAP 13 on research and development expenditure; SSAP 14 and SSAP 16 both include something concerning goodwill; the ASC published a discussion paper in 1980 on goodwill, and SSAP 22, 'Accounting for Goodwill', was issued in December 1984.[1] SSAP 2 requires that, where significant, the accounting policies relating to intangible assets should be disclosed.[2]

The Companies Act 1985 permits goodwill to be shown as an asset only if it was acquired for valuable consideration; the Act is not concerned with goodwill arising on consolidation. The same Act also refers to concessions, patents, licences, trade marks and similar rights and assets. It allows amounts in respect of these assets to be included in the balance sheet if either

(a) the assets were acquired for valuable consideration and are not required to be shown under goodwill; or

(b) the assets in question were created by the company itself.

Where intangible assets (apart from goodwill) are capitalized, they must always be amortized over their estimated useful life.

The UK was behind other countries in recommending accounting policies relating to intangible assets. There is a standard on intangible assets in the USA, and both the EEC 4th Directive and 7th Directive have a lot to say on goodwill;[3] all of these have influenced the UK requirement, although they have not led to uniformity in practice in the different countries.

This can be seen by looking at just one problem, namely, amortization policy for intangible assets. APB Opinion no. 17 in the USA states that:

> the value of intangible assets at any one date eventually disappears, and the recorded cost of intangible assets should be amortized by systematic charges to income over the periods estimated to be benefited. The cost of each type of intangible should be amortized on the basis of the estimated life of that specific asset. . . . The period of amortization should not, however, exceed 40 years.[4]

SSAP 22 required that purchased goodwill should normally be eliminated immediately upon acquisition.

4.2 Goodwill

Goodwill is defined in SSAP 22 as 'the difference between the value of a business as a whole and the aggregate of the fair values of its separable net assets'.[5] Separable net assets are those assets (and liabilities) that can be identified and sold (or discharged) separately without necessarily disposing of the business as a whole. They include identifiable intangibles.[6] Goodwill is an asset that represents the above-normal earning potential of a business. If only the land and building, plant and machinery, working capital and other individual assets of a business are considered, it might appear that a certain level of profits will be earned, given an expected overall return on assets. If a higher level of profits is expected to be earned, this is because the business enjoys goodwill. It could arise because of the firm's good reputation, customer loyalty, an advantageous location or a superior management team (technically, only if paying less than their marginal product in terms of rent or salaries). All these are factors that affect profits but do not appear as assets being purchased.

4.2.1   Value of goodwill

Goodwill can arise in a number of different situations, and the accounting treatment can vary between one situation and another. In order to put the various treatments in perspective, it is useful to consider how goodwill would be valued theoretically in terms similar to those applicable to the concept of pure economic income introduced in Chapter 1. The value of a business could be computed as follows. An estimate could be made of its expected future stream of net income, its profits. These could be discounted at a rate that represents the normal rate of earnings in the type of business in which it is engaged, then this value could be compared with the fair value of its net assets; the difference would be goodwill. Goodwill is the excess of the present value of the expected future earnings over the fair value of the asset. If, by any chance, the present value of the future earnings is less than the fair value of the net assets, 'negative goodwill' exists.

If the business has built up its own reputation, it creates a premium. The total value of the business will be greater than the aggregate of the fair value of the net identifiable assets. This is called 'inherent goodwill' or 'non-purchased goodwill'. No accounting entries are involved; it is not shown in the balance sheet, as it is not the function of a balance sheet to show the total overall value of the business. Goodwill enters into accounting records only when it is purchased, when one business acquires all or part of another business. The purchasing business may absorb the whole of another business or acquire a subsidiary or associate. The price paid in terms of cash or shares normally exceeds the accounting values of the assets acquired. The business is worth more than the collection of assets. The excess is called 'purchased goodwill'. If it is a subsidiary that is being acquired, then consolidated accounts need to be prepared, and the goodwill involved is called 'goodwill arising on consolidation'. The appropriate valuation and the accounting entries involved are covered in Chapters 10 and 11.

In economic terms, there is no difference between inherent goodwill and purchased goodwill, but the accounting treatment differs. The existence of purchased goodwill is validated by a transaction, but no such evidence exists for inherent goodwill. In the case of purchased goodwill, there is less judgement involved in establishing the value. A market transaction has taken place. A value has been established, however subjective.

SSAP 14 indicates that the premium or discount on acquisition (goodwill or negative goodwill) is the difference between the purchase consideration and the value ascribed to net tangible assets and identifiable intangible assets. This standard became effective from 1 January 1979. Prior to this date, some businesses measured goodwill on consolidation as the difference between the purchase consideration and the book value of the net assets acquired. SSAP 14 makes clear that it should be the difference between the purchase consideration and the fair market value of the net assets acquired. This might involve revaluing the assets of the subsidiary.

SSAP 16, which considered current cost accounting, did not attempt to resolve the issue of goodwill; it did not, for example, discuss the time period over which goodwill should be written off. The standard did, however, have implications for goodwill. Goodwill on consolidation is intended to be the genuine revaluation surplus at the time of acquisition. A problem can arise as to how to determine the fair market value of the assets acquired. Current cost accounting helps in that it is possible to use the current cost values of assets that have been calculated for SSAP 16 purposes as the fair value of assets.

The discussion so far has been concerned with the treatment of goodwill in the consolidated accounts. There is also the problem of treatment in the individual accounts of the holding company. With the 'cost method' of carrying the investment in the holding company's books (see Chapter 9), it is usually acquisition cost that determines the size of the balance in the 'Investment in subsidiary' account. This asset is shown as a single figure and is not broken down to show the value of each type of asset acquired. The goodwill purchased will not therefore appear as a separate item in the accounts of the holding company. The standard expresses the opinion that there is no need to consider reducing, i.e. amortizing, in the accounts of the holding company, any goodwill element in the purchasing price.[7]

If there has been a permanent diminution of value of the investment in subsidiary, the balance on this account will need to be written down. If there has been a permanent increase in value, with the 'cost method' of carrying the investment, the balance would not normally be written up. Even if it were, it would be incorrect to consider writing up the goodwill element of this balance as this would represent the inherent goodwill of the group.

Up to now we have been considering subsidiary companies. SSAP 1, 'Accounting for the Results of Associated Companies' (revised in April 1982), proposes that the premium paid on the acquisition of an associate should be identified and separately disclosed in the consolidated balance sheet of the investing group.[8] Where consolidated accounts are produced, the treatment of goodwill on the acquisition of an associate is as above.

If an investing company acquires an associate but does not have to produce consolidated accounts, it needs to disclose certain relevant information (see Chapter 9). Again, as with the individual accounts of the holding company with subsidiaries, no individual goodwill account will be opened. The net assets acquired are represented by the one figure in the balance sheet, 'Investment in associated companies'.

4.2.2   Amortization

Goodwill is not a permanent asset. A business does not enjoy for ever the factors that contribute to the goodwill. There are differences of opinion as to the period of time over which goodwill should be amortized.

Companies in the UK have traditionally had a great deal of freedom as to how they would write off goodwill, however it arose; but, as previously mentioned, the EEC Fourth Directive, which could affect accounting practice in the UK, requires that goodwill acquired for valuable consideration normally be written off over a maximum period of five years.

The Companies Act 1985 (sch. 4, para. 21) requires that the period chosen for amortization should not exceed the useful economic life of the particular goodwill, and that the reason for choosing that period should be disclosed.

The EEC 4th Directive and the Companies Act 1985 section does not apply to group accounts, and therefore its reference to goodwill applies only to goodwill purchased as an individual asset and not to goodwill arising on consolidation. The EEC 7th Directive deals with group accounts and proposes that goodwill arising on consolidation should be written off within five years, but it would permit the extension of the period to the length of the economic life of the goodwill. SSAP 22 covers group accounts, and as previously stated, the preferred policy is for immediate elimination.[9]

For many UK companies, this fast write-off policy will not cause concern. In fact, in the survey of 300 companies' financial statements,[10] it is shown that the stated accounting policy for goodwill for the majority of the companies in the annual surveys is, and has been, to write it off in the year of acquisition.

Many groups have changed their policy from capitalization (with or without amortization) to immediate elimination against reserves. This is the simplest policy, and also has the advantage of not requiring a regular charge in the profit and loss account.

A policy of this nature was probably followed by GEC plc for the year ended 31 March 1987, when they published a much shorter version of the accounts policy note: 'Goodwill. Purchased goodwill is written off directly against reserves.' But which reserve should be used? Most companies use the profit and loss account balance, but there are alternatives.

One method of eliminating purchased goodwill that has been popular is to write it all off, or as much as is possible, against any share premium that was created when the goodwill was purchased. In a share-for-share exchange, the shares of the purchasing company are being issued in exchange for the assets and goodwill of the other company, and these shares are normally valued at a price in excess of their nominal value.

Although a tidy solution to the problem, this approach at eliminating goodwill can be regarded as wrong in principle. It is in effect reducing the contributed capital of the purchasing company. If the shares issued were of 'no par' value, it is quite apparent that the contributed capital is being reduced. Further, the valuation of the goodwill, and the decision on the issue price of the shares and hence the size of the share premium, are separate and distinct issues. Another point is that goodwill is an asset; therefore to treat it as an expense by writing it off in the year in which it is purchased is to be inconsistent. It is only if it is believed that goodwill is so intangible, if it is believed the evidence that it will produce future receipts is so vague, that the treatment of immediate write-off can be justified.

The attitude of the standard-setting body in the USA is that the period of write-off should be the number of years of useful economic life of the goodwill, and the ASC in SSAP 22 offers this as an alternative method. This is theoretically sound. However, it is only if one considers the vague factors that contribute to goodwill that one begins to doubt whether in practice anyone can estimate such a useful economic life. For example, how long can one expect the superior management team or the good labour relations to continue? How long can a favourable association with another company continue or a position of market dominance be maintained? It is possible to talk about the useful economic life of goodwill, but the life is indeterminate; usually a business has to resort to deciding on an arbitrary period of time. If this is accepted, the debate becomes one of deciding whether the arbitrary period should be short—the attitude favoured by the balance of the EEC countries—or long, as favoured in the UK and USA.

This admission that the period must to some extent be arbitrary was in fact, recognized in the 1980 ASC discussion paper, which contains a proposal that the useful economic life of the goodwill should never exceed a period determined by multiplying the PE ratio by a predetermined figure.[11] The figure mentioned in the discussion paper as a guideline was $2\frac{1}{2}$. A business with a PE ratio of 10 to 1 would, according to the proposal, have to write off its goodwill in not less than 25 years. When the need to resort to such arbitrary formulae is recognized, it is clear evidence that the real issue is one of rapid versus gradual write-off.

SSAP 22, Appendix 1, provides a summary of the 'factors to be considered in determining the useful economic life of purchased goodwill'. These factors should be assessed at the time of acquisition and include 'expected changes in products, markets and technology; expected period of future service of certain employees; and expected future demand, competition or other economic factors which may affect current advantages' (para. 2).

It would appear that there is no necessity to use the reserve designated 'Revaluation reserve' or any other existing account for this purpose. In effect, this produces an example of a 'dangling debit'. Although the name conjures up some strange images, it is in reality not very exciting. All it means is that, instead of the goodwill being shown on the asset side of the balance sheet, it is presented on the liabilities side as a deduction from shareholders' interests.

This is not in fact eliminating goodwill from the accounts, not recognizing the wasting asset nature of goodwill, but the method has been used by at least one public quoted company. In the accounts to 31 December 1984, GKN plc included in its total capital and reserves £771.5 million, a deduction of £67.7 million in respect of goodwill arising on consolidation. The accounts to 31 December 1986 showed a slight change, not material enough to be identified as a change in accounting policy, as the policy for goodwill remained '... deducted from reserves'. However, the note relating to reserves included the following statement: 'Goodwill arising on consolidation is now deducted from Other Reserves. The comparative figures for 1985 have been restated to reflect the change in presentation.' This had the effect of showing the net balance of the 'Other reserves' as £(22.7) million out of a total of £403.2 million.

4.2.3 Negative goodwill

This can arise in consolidated accounts where the vendors of a business are anxious to sell and do so at a price less than the aggregate value of the net assets involved. It could arise as the result of the incorrect valuation of assets by the vendor, where for example the value of stocks was not realized, or it could arise when future losses or reduced profits are expected.

The ASC discussion paper recommended that negative goodwill should normally be treated as the exact reverse of positive goodwill.[12] It should be amortized over time, by taking a credit to the profit and loss account, which is shown as a reduction in the depreciation charge. However, the standard requires that negative goodwill be credited directly to reserves (para. 33).

Appendix 2 of SSAP 12 confirms that the initial transfer to reserves represents unrealized profits. As the assets acquired, which give rise to the negative goodwill, are realized by depreciation or sale, the proportionate amount may be transferred from the unrealized to the realized reserves. This is in contrast to IAS 22, which permits allocation over the assets' acquired or deferred income.

4.2.4 The future

At the moment of writing, pure goodwill (as defined at the beginning of this section) for an individual company does not appear to be a controversial topic. The discussion and variety of practice generally relate to goodwill (or the net premium) arising on consolidation. This will need to be legislated for with respect to the implementation of the EEC Seventh Directive, and the Accounting Standards Committee agreed in June 1987 to undertake an urgent review of SSAP 22 (and SSAP 23, 'Accounting for Acquisition and Mergers'). Some commentators support the theoretical arguments that justify amortization – basically, that goodwill is an asset that produces earnings and should be written off against those earnings. But the usual basis of calculation is the difference between the aggregate of separate valuation of tangible and intangible assets and a stock market price on a particular date—with both the valuation and the price being subject to wide variations.

4.3 Research and development

There are various categories of research and development expenditure, and it is permitted under the relevant standard to capitalize certain items of such expenditure, namely those that are incurred with a longer-term payoff in mind, where the expected returns are reasonably certain.[13]

Research activity can be divided into three broad categories:
(a) pure research, which is undertaken to advance knowledge in general and about which it is uncertain where the results will lead;
(b) applied research, which entails using the knowledge obtained in pure research and trying to apply it in an area of interest to the business;
(c) development, which is work undertaken to develop a new product or process, or to improve an existing product or process, and involves using ideas obtained through applied research.

These classifications are broad, and in certain industries it is difficult to distinguish between applied research and development expenditure. It can also become a problem to distinguish between development expenditure and production costs.

The accounting entries to record most items of research expenditure would charge the amount involved as an expense in the profit and loss account of the year in which the expense is incurred. It can be argued that in certain situations the accrual concept should be followed, and the costs should be matched against the revenue. If the revenue resulting from the expenditure is not to be received until the next accounting period or any subsequent period, then the expenditure should be capitalized and written off in the periods when the revenue is to be received. Many applied research and development activities, for example the development of a new type of aero engine, will not result in immediate returns, and so it is argued that the matching concept should be applied, with the expenditure amortized over the period in which the benefits will arise.

An alternative line of reasoning is that the prudence concept should be invoked. Revenues and profits should not be anticipated, particularly in such high-risk areas as research activity. The revenues and profits should be recognized only when they have been realized, when they are certain. The decision therefore on whether to capitalize research and development activity is a question of balancing the matching concept with the prudence concept.

SSAP 13 recommends that expenditure on pure and applied research should be charged against the profit and loss account of the year in which the expense is incurred.[14] The return can be uncertain, and so the arguments for prudency are stronger than those for matching. Expenditure on these items is usually part of the continuous activities of the business, designed to maintain its competitive position in the industry, and so it is difficult to link the expenditure with any particular items of revenue.

The standard recognizes that it is possible to capitalize certain types of development expenditures and match the costs against the future revenue. There are, however, a number of tests that have to be passed before such matching is justified. It is necessary to be able to clearly identify a particular project from which the revenue will arise and on which the expenditure has been incurred:

The outcome of such a project would then need to be examined for
  (a) its technical feasibility and
  (b) its ultimate commercial viability considered in the light of factors such as:
    (i)   likely market conditions (including competing products)
    (ii) public opinion
    (iii) consumer and environmental legislation.
Furthermore a project will only be of value:
  (a) if further development costs to be incurred on the same project together with related production, selling and administration costs will be more than covered by related future revenues and
  (b) adequate resources exist, or are reasonably expected to be available, to enable the project to be completed and to provide any consequential increases in working capital.[15]

The opinion is expressed in the standard that 'the future benefits of most development projects would be too uncertain to justify carrying the expenditure forward. Nevertheless, in certain industries it is considered that there are a number of major developments that satisfy the stringent criteria.[16] Because of the uncertainties, it is emphasized that different persons having different knowledge will need to be involved in assessing the technical, commercial and financial viability of the project. At the time of preparing each balance sheet, the unamortized balance of the development expenditure will need to be examined to be sure that it still fulfils the criteria for carrying forward.

As well as carrying forward the direct costs of certain development expenditure, there is also the question of what to do with any fixed assets employed in research and development activities. The use of such assets, say a research laboratory with all its equipment, will benefit the business over a number of accounting periods. It should therefore be capitalized as with any other fixed asset, and written off over its useful life. The annual depreciation charge will be included in the profit and loss account as part of the expenditure on research and development.

There is another situation in which it is permitted to carry forward development expenditure:

This is where companies enter into a firm contract:
(a)   to carry out development work on behalf of third parties on such terms that the related expenditure is to be fully reimbursed or
(b)   to develop and manufacture at an agreed price which has been calculated to reimburse expenditure on development as well as on manufacture.
Any such expenditure which has not been reimbursed at the balance sheet date should be included in work in progress.[17]

In the annual surveys of 300 company accounts, of the companies that identified their treatment of research and development expenditure, the majority wrote off all such expenditure in the year in which it was incurred. In 1980 only 34 carried forward some element of the expenditure,[18] and in the 1985–86 survey the percentage of a different sample had fallen to 2. Included in that percentage are those that carried forward expenditure on product development, or on production costs incurred with a view to the extraction of minerals (although SSAP 13 is not specifically concerned with the extractive industries), and those that separately identified fixed assets providing facilities for research and development.

SSAP 13 requires that development expenditure that is deferred be separately disclosed in the accounts, that the accounting policies relating to such items be clearly explained, and that the movement over the accounting period in the deferred development expenditure be shown. The International Accounting Standard on this subject, IAS 9, which has not been adopted in the UK, requires that the total amount of research and development costs charged as an expense in a year (including the amortized part of such deferred costs) be disclosed in the financial statements of a company.[19] This disclosure is in addition to all that is required by SSAP 13, 'Accounting for Research and Development'. There is also considerable pressure for such disclosure from international organizations, such as the United Nations, which are concerned about the activities of transnational companies.

The Companies Act 1985 requires that, where development costs are shown as a asset, a note must appear in the accounts explaining the reasons for capitalizing the costs and explaining the write-off policy (sch. 4, para. 20(2)). The directors' report must also contain an indication of the activities (if any) of the company and its subsidiaries in the field of research and development.

There has been discussion in the UK as to whether there should be a disclosure of the total research and development efforts of companies. There is no such requirement at the time of writing; there is however a proposal to do so in the current exposure draft on this topic.[20]

As a guide to the activities that are typically excluded from research and development, paragraph 7 of the exposure draft lists the following:
(a) routine design, testing and analysis either of equipment or product for purposes of quality or quantity control;
(b) routine or periodic alterations to existing products or processes, even though these may represent improvement;
(c) operational research;
(d) trouble-shooting in connection with breakdowns during commercial production;
(e) legal and administrative work in connection with patent applications, records and litigation and the sale or licensing of patents;
(f) activity, including design and construction engineering, relating to the construction, relocation, rearrangement or start-up of facilities or equipment other than facilities or equipment whose sole use is for a particular research and development project.

There have been some suggestions that this list is based on a manufacturing or scientific laboratory environment, whereas much of the current expenditure of this nature is in connection with the services (particularly financial service) environment. These other intangibles are considered in the following section.

IAS 9 does give some guidance on the type of costs that may be capitalized. Research and development costs should include

(a) the salaries, wages and other related costs of personnel;
(b) the costs of material and services consumed;
(c) the depreciation of equipment and facilities;
(d) related overhead costs;
(e) other costs, e.g. the amortization of patents and licences;

in so far as these expenses relate to research and development activities.

4.4   Other intangibles

The Companies Act 1985 specifically refers to some other intangible assets—concessions, patents, licences, trade marks—but it is accepted that there could be others, e.g. know-how, computer software, market research, advertising, the education and training of staff for new projects, rights to publish books and magazines, and the 'golden hello's' in respect of new staff. It is possible to see a rapid expansion of expenses that could be capitalized and subsequently amortized as part of the principle to recognize substance over form in order to ensure that assets and rights to service potential are included in the balance sheet, and an appropriate amount charged against the profit and loss account for the appropriate period.

4.4.1   Market research expenditure

Expenditure on market research or advertising can be treated in the same way as that on research and development. It is possible that, within an accounting period, a business will invest heavily in market research or advertising—not the usual annual expenditure on such items, but that incurred in connection with a new promotion. Not all the returns expected to result from such promotional activities may be realized by the end of the accounting period. Following the matching principal, it is reasonable to carry forward such expenditure.

SSAP 13 allows for this carry-forward, as long as the expenditure satisfies the criteria mentioned above for research and development expenditure. The capitalized expenditure should be separately disclosed in the balance sheet. It is in fact extremely rare for advertising and market research expenditure to be carried forward; it is generally written off in the year in which it is incurred.

4.4.2   Exploration costs

For companies engaged in the extractive industries, such as mining and oil, the accounting treatment of exploration costs is of considerable importance. There is no accounting standard on this subject in the UK, although there is a history of standards on the subject in the USA.[21] Companies in the mining and oil industries have continually to be exploring for new reserves. The expenditure on such exploration is usually high. The accounting problem arises because some of these explorations are successful and some are not; some lead to future returns and some do not.

If the matching principle were to be applied, then, as with research and development expenditure, the costs would be carried over to the period when the returns were expected to be realized. But one of the criteria to be satisfied to justify carrying over is that the outcome of such a project has been assessed with reasonable certainty. It is difficult to be able to do this in the extractive industries. It was because of the range of reporting practices being used that it was found necessary to bring out a standard on this subject in the USA.

The 'successful efforts' approach can be contrasted with the 'full-cost' approach. In this latter approach the entire exploration costs are capitalized, whether or not the project is successful. The issue of which approach should be used is of considerable concern in the oil and natural gas industry, where much of the exploration merely leads to finding 'dry holes'. The advocates of the full-cost approach argue that finding a number of dry holes is all part of the process of discovering one hole in which there is oil or gas; the total costs of finding an income-producing hole should therefore include the costs of dry holes. Clearly, the alternative accounting treatments can have a considerable effort on the profits reported for a particular year.

There are a number of other possible approaches to the problem, as the following two examples will indicate. An interesting approach to exploration and development costs is that of the Rio-Tinto Zinc Corporation. During the initial exploration stages of a project, the company charges all the costs against the current year's profit. When, however, expenditures on a project have reached a 'promising stage', the exploration and development costs, including the costs incurred on evaluating the project to establish its commercial viability, are carried forward and are transferred to pre-production expenditure if the project proceeds. If a project does not prove viable, all irrecoverable costs associated with the project are written off. Where expenditure is carried forward in respect of a project that will not proceed to commercial development for some time, provision is made against the possibility of non-development by a charge against profits over periods of up to seven years. All pre-production expenditure is carried forward, and when commercial production commences, this expenditure is charged against profit on the same basis as any property, plant or equipment.

4.4.3   Patents, trademarks, etc.

A number of references have already been made to such intangibles as patents, trademarks and franchises. The requirements of sch. 4, 2 of the Companies Act 1985 apply to amounts in respect of these items in a similar manner to goodwill, so that they can be included in a company's balance sheet under this item only if

(a) the assets were acquired for valuable consideration and are not required to be shown under goodwill; or

(b) the assets in question were created by the company itself.

They are subject to the usual requirements applicable to all fixed assets. If the expected returns can be identified with a reasonable degree of confidence, then the costs can be spread over time. The asset would be valued, a write-off period established, and the asset written down each year of its useful economic life. In practice, many are written off in year of acquisition.

Quoted advertising agencies have recently been involved in a high level of acquisitions, which means that goodwill usually amounts to a substantial sum. This may be because of a reluctance to value the other intangibles that would be present in this type of business.

Whatever this asset is called, it will require amortization or immediate write-off against reserves. The effect on future reported profits encourages companies to make the latter choice, but this means that no charge ever appears in the profit and loss account for the use of these assets, or at least not in respect of the full cost of acquisition of the assets.

The publishing industry has a particular type of asset, usually known as 'publishing rights'. One accounting policy, that of the publishing firm Reed International, in its accounting policy in the accounts to 30 March 1986, states that, as these rights have no finite life, amortization is not provided. Subject to annual review, any permanent impairment of value is written off against profit.

In the accounts to 30 June 1983, however, another firm, News International plc, changed its policy: ' ... the Directors have decided to amortise goodwill (including publishing rights, titles and benefits) over 20 years.'

Notes

1. SSAP 13: 'Accounting for Research and Development', ASC, 1977; SSAP 14: 'Group Accounts', ASC, 1979; SSAP 16: 'Current Cost Accounting', ASC, 1980; 'Accounting for Goodwill—A Discussion Paper', 1980; SSAP 22; 'Accounting for Goodwill', ASC, 1984.
2. SSAP 2, 'Disclosure of Accounting Policies', ASC, 1972.
3. Accounting Principles Board, Opinion 17, 'Intangible Assets', 1970, with subsequent interpretations; European Economic Community, 4th Directive, 'Accounting Presentation and Disclosure'; 7th Directive, 'Group Accounts'.
4. Accounting Principles Board, Opinion 17.
5. SSAP 22, para. 21.
6. Ibid., para. 22.
7. SSAP 16, para. 53.
8. SSAP 1, 'Accounting for the Results of Associated Companies', ASC, (revised) 1982, paras. 26(b) and (c).
9. SSAP 22, para. 7.
10. L. C. L. Skerratt (ed.), *Financial Reporting: A Survey of UK Published Accounts*, ICAEW, various years.
11. ASC, 'Accounting for Goodwill', para. 1.7.
12. Ibid., paras. 7.5 and 7.8.
13. SSAP 13, December 1977.
14. Ibid.
15. Ibid., paras. 8 and 9.
16. Ibid., para. 11.
17. Ibid., para. 14.
18. Skerratt, *Financial Reporting*, 1980.
19. International Accounting Standards Committee, IAS 9.
20. ED 41, 'Accounting for Research and Development', ASC, June 1987.
21. See Financial Accounting Standards Board, SFAS 19, 'Financial Accounting and Reporting by Oil and Gas-producing Companies', 1977; and SFAS 25, 'Suspension of Certain Accounting Requirements for Oil and Gas Companies', 1979.

Further reading

Brookes, M., 'Setting a standard for best practice on accounting in the UK oil and gas industry', *Accountancy Age*, 12 November 1987.

Comiskey, E. and C. Mulford, 'Adding to an international pot of pourri', *Accountancy*, May 1987.

Gray, R. H., 'Accounting for R&D: A Review of Experiences with SSAP 13', ICAEW Research Paper, 1986.

Hope, T. and R. Gray, 'Power and policy-making: the development standard', *Journal of Business Finance and Accountancy*, Winter 1982.

Lee, T. A., 'Goodwill: an example of will-o'-the-wash accounting', *Accounting and Business Research*, Autumn 1971.

Moore, K., 'The goodwill saga—let's not drag it out any longer', *Accountancy*, August 1980.

Oil Industry Accounting Committee, 'SORP—Accounting for Oil and Gas Exploration and Development Activities', ASC, October 1987.

Rutteman, P., 'Where has all the goodwill gone?', *Accountancy*, August 1987.

Woolf, E., 'Goodwill: SSAP 22 the best answer?', *Accountancy*, August 1987.

Questions

1. SSAP 13, *Accounting for research and development* (1977), lays down requirements for the treatment of R & D expenditures in published financial statements.

    Required:
    (a) Discuss the PRACTICAL problems of revenue-cost matching that SSAP 13 poses for the accountant who prepares the published financial statements of a company that engages in research and development in the course of its ordinary activities. (10 marks)
    (b) State with reasons, for each of the three following cases, how you would deal with, and disclose, the R & D expenditures in the accounts of a pharmaceutical (drug) company:
    (i) During the financial year, the company has spent £500,000 on a new project to develop a drug to treat cancer. It is expected that it will take at least three years to establish whether the drug is likely to be effective or not, and if it is, it will take at least another two years to produce a marketable product.
    (ii) In previous years, the company has spent a total of £2,000,000 on developing a new tranquilliser, and has carried this expenditure forward in the books. In the current year the project is completed at a cost of £400,000, and the drug is launched on the market, with sales of £1,500,000 in the second half of the year. It is expected that the new drug will lead the market for two years (from launching) before a successful competing product appears, with total sales in that time estimated at £10,000,000. The tranquilliser drug will remain marketable for another two years after that, with estimated further sales of £5,000,000 before it is withdrawn. The profits on the new drug are forecast at £8,000,000 in the first two years (£1,000,000 of this sum arising in the second half of the current year), and at £2,000,000 in the following two years—exclusive, in all cases, of development costs.
    (iii) In previous years, the company has spent, and carried foward in the books, a total of £10,000,000 on developing a cure for influenza. During the current year it is decided to terminate this project, as test results in the current year have proved adverse. (15 marks)
    (25 marks)
    ACCA, 3.1, AFA, June 1986

2. Newprods plc has an extensive research facility involved in the research, development and promotion of various projects. The managing director wishes to comply with SSAP 13 and seeks your advice as financial director.

    Information regarding the research department's activities for the year ended 31st July 1986 is given below:

    (1) £750,000 spent on a new gas ionising plant. Such plant is highly specialised and has minimal scrap value due to contamination. It has an expected life of 10 years and came into use from 1st July 1986.

    (2) A contract was entered into with a cosmetics group on a cost plus 25% basis to develop a kissproof lipstick. So far Newprods plc has incurred costs of £90,000 and has received £25,000 on account. Further costs of £35,000 to complete the contract are expected before 31st July 1987. The balance of the contract price is to be settled on completion.

    (3) Dr Zod, a nuclear physicist, was employed at a cost of £25,000 to conduct investigations into sub-atomic wave motions. This work is vital to the future success of several current projects.

    (4) £250,000 has been spent on the research and development of a new audio product: 40% is attributable to development. The product will not be marketable until 1988. Further total costs of some £400,000 are estimated, but financial backing is available from institutions and there are no doubts over the technical feasibility of the product. It is expected to have the same impact on home entertainment as television.

(5) Wallop, a new low alcohol beverage, was launched on 1st February 1986 with an expected market life of four years. During the year £20,000 was spent on advertising. Development expenditure brought forward amounted to £300,000.

Requirements

(a) Draft for Newprods plc an accounting policy note covering research and development expenditure and show how items (1) to (5) above should be reflected in its statutory accounts. State clearly your assumptions. (10 marks)

(b) Critically evaluate the accounting treatment and disclosure required by SSAP 13. (8 marks)
(18 marks)
ICAEW, PE II, FA II, December 1986

3. The treatment of goodwill in published company and group accounts has been a highly controversial topic for several decades.

Required:

(a) Discuss critically the methods of goodwill accounting that are in common use in companies and groups, with reference to both positive and negative goodwill. (15 marks)

(b) Give your views as to the methods of goodwill accounting that are most suitable for general use by companies and groups. (10 marks)
(You may refer to relevant accounting standards and/or exposure drafts.)
(25 marks)
ACCA, 3.1, AFA, June 1986

4. You are required to answer the following questions in accordance with SSAP 22, 'Accounting for Goodwill':

(a) (i) Explain the nature and meaning of goodwill. (5 marks)
   (ii) What TWO methods does SSAP 22 allow for accounting for purchased goodwill, which does it prefer and why? (6 marks)

(b) How should you account for the following in a consolidated balance sheet? Explain the reasons for your answers:
   (i) a sports clubhouse which is valued on the basis of its trading potential in the balance sheet of a subsidiary (4 marks)
   (ii) a valuable patent which is owned by a subsidiary company but not included in its balance sheet. (4 marks)

(c) What effect may the accounting policy adopted for goodwill have on the legal ability to pay dividends? (6 marks)
(25 marks)
ACCA, 2.8, RFA, June 1986

5. In preparing its financial statements for the year ended 30th June 1985, Metals plc decides to adopt the requirements of SSAP 22—'Accounting for Goodwill'. On 1st July 1984, Metals plc, which had no subsidiaries previously, made the following acquisitions:

(1) The following assets were purchased for cash at the amounts shown from the Receiver of Tin Ltd:

	£'000s
Freehold factory and associated plant	465
Stocks and work in progress	847
Knowhow	188

Included in the knowhow figure were certain patents with a fair value of £110,000. The balance represents the amount necessarily paid to secure the deal with the Receiver.

(2) The share capital of Manganese Ltd was purchased from the Ferric Group plc at a cash cost of £2,312,000. Manganese Ltd had not been profitable and the net assets acquired had a fair value of £2,460,000.

(3) The share capital of a private company, Copper Ltd, was purchased at a cash cost of £647,000. The book amounts of the assets and liabilities of that company, considered to be at a fair value, were:

	£'000s
Plant and equipment	324
Current assets	512
Current liabilities	(487)

(4) The share capital of Zinc Ltd was purchased by the issue of 3 million ordinary shares of 25p each at an agreed value of 126p per share to cover the following net assets:

	£'000s
Freehold factory and associated plant	1,728
Goodwil at cost	100
Current assets	3,126
Current liabilities	(1,174)

At the time of acquisition it was considered that the freehold factory should be revalued upwards by £80,000.

In complying with SSAP 22, Metals plc resolves not only to write off goodwill immediately, but also to maintain the maximum value of distributable reserves. In the opinion of the directors, the economic life of any goodwill on these acquisitions is 5 years including the year of acquisition.

The balances at 30th June 1984 on the reserves of Metals plc were:

	£'000s
Share premium	1,126
Other reserves (non-distributable)	175
Profit and loss	478

The retained profit for the year ended 30th June 1985 was £368,000 for the group including £176,000 for the parent company.

Requirements

(a) Draft the accounting policy note for goodwill to be included in the group financial statements of Metals plc at 30th June 1985. (4 marks)

(b) Prepare the notes to the group financial statements of Metals plc at 30th June 1985 covering goodwill and reserves. (9 marks)

(c) Describe the factors which should be considered in determining the useful economic life of purchased goodwill. (8 marks)

(21 marks)

ICAEW, PE II, FA II, July 1985

6. A company in the oil business covers the activities associated with exploration, development, production and sale of crude. It operates in four geographical areas. Data relating to expenditure, sales and reserves for the first three years are shown below:

Year 1

	Area A	B	C	D	Total
Costs £'000s					
Exploration	1,000	1,000	—	—	2,000
Development	2,000	—	—	—	2,000
Production	500	—	—	—	500
Output & Sales—units	500	—	—	—	500
£'000s	2,500	—	—	—	2,500
Estimated reserves at year end—units	2,500	1,000	—	—	3,500

Year 2

	Area A	B	C	D	Total
Costs £'000s					
Exploration	—	1,000	3,000	—	4,000
Development	500	1,000	—	—	1,500
Production	2,000	—	—	—	2,000
Output & Sales—units	2,000	—	—	—	2,000
£'000s	10,000	—	—	—	10,000
Estimated reserves at year end—units	2,000	3,000	1,000	—	6,000

Year 3

Costs £'000s	Area A	B	C	D	Total
Exploration	—	7,000	—	2,000	9,000
Development	—	2,000	4,000	500	6,500
Production	1,500	3,000	1,000	—	5,500
Output & Sales—units	2,000	2,000	1,000	—	5,000
£'000s	10,000	10,000	10,000	—	30,000
Estimated reserves at year end—units	—	4,000	—	2,000	6,000

There are at least three recognized methods of accounting for exploration and development expenditure:

(1) Current expense, in which all expenditure is written off in the year it is incurred.

(2) Conventional, one variation of which writes off in the year of incurrence all expenditure which is not likely to be recovered from production in the particular area. A maximum amount of £2,000 per unit is carried forward for recovery from future production and sale.

(3) Full cost, or total cost, which assumes that all exploration and development costs contribute towards the discovery of reserves irrespective of the particular area in which they are spent. Again, a maximum amount of £2,000 per unit would be carried forward for recovery from future production and sale.

You are required:

(a) to calculate and present in a comparative form the reported profit for each year using the three methods, and

(b) to comment on the relevance of the alternative methods for internal and external reporting.

(25 marks)

ICAEW, FE II, AA II, May 1974

5. Leasing transactions

In this chapter and in Chapter 16 we consider a number of situations in which the issue is how far the accountant is guided by the legal form of a transaction and how far by the substance of the transaction. With each of these situations there is either no legal or accounting requirement, or (until recently) no such clear requirement to disclose the transaction in the financial reports of the companies concerned. If such transactions are not disclosed in the financial accounts because of a strict following of the legal position, the question that arises is, Do the accounts give a true and fair view of the state of affairs of the business? Such transactions can result in what has become known as 'off-the-balance-sheet financing'. Until recently leasing was such a method of financing.

These transactions, which resulted in non-recognition (i.e. did not appear in the balance sheet and the profit and loss account) and often even in non-disclosure (i.e. not even appearing in the notes to the accounts), are special-purpose transactions. On occasions they have been specially designed so that they do not have to be recognized in the financial accounts.

A special-purpose transaction is 'one which combines or divides up the benefits and obligations flowing from it in such a way that they fall to be accounted for differently or in different periods depending on whether the elements are taken step by step or whether the transaction is viewed as a whole'. With a leasing transaction, the benefits from using a leased asset flow to the lessee over time. Legally, the lessee does not at any time own the asset. If the lessee uses the asset for all its useful life, by the end of that period he will have received the same economic benefits from it as if he had been the legal owner. If the leasing transaction is viewed as a whole, the lessee has the equivalent of an asset; if it is viewed step by step over time, the lessee does not own an asset.

In accounting for assets, the straightforward asset acquisition transaction is either a straight exchange of the asset for the buyer's cash or a credit transaction in which the buyer is expected to settle his account within the usual credit period. Many transactions are not this simple. For example, finance may be made available to buyers to help and encourage them to use an asset. For a transaction of this type, payments may be made over several years so that, at many year-ends, the exchange is not completed. When transaction agreements are made which will be fulfilled only in the future, these are classed as 'executory contracts'. Hire purchase agreements and leases, as well as contracts for the long-term supply of raw material, can all be described by the legal term 'executory contracts'.

These contracts create some accounting problems. The concept of pure economic income introduced in Chapter 1 would indicate that future implications of an executory contract should be anticipated, but such anticipation will not always represent the legal reality. The principle of substance over form would commend the recognition of these significant implications. If the transaction is effectively obtaining the use of an asset, even though this is not the legal position, it is appropriate to report it as if a purchase has taken place; if leasing provides additional debt capital, then to exclude the effects from the balance sheet will distort the disclosed gearing. Identifying, quantifying and presenting the relevant matters to be reported remain problems, and they are the concern of this chapter.

We will begin by considering the leasing transaction from an accounting point of view. Leasing was once referred to as an off-the-balance sheet method of finance. However in the UK, following the introduction of SSAP 21, for accounting periods commencing after 1 July 1987, details about many leasing transactions need to be disclosed in the balance sheet.

5.1 Accounting for leases

The Accounting Standards Committee in the mid-1970s set up a working party to examine the accounting problems associated with leasing contracts. A standard on the subject (SSAP 21) did not appear until 1984. This delay reflects the controversy surrounding the issue. The conflict largely revolved around the issue of whether financial accounts should reflect the legal form of a transaction or its practical substance. The standard was a bold step forward, stating that in certain situations substance should take precedence over legal form.

A lease agreement is one in which one party (the lessee) obtains the use of an asset for a period of time, while the legal ownership of that asset remains with the other party (the lessor). The leasing agreement, unlike a hire purchase agreement, does not give the lessee (equivalent to the hirer) the right to final ownership. If, say, a manufacturing or transport business wishes to obtain the use of an asset, without necessarily wanting to own the asset, then leasing is a possibility. In the UK, before SSAP 21, the lessee could use the asset perhaps for substantially all its useful life, taking on all the risks that would go with ownership, and still not show the asset, or the leasing liability, on its balance sheet. This is an example of 'off-the-balance-sheet' financing. The ASC pointed out in the introduction to the standard that,

> When a company is leasing a substantial amount of assets instead of buying them, the effect is that, unless the leased assets and obligation are capitalised, potentially large liabilities build up off the balance sheet; equally, the leased assets employed are not reflected in the balance sheet. These omissions may mislead users of a company's accounts—both external users and the company's own management.

Leasing showed tremendous growth in popularity during the 1970s and early 1980s. In 1965 new assets acquired by means of leasing totalled £52 million; by 1977 this had increased to £930, and by 1981 it was £3,300 million. The Department of Trade and Industry estimated that, in 1982, assets acquired to be leased out accounted for 26 per cent of the total investment in that year in plant machinery and vehicles by manufacturing, distribution and service companies. Leasing was clearly big business. The possibility that the accounts of many companies could mislead users because they did not give a true and fair view meant that the accounting profession could not ignore the issue.

The US standard-setters had encountered difficulties in introducing a standard on leasing. The FASB issued SFA 13 in 1976, but it proved necessary over the next few years to issue a number of interpretations of the standard and changes in the standard. The problem was one of deciding on the appropriate dividing line between a lease in which the lessee is obtaining similar rewards and risks from using an asset as if he were the owner, and a lease that is just providing a means for using an asset to give short-term benefits. The UK standard-setters encountered a similar problem. As in many situations in accounting where arbitrary lines have to be drawn, or where matters of judgement are involved, it gives the opportunity for preparers of accounts to make decisions, or to arrange the legal form of the transaction, which will enable them to adopt the practice that best suits their interests. This is what happened in the USA. The revisions to the standard were necessary to try to prevent certain companies altering leasing deals so as to avoid having to show them in their balance sheet.

5.1.1 The problems

Leases can be subdivided into two types, the finance lease and the operating lease. The basis of this subdivision reflects the economic rather than legal form of the transaction.

A finance lease is a contract that in many ways commits the lessee to substantially the same extent as an outright purchase. This form of contract is adopted to combine the acquisition and use of the asset with financing arrangements between lessee and lessor. A number of features may identify a finance lease: the contract is non-cancellable for a major part of the useful life of the asset; the payments during the non-cancellable period amount in total to almost as much as, if not more than, the outright purchase price; the lessee will take on most of the risks of obsolescence; and it is usual for the responsibilities for repairs, maintenance and insurance to be transferred to him.

The major theoretical issue that arises concerns the validity of recognizing the asset in the balance sheet of the lessee despite the lessee's lack of legal title. Of course, the lessee does have a legal right to the services of the asset during the period of the agreement. The capitalization of the asset and future liability is regarded by the ASC as superior to the limiting of disclosure to notes in the accounts; it can be argued that the latter treatment uses the notes to correct omissions in the balance sheet, whereas the purpose of notes is to provide greater detail. The move towards capitalizing leases has other theoretical implications. A lease is not the only contract that provides a supply of future services (the use of the asset) in return for agreed regular future payments; agreements with such future implications, known as executory contracts, include long-term contracts for material supplies and long-term employment agreements.

Technical and practical issues cannot be ignored. Although the difference between a typical operating lease and a finance lease can be clearly defined, contracts can be drawn up which are not easily classified. Setting specific limits on what constitutes a finance lease is subjective. Methods of valuing both the asset and the future payments are not without difficulties. The outright purchase alternative may not be available, or the purchase price may be set artifically high to discourage outright purchase. In either case, a valuation method must be arbitrarily selected.

In valuing the amount of the lease payments to be collected by the lessor, it may be necessary to give some consideration to the possibility that the lessee may fail to pay, or to the fact that unpredictable costs may have to be met by the lessor. Further, maintaining the compatibility between lessor and lessee reporting may be made complex by the incidence of the taxation effects relating to the lease.

5.1.2   Finance lease versus operating lease

The dividing line between the two types of leases is important, because the accounting treatment of the two differe fundamentally. SSAP 21 states that 'a finance lease should be capitalised by the lessee, that is, accounted for as the purchase of rights to the use and enjoyment of the asset with simultaneous recognition of the obligation to make future payments'. Under an operating lease, only the rental will be taken into account by a lessee, on a month-by-month or year-by-year basis.

The distinction between the two types of lease could have been based on a number of criteria. It could have been based on the useful economic life of the asset. For example, it could be said that it is a finance lease if in the lease agreement the primary period for which the asset is leased is at least 75 per cent of its estimated economic life. The distinction could have been based on value, that is on the relationship between the total amount paid by the lessee during the primary lease period and the cost to the lessee of purchasing the asset at the date of the inception of the lease. In the USA a finance lease is sometimes referred to as a full-payout lease. The distinction could have been based on the wording of the lease with regard to the risks and rewards attached to using the asset.

The ASC in fact decided to base its definition on the latter two considerations:

> a finance lease is a lease that transfers substantially all the risks and rewards of ownership of an asset to the lessee. It should be presumed that such a transfer of risks and rewards occurs if at the inception of a lease the present value of the minimum lease payments, including any initial payment, amounts to substantially all (normally 90 percent or more) of the fair value of the leased asset. The present value should be calculated by using the interest rate implicit in the lease. If the fair value of the asset is not determinable, an estimate thereof should be used.

However, the ASC goes on to say that 'the presumption that it should be classified as a finance lease may in exceptional circumstances be rebutted if it can be clearly demonstrated that the lease in question does not transfer substantially all the risks and rewards of ownership (other than legal title) to the lessee.'

An operating lease is defined as a lease other than a finance lease.

There are therefore two possible tests for determining whether or not a lease is a finance lease. One is based on terms and conditions, the other on the present value of the lease payments. The first involves interpreting the terms of the agreement. This means considering the provisions relating to such issues as cancellation, rental reviews, renewal options and the treatment of any residual value. With some leasing contracts, the lessee is given the option at the end of the primary lease period of entering into a further agreement for leasing the asset; this would suggest that it is a finance lease. The size of the estimated residual value at the end of the primary period is important, as is the question of who will receive such residual value. The lessee on occasions guarantees a residual value to the lessor. In other situations, when fluctuations in the market value of the residual are expected, and it is agreed that the lessee will receive the residual value based on the actual sale proceeds, this suggests a finance lease, with the risks and rewards being born by the lessee. On some occasions the contract allows for the residual value to be divided between the lessee and lessor: they share the risks of ownership.

In fact, in many cases in the UK the benefit of any residual value at the end of the lease period is passed on to the lessee. The lessor must not, however, sell the asset to the lessee at the end of the lease agreement, as this would cause tax problems. The benefit of any residual value is usually passed on either by a sale of the asset to a third party, after the end of the primary period, with perhaps 95 per cent or more of the proceeds being passed on to the lessee by way of a rental rebate adjustment, or by the lessee continuing to lease the asset for a secondary period at a very low (peppercorn) rental. Clearly, if such conditions are written into the leasing contract it would indicate a finance lease.

Most leases are written in terms of a fixed interest rate. But in some contracts the lessor can vary the terms of the agreement during the leasing period, so as to take advantage of changing market conditions; some rental payments are based on the performance of the lessee; and in some leasing contracts the lessee can cancel the lease, paying comparatively little compensation to the lessor.

An analysis of the above and other significant points in particular contracts should help to determine what risks, if any, the lessor has retained, and what risks have been transferred to the lessee. In many cases it is possible to identify whether or not a lease is a finance lease from the terms and conditions in the contract. However, where it is not possible to identify a lease from the conditions in the contract it is necessary to carry out a present-value calculation to ascertain whether the lease payments amount to more or less than 90 per cent of the fair value. In examination questions on leasing, it is frequently necessary to carry out such calculations!

A simple example, based on the 90 per cent of the fair value rule, is as follows.

Case A

The purchase price in the market of a computer Model XT is £10,000. A leasing company offers to lease the computer to Company X in return for eight quarterly rental payments, each of £1,000, over two years. The lease payments are to be made in advance each quarter. The interest rate payable on similar leasing deals is 4 per cent per quarter. Is this a finance lease or an operating lease?

In determining whether or not a lease can be classed as finance or operating, the standard states that, when the present-value calculations are made, the discount rate used should be the interest rate implicit in the lease. This is a calculation to be undertaken by the lessee, based on the cash flows of the lessor, i.e. the leasing company. How, when this cash flow information is not available to the lessee, this implicit rate can be estimated will be considered later in the chapter. It is not always easy, and the standard recognizes this, and allows as an alternative discount rate 'the rate which a lessee would be expected to pay on a similar lease'.

To keep this example simple, it is the latter rate that we shall use in the calculations. In normal circumstances it would be close to the rate implicit in the lease.

It should be remembered that one way to answer the question would be to examine the wording of the leasing contract to ascertain whether substantially all the risks and reward of ownership have been transferred. For example, does the lessee or the lessor pay the insurance costs? Does the lessee pay for maintenance? Without the information required to answer these questions, this case must be decided on the basis of the financial arrangements only.

The present value of the lease payments is

$$£1,000 + \frac{£1,000}{(1.04)} + \frac{£1,000}{(1.04)^2} \cdots \frac{£1,000}{(1.04)^7} \quad \begin{aligned} &= £1,000 + £1,000 \times a_{\overline{7}|0.04} \\ &= £1,000 + (£1,000 \times 6.0021) \\ &= £7,002. \end{aligned}$$

This is less than 90 per cent of the fair value of the asset and supports the view that this is an operating lease.

Case B

This is a similar situation to the above, except that this time the primary period of the leasing arrangement is three years instead of two. The present value of the lease payments can be easily calculated. The present value of 11 future payments of £1 each, with an interest rate of 4 per cent per period, can be ascertained, by examining the present value of an annuity table, to be £8.7605. This means that, the future payments of £1,000, together with the initial payment, give the present value of the lease payments which is £9,760. This is more than 90 per cent of the fair value of the computer, and so the presumption in this second case is that it is a finance lease.

Certain terms need to be explained. First *fair value* is defined as 'the price at which an asset could be exchanged in an arm's-length transaction less, where applicable, any grants receivable towards the purchase or use of the asset'.

The definition of a *finance lease* refers to minimum lease payments. These are the payments the lessee guarantees to make to the lessor during the lease term. The *lease term* is defined as 'the period for which the lessee has contracted to lease the asset and any further terms for which the lessee has the option to continue to lease the asset, with or without further payment, which option it is reasonably certain at the inception of the lease that the lessee will exercise'.

In many leasing agreements reference is made to what will happen to the asset at the end of the 'primary' lease period. As mentioned above, sometimes the lessee will arrange to benefit from the sale of the asset at the end of the lease period, and sometimes he will continue to lease (during a secondary period) at an agreed rate, perhaps even a peppercorn rent.

Whether these arrangements for the sale of the asset or the leasing for a secondary period are taken into account in calculating the minimum lease payments for accounting purposes depends on whether or not the amounts involved are guaranteed. If they are not guaranteed by definition, they cannot be part of the 'minimum' lease payments.

One further expression needs to be clarified. The present value of the lease payments is to be calculated using, where it can reasonably be calculated, the interest rate implicit in the lease. This rate is defined in the standard as the discount rate that at the inception of a lease, when applied to the amounts which the lessor expects to receive and retain, produces an amount (the present value) equal to the fair value of the leased asset. If the interest rate implicit in the lease is not determinable, it should be estimated by reference to the rate which a lessee would be expected to pay on a similar lease.

It should be noted that this bases the interest rate implicit in the lease not on the lessee's cash flows, but on the lessor's cash flows. This means taking into account the fair value of the leased asset, net of any grants and tax credits receivable by the lessor, and the guaranteed lease payments plus (or less) any unguaranteed residual values and the related tax charges.

By way of illustration, let us assume that the fair value of an asset is £100,000, and the finance company (the lessor) receives grants of £30,000. The asset is leased for a three-year period, and the lessor is to receive £30,000 per annum, payable in arrears. The lessor expects the asset to have a residual value at the end of the period of £20,000, which will be shared with the lessee.

To determine the interest rate (r) implicit in the lease, the following equation needs to be solved:

$$£100,000 - £30,000 = \frac{£30,000}{(1+r)} + \frac{£30,000}{(1+r)^2} + \frac{£40,000}{(1+r)^3}.$$

The solution is that the rate of interest implicit in the lease is 19 per cent (to the nearest whole number). These sums are based on the lessor's cash flow. It is a simplified example as it ignores the annual tax position and the financing arrangements of the leasing company.

5.1.3 Accounting by lessees—finance lease

Having determined that a particular lease should be classified as a finance lease, the next issue to consider is how the entries will appear in the books of account. We will first deal with the entries for a finance lease in the books of the lessee.

To illustrate we will use an example. Leek plc, a finance company, leases an asset to Wythall Ltd on 1 January 1987. Under the terms of the lease, Wythall is responsible for all the maintenance and insurance, and has to make rental payments of £500 every six months for five years, the first payment being required on 1 January 1987.

In this example we have a finance lease, so we need to decide the value at which the leased asset will be capitalized. The standard states: 'At the inception of the lease the sum to be recorded both as an asset and as a liability should be the present value of the minimum lease payments, derived at the interest rate implicit in the lease.'

We have already discussed the meaning of the expression 'interest rate implicit in the lease'. Let us assume in this example that there is no residual value at the end of the lease. The fair value of the asset is estimated to be £4,050. We have to determine the implicit interest rate (i), where

$$4,050 = 500 + \sum_{j=0}^{9} \frac{500}{(1+i)^j}$$

$$3,550 = \sum_{j=0}^{9} \frac{500}{(1+i)^j}$$

$$\frac{3,550}{500} = \sum_{j=0}^{9} \frac{1}{(1+i)^j} = 7.10.$$

At this stage we have ignored any grants and capital allowances that might benefit the lessor.

The first £500 payment is not discounted as it is paid at the beginning of the lease period. Present value of annuity tables show that 7.1078 represents an interest rate of 5 per cent per period for an annuity for nine periods. We will take this 5 per cent as the implicit interest rate.

The present value of the minimum lease payments is therefore [£500 + £500 (7.1078)], which (rounded off) equals £4,050, which in the case equals the fair value of the asset. This is not always the situation; it depends on the cash flows of the lessor. These are discussed, with examples, in Section 5.1.4.

The standard does try to minimize the calculations required; it states: 'In practice in the case of a finance lease the fair value of the asset will often be a sufficiently close approximation to the present value of the minimum lease payments and may in these circumstances be substituted for it.'

It emphasizes, however, that where there is a difference it is the minimum payments that should be capitalized, not the fair value:

> The combined benefit to a lessor of regional development and other grants, together with capital allowances, which reduce tax liabilities, may enable the minimum lease payments under a finance lease to be reduced to a total which is less than the fair value of the asset. In these circumstances, the amount to be capitalised and depreciated should be restricted to the minimum lease payments. A negative finance charge should not be shown.

In our example we can now make the initial entry:

Dr Leased asset	4,050	
Cr Liability under lease		4,050

The second step is to determine how each lease payment shall be divided between the interest element and the capital repayment element. This will enable us to reduce the liability under the lease each period, to reflect the capital repayment. We will also have to depreciate the asset. The asset needs to be depreciated over a period that is the shorter of the lease term and its useful life. Clearly, the two periods need not be the same.

It should be appreciated that, although at the inception of the lease the value of the asset will equal the value of the liability, this concurrence need not occur again until the end of the lease period. The two items are usually being written down at different rates.

Interest and capital repayment

There are a number of possible ways of spreading the interest charge over the period of the lease. The standard states: 'the total finance charge should be allocated to accounting periods during the lease term so as to produce a constant periodic rate of charge on the remaining balance of the obligation for each accounting period, or a reasonable approximation thereto.' Theoretically, the best method is the annuity method, an example of which follows. (A good approximation is given by the sum-of-digits method (sometimes called the Rule of 78) which is illustrated below.)

Annuity method

The total payments (£500 × 10)	£5,000
less 'Cost' (fair value or PV of lease payments)	4,050
Total interest payable	£ 950

Our problem is to distribute this £950 over ten periods, each of six months. We know that the interest rate being charged is 5 per cent on the outstanding debt for each period; therefore we can calculate how much of each rental payment represents interest, the remainder of the rental being capital repayment.

	Opening balance of liability	Payment	Capital	Interest 5%	Closing Balance of liability
1/1/87	4,050	500	500	0	3,550
1/7/87	3,550	500	322	178	3,228
1/1/88	3,228	500	338	162	2,890
1/7/88	2,890	500	355	145	2,535
1/1/89	2,535	500	373	127	2,162
1/7/89	2,162	500	392	108	1,770
1/1/90	1,770	500	411	89	1,359
1/7/90	1,359	500	433	67	926
1/1/91	926	500	453	47	473
1/7/91	473	500	473	27	0
		5,000	4,050	950	

The interest element of the 1/7/87 payment is calculated as 5 per cent of £3,550, which is £178. All other interest payments are calculated in a similar way: 5 per cent on the opening balance on the liability for the period.

The journal entries in the first year would be

1/1/87	Dr Liability under lease £500	
	Cr Cash	£500
1/7/87	Dr Liability under lease	322
	Interest charge	178
	Cr Cash	500
31/12/87	Dr Interest charge	162
	Cr Accrued interest	162

At the end of the first year, the 'Liability under lease', shown on the liabilities side of the balance sheet, would be £3,228 (i.e. £4,050 − £500 − £322). The interest charge in the profit and loss account would be £340, that is, the £178 paid plus the accrued interest of £162 payable on 1 January 1988.

The leased asset has to be depreciated. Let us initially assume that its useful life is six years; it will be depreciated over the shorter period, namely the five years of the leasing contract. For simplicity we will assume straight-line depreciation, that is £810 per annum, which will be charged to the profit and loss account.

The net value of the leased asset in the balance sheet at the end of the first year will be £3,240 (i.e. £4,050 − £810). By chance, in this case the value of the asset is not so different from the value of the liability. By the end of 1988 the difference will be greater: the liability will be £2,535 (i.e. £3,228 − £338 − £355), and the asset £2,430 (i.e. £3,240 − £810).

The total charge to the profit and loss account in the first year will be £1,150, that is, interest of £340 plus depreciation of £810 — in this case not so different from the actual cash payment of £1,000 for the year. The total charge to the profit and loss account in 1988 will be £1,082, being depreciation plus the interest element in the rental payments.

It has been mentioned that the asset is to be depreciated over the shorter of the lease term and its useful live. Normally the lease term will be shorter, for one could argue a company would not wish to lease an asset whose useful economic life was less than the lease period. Occasionally, however, one does come across examples where the company wishes to adopt a rapid depreciation policy and so a short economic life is adopted.

Sum of digits

The above example was based on the actuarial method of apportioning interest charges. Another popular method is the sum of digits. The sum of the digits of the periods is determined and the total interest is allocated on the basis of the digit for each period as a proportion of the sum of digits. Taking the sum of the digits from 1 to 9 equals 45. The first period's interest charge is therefore 9/45 of this total interest; this amounts to £190. The second period would be 8/45 of the £950; the third 7/45 etc. It will be seen that the interest charged per period under this method does not differ very much from that arrived at under the annuity method. It generally provides a good and acceptable approximation.

Disclosure

We will now consider the disclosure requirements with regard to finance leases. SSAP 21 states that the gross amount of assets held under such leases, together with the related accumulated depreciation, 'should' be shown in the balance sheet. The appropriate accounting entries have been illustrated above. The value needs to be shown for each major class of asset. The annual (period) depreciation charge relating to assets held under lease for each major class of asset also needs to be shown in the profit and loss account.

The standard does however allow for an alternative treatment in that rather than showing leased assets separately from the fixed asset the company owns, the two can be integrated. When this alternative treatment is adopted, it is necessary to disclose by way of a note the net amount of assets held under finance leases that has been included in the net asset total, and also the amount of depreciation for the year that relates to assets held under finance leases that is included in the profit and loss account charge.

We have dealt above with the asset part of the balance sheet, and with the depreciation charge. With respect to the liability, the standard states that the amounts of the obligations relating to finance leases (net of finance charges allocated to future periods) should be disclosed separately from other obligations and liabilities. This disclosure need not be on the face of the balance sheet; the leasing obligation can be integrated with other liabilities, provided a note to the accounts discloses the leasing element included in the total.

In the notes to the accounts, the leasing obligations should be analysed, showing the amounts payable in the next year, the amounts payable in the second to fifth years inclusive from the balance sheet date, and the aggregate amounts payable thereafter. This can be shown as the set of figures relating to just finance leasing obligations; alternatively, if in the balance sheet the leasing figures are integrated with other liabilities, an analysis of the payments over time can be similarly integrated. When the obligations are integrated they will be shown within the 'creditors due within one year' figures and the 'creditors due after more than one year'.

By way of example, the 'Notes on the accounts' of Lucas Industries plc for 1987 indicated their accounting policy with respect to leasing. The actual group accounts showed that the net plant and equipment figure of £338 million included leased assets with a net value of £65 million. The 'creditors payable within one year' included finance leasing obligations of £19 million, and the 'creditors payable after more than one year' included finance leasing obligations of £33 million. The notes concerning the profit and loss account items showed that the depreciation on leased assets was £8 million and the interest paid on finance leases was £3.2 million.

5.1.4 Accounting by lessees—operating lease

The accounting treatment of operating leases is relatively straightforward. SSAP 21 states that the rentals payable under such a lease 'should be charged on a straight-line basis over the lease term, even if the payments are not made on such a basis'.

Not all leasing deals require equal periodic payments. Deals can be arranged to suit lessees' individual needs—to fit in with seasonal cash flow for example. The standard adopts the principle of matching; the benefits are assumed to be spread evenly over time, and so the charge to the profit and loss account should be on an even basis. The standard does, however, allow for the use of 'another systematic and rational basis' where this is more approriate than the straight-line basis.

The accounting entries for an operating lease are not too complicated—a charge to the profit and loss account, with a possible entry as an accrual or payment in advance if the cash payments in a period are not the same as the annual charge. There is of course no capitalization of the asset involved.

Disclosure

Where leases are to be treated as operating leases, SSAP 21 requires that the total of operating lease rentals charged as an expense in the profit and loss account should be disclosed, with the figure divided between amounts payable in respect of the hire of plant and machinery and in respect of other operating leases. Further, the lessee is required to disclose the payments that he is committed to make during the next year, in the second to fifth years' inclusive, and over five years. The future commitments in respect of leases of land and buildings need to be shown separately from commitments on other operating leases.

This information, together with that required for finance leases, provides users of the accounts with important information regarding future commitments. These payments are just as much a fixed charge against future income as is interest on medium- and long-term borrowings.

5.1.5 Accounting by lessors—finance lease

The most controversial issue surrounding the accounting treatment of a finance lease in the books of the lessor concerns when, within the lease period, the profit is to be recognized. Are the profits earned when the cash is invested, evenly over the period of the lease, or when the final payment is made? If one adopted an ultra-conservative approach, one could argue that no profits should be shown in the accounts until late in the lease period—until, in fact, the total lease payments actually received exceeded the net cost of the asset to the lessor plus any financing charges. This is in fact not the approach the leasing companies adopted before there was a standard, and it is not the practice to be adopted following the standard.

When 100 per cent first-year capital allowances were possible, the amount of cash the lessor had invested in the lease deal declined rapidly over the leasing period. In many cases the cash initially invested had been fully recovered halfway through the lease period. The leasing companies were keen to relate the profit shown in any year to the balance of the capital they had invested in the leased asset in any year. This was the practice adopted in the leasing industry at the time a standard was under discussion. The Accounting Standard Committee accepted the point of view of the leasing industry. The standard states: 'The total gross earnings under a finance lease should normally be allocated to accounting periods to give a constant periodic rate of return on the lessor's net cash investment in the lease in each period.'

It should be noted that this is referred to as the 'normal' treatment. Alternative methods are allowed. Paragraph 39 of the standard states that, 'In arriving at the constant periodic rate of return, a reasonable approximation may be made.'

There are a number of ways in which the profit can be spread over the period of the lease to give approximately a constant annual rate of return, including the rule of 78, the actuarial method based on either before- or after-tax return and the investment period method. These alternative methods are illustrated in the guidance notes accompanying the standard.

The standard requires the allocation of gross earnings to give a constant periodic rate of return on the net cash invested in the lease in each period. The net cash investment in a lease at a point of time comprises the cost of the asset plus or minus the following relevant payments or receipts:

(a) government or other grants receivable towards the purchase or use of the asset;
(b) rentals received;
(c) taxation payments and receipts, including the effect of capital allowances;
(d) residual values, if any, at the end of the lease term;
(e) interest payments (where applicable);
(f) interest received on cash surplus;
(g) profit taken out of the lease.

The calculation of the constant rate of return is somewhat complicated. It requires a detailed cash flow projection and then the allocation of the profit figures over the years of the lease to give a constant annual rate of return. The method that is the most accurate is the actuarial method after tax, but this is also the most complex. A method that gives a good approximation is the investment period method.

Investment period method

The investment period method allocates gross earnings over the periods of the lease agreement according to the level of cash investment in each period by the lessor as a proportion of the sum of the cash invested at the start of each period. Earnings are allocated only over the periods of the lease in which the lessor still actually has cash invested, that is, before there is a positive cash balance.

Example 5.1

The Ryton Leasing Company leases an asset on 1 January 1988 on a four-year lease to Lawson Ltd. The rental payment is £1,000 per annum, payable in advance on 1 January of each year. The residual value is expected to be zero. The corporation tax rate is 35 per cent, and the capital allowances are 25 per cent per annum on a reducing balance basis. Tax is payable six months after the year end. The asset cost Ryton £3,000. The lessor borrows funds to finance the leasing business at an interest rate of 12 per cent per annum, payable annually. When cash surpluses arise the lessor is able to use the funds to finance other leases, thereby saving the 12 per cent borrowing cost.

Table 5.1 shows the cash flow projection. The estimate of tax to be paid on the 1988 profits is arrived at as follows:

Rentals (earnings)		£1,000
Capital allowance	£750	
Interest paid	240	990
Earnings subject to tax		10
Tax 35%		4

A similar calculation is made for the following years. It should be noted that interest payable has been deducted in arriving at taxable profit.

Table 5.2 shows the summary of the final results of the four-year lease. The annual interest charge for a year is based on the average net cash invested for that year as shown in Table 5.1. The cash flows shown conform with the figures needed for the investment period method. If the full actuarial method after tax is used a complication arises, because under this method profits are assumed to be periodically taken out of the lease. This means they are recognized in the profit and loss account each year, and are assumed distributed or spent, thereby increasing the borrowing required in the leasing cash flow calculation and consequently the interest charges. (This point will be returned to later.) 'Gross earnings' is defined in the standard as the lessor's gross finance income over the lease term, representing the difference between the total of the minimum lease payments (and any unguaranteed residual value) and the cost of the leased asset less any grants receivable.

The problem we are faced with is how to allocate the total gross earnings of £1,000 over the four-year period. In Table 5.3, the apportionment has been based on the ratio of the net cash invested in the lease at the beginning of each period, as a proportion of the sum of the annual net cash invested figures before there was a positive cash balance.

The profit and loss account for the four years is shown in Table 5.4. We have allocated the gross earnings to give approximately a constant rate of return on net cash invested. When large

TABLE 5.1   The cash flows of the lessor

Date	Transaction	Receipt	Payment	Net cash invested
1/1/88	Purchase of asset		3,000	(3,000)
1/1/88	Rental received	1,000		(2,000)
31/12/88	Interest paid		240	(2,240)
1/1/89	Rental received	1,000		(1,240)
1/7/89	Tax paid for 1988		4	(1,244)
31/12/89	Interest paid		150	(1,394)
1/1/90	Rental received	1,000		(394)
1/7/90	Tax paid for 1989		100	(494)
31/12/90	Interest paid		53	(547)
1/1/91	Rental received	1,000		453
1/7/91	Tax paid for 1990		184	269
31/12/91	Interest earned	43		312
1/7/92	Tax refund	78		390

TABLE 5.2   Results from the lease contract over the four-year period

	£
Rentals received	4,000
less Cost of asset	3,000
Gross earnings	1,000
Interest paid (less earned)	400
Profit before tax	600
Taxation (35%)	210
Profit after tax	390

TABLE 5.3   Apportionment of gross earnings

Date	Net cash invested	Gross earnings		Capital repayment
1/1/88	£2,000	$\dfrac{2,000}{3,634} \times 1,000 =$	550	450
1/1/89	1,240	$\dfrac{1,240}{3,634} \times 1,000 =$	341	659
1/1/90	394	$\dfrac{394}{3,634} \times 1,000 =$	109	891
1/1/91	0		0	1,000
	£3,634		£1,000	£3,000

first-year capital allowances were available, a further stage was usually necessary, namely to make allowance for deferred taxation. This is no longer necessary, as there is now no large tax credit in the year of purchase to be spread over the life of the asset.

The 'profit after tax' figures for the four years, based on the tax payments in the cash flow statement, are £306, £91, (£128) and £121, respectively. The fourth year shows a net profit largely because of the balancing tax charge on the asset. The reason for the high net profit in the first two years is because the leasing company chose to take its gross profit in line with the level of actual cash invested.

It should be noted that the tax payments shown in the cash flow calculations (Table 5.1) were based on the rentals received each year being classed as income, with deduction for depreciation and actual interest paid. They were not based on the split of the rentals between gross earnings and capital repayment (as in Table 5.4), which is used for accounting reporting purposes.

TABLE 5.4   Profit and loss account

	1988	1989	1990	1991	Total
Rental	1,000	1,000	1,000	1,000	4,000
less capital repayment	450	659	891	1,000	3,000
Gross earnings	550	341	109	0	1,000
Actual interest paid/received	240	150	53	(43)	400
Profit before tax	310	191	56	43	600
Tax paid	4	100	184	(78)	210
Profit after tax	306	91	(128)	121	390

Balance sheet entry

The lessors should not disclose the plant, equipment or whatever is being leased as assets in their balance sheets even though they are legally the owners: they will in fact be shown as assets in the accounts of the lessees. The lessor records the fact that the lessee is a debtor. The debt is valued as the net investment in the lease at the balance sheet date after making any necessary provision for bad or doubtful debts. The net investment at any point of time comprises the minimum lease payments plus any unguaranteed residual values still to be received by the lessor, less the gross earnings allocated to future periods.

In our example, the minimum guaranteed interest payments equal £4,000, and there is no residual value. The gross earnings that have been allocated to future periods are £1,000. Therefore the net investment at the inception of the lease is £3,000; this is equal to the cost of the assets less any grants receivable by the lessor.

In the first year the gross earnings recognized in the profit and loss account are £550. This means that, at 31 December 1988, £450 gross earnings remain allocated to future periods. At that date there are only three years' lease payments to be recieved (£3,000), giving a net investment to appear in the balance sheet at 31 December 1988 of £2,550.

TABLE 5.5 Allocation of earnings to future periods

	Minimum lease payments still due	Gross earnings to be allocated to future periods	Net investment
1/1/88	4,000	1,000	3,000
31/12/88	3,000	450	2,550
31/12/89	2,000	109	1,891
31/12/90	1,000	0	1,000
31/12/91	0		

The journal entries would be as follows:

Date	Account	Dr	Cr
1 Jan. 1988	Debtor: Lawson Ltd	3,000	
	Equipment		3,000
1 Jan. 1988	Receipts under lease	1,000	
	Profit before tax		550
	Debtors		450
1 Jan. 1989	Receipts under lease	1,000	
	Profit before tax		341
	Debtors		659
1 Jan. 1990	Receipts under lease	1,000	
	Profit before tax		109
	Debtors		891
1 Jan 1991	Receipts under lease	1,000	
	Debtors		1,000

Actuarial after tax method

In this method, a profit is taken out of the cash flow calculations each year. This is of course recognized as income in the profit and loss account. Whether or not this results in an actual cash outflow for the lessor depends on other decisions. The guidance notes to SSAP 21 assume in their actuarial example that the profits are used to pay overheads and dividends. If this happens, it will increase the amount of cash that needs to be invested in the lease at any point in time, and so not only will it be necessary to take account of interest payable on money borrowed to acquire the asset, but it will also be necessary to take account of interest payable on money transferred to the profit and loss account and spent.

This leads to a very complicated calculation that goes round in circles. It is necessary to have a zero cash balance at the end of the lease period; a rate of profit has to be calculated that gives an equal rate of return each year on the cash invested; but the level of cash invested each period is itself influenced by the profit taken out and the interest that has to be paid on this additional outflow. The problem can be solved either by trial and error, (which would be necessary in an exam if the rate of profit being earned was not given) or, as in practice, by an iteration procedure using an appropriate computer program.

There is a modified version of the actuarial after-tax method which is sometimes mentioned in books, but this does not take into account the interest on the funds that have been borrowed either for the purpose of financing the acquisition of the leased asset or for the financing of any cash flow taken out as profits. It does not give a very accurate approximation to the true rate of profit earned.

Taking the above example, adopting the complete actuarial after-tax approach to allocate earnings gives profits after tax in the four years of £150, £104, £57 and £4, respectively. This is a smoother series of figures than those obtained using the investment period method. It will be noted that these total only £315, less than the after-tax profit with the investment period method (£390). This is because the profits taken out each year add to the cash invested each year, and hence to the interest charge. The investment period method assumes that, although profits are credited to the profit and loss account each year, no actual cash relating to these profits is taken out of the business until the end of the lease period. The detailed calculations for the complete actuarial method are shown in Table 5.6.

TABLE 5.6   The complete actuarial method

Date	Net cash investment	Rental received	Tax paid	Interest paid	Profit taken out ($7\frac{1}{2}\%$)	Net cash investment at end
1/1/88	(3,000)	1,000				(2,000)
31/12/88	(2,000)			240	150	(2,390)
1/1/89	(2,390)	1,000				(1,390)
1/7/89	(1,390)		4			(1,394)
31/12/89	(1,394)			167	104	(1,665)
1/1/90	(1,665)	1,000				(665)
1/7/90	(665)		94			(759)
31/12/90	(759)			91	57	(907)
1/1/91	(907)	1,000				+93
1/7/91	+93		180			(87)
31/12/91	(87)				4	(91)
1/7/92	(91)		(91)			0

Notes:

The tax for each period is based on taxable profits which equal rentals received, less capital allowances, and interest paid.

The interest paid is derived from an annual charge of 12% on the average net cash invested during the 12-month period.

The annual profit taken out is the complicated figure. It is based on the rate of return on the net cash invested at the end of each period that allocates the total profit over the life of the lease.

If this example is reworked using the 'modified' actuarial method, that is, ignoring the interest charge on the cash invested each year, it gives misleading figures. If a relatively simple set of calculations is needed, it is recommended that the investment period method be used to obtain the approximate constant rate of return rather than the modified actuarial method.

Disclosure

The lessor is required to disclose the net investment in finance leases at each balance sheet date. The net investment is of course not the asset, which is being capitalized by the lessee, but the amount due from the lessee, after making provision for items such as bad and doubtful rentals. This will be shown in the balance sheet as a debtor. Also to be shown is the gross amounts of assets held for use in operating leases and the accumulated depreciation relating to these assets. These operating lease assets are shown as fixed assets.

Notes should show the policy adopted for accounting for operating and finance leases. The aggregate rentals received during a period in respect of each type of lease should be shown, together with the cost of any assets acquired during the period for the purpose of letting under finance leases.

The 1986 annual reports of the Big Four banks present a confusing picture. Lloyds' policy is that 'income from leasing transactions is credited to the profit and loss account in proportion to the net funds invested using the investment period method.' Barclays' policy is that 'Net leasing income under 'finance leases is now taken to profit using an actuarial method to give a constant periodic return on the net cash investment.' Barclays point out that, with effect from January 1986, their policy for allocating income from finance leases was changed from the investment period method to the actuarial method, which the directors believe 'gives a fairer presentation of the group's leasing business'. Barclays and Lloyds clearly disagree. The Midland and National Westminster Banks do not make their positions clear. Midland just say 'income from leasing contracts ... is credited to profit and loss account in proportion to the funds invested.' The National Westminster use similar wording. No attempt was made to explain to users of accounts how the income was being spread over time.

5.1.6   Accounting by lessor–operating leases

As mentioned, an asset held for use in operating leases should be recorded as a fixed asset and depreciated over its useful life.

The standard requires that rental income received, excluding charges for services such as insurance and maintenance, be recognized on a straight-line basis over the period of the lease. This is normally required even if payments are not made on such a basis, 'unless another systematic and rational basis is more representative of the time pattern in which the benefit from the leased asset is receivable'. This is similar treatment to that recommended for the lessee under an operating leasing deal.

5.1.7   Sale and leaseback transactions

In a sale and leaseback arrangement, one business sells an asset, say a building, to another business, usually an insurance or finance company. As part of the same contract, the new purchaser of the asset agrees to lease the building back to the vendor for an agreed period of time. This leasing deal can result in either a finance lease or an operating lease.

In the case of a building, the seller/lessee could obtain use of the building for more or less all its useful life, with all the risks and rewards from using the building being the same as if it legally owned the building: a finance lease. If it is a piece of land that is the subject of the deal, the leasing period could be for a relatively short period of time with most of the risks and rewards remaining with the purchaser/lessor: an operating lease.

When the asset is initially sold by the lessee to the purchaser/lessor, the lessee can make a profit or loss, depending on the difference between the sales price and the book value of the asset. The accounting issue is whether this profit or loss should be recognized all at once at the time the contract is signed, or spread over the life of the leasing contract.

One argument is that the profit or loss has been made as a result of negotiating at a point in time, so the financial consequence of the deal should be immediately recognized. The alternative argument is that the settlement of the selling price is not independent of the agreed rental payments. It would be possible for the seller/lessee to receive a very high selling price, show a large profit, and then pay high rental payments to recompense the purchaser/lessor. Alternatively, the selling price could be low, and a loss could result for the seller/lessee, followed by low rental payments.

SSAP 21 states that, with a finance lease, 'any apparent profit or loss should be deferred and amortised in the financial statements of the seller/lessee over the shorter of the lease term and the useful life of the asset.' Clearly, the profit is not all to be taken, or the loss all to be recognized, at the time of sale.

With an operating lease, any profit or loss of the seller/lessee should be recognized immediately, 'provided it is clear that the transaction is established at fair value'.

If the sale price is below fair value, any profit or loss should be recognised immediately except that, if the apparent loss is compensated by future rentals at below market price, it should to that extent be deferred and amortised over the remainder of the lease term (or if shorter, the period during which the reduced rentals are chargeable); If the sale price is above fair value, the excess fair value should be deferred and amortized over the shorter of the remainder of the lease term and the period to the next rent review (if any).

5.2   Hire purchase contracts

Leasing contracts are described in legal terms as executory contracts. Hire purchase contracts and contracts for the long-term supply of a raw material are also executory contracts. Payments are made over a number of years, so that, at the end of a number of accounting periods, the transaction may not be completed. Such contracts create accounting problems. The concept of pure economic income introduced in Chapter 1 would indicate that future implications of an executory contract should be anticipated, but such anticipation would not always represent the legal reality. The principle of substance over form would, however, commend the recognition of these significant implications. Two types of sales by instalment will be considered: hire purchase, and the instalment credit sale.

Under a hire purchase agreement, goods are supplied to a customer on hire with the option to purchase at the end of a hire period. The purchase price at the end of the hire period is agreed as part of the original agreement and is usually represented by the payment of a final hire charge. Three characteristics of such a contract can be identified: periodic payments over a relatively long period of time, ownership remaining with the supplier until the last payment is made, and uninterrupted use by the hirer.

In an instalment credit sale, periodic payments would be found again. Here, however, title to the goods passes from the supplier when delivery is made, and a binding debt is created which cannot be avoided by returning the goods. Often the contract allows the supplier to repossess the goods in cases of default.

Despite the legal difference in the timing of change of ownership, the economic effects of both categories of instalment sale are very similar, and this is reflected in their accounting treatment. Although in law a hire purchase agreement is only a contract of hire with an *option* to purchase, generally accepted accounting practice assumes that it is intended to complete the purchase. The goods that are the subject of a hire purchase agreement are brought into the accounts of the purchaser as assets. The goods are being treated as if the purchaser is the owner as soon as delivery is made. The adjusted outstanding instalments are shown as a liability due to the supplier. In the accounts of the supplier, the transaction is treated as a sale, the buyer being a debtor for the outstanding payments.

Both types of instalment sale can be put into effect either directly or by the introduction of a finance company as an intermediary. In the former case, the supplier provides the finance. In the latter case, the finance company purchases the goods from the suppliers and lets these goods on hire purchase or sells them on instalment credit to the customer. It is common for the dealer to make the agreement with the customer on behalf of the finance company and he may collect the instalments on its behalf. Each arrangement has different accounting implications. Where a finance company is involved, it makes a profit mainly from the provision of finance rather than on the goods themselves. Where a dealer provides the finance, it will be necessary to give separate consideration to both the profit from the trading transaction and that from the financing arrangement.

SSAP 21 is concerned with both leasing and hire purchase. It was not intended that the standard should change the existing practices with regard to hire purchase contracts for either the hirer or the finance company. The accounting treatment of a hire purchase contract is now similar to that of a leasing contract. Hire purchase contracts are similar to a finance lease, and should be treated in a similar way, with similar disclosure to that described above. A few hire purchase contracts are similar to operating leases and so receive similar accounting treatment.

Normally a hire purchase contract contains a purchase option for the hirer to acquire the asset at a bargain price at the end of the hire period. Such a contract is usually non-cancellable and can be clearly seen to be similar in nature to a finance lease.

Because it is usually reasonable to assume that the hirer will exercise the option, the minimum hire payments include the hire charges plus the option price. These payments, discounted at the interest rate implicit in the contract, will equal the fair value of the asset. This will be the amount capitalized, and it will be depreciated over the estimated useful life. The annual finance charge to the profit and loss account will be calculated in the same way as with a finance lease.

The asset and liability will be shown in the balance sheet in the same way as with an asset used under a finance lease. The liability under the hire purchase contracts will be the net investment, that is, the future payment less the future financing charges.

From the point of view of the finance company, in accounting for the transaction as a sale, careful appraisal is needed in measuring the income for a particular period. The finance company's role as a financier, and the relatively long collection period involved, make it inappropriate to recognize as profit at the time of sale the excess of the sum of the instalments over the cost of the goods supplied. All costs that relate to an instalment sale should be considered.

To be consistent with the matching principle, the timing of recognition of the gross profit and expenses should be coordinated. Two general approaches are available. (1) Gross profit is not recognized until instalments received (collections) exceed the cost of the goods supplied; all subsequent receipts are then recorded as realized gross profit. (This is an extremely conservative approach, and would only be suited to cases where unusual risks are considered to exist.) (2) Each collection is regarded as a partial recovery of cost and a partial realization of gross profit. SSAP 21 states that, with 'a hire purchase contract which has characteristics similar to a finance lease, the allocation of gross earnings should give a constant periodic rate of return on the finance company's net investment'. This apportionment of the gross profit can be carried out by number of methods with varying merits. The two most relevant are the annuity method and the sum of digits method, both of which have been explained in connection with leasing.

5.3 Sales type leases and hire purchase contracts

One type of leasing or hire purchase deal is that arranged by a manufacturer or dealer who uses the availability of a leasing or hire purchase arrangement as a means of marketing the product produced or traded by the firm. The problem with this arrangement is determining when, if at all, the profit on the sale or leasing arrangement should be recognized.

Where the supplier of the goods acts as a dealer and financier, any resulting income will be attributable to both of his activities. The gross profit (i.e. the down payment plus instalments less the cost of goods supplied) needs to be divided into two components:
(a) the dealer's profit attributable to his activities as a dealer;
(b) the income related to the provision of finance.

There are two methods of treating the dealer's profit. The first recognizes all dealer's profits in the period in which the agreement is made. The second spreads this profit over the collection period of a hire purchase agreement, on the grounds that it reflects the legal position whereby title to the goods is not transferred until the final instalment is paid. When the assumption that the purchase will be completed appears valid, the first method will be more consistent with the recognition of income from normal sales.

SSAP 21 makes the point that no selling or dealer's profit should be recognized under an operating lease. The asset is not 'sold'; the risks and rewards of ownership are not transferred to the lessee.

With a finance lease, the selling profit should be restricted to the excess of the fair value of the asset (as defined in SSAP 21) over the manufacturer's or dealer's cost less any grants receivable by the manufacturer or dealer. The fair value is the arm's-length selling price less grants. This profit can be recognized at the time of the inception of the leasing deal. Any earnings resulting from the finance charges paid by the lessee will be recognized in the normal way over the period of the lease.

Further reading

Abdel-Khalik, A. R., 'The Economic Effects on Lessees of FASB Statement no. 13, Accounting for Leases', FASB, 1981.

Accounting Standards Committee, SSAP 21: 'Accounting for Leases and Hire Purchase Contracts', 1984.

Birnberg, J. G., 'The reporting of executory contracts', *Accounting Review*, 4 October 1965.

Carr, J., 'Why accounting for leases is inconsistent', *Accountancy*, July 1985.

Clarke, T. M., *Leasing*, McGraw-Hill, Maidenhead, Berks, 1978.

Glynn, J. J., 'Accounting for leases, 1: On the question of capitalisation', *The Accountant*, November 1979.

International Accounting Standard Committee, E 19: 'Accounting for Leases', 1981.

Rickwood, C. P., 'Accounting for leases, 2: Some problems of standardisation', *The Accountant*, November 1979.

Taylor, P. and S. Turley, 'Views of management and accounting for leases', *Accounting and Business Research*, Winter 1985.

Tomkins, C., J. Lowe and E. Morgan, *An Economic Analysis of the Financial Leasing Industry*, Saxon House, Farnborough, Hants, 1979.

Questions

1. SSAP 21, Accounting for Leases and Hire Purchase Contracts, was recently published, and incorporated, largely unchanged, the proposals made originally in ED 29.
    You are required to:
    (a) state concisely the difference between operating and finance leases giving an example of each
                                                                                    (5 marks)
    (b) summarise the main requirements excluding those relating to disclosure and transitional arrangements affecting lessees   (5 marks)
    (c) discuss the reasons which have led to the adoption of the requirements of SSAP 21   (8 marks).
                                                                                    (18 marks)
                                                       ICAEW, PEII, FAII, December 1984
2. Queen Ltd manufactures 'Magic' and to improve efficiency has scrapped all its existing plant and replaced it as follows:

(1) On 1st December 1985 Queen Ltd agreed to rent an 'Imperial Wizard' from Deacon & Taylor at a cost of £1,500 per month payable in advance. The agreement is terminable at three months' notice by either party.

(2) On 1st June 1986 Queen Ltd entered into an agreement with May for the lease of a 'Gandalf'. Terms included:
   (a) neither party could cancel;
   (b) Queen Ltd is to have responsibility for maintenance;
   (c) 6 instalments of £7,500 are payable half yearly in advance.
   The cash price of a Gandalf on 1st June 1986 was £40,000 and the machine is considered to have a residual value of £5,000 at the end of a 5-year life. The rate of interest implicit in the lease is 5.0% semi-annually.

(3) A 'Merlin' was bought on 1st September 1986 from Mercury Ltd. The price of £120,000 is payable in 10 equal quarterly instalments starting 1st September 1986.
   A Merlin is expected to have negligible value at the end of its 12-year life.

Other than the above items no amounts were unpaid at 30th November 1986. Queen Ltd uses a straight-line basis for depreciation from the date of purchase.

Requirements

(a) Show how the above should be reflected in the financial statements, including the notes thereto of Queen Ltd at 30th November 1986 in accordance with SSAP21. The accounting policy note is not required.   (10 marks)
(b) Discuss and explain the rational for the accounting treatments in the standard   (10 marks)
                                                                                          (20 marks)

ICAEW, PEII, FAII, December 1986

3. Bedrock plc is to lease a machine on 1st January 1986. Under the terms of the lease, Bedrock is to pay £5,000 at the start of the lease, followed by five annual payments of £5,000 commencing on 31st December 1986. From 1991 Bedrock is to pay £1 per year to continue to lease the machine. The machine has an expected life of eight years. Bedrock is to be responsible for all the maintenance and insurance costs of the machine. Accounts are prepared for the year ending 31st December. The rate of interest being charged by the leasing company is 7% per annum.

You are required:

(a) using the annuity method, to show all the journal entries relating to the leasing deal, and the asset as it would appear in the balance sheet of Bedrock plc for the years 1986 and 1987. Show the schedule of payments;   (13 marks)
(b) to discuss the problems that arise in accounting theory from the capitalisation of financial leases, and
                                                                                          (7 marks)
(c) to say how the Accounting Standards Committee in the UK has decided to resolve the issue of whether or not to capitalise leases.   (5 marks)
                                                                                          (25 marks)

6. Accounting for pensions

6.1 Introduction

The subject of accounting for pension costs has been a controversial issue for a number of years. The topic first appeared on the programme of the ASC in the early 1970s, but it was a decade later before the first Exposure Draft was issued.

The problems we are concerned with arise in connection with occupational pension schemes. The State Earnings Related Pension Scheme (SERPS), which is administered by the Department of Health and Social Security, is not given detailed attention in this book as it is a topic for public sector accounting. For many years an employer has been able to contract-out employees from the state scheme, as long as the occupational scheme provides at least the level of earnings-related pension that would otherwise have come from SERPS.

In addition to occupational schemes organized by employers, there are personal pension schemes. A personal pension scheme consists of a contract between an individual and a financial institution, such as an insurance company, bank, building society or unit trust. From 1988 it has been possible for an individual employee to contract-out of SERPS, and also out of an occupational scheme (except if it is non-contributory or provides death benefits only), and take out a personal pension scheme instead, or indeed not enter a scheme at all. Compulsory pension scheme membership was abolished in 1988.

Our concern in financial accounting is with the occupational pension schemes. There are really two different aspects of the problem. One deals with the financial report of the trustees of a pension scheme to the members of the scheme. In 1982 the ASC published a discussion paper on the subject of the accounts of pension schemes and this led to a statement of recommended practice on 'Pension Scheme Accounts'.

The other aspect of the problem, the recognition, measurement and disclosure of the cost of pensions in the financial accounts of employers, was the subject of ED 32, issued in 1983. This exposure draft was concerned primarily with disclosure. It was followed by a statement of intent on 'Accounting for Pension Costs' in 1984, a further exposure draft, ED 39, with the same title, in 1986, and eventually a standard, SSAP 24, in 1988. This particular issue has therefore been under discussion for a long time.

The later exposure draft was not well received by many large companies, who submitted evidence to the ASC, suggesting that the proposals were illogical, vaguely worded and contravened the concept of prudence. In particular, they were critical of the suggestion that 'the normal period over which material deficiencies or surpluses should be spread for accounting purposes is the expected average remaining service lives of the employees'. They pointed out that in practice the estimate of the average remaining service would be extremely arbitrary. Also, a significant part of any surplus would be due to individuals who are no longer members of the fund. The ASC, having considered the comments arising from the exposure draft, produced a standard SSAP 24, 'Accounting for Pension Costs'.

The proposals in ED 32 have not been followed by many companies. Companies have increased the amount of information they reveal about pension matters, but they do not always follow the recommended accounting treatment with regard to the spreading of surpluses and deficiencies over time.

At the end of 1987, the only specific disclosure requirements were those required by company law. The Companies Act 1985 states that the profit and loss account should show the charge for pension costs and that particulars of any pension commitment should be disclosed whether or not provision has been made in the accounts.

The reasons why accounting for pensions has taken on increasing importance is (1) because of the growth in the number of private pension schemes, (2) because of the increasing levels of contributions that have to be paid into the schemes, and (3) because of the size of the surpluses or deficits that have arisen in many schemes over recent years. Many firms have opted out of the state pension schemes and have started their own schemes. As the size of pensions being paid to past employees and to be paid to present employees increases, so does the scale of contributions. It has been estimated that in the average company pension costs represent about 5 per cent of total staff costs and 17.5 per cent of historic cost profit on ordinary activities before taxation. However, because there is a very wide variation in company profit performance, this last percentage shows considerable variation from one company to another. The average percentage indicates that pension costs can have a significant effect on a company's profit performance.

As will be explained below, the measurement of the costs of a pension scheme to a company can involve a considerable amount of estimation. It depends on what assumptions are made; it involves forecasting the future. The cost, therefore, can be a matter of opinion—albeit an expert's opinion. Nevertheless, the annual cost disclosed and the details given regarding future commitments affect the interpretation placed upon a company's profit performance and financial status. The treatment of pension costs can affect share price. In September 1985, Lucas Industries announced that there was a 'surplus' in the company pension scheme, which would mean a 'contribution holiday'. This would mean a saving on the expected cash outflow for Lucas of approximately £20 million in both the current year and the following year. The result of this announcement was that the share price of the company rose by 10 per cent.

From a firm's point of view, there can be two elements to the cost of a pension scheme: (1) the regular payment the firm makes to the scheme, which is known as the employers' contribution, and (2) a possible lump-sum payment which can arise if it is estimated that the assets of the scheme are less than the liabilities. Over the period 1963–79, the average return on the investments made by private sector pension funds was 8.2 per cent per annum, but wages were increasing at an average annual rate of 11.4 per cent. In most schemes the pensions paid to an individual are related to the wages paid to that individual at or near the time of retirement. During this period the assets of the typical scheme were increasing at a slower rate than the liabilities, which are based on wage levels. This deficit meant that many companies needed to make lump-sum payments into the scheme, an additional cost.

The position was reversed during the 1980s. Over the period 1980–85, wages rose on average only by 10 per cent per annum, whereas the average private sector pension fund was earning 21 per cent per annum. As a result, pension scheme assets increased faster than liabilities. The schemes were in surplus. How were the surpluses to be treated? Should they be left to grow, used to reduce the pension fund costs of the firms, or perhaps to reduce the cost to the members of the scheme? These issues will be discussed below.

6.2 Types of scheme

Before dealing with the accounting and financial issues connected with pension schemes, there are a number of definitional matters that need to be dealt with. The variety of possible schemes can be classified under the following headings:
- externally funded versus internally funded;
- contractual versus non-contractual;

- defined contributions versus defined benefits;
- projected benefits versus vested benefits.

The most common schemes in the UK are externally funded, contractual, with defined benefits based on projections of income. Each permutation has slightly different accounting problems. The emphasis in this chapter will be on the permutation that is most common.

6.2.1   External versus internal funding

It is usual in the UK for a company to set up a trustee-administered fund to provide for pensions for its employees. The company will make payments into the fund. If the pension scheme is contributary, the employees will also be making payments into the fund based on their level of pay. Not all schemes are contributary; a non-contributary scheme is one in which all the payments into the administered fund are made by the employer. Both of these arrangements are known as externally funded schemes. The trustees can either administer the fund themselves, making their own investment decisions, or use the services of an insurance company or specialist fund manager, which is often the policy with smaller schemes.

The trustees of the fund usually comprise directors of the company, employee representatives and outsiders with relevant experience or worthy reputations. The fund is a separate legal entity, independent of the company whose employees will benefit from the pension scheme.

The trustees or insurance company managers administering the fund can invest where they wish—in property, equity shares, the money market or even insurance policies. They are even free to purchase the equity shares of the company whose pension fund they are administering. Indeed, this is a quite common practice; in the early 1980s Lucas Industries pension scheme was said to own somewhere in the region of 25 per cent of the equity shares of Lucas itself.

Such a shareholding by a firm's own pension fund can be a very useful defence weapon for a company wishing either to keep potential predators at bay or to make it difficult for any actual takeover bidder to succeed. The danger is that, in the case of failure by the employing firm, the employee will not only lose a job but also suffer a fall in value of the assets of his pension fund.

It is not essential for a company/employer to set up an external funded pension fund: pensions can be provided through an internally financed scheme. Under such a scheme contributions are reinvested within the employer's own business. There may be no separately identified fund within the business, the actual cash for pension payments being on a pay-as-you-go basis. Contributions are invested in the business, and as pensions need to be paid they are paid out of the general funds of the business. With these internally financed schemes, provisions may be made in the balance sheet to meet the costs of future pension benefits. The provision may be matched by an identified fund of assets, with benefits paid out of the earmarked fund. If this is the case, the accounting situation is similar to that for an externally funded scheme.

6.2.2.   Contractual schemes

Two more areas of classification need to be explained. The schemes referred to above are of a contractual nature. The employer agrees to pay a pension to the employees, at a rate usually based on a formula taking into account the level of an employee's pay at or near the time of retirement and his number of years of employment with the business. This can be contrasted to an alternative arrangement whereby an employee receives an *ex gratia* pension. The employee does not receive a guarantee that a pension will be received upon retirement; there is no contractual arrangement. No accounting problems arise with this method. It is, however, no longer a very common arrangement.

The other classification problem that is important arises because there are in fact two types of contractual scheme: defined contribution schemes and defined benefit schemes. Under the former, decisions are made as to the level of contributions that will be paid into the scheme. These accumulated contributions plus the earnings made from their investment provide a sum out of which pensions are paid. The level of the pensions that are paid depends on the funds available. There is no guarantee concerning the level of the benefits to be received, only on the contributions that will be made. Once the employer has made the agreed level of contribution, he will have discharged his obligation to the scheme. The cost to the employer is known. It is the amount of contributions payable in respect of the particular accounting period. As a result it does not cause any accounting problems.

Accounting difficulties arise when it comes to measuring the cost to the employer of the most widely used type of scheme, the defined benefit scheme. Here it is the benefit to the employee that is guaranteed. At any point in time, an employee will not know precisely what level of pension he will receive upon retirement, but he will know that it will be a percentage of his final salary, or of his average salary in the final years of employment. What the final salary will be depends of course on promotion and general wage increases. So the benefits to the employee are not certain; therefore the costs to the employer are also uncertain. The employer will not even know what the future level of contributions will have to be, but he does know that, if at any point in time the value of the assets of the pension fund do not cover the estimated liabilities, the employer will have to make up the shortfall, the deficit.

In evaluating the cost of providing future pensions, actuaries play a major role. Actuarial valuations consider a number of relevant variables, including the numbers in the scheme, their age distribution, retirement age, life expectancy, turnover, future salaries and benefits of the scheme. The fund required to meet commitments is calculated by actuaries considering the forms of investment made and to be made, interest rates and expected capital gains from investments. Annual costs can be calculated from the actuarial values.

To reflect the implications of pensions, accounts must report the current effect on cost of the future commitment. There are many possible solutions, but two general approaches can be identified: the vested benefit method and the projected benefit method. The latter is favoured in the UK. Vested benefits are those that would arise even if employees did not continue in employment; they represent those benefits that are due to employees on the basis of service and contribution to date. Projected benefits represent the present value of the total benefit which actuarial estimates predict will be payable to the existing work-force during their lifetime.

The required annual cost can be calculated under this latter method by finding the constant annual amount that will provide for the estimated projected benefits for individuals and then accumulating for all individuals in the scheme. A number of actuarial methods are employed which give results that approximate to the desired annual cost.

The choice of methods will depend on the view taken on the reporting objective. If the aim is to identify what cash flow is required to meet existing commitments, the vested benefit method is adopted. An attempt to ensure that current shareholders bear their proper share of the employment cost of the current work-force considers a different time-scale. It is more congruent with the projected benefit method, which also is more in line with the going concern assumption. Both methods attempt to carry out matching by quantifying this part of the current remuneration and including it as an expense.

The accounting problem for the employer is to determine how the total cost of providing pensions should be allocated to accounting periods. SSAP 24 indicates that the ASC believes that the matching principle should apply and the cost of pensions should be matched with the benefit derived from the employee's service. This means charging the cost of pensions against profits on a systematic basis over an employee's service life. It is referred to as 'the income approach'.

6.3 The financing of pensions

6.3.1 Regular costs

A pension scheme obtains funds from employees' contributions, from employers' contributions and from capital gains and income arising from the investments it has made over a number of years. Employees' contributions are a percentage of their earnings. Employers' normal annual contributions are usually also based on a percentage of the employees' pensionable earnings. These are referred to as 'regular costs'. No problems arise in connection with these costs; the employing company makes a payment each year to the pension fund, and this regular payment is charged to the profit and loss account so that the costs are related to the benefits derived from the employees' services, the remuneration paid to the employee being the best measure available of the benefits received. The funds paid to the scheme each year are equal to the cost recognized in the accounts, subject to possible payments in advance or in arrears.

6.3.2 Irregular costs

Accounting problems arise in dealing with variations from regular costs. These 'irregular costs' can arise because of
(a) surpluses or deficiencies in the pension fund;
(b) retroactive changes in conditions of membership or in benefits to be received;
(c) increases in the level of pensions already being paid or deferred pensions not previously provided for;
(d) retroactive effects of changes in assumptions.
    We shall now consider each of these irregular costs. However, in order to understand how surpluses or deficiencies arise, it is first necessary to understand how a pension fund works. As already mentioned, most pension schemes are wholly or partially externally funded. The fund is continually receiving contributions from employees and employers. The manager of the fund invests the income 'to build up assets in a prudent and controlled manner'. The investments generate income and capital gains.
    Pension funds are in fact very large investors. Between the end of 1962 and 1984, private pension fund assets increased from £2.5 billion to £77.8 billion. This growth of funds flowing into pension schemes has been stimulated by several factors, one of which is favourable tax treatment. All contributions to approved schemes, whether by employer or employee, are deductible from taxable income. All income and gains from the investments of the funds are tax-exempt.
    The funds flowing into the scheme are invested by trustees, and at any time it is possible to value the assets of the pension scheme, and to estimate what the value will be at any future date.
    The liabilities can also be valued. An actuary estimates the amounts needed to provide for pensions. This

> ... is essentially the discounted value of the future cash flows of the pension scheme. It will be based upon assumptions about such matters as future rates of inflation, pay increases, earnings on investments, numbers of employees joining the scheme and the probability that employees will die or leave before they reach retiring age.
> The Actuary has to make a judgement as to the balance between funds available now and in the future against benefits due to be paid. Commonly he will make projections of the expected income and outgoings. Since these will extend until the expected date of death of the last pensioner the projections are extremely long term.

It is difficult to estimate the future commitments of the fund. As the exposure draft points out, it depends on the number of members in the scheme, how many will remain in the scheme until pensionable age, their life expectancy, the earnings of members when they retire and the rate of inflation. Having made estimates of the present value of future outflows and inflows, it may be found that the fund has a surplus or a deficit. These are referred to as 'experience' surpluses or deficiencies. It is the treatment of these surpluses or deficiencies, these irregular amounts, that causes accounting problems.

But before explaining the recommended accounting treatment, it should be mentioned that there are two fundamentally different sets of assumptions that can be made when valuing pension provisions: one is a discontinuance valuation, the other a going concern valuation.

The former is concerned with judging whether the existing assets are sufficient to secure the benefits of existing pensioners and existing employees on the assumption that the scheme is to be wound up on the valuation date. This does not imply that the scheme is actually expected to be wound up on that particular day, but it is an approach that can be employed as a means to test the solvency of the scheme.

The market value of the fund assets, or alternatively the present value of future investment returns, is compared either with the sum of present values of existing liabilities for current and deferred pensions plus the accrued benefit of existing members based on their current pay and service to date, or with the cost of purchasing the benefits from an insurer. It is assumed that no new members will be admitted and that no further contributions will be paid by either the members or the employer.

The going concern method of valuation allows for expected future pay increases, and for expected increases in contributions. It is the valuation of a dynamic situation. Other crucial assumptions concern the flow of new entrants to the scheme and their ages, the people leaving the scheme and their ages, and the returns earned on the investments.

If, on valuation, the liabilities of the fund are judged to be in excess of the assets of the fund, there is a deficiency. As mentioned earlier, this was often the case during the late 1970s and early 1980s. If on the other hand the assets of the fund exceed the liabilities, the fund is in surplus. Such was the case in the mid-1980s. In either case, something needs to be done to rectify the situation.

6.3.3 Deficits

The funding of a deficiency in a scheme that has been in existence for some time can be handled in a number of ways. Contributions to the fund can be increased; this could be done either by extra payments into the fund over future periods or by the payment of a single sum, a lump-sum additional contribution. Quite often the employer makes a single payment; from the employer's point of view, this is a 'cash outflow'.

During the early and mid-1970s, many companies made additional contributions to their pension schemes in order to cover deficits. The deficits had arisen because of negative real rates of return on investments coupled with high wage increases.

There are really two accounting questions to be considered: how the deficit is to be funded, and over what period it would be appropriate to charge the deficiency in the accounts. Even if a single lump-sum payment is made to cover the deficit, it does not mean that from an accounting point of view the charge need be all against the profits of the period of the payment. It is not a prior-year adjustment; the deficiency is part of an ongoing process of revising estimates of liabilities. It is referred to as an 'experience deficiency'.

It is argued that it is not appropriate to charge the entire deficiency against profits in one accounting period, except when the deficiency is directly caused by an extraordinary event such as the closure of a major division.

In fact, in the mid-1970s, many of these additional contributions were treated in the accounts as extraordinary items or exceptional items. The ASC is now proposing that deficiencies should be treated in a different way.

In accordance with the accounting objective of matching, the cost of the deficiency should normally be spread over.

> the expected average remaining service lives of the employees in the scheme after making suitable allowances for future withdrawals. In many cases this period may be ten to twelve years. Prudence, however, may sometimes indicate that a period shorter than the expected average remaining service lives of employees is necessary for the recognition of a material deficiency. This may occur, for example, if the membership profile is such as to render the expected average remaining service lives too extended a period for the recognition of cost in respect of employees expected to retire in the very near future.

6.3.4   Surpluses

Let us turn to the situation that arose in the 1980s, when a number of pension schemes found they had funds surplus to their needs; the actuarial value of their assets exceeded the actuarial value of their liabilities. Inflation rates and wage increases had been lower than had been assumed, and because of redundancies the number of employees remaining with the company to retirement age was less than expected, with the result that liabilities were being revised downwards. This, with the higher rates of return that had been earned on investments for a number of years boosting the value of the assets, led to surpluses. At the end of 1985, a study by the London Business School estimated that on aggregate the level of pension scheme surplus was 30 per cent of total pension scheme assets.

With a surplus in the scheme, a number of funding possibilities arise.

(a) The rate of future annual employee and/or employer contributions could be reduced for up to five years.
(b) The employee and/or employer could take a contribution-free holiday for up to five years.
(c) The employer could receive a refund of some of the surplus from the scheme, subject to a special tax charge.
(d) The benefits payable to members of the scheme upon retirement could be increased.
(e) A combination of the above.

The Finance Act 1986 placed controls on the amount of surpluses that pension schemes could maintain. Pressure was placed on the schemes to reduce the surpluses. An approved pension scheme enjoys many tax privileges, so the tax authorities are in a good position to influence the actions of individual schemes. If a scheme wished to retain its tax-approved status, it became necessary for it to follow a certain policy with respect to any surplus. Under these requirements, schemes must determine every three years the size of any surplus, on a standard actuarial basis. If the scheme's assets are more than 105 per cent of its past service liabilities, then in order to retain its full tax exemption it is necessary to reduce assets to the 105 per cent level.

An administrative procedure was introduced in 1986 for dealing with surpluses. Following a valuation, a report has to be submitted to the Superannuation Funds Office giving details of the proposal. If the Office is not satisfied, it has considerable power, being a government department, to prevent a company from going ahead with its proposal.

Of the possible ways of reducing the surplus, the payment from the scheme to the employer is not easy, but in fact a number of schemes have made such refunds. Such payments need Inland Revenue approval. This requirement is justified on the grounds that the assets were built up as a result of a privileged tax position. The employer's contributions and possible lump-sum payments were tax-deductible expenses. Such a refund to the employer would need to be permitted in principle by the trust deed setting up the scheme, and would have to be agreed to by the scheme's trustees. If a trust deed prevented such a repayment, the Occupational Pension Board is authorized to change the trust deed, subject to any conditions they think appropriate.

If it is the company that is to receive a refund of a surplus, 40 per cent needs to be deducted to satisfy the taxation requirement. Although the tax will be paid to the Inland Revenue by the trustees of the fund, payment is the responsibility of the employer and should be accounted for by the employer. If the refund is to be taken to the profit and loss account as an exceptional credit or extraordinary item, the tax payable has to be taken into account. The reported profit will benefit, therefore, by the net refund of the surplus.

The most popular ways of reducing a surplus are by contribution-free holidays and a reduction in contributions. The aim must be to eliminate the surplus within five years. With the increased benefits approach, the improvements should relate to past, not future, service.

6.4 Accounting treatment

Part of the terms of many pension agreements is a requirement for regular pension costs to be funded in full. If this is the case, the accounting entries are a credit to cash and a debit to regular pension costs. The various calculations and entries can be illustrated in a single example in which irregular contributions arise and are amortized and funded over different periods. Consider a new scheme for which actuarial calculation determines that normal costs are £10,000 per annum, past service costs are £50,000 and the appropriate rate of interest is 8 per cent. It is decided to amortize the special contribution over three years but fund it over five years. Short periods have been chosen to minimize calculations. Annuity tables are used to obtain the annual expense and funding, and interest is imputed on the outstanding liability or deferred charge. Since amortization exceeds funding, liabilities rather than deferred charges will arise in this case.

The annual funding of the special contribution is

$$£50,000 \div a_{\overline{5}|0.08} = £12,500.$$

The annual allocation of the special contribution is

$$£50,000 \div a_{\overline{3}|0.08} = £19,400.$$

A schedule showing the impact of the special contribution can be prepared:

Year	Allocation	8% interest on outstanding liability	Past service cost	Funding	Change in liability		Outstanding liability
	£	£	£	£	£		£
1	19,400	—	19,400	12,500	6,900	Cr	6,900
2	19,400	552	19,952	12,500	7,452	Cr	14,352
3	19,400	1,148	20,548	12,500	8,048	Cr	22,400
4	—	1,792	1,792	12,500	10,708	Dr	11,692
5	—	808	808	12,500	11,692	Dr	—

The entries for the first year are:

Dr	Normal pension cost	£10,000	
Dr	Past period service cost	19,400	
Cr	Pension fund liability		£6,900
Cr	Cash		22,500

For the second year:

Dr	Normal pension cost	£10,000	
Dr	Past period service cost	19,952	
Cr	Pension fund liability		£7,452
Cr	Cash		22,500

Much of the above discussion on surpluses and deficits relates to the funding position, that is the cash flow position. The accounting standard on pensions recognizes that the financial treatment of a surplus or deficit might differ from the accounting treatment. The financial position of the sponsoring employer may cause the pattern of cash flows between it and the scheme to be erratic. For example, if the scheme is over-funded, rather than reduce the future ongoing contribution rate, the employer may take a contribution-free holiday or withdraw some of the surplus from the pension scheme. While such arrangements may be valid for funding purposes, it can be argued they will not provide a satisfactory basis for determining the pension charge in the accounts.

Prior to the issue of the exposure draft, the most common treatment adopted in practice for the treatment of surpluses was to charge against profits the contributions actually made towards pensions during an accounting period. This was equating the actual funding with the accounting cost. The proposals contained in the exposure draft differed from this practice. As mentioned earlier, the proposal was to spread the cost of pensions over the service life of the employees. If adopted, this would reduce the volatility of the pension cost charge; the volatility would be less than if based on the actual contributions, the cash flows. After the issue of the exposure draft, some companies changed their accounting treatment to conform with the recommendations, while others did not.

As a result of an experience surplus, contributions might be reduced. If this results in a reduction in 'regular' payments for a limited period, the recommendation is that the actual contribution paid should not be used as a basis for the charges in the accounts. It should be treated in an analogous fashion to an experience deficiency, with the amount saved being taken to the balance sheet and spread over time.

If the company receives a contribution-free holiday, it is also suggested that it is inappropriate to credit the entire benefit against the profits in one accounting period. If the employing company receives a lump-sum payment, it is recommended that such a benefit be spread over the average remaining service life of employees. It must be remembered that this has not occurred because of a change of accounting policy, or because of fundamental errors that rule out treatment as a prior-year adjustment. One possible accounting treatment would be to treat the full repayment as an exceptional item in the year it is repaid, but this is not recommended as the normal practice.

As mentioned, where the employer benefits from a contribution-free holiday, the proposed standard recommends that the reduction in cost be taken into account by adjusting the current and future costs charged in the accounts. This reduces the amount of the 'regular' pension costs charged each year, and it is a prudent approach. An interesting practical question, however, is over how many years the saving from the reduction in cost should be spread.

In 1986 many companies reported increased profits arising from their treatment of pension surpluses. If the spirit of the exposure draft had been followed, the savings would have been spread over an extended period — the average service life of employees. This would have meant smaller boosts to profits in any one year.

It is important, therefore, that certain basic accounting rules are laid down; otherwise one could find certain companies boosting their profits in years when they needed to be taking the savings arising from pension surpluses into account. This 'creative' accounting technique could be used to assist a company's profit forecast when it is faced with a takeover bid.

If the recommended accounting treatment of surpluses and deficiencies is followed, there will be occasions in which the charge to the profit and loss account in respect of pension costs will not equal the contributions actually paid in a year. The following examples, based on those in Appendix 2 of ED 39, illustrate the recommended treatment of surpluses and deficiencies. They are to some extent simplified in that they do not take interest into account.

Example 6.1: Deficiencies

The actuarial valuation at 31 December 1980 of a company's pension scheme showed a deficiency of £180 million. The actuary recommended that the company eliminate the deficiency by making payments into the scheme of £60 million in each of the next three years. The regular employer's contributions of £20 million per annum would continue to be paid.

The average remaining service life of employees in the scheme at 31 December 1980 is estimated to be ten years.

From an accounting point of view, and assuming no change in circumstances, the annual charge in the profit and loss account for pension costs in each of the years 1981–90 will be £38 million. This is the regular charge of £20 million plus £18 million, this latter figure being the £180 million deficit spread over the estimated remaining service life of employees.

In fact, it is most likely that this figure of £38 million will vary in future years. Further actuarial valuations will take place, and the regular payments themselves are most likely to change in line with wage increases and changes in the number of employees. As at 31 December 1980, the £38 million per annum is the best estimate available.

The funds actually flowing from the company to the pension fund will be £80 million in each of the next three years (1981, 1982 and 1983) and £20 million in each of the following seven years (1984–90).

The difference in the amounts funded and the amounts charged in the profit and loss account will be treated as a prepayment. The journal entry in the first year would be

Dr	Pension cost	£38m	
Dr	Prepayment pension	£42m	
Cr	Cash		£80m

The details of the profit and loss account charge, the cash outflow, and the balance in the prepayment account for each year is as follows:

	1981	1982	1983	1984	1985	1986	1987	1988	1989	1990
Cash outflow (£m)	80	80	80	20	20	20	20	20	20	20
Pension cost (£m)	38	38	38	38	38	38	38	38	38	38
Balance on pre-payments a/c (£m)	42	84	126	108	90	72	54	36	18	0

Example 6.2: Surplus

The actuarial valuation of a company's pension scheme at 31 December 1986 showed a surplus of £90 million. The actuary recommends that the company eliminate the surplus by taking a contribution-free holiday in each of the next three years. After that the regular contributions of £30 million would be continued.

The average remaining service life of employees is estimated to be nine years.

Assuming no change in circumstances, the annual charge to the profit and loss account for the next nine years as proposed in the exposure draft would be £20 million; that is,

the regular cost   *less*   (surplus/average remaining service life)
£30m   –   (£90/£9)m

The funding would be

      1987, 1988, 1989   nil
      1990–95   £30m

The difference between the amounts funded and the profit and loss account charge would be recognized as a provision. The journal entry in the first year would be:

Dr   Pension cost   £20m
Cr   Provision for pension   £20m

The details of the profit and loss charge, the cash outflow and the balance on the provision account for each year are as follows.

	1987	*1988*	*1989*	*1990*	*1991*	*1992*	*1993*	*1994*	*1995*
Cash outflow (£m)	0	0	0	30	30	30	30	30	30
Pension cost (£m)	20	20	20	20	20	20	20	20	20
Balance on provisions a/c (£m)	20	40	60	50	40	30	20	10	0

It is emphasized these are the entries recommended in the standard. Prior to its issue, many companies showed as a charge in the accounts the actual contribution they paid in that year. So in the above example there would be a zero pension cost shown in years 1987 and 1988.

The fact that Lucas Industries plc benefited from a contribution-free holiday in 1986 has already been referred to above. In fact, the company did not actually disclose the exact financial effects of the two-year cessation of contributions, although it was reported in the press that pre-tax profits would benefit by £20 million in each of the two years. The financial accounts do show that in 1985 the pension costs charged to the profit and loss account were £38.8 million; in 1986 this had dropped to £8.4 million. Not all of this reduction can be attributed to the contribution-free holiday. The surplus and the suspension of contributions is explained in the notes to the accounts as follows:

> Actuarial valuations of the funds are carried out regularly as prescribed by the trust deeds and rules. Following the most recent valuations by R. Watson and Sons of the two principal funds—Lucas Staff Pension Fund and Lucas Works Pension Fund—the actuary reported to each fund's trustees that the assets of each of the funds at 31 March 1985 were sufficient to secure the benefits then in course of payment and the accrued benefits prospectively payable, based upon current earnings in the case of members in service.
>
> Since that report the actuary has concluded actuarial valuations to ascertain the rate of company contribution required to maintain the satisfactory position reported as at 31 March 1985. The position revealed is that, if company and member contributions continue at their present percentage rate but with a two-year cessation of company contributions, then there would still be a surplus in both funds. The company has suspended contributions for a period of two years commencing 1 August 1985 and has also improved members' benefits from the surpluses in funds.

6.4.1   Other irregular changes

At any point in time, changes in actuarial valuation methods can affect the cost of past services, as can changes in assumptions relating to the calculation of the cost of past services. Such retroactive changes can give rise to deficiencies and surpluses and from an accounting point of view should be treated in the same way as the deficiencies and surpluses referred to above. That is spread over the average remaining service life of employees.

Another change that can affect pension costs is when the benefits arising from belonging to the scheme, or the conditions for membership of the scheme, are altered. Any decision to change must take place at a certain point in time. It is not anything relating to the past that has altered: any advantages resulting from the change will benefit the employer in the future. For example, an increase in the level of pensions should make it easier in the future to recruit employees and to retain present employees. The exposure draft expresses the opinion, therefore, that it would normally be excessively prudent to write off the cost wholly or partly in the period in which the improvement is granted. As with other irregular costs we have referred to above, the proposal is that extra cost resulting from these changes should be written off over the average remaining service life of the employees.

Finally, any increases in the rate of pension already being paid and any increases in the rate of pension to be paid that could arise either from the pension scheme rules or from changes in the law should again be charged over the service life of the employees. If for any reason because of the changes a surplus or deficiency arises, these should be treated in the ways referred to above for such items.

6.5   Disclosure requirements

The exposure draft states that: 'Sufficient information should be disclosed to give the user of the financial statements a broad understanding of the significance of the pension arrangements.' The items that it is recommended be disclosed are listed. For a defined benefit scheme, these include details of the accounting policy and (if different) the funding policy, the actuarial valuation method used, and the pension cost charge for the period, distinguishing between the regular cost and the variations from the regular cost. It will also be necessary to give an indication of any expected significant changes in relative future costs.

As at the beginning of 1988, there were no requirements to disclose surpluses or deficiencies. Many companies do not in fact disclose the size of the surplus or deficit. The majority of companies place the benefits they receive from pension surpluses in the above-the-line results on ordinary activities. With a refund this is shown as an exceptional credit; with reduced contributions it is reflected in a lower charge for pension costs.

An example of a company quantifying a surplus and bringing it into their accounts as a refund is Massey Ferguson Holdings Ltd, in its 31 January 1986 accounts:

The actuarial valuation of all of the Massey-Ferguson and Perkins Engines UK Pension Schemes, based on the projected unit method revealed a past service surplus of £17.6 million as at 31 January 1985. The past service surplus as at 31 January 1983 of £33.8 million is being written back to revenue over a three-year period on an annuity basis of which this is the final year.

The amortization of the surplus referred to is shown as an exceptional credit of £12.35 million in the 1986 profit and loss account. This entry reflects the refund of a surplus. The regular pension cost is shown in the accounts as £7.68 million. Many companies, although not quantifying the actual total surplus, do identify any benefit for the year from a refund as an exceptional credit in the profit and loss account.

The accounting treatment usually adopted with regard to reduced annual contributions or a contribution-free holiday is either to reduce the amount of the 'regular' pension cost shown in the profit and loss account, or to show no payment at all, and to refer to this fact in a note. Often the size of the overall surplus is not disclosed. The Lucas Industries surplus referred to above was not quantified in the accounts, although an indication of the magnitude of its effect on profits was reported in the press. The company made a statement on its pension surplus independently of any results announcements. The treatment in the accounts was to show a pension cost in the profit and loss account which reflected the employer's contributions actually made in the year, which were much lower than in previous years.

The actual practice followed, and the recommendation in the exposure draft, is to allow the benefits from the surplus to affect the profit above the line. It is only if the surplus or deficiency arises as the result of an extraordinary event that it should be treated as an extraordinary item. Such a situation can arise when there have been substantial redundancies, leading to more assets being available in the pension fund than are needed to meet the reduced pension commitments.

6.6 Pension scheme accounts

The Occupational Pension Scheme (Auditors) Regulations 1987 complement the requirements imposed on certain scheme trustees by the Disclosure of Information Regulations 1986 to produce audited accounts. The regulations cover the information to be supplied to members by employers and trustees.

The exact details to be shown in the accounts has been left to the accounting profession. The Statement of Recommended Practice on this subject (SORP 1) states that, for the annual financial report to be meaningful, it should be audited, and should contain an actuarial report, an investment report and a comment on the overall position of the scheme.

The accounts should give details of all the significant accounting policies adopted, for example any departure from the accruals concept that might arise in connection with contributions, investment income or benefits. The methods adopted for assessing the market value of assets, the method of foreign currency translation and the treatment of interest on property development are other matters on which it would be appropriate to disclose the accounting treatment.

The accounts themselves should comprise a revenue account and a net assets account. The revenue account would record the financial inflows and outflows of the scheme over a year. It would include details of contributions receivable from employers and members, giving details of normal and additional payments. It would show investment and any other source of income, including transfers from other schemes. The outflow would include pension and lump-sum payments, death benefits and refunds of contributions, and grant transfers out of the scheme. The administrative costs also need to be disclosed.

The net asset account would show the 'worth' of the scheme at the year end, the valuation being based on market values. This net asset statement would list all the investments and assets, showing for example the holdings of fixed-interest securities, equities, property, cash, financial futures and insurance policies. Any long-term borrowings, and the current assets and liabilities, would also appear.

It is necessary to reconcile the change in the balance of funds, the 'net assets', over the year with the annual additions less withdrawals from the revenue account, and any changes in the investments, whether realized or unrealized. This could be done by means of a statement similar to a traditional flow-of-funds statement, which the SORP suggests might be entitled a 'movement of funds statement'. The SORP does allow for alternative terminology for all the pension scheme statements that have been suggested.

Further reading

Accounting Standards Committee, ED 39, 'Accounting for Pension Costs', ASC, 1986.

Dewhirst, J. F., 'A conceptual approach to pension accounting', *Accounting Review*, April 1971.

International Accounting Standards Committee, IAS 19, 'Accounting for Retirement Benefits in the Financial Statements of Employers', IASC, 1983.

McLeish, D., 'Setting a standard for pension costs', *Accountancy*, March 1980.

Napier, C. J., *Accounting for the Cost of Pensions*, ICAEW, 1983.

The Times Special Report, 'Pensions', 7 October 1986.

Wilkins, R. M., 'Pension surpluses in company accounts', in *Financial Reporting 1986–87: A Survey of UK Published Accounts*, ICAEW, 1987.

Questions

1. A. P. Canning Ltd has agreed to adopt a non-contributory employee pension plan commencing with the year ended 31st December 1981. On the basis of actuarial calculations and other information it is decided that:
   (1) the past period service costs amount to £80,000
   (2) the normal costs for 1981 are £100,000 and for 1982 £125,000
   (3) since the company has an excess of ready cash, past period service costs were funded in full on 31st December 1982 and are to be amortized over the ten years
   (4) the appropriate rate of interest is 12%.

   Required:
   On the basis of your calculations, present the entries which reflect the above in the accounts for the years 1981 and 1982.

2. The directors of Richelieu plc have received a report from their actuaries dealing with each of the company's two non-contributory pension schemes, based upon data at 1 January 1987.

   Extracts from the report are as follows:

   "Works Scheme
   The closure of the Buckingham division (a material business segment) in June 1987 will require an immediate contribution of £2 million to ensure that the assets of the Scheme are sufficient to cover the liabilities in respect of the accrued benefits of the former employees at that location.

   Other assets of the Scheme were insufficient to cover the liabilities in respect of the prospective benefits for continuing employees. The extent of the deficiency was some £5.5 million. It is recommended that one lump sum payment of £3 million be made on 31 December 1987 followed by a payment of £2.7 million on 31 December 1988, and that contributions thereafter be at the rate of £1 million per annum until 31 December 1995 and £800,000 per annum thereafter.

   The average age of the continuing employees is 50 years, their average retirement age is 61 years and benefits are determined by pensionable salary at date of retirement.

   Staff Scheme
   A surplus in respect of prospective benefits of £2.2 million has been disclosed by the valuation, partly due to changes in the actuarial assumptions. It is recommended that a contribution holiday be taken in 1987 and 1988 and thereafter that contributions be £400,000 per annum to 31 December 1990 and £750,000 per annum thereafter. The age profile of this Scheme is similar to that of the Works Scheme. Benefits are determined by pensionable salary at date of retirement."

   Requirements
   (a) On the assumption that the actuaries' recommendations are accepted, calculate the amounts to be included with respect to the pension schemes in the profit and loss account and balance sheet of Richelieu plc for the year ending 31 December 1987 in order to comply with the provisions of ED 39 and draft all the appropriate notes thereto.   (10 marks)
   (b) Explain the importance of the assumptions made in actuarial valuations.   (3 marks)

(c) Identify and evaluate the relative merits of the treatment of actuarial surpluses and deficits proposed in ED 39 with alternative methods of accounting for such items.   (5 marks)

(18 marks)

Note: Ignore taxation considerations.

ICAEW, PEII, FAII, December 1987

3. The Secretary of the pension scheme for Park Industries plc has written to you as the scheme's auditors indicating that he wishes to observe current best practice in the annual report as recommended in SORP 1. He enclosed the following information on the scheme for the year ended 31st March 1986:

(1) Balances

	£'000
Employer's contributions	1,246
Employees' contributions	642
Transfers from other schemes	230
Dividends received (net)	2,196
Interest received (net)	217
Pensions paid	1,261
Lump sum benefits	576
Transfers out including refunds	650
Expenses	124
Cash balances	2,164
Overdraft	27
Accruals	37
Creditors	74
Due from employers	44
Tax recoverable	116
Debtors	81
Balance of fund on 1st April 1985	55,978

(2) Investments

	31st March 1986	
	Cost	Market value
	£'000	£'000
UK gilt edged securities	3,600	4,380
UK listed securities		
Ordinary stocks	33,290	49,665
Loan stocks	1,400	650
Overseas listed securities	7,400	9,675
	45,690	64,370

Market value of investments on 31st March 1985: £54,327,000.

On 31st March 1986 the scheme purchased 6% of the ordinary share capital of Field plc, a listed company, at a cost of £600,000, which is also to be taken as the market value. This purchase has not yet been paid for or recorded in the books of the scheme.

In the year ended 31st March 1986 investments costing £4,550,000 were sold for £14,068,000.

(3) The rate of income tax for the year was 30%.

(4) Audit and accountancy charges of £20,000 will be paid by Park Industries plc.

Requirements

(a) Present the information provided in a form suitable for inclusion in the accounts of the pension scheme for Park Industries plc.   (10 marks)

(b) Identify the separate elements of a pension scheme's annual report and outline the objectives of each of those elements.   (8 marks)

(18 marks)

ICAEW, PEII, FAII, December 1986

4. Union leaders recently accused Lucas plc of 'pension piracy'. They claim that there is £158 million surplus in the staff and works pension funds. The company announced proposals to extend an existing two-year contribution holiday for another two years. 'They are plundering the pension fund to pay their shareholders' dividends', claims the union. The union sees it as taking money out of members' pockets.

The members have to continue to pay into the fund during a time when the company is enjoying a contribution-free holiday.

Lucas claims that, unless a reduction is made in the surpluses, their reported results will be such that the Inland Revenue will intervene with massive tax claims.

You are required to:
Discuss the issues involved in this case, paying particular attention to the recommended accounting practices with regard to pension costs, and the possible economic consequences of the Lucas accounting policies. (25 marks)

5. SSAP 24, 'Accounting for Pension Costs', and Statement of Intent (SOI), 'Accounting for Pension Costs' (1986), constitute the Accounting Standards Committee's latest pronouncements on relevant disclosure requirements.

Required:
(a) Describe six matters which are recommended by the ASC for disclosure by companies in financial statements. (9 marks)
(b) (i) Describe factors an actuary takes into account when producing the 'actuarial valuation' of a company's pension obligations.
(ii) Discuss the nature of such a valuation and explain how it has an impact on financial statements.
(iii) Discuss whether the valuation is based on the discontinuance principle. (6 marks)
(c) On occasions the actuarial valuation discloses a surplus or deficiency in the pension fund. Discuss how a company should respond to such a surplus or deficiency from a financial point of view. (5 marks)
(d) Relate the accounting principles of prudence and matching to the possible treatment of pension costs. (5 marks)
(25 marks)

7. Extraordinary items and other income categories

7.1 Income demarcation

A fundamental question to be answered by accounting for any continuing business entity is what to incude in each period's results. Businesses do not come to a halt at the end of each financial year for the convenience of accounting. To be successful, normally they have to continue in business and Chapter 1 set out the postulate of going concern which requires that entities must be assumed to continue unless there is evidence to the contrary. That chapter examined how the accounting process attributes charges to periods in its discussion of the accruals postulate. A potential conflict was identified between measuring profit on the basis of transactions attributed to a given period and measuring the change in opening and closing balance sheet values. The process of measuring periodic profit from transactions was described in terms of recognizing revenue when it is realized: costs that match to the creation of that revenue are deducted; other increases in value are regarded as unrealized.

The manner in which profit is recognized in particular periods has important implications. It may contribute to predictions of future success and to dividend flows; legal restrictions limit the size of dividend distributions by identifying that profit which is distributable.

This chapter gives attention to the boundaries of profit, examining how relevant information is presented to reflect the impact of unusual events as well as those before and after the period of report. The boundaries applied in identifying distributable profits are also discussed.

In measuring the performance of an accounting entity over its lifetime, all economic changes may be relevant. However, for the going concern, any particular income figure can be regarded as an interim indicator rather than a result. It may be viewed as useful only in relation to past progress and to any indications it may provide for future performance. In this context it may be informative to classify the potential changes in balance sheet values on the basis of their relationship with other periods. However, views differ, and three concepts of income are commonly put forward which result in contrasting treatment of the reporting of profit: the normally recurring, the current operating and the all-inclusive concepts of income. These set out profit boundaries in terms of the nature of the items. Further differences arise from policies setting out profit boundaries in terms of timing.

The *normally recurring* concept of income is put forward as useful for making predictions of future income and dividends. The inclusion of an event that is so rare and unusual in the experience of a particular business that it is not likely to happen again may distort an otherwise smooth trend of profits. With many accounting activities actually leading to a smooth profit trend, echoing the smoothing of the economic concept of income, exclusion of the non-recurrent would seem to have some validity. It may also be argued that it offers a better basis for comparison of underlying performance, not only from year to year but also between businesses.

This concept is not without its criticisms. A specific disadvantage lies with the difficulty in identifying which items are to be classified as non-recurrent. It may be that an event experienced in one period may not have occurred previously, but this does not prevent its regular recurrence in the future. Recurrence of similar but not identical events might be put forward as grounds for regarding each event as unique. The classification is dependent on prediction and is subjective, making external assessment difficult.

As the name suggests, *current operating* income restricts inclusion to the results that relate to operations in the current period. It attempts to measure the performance due to the present management in dealing with the normal activities of a business. It is suggested that a better basis for comparison with other businesses is provided by directing attention to operating activity, referring to the fulfilment of business objectives in terms of converting inputs into commercially valuable outputs. This is offered as an indication of competitiveness.

The focus on current income is not necessarily intended to exclude the impact of past decisions on the present (although this is taken up later in connection with accounting under conditions of price level change). It does suggest the exclusion of changes that come to light in a particular period because although they occurred in a previous period they failed to be recognized.

The identification of current operating items may be less subjective than an attempt to identify normally recurring income, but both offer scope for the non-disclosure of economic change.

Those advocating the *all-inclusive* concept would want all changes to be disclosed by being passed through the profit and loss account. No omissions would mean that income can be aggregated over a sequence of years to show the total income over the extended period. This would remove effects of subjectivity, reducing opportunities for manipulation.

Support for this approach is strengthened by permitting the classification of all-inclusive income into recurring and non-recurring, or operating and non-operating, components. This combines the information content of the two concepts.

These considerations have been the subject of a number of pronouncements. The International Accounting Standards Committee issued IAS 8, 'Unusual and Prior-period Items and Changes in Accounting Policies'.[1] The ASC issued a standard, SSAP 6, 'Extraordinary Items and Prior-year Adjustments', in April 1974;[2] this was revised first in June 1975, next in 1978 and then more extensively in August 1986. The impact of the future on current disclosures was dealt with in SSAP 17, 'Accounting for Post-balance-sheet Events',[3] and SSAP 18, 'Accounting for Contingencies',[4] both issued in August 1980. The various aspects are dealt with in the following sections of this chapter.

7.2 Extraordinary items

Separating unusual items from the total income figure can have significant utility. The standard, SSAP 6, has directed attention not only to the identification of such unusual items but more particularly to whether or not they should be included in the profit and loss account or recorded directly in reserves. The Companies Act 1985 requires that 'every profit and loss account of a company shall show the amount of the company's profit or loss on ordinary activities before taxation' (4 sch. 3(6)). SSAP 6 adopts an all-inclusive view, arguing that 'the profit on ordinary activities alone is not appropriate for all the uses to which financial statements are put', and that profit and loss should include all extraordinary items to improve comparability and avoid items being overlooked over a series of years.

However, the standard was unable to require all changes in reserves to be passed through the profit and loss account because this would have conflicted with both company law and some other standards.[5] The Companies Act 1985 does not permit surpluses on the revaluation of assets (see Chapter 3) to be included in the profit and loss account (4 sch. 34). An unrealized surplus should be credited directly to reserves, but deficits should be charged to profit and loss unless arising in respect of an asset that had been revalued, whereupon the deficit should be charged first against that surplus. Standards dealing with foreign currency (see Chapter 12) and goodwill (see Chapters 4 and 10) permit adjustments direct to reserves. A further direct adjustment, prior-year items, is dealt with in the next section.

The standard defines extraordinary items as

> material items which derive from events or transactions that fall outside the ordinary activities of the company and which are therefore expected not to recur frequently or regularly. They do not include exceptional items, nor do they include prior-year items merely because they relate to a prior year.

Exceptional and prior-year items will be discussed later in this chapter. The definition given shows that an attempt has been made to combine all three concepts of profit, requiring (a) extraordinary items to be included in the profit and loss account, and then restricting the items to those that (b) are not ordinary and (c) are not expected to recur frequently or regularly. There is a presumption here, and in the exposure draft ED 36 which preceded this revision,[6] that normally recurrent and current operating concepts are equivalent. In ED 36 the two concepts were used as if they were interchangeable. The definition indicates that infrequency or irregularity follows from being outside ordinary activities. The impact of earthquakes may be all too frequent in certain areas, but suffering these hazards would not be regarded as part of a company's normal operating activities. The terms 'frequent' and 'regular' are not defined in the standard, and interpretation becomes a matter of opinion and judgement.

The definition of ordinary activities is also framed widely to exclude only items both non-recurrent and non-operating:

> Ordinary activities are any activities which are usually, frequently or regularly undertaken by the company and any related activities in which the company engages in furtherance of, incidental to, or arising from those activities. They include, but are not confined to, the trading activities of the company.

Although materiality is a requirement for an item to be extraordinary, size alone is insufficient: the circumstances of the event and the company must also be considered. It is possible for an event to be extraordinary for one company but not extraordinary for a company in the same group or for a holding or subsidiary company within a group.

The standard presents some examples where material profits or losses *may* be extraordinary items:

(a) the discontinuance of a business segment either through termination or disposal;
(b) the sale of an investment not acquired with the intention of resale, such as investments in subsidiary and associated companies;
(c) profits or losses on the disposal of fixed assets (see para. 15);
(d) provision made for the permanent diminution in value of a fixed asset because of extraordinary events during the period;
(e) the expropriation of assets;
(f) a change in the basis of taxation, or a significant change in Government fiscal policy.

Examples (c), (d) and (f) were all added as part of the 1986 revision.

7.2.1   Disposal and terminated units

The reference in example (c) above to paragraph 15 is to indicate that the treatment of profits or losses on the disposal of fixed assets is dependent on the nature of the event giving rise to the disposal. It is recognized that businesses will need to dispose of assets from time to time as part of the normal operating function, perhaps updating in response to technological progress. Since companies are not usually in business with the objective of discontinuing business segments, such action would typically be 'extraordinary'. However, some conglomerate holding companies do operate by the regular acquisition of and disinvestment in subsidiaries. For them, the 'extraordinary' classification would be inappropriate.

The current US standard[7] is more restrictive in this matter and does not consider disposals of business segments eligible for 'extraordinary' treatment. A notable feature of the 1986 SSAP 6 revision was to exclude the applicability in the UK of the 'extraordinary' classification to cases of business reorganization that do not involve closure of the complete segment. Paragraph 14 states:

> Programmes of reorganisation which, although involving redundancies and a reduction in the level of activities, do not amount to the discontinuance of a business segment, are not extraordinary. Such reorganisations are a normal business process and therefore form part of the ordinary activities of a company. Their costs are charged in arriving at profit or loss on ordinary activities, and shown as an exceptional item if material.

Business segments are also defined tightly, as readily distinguishable, separately identified business components, each normally having its own product line or market. These restrictions were a response to the growth in reorganization programmes in the competitive environment of the early 1980s. It was considered that companies were abusing the latitude the previous standard offered by including any redundancy or reorganization costs as 'extraordinary'. The expansion and contraction of activity level and its costs must now be considered as part of a company's flexibility in response to changing market conditions, provided the entire business segment is not abandoned.

Termination of a business activity raises interesting measurement issues. An accruals approach requires that the full impact of a decision to shut down a business segment must be reflected in the accounts of the period of the decision. Another fundamental concept—prudence—is met by providing for all the losses that a decision to discontinue might create. The standard lists eight types of costs that are likely to result from segment shutdown:

(a) redundancy costs (net of government contributions);
(b) costs of retaining key personnel during the run-down period;
(c) profits or losses arising from the disposal of assets, including anticipated ongoing costs such as rent, rates and security;
(d) pension costs;
(e) bad and doubtful debts arising from the decision to close;
(f) all debits and credits arising from trading after the commencement of implementation;
(g) any losses arising from penalty clauses in contracts.

However, the costs may not all be incurred in the same period. The standard implements the accruals and prudence concepts by advocating that all the consequences of the shut-down be included in the period of the decision. Provisions for future losses which can be anticipated are to be made, and it is also appropriate to reduce losses by future gains that are expected with reasonable confidence; a particular example of the latter would be gains from land which can be revalued upwards on a disposals basis. The support for such treatment is found in paragraph 12:

> Such provisions are not prevented from being treated as extraordinary items merely because they occur and are recognised over a number of accounting periods where this is either the ongoing result of a single decision or because of a number of separate decisions.

Providing for the future impact of a prolonged shut-down intending to reflect prudence may have the opposite effect. Extraordinary losses in the initial year may be increased, but ordinary profits may remain intact. In subsequent years asset write-downs reduce subsequent depreciation charges and increase the return on assets. Rutherford and Wearing examine the case of British Airways, where these effects also included a reduction in operating costs resulting from the savings in staffing following redundancies.[8] The series of profits and returns may be considerably enhanced by adoption of the standard treatment.

7.2.2   Taxation

The Companies Act 1985 (4 sch. 53) requires taxation on extraordinary profit or loss to be shown separately, and the standard states that the tax effects resulting from extraordinary items are themselves extraordinary, even if recognized in a different period to that of the profit and loss. The tax is to be calculated by computing the change in tax with and without including the extraordinary items.

The standard also indicates that a tax charge or credit may itself be extraordinary, and an illustration of this is included in the examples reproduced earlier in the chapter. The computation of such an item is considered in the following chapter. The treatment as extraordinary may have removed a large loss from the results of many companies, but this classification would not have followed from other ASC pronouncements on this subject. Paragraph 17 of this standard (SSAP 6) suggests, in relation to prior-year items, that estimating future events will require reappraisal as additional information is obtained, and paragraph 17 of ED 36 states that corrections and adjustments 'are the natural result of estimates inherent in accounting and more particularly in the periodic preparation of financial statements'.

7.2.3   Presentation

The Companies Act 1985 lays down a number of disclosure requirements, in relation to extraordinary items, requiring separate disclosure. The profit and loss formats require analysis under four headings: extraordinary profit, extraordinary charges, extraordinary profit or loss, and tax on extraordinary profit or loss. The analysis of extraordinary items can be provided in a note rather than on the face of the profit and loss account. Under the standard, the extraordinary profit or loss should come after profit or loss on ordinary items and before the profit and loss for the year from which dividends and other appropriations are deducted. The legal requirement for 'particulars' of these items is amplified in the standard stipulation that 'An adequate description of each extraordinary item should be given to enable its nature to be understood.'

A survey of published accounts revealed that, for financial reports issued during the year to 30 June 1987, 476 extraordinary items were reported by 300 major industrial and commercial companies.[9] The most common items resulted from disposal of assets, investments, businesses or subsidiaries (195) and from discontinuance, reorganization and redundancy (137). Although only 24 companies reported takeover bids or defence costs, 75 per cent of these were reported as extraordinary. One of special note was supplied by Guinness plc following its controversial but successful bid for Distillers.

The decision to classify as 'extraordinary' has important implications, two of which deserve particular note. First, calculation of the much-used earnings-per-share figure (see Chapter 15) is normally based on profit before extraordinary items. Despite the tighter wording of the revised standard, it remains a source of potential differences in treatment between companies, expecially if there is a view that management can be regarded as responsible for their ordinary activities whereas the extraordinary are the result of random factors beyond their control. A contrary view would see a key top management entrepreneurial skill to be anticipating and avoiding major catastrophes while finding beneficial opportunities.

7.2.4 Exceptional items

Although items that are abnormal in size or incidence may not be classified as extraordinary, either because of their frequency or because of the manner in which they relate to the company's activities, there is a need to give them separate disclosure in order to present a true and fair view. The standard supports this treatment, requiring, in addition to separation of the exceptional amounts, adequate description to permit them to be understood. The Companies Act 1985 has similar requirements. The standard provides examples:

(a) redundancy costs relating to continuing business segments;
(b) reorganisation costs unrelated to the discontinuance of a business segment;
(c) previously capitalised expenditure on intangible fixed assets written off other than as part of a process of amortisation;
(d) amounts transferred to employee share schemes;
(e) profits or losses on the disposal of fixed assets (see para. 15);
(f) abnormal charges for bad debts and write-offs of stock and work in progress;
(g) abnormal provisions for losses on long-term contracts;
(h) surpluses arising on the settlement of insurance claims;
(i) amounts received in settlement of insurance claims for consequential loss of profits.

The survey of 1986/87 accounts revealed 720 disclosures of exceptional items by the 300 companies, pension costs being the most common of these.[10]

Some recent examples of disclosures illustrate how the dividing line between 'extraordinary' and 'exceptional' is interpreted in practice. In their accounts for the year to 29 March 1986, the costs of the unsuccessful offer for Distillers by Argyll Group plc are treated as extraordinary. Note 8 shows the disclosure:

8.0 Extraordinary Items

	1986 £'000s	1985 £'000s
Cost of the unsuccessful offer for The Distillers Company p.l.c., less taxation relief of £5,680,000	(48,031)	—
Profit on disposal of shares held in The Distillers Company p.l.c., less taxation charge of £5,963,000	13,913	—
Future costs of restructuring of physical distribution and retail trading identities, less taxation relief of £4,844,000	—	(10,064)
Costs of reduction of investment in Scotch whisky production	—	(1,440)
	(34,118)	(11,504)

One year later, the same group treated the costs of reorganization of its Safeway and Presto operations as exceptional. The chief executive's review explained:

Excluding the new capital investment in store conversions, initial estimates of the fixed asset write-offs and revenue costs of the Safeway 1990's programme would indicate that these costs should not exceed £90 million before taxation. A substantial proportion of these costs will be charged in the current year as an exceptional item with the balance being similarly charged, as incurred, over the succeeding three years.

The final cost estimates will be identified with the announcement of the Company's interim results in December. None of these costs has been reflected in accounting for the purchase cost of Safeway since the restructuring affects principally Presto and not Safeway.

This might appear prudent, but the stock market reaction to this, combined with an announcement of a rights issue, was adverse, dropping some 10 per cent. Other shares in the stores sector were also marked down, it would seem owing to concern of prudent policies elsewhere.

The Dee Corporation plc treated the costs of integrating Fine Fare into the group as extraordinary.[11] Note 7 to the accounts for the period ended 25 April 1987 showed:

7. Extraordinary Items	1987
	£m
Write-down of loan investment in Amalgamated Foods Limited (note 11)	2.4
Integration of Fine Fare with Gateway:	
Closure and integration costs incurred in the period	19.2
Provision for closure and reorganisation costs	33.5
	55.1

The above items are net of taxation of £26.5m.

7.3 Prior-year adjustments

Changes may fail to be recognized in the periods in which they occur but may come to light later. Although rigid application of an all-inclusive income approach would require them to included when they are discovered, they would not necessarily be regarded as current items. It was recognized in Section 7.2.2 that, in order to carry out periodic reporting, the accounting process requires estimates of the future to be made (eg. in providing for doubtful debts or depreciation), and these estimates can be expected to require correction and adjustment. These changes in the estimate are normal and recurring and arise from information becoming available in the current period. There is no need to relinquish the all-inclusive concept of income in these cases, and the items should be dealt with in the year in which they are recognized.

The standard specifies two cases in which it would be inappropriate, in presenting a true and fair view, to include items in the current year's profit and loss since they relate to a previous period. These are defined as 'material adjustments applicable to prior years arising from changes in accounting policies or from the correction of fundamental errors' (SSAP 6, para. 31).

As described in Chapter 1, SSAP 2 included consistency of accounting treatment from one period to the next among the fundamental concepts of accounting.[12] As a result, change in accounting policy should be made only if it can be demonstrated that the new policy is preferable to the one it replaces. When such a change in policy does occur, amounts for corresponding periods need to be restated on the same new basis as amounts for current periods. The cumulative adjustments that apply to previous years have no bearing on the results of the current year and should be excluded from the current year's profit and loss. Cumulative restatement will require the adjustment of the opening balance of retained profits. SSAP 6 requires this adjustment to be made and its effect disclosed as a movement in reserves.

Fundamental errors as compared with corrections of accounting estimates should occur only in exceptional circumstances. However, if an error occurred in a prior year's accounts and was sufficiently fundamental that it would have undermined their truth and fairness, so that those accounts would have had to be withdrawn had the error been discovered before presentation to a general meeting, a correction is necessary. It would be inappropriate to include the correction in the current year's profit and loss; correction requires a restatement of the prior year, resulting in a need to adjust the opening balance on retained earnings.

7.3.1 Presentation and movement on reserves

The original SSAP 6 required a statement of retained profits/reserves showing any prior-year adjustment to follow immediately after the profit and loss account for the year. The 1986 revision permitted, as an alternative, the movement in reserves to appear in a note with reference to the existence and location of the note being made on the face of the profit and loss account for the year. The reserve movements should include only the effect of retained profits plus those changes in shareholders' equity arising from prior-year adjustments or other changes explicitly permitted by accounting standard or legal requirement. The Companies Act does not give explicit recognition to prior-year adjustments but does state that, 'where any amount relating to any preceding financial year is included in any item in the profit and loss account, the effect should be stated' (4 sch. 57).

Correction of fundamental errors made in a prior period will be recorded in the books by opening a prior-period adjustment error correction account, which will reflect the error that has been corrected. For example, for a company with a year-end on 31 December it was discovered in 1989 that in 1988 plant costing £100,000 with a five-year life was written off instead of being capitalized. The entry required in 1989, assuming it has been decided that the error was material, would be:

Plant	£100,000	
Accumulated depreciation		£20,000
Prior-period adjustment, error correction		80,000

In addition, there may be some effect on the tax charge.

Also, it will be necessary to ensure that the depreciation charge for 1989 is correct. This may necessitate an adjusting entry (depending on when the error is discovered), but the prior-period adjustment account should not be used for this current-year adjustmemt.

7.4 Post-balance-sheet events

Just as recognition in the current period of an event relating to a previous period raised the question of whether or not the resulting effect should be reflected in the accounts of the current or the prior period, matters may occur or come to light after the end of an accounting period which may have a bearing on that period's results or financial position. Annual accounts may well take three or four months to finalize, and it would be very narrow-minded to regard the balance sheet as restricted to the presentation of balances on the companies' ledgers at the end of trading on the balance sheet date: it might result in not presenting a true and fair view of the financial position at that date, given that the view is taken with the benefit of subsequent knowledge. It would seem reasonable to expect that, when directors give their approval to a company's financial statements, they should not ignore information simply because they became aware of it only after the end of the financial year.

This was first given recognition in the Companies Act 1981 and is now embodied in the 1985 Act (7 sch. 6a), which requires the directors' report to contain 'particulars of any important events affecting the company or any of its subsidiaries which have occurred since the end of the financial year'.

The ASC had earlier, in August 1980, issued a standard (SSAP 17) which contrasts with the Act in directing attention to the accounts and the accompanying notes rather than the directors' report. In the standard, post-balance-sheet events are defined as 'those events both favourable and unfavourable which occur between the balance sheet date and the date on which the financial statements are approved by the board'. For group accounts the date would be when the holding company board approves the group accounts. This clearly defines the cut-off date for the recognition of events. It does not define their treatment, and has to turn to the question of whether or not such occurrences require accounts to be modified. In meeting the needs of periodic reporting, it would be inappropriate to change a company's results to include transactions occurring simply because the directors are aware of them.

SSAP 17 sets out two categories of events: adjusting and non-adjusting. Adjusting events provide additional evidence relating to conditions existing at the balance sheet date. Clearly, these events would contribute to the measurement of results and financial position within the accounting period so that financial statements 'can be prepared on the basis of conditions existing at the balance sheet date' but using later knowledge of those conditions. As the name suggests, material adjusting events will require changes to be made to the amounts included in published accounts as part of normal accruals and provisions.

One aspect given specific mention in the standard is that of 'going concern'. As discussed in Chapter 1, accounts are prepared on a going-concern basis unless there is evidence to the contrary. Evidence may be provided in the post-balance-sheet period, particularly by a deterioration in performance or position. This could require considerable changes in amounts reported, notably because assets would need to be written down to break up values. Fixed assets that may have been of substantial value to an ongoing operation may be of such a specific nature that they are relatively worthless on breakup. Work-in-progress for which completion is not anticipated may become scrap. In addition, provisions may need to be made for redundancy payments, for example. Certain statutory or conventional items have traditionally been adjusted, including dividends proposed and reserve appropriations. The standard provides a useful list of examples of adjusting events:

(a) *Fixed assets* The subsequent determination of the purchase price or of the proceeds of sale of assets purchased or sold before the year end.
(b) *Property* A valuation which provides evidence of a permanent diminution in value.
(c) *Investments* The receipt of a copy of the financial statements or other information in respect of an unlisted company which provides evidence of a permanent diminution in the value of a long-term investment.
(d) *Stocks and work in progress* (i) The receipt of proceeds of sales after the balance sheet date or other evidence concerning net realisable value of stocks.
                              (ii) The receipt of evidence that the previous estimate of accrued profit on a long-term contract was materially inaccurate.
(e) *Debtors* The renegotiation of amounts owing by debtors or the insolvency of a debtor.
(f) *Dividends receivable* The declaration of dividends by subsidiaries and associated companies related to periods prior to the balance sheet date of the holding company.
(g) *Taxation* The receipt of information regarding rates of taxation.
(h) *Claims* Amounts received or receivable in respect of insurance claims which were in the course of negotiation at the balance sheet date.
(i) *Discoveries* The discovery or errors or frauds which show that the financial statements were incorrect.

By way of illustration, debtor information may affect the provision for bad debts.

Since non-adjusting events occur subsequent to the year-end, and concern conditions that did not exist at the balance sheet date, they do not alter estimates or other amounts in financial statements. However, if they are material, their disclosure may be needed to ensure that the statements are not misleading. SSAP 17 requires this disclosure in notes, providing information on the nature and the financial effect of the event, and giving separate disclosure of the taxation implications; if it is not practical to estimate financial quantities, this should be stated.

Mergers and acquisitions tend to be of significance and are a common example of non-adjusting events. A case of a takeover occurring after the year-end but treated as an adjusting event attracted considerable attention and resulted in a Department of Trade statement.[13] The case, which concerns Argyll Foods Ltd, the subject of an earlier example in this chapter, is discussed further in Chapter 10. The company directors included in their group consolidated statements for the year ended 31 December 1979 the accounts of Morgan Edwards Ltd, even though the acquisition did not take place until 25 March 1980. This was justified on the grounds that this was necessary to produce a true and fair view. Even though negotiations for the purchase had commenced in November 1979, Morgan Edwards was not a subsidiary and therefore not part of the group at the balance sheet date.[14]

SSAP 17 was issued in August 1980, and the accounts of Argyll were approved at the company's AGM in September 1980. It is interesting to note that the SSAP included mergers and takeovers in their list of examples of non-adjusting events. Other possible examples are:

(a) raising of additional share or loan capital;
(b) purchases and sales of major fixed assets and investments;
(c) losses of fixed assets or stocks as a result of catastrophes such as fire or flood;
(d) changes in foreign currency exchange rates;
(e) liabilities arising from subsequent events, including contingent liabilities (e.g. claims and other litigation);
(f) political events and other government action, including nationalization.

The standard emphasized a post-balance-sheet event of note. This is 'the reversal of maturity, after the year-end, of a transaction entered into before the year-end, the substance of which was primarily to alter the appearance of the company's balance sheet'. This type of transaction is popularly described as 'window-dressing', and it became apparent right from the time of issuing ED 22, the exposure draft that preceded SSAP 17, in March 1978, that the incidence and impact of window-dressing was a matter of concern. More recently the ICAEW has issued TR 603, 'Off-balance-sheet Finance and Window Dressing' and the ASC issued ED 42, 'Special-purpose Transactions', which aim to tackle some of these problems. These are the subject of Chapter 16.

One other issue that has been contentious in the past was new share or loan issues. The decision to make an issue may take place during a period for subsequent implementation. One practice has been to adjust the results for the effects of such a decision. Grand Metropolitan took this view in relation to their accounts for the year ended 30 September 1975. As a result, at the year-end share capital of £149 million included £29 million in respect of a rights issue announced on the last day of the financial year. Even though cash was not received until October, adjustments were made, reducing the bank overdrafts and short-term borrowings reported as at 30 September 1975. SSAP 17 includes this as an example of an event that would normally be non-adjusting.

7.5 Contingencies

The close relationship between contingencies and post-balance-sheet items enabled the IASC to include both in the same international standard (IAS 10). Similarly, to coincide with the issue of SSAP 17, the ASC issued SSAP 18, 'Accounting for Contingencies', in August 1980. This defines a contingency as 'a condition which exists at the balance sheet date where the outcome will be confirmed only on the occurrence or non-occurrence of one or more uncertain future events'. A contingent gain or loss is a gain or loss dependent on a contingency. It does not refer to uncertainties surrounding accounting estimates including, for example, fixed asset lives.

Although both gains and losses are covered by this definition, the prudence concept will mean that the disclosure of contingent gains are rare. The standard explains this: 'contingent gains should not be accrued in financial statements.' Despite the informative value of making disclosures in notes about the impact of contingencies, prudence plays a role here also: 'a material contingent gain should be disclosed in financial statements only if it is probable that the gain will be realised.' It is not surprising that there are few cases of gains that were both probable and dependent on the outcome of uncertain events.

One reference is included in the *Survey of UK Published Accounts 1982–83* (none for the previous year), while 269 of the 300 companies surveyed included contingent liabilities.

The Companies Act (44 sch. 50) refers only to contingent liabilities, identifying guarantees, charges on assets, contracted and authorized capital expenditure and pension commitments for which no provision has been made. The standard provides the example of a legal claim.

The required treatment of material contingencies is disclosure in notes to published statements. The disclosure should include information to show the nature of the contingency and the uncertainties affecting the outcome, and where possible a prudent estimate of the financial effect of the contingency.

Burnett & Hallamshire Holdings plc include the following note under contingent liabilities for the year ended 31 March 1984:

(a) The Company and relevant subsidiaries have given guarantees amounting to £41.25m (1983—£6.3m) in respect of certain contracts and undertakings entered into in the ordinary course of business.

This was to prove a note of some significance. The *Financial Times* of 24 January 1986 reported a situation of some difficulty a year later, indicating that the guarantees made by the company included some of considerable size for hire purchase commitments.[15] The contingent liabilities reported in 1984 resulted in a need to make adjustments in the balance sheet at 31 March 1985:

Balance Sheet Totals

	Adjusted Group 1985 £000s	Group 1985 £000s	Group 1984 £000s
Fixed assets	127,360	103,023	133,526
Current assets	71,564	57,335	118,041
Creditors—within one year	(100,545)	(87,916)	(80,261)
	98,379	72,442	171,306
Creditors—over one year, provisions and accruals	102,617	76,680	62,954
Net (liabilities) assets	(4,238)	(4,238)	108,352

7.6   Disclosure of distributable profits

When the concept of capital maintenance was introduced in Chapter 1, it was used as an element in setting the dimensions for accounting measurement. However, the law has made use of the concept by requiring that any distribution to its shareholders must be made only out of profits available for the purpose (Companies Act 1985, sec. 263). For all but investment and insurance companies, the profits available are realized profits not previously distributed or capitalized. In addition, only realized profits can be included in the profit and loss account (4 sch. 12).

In the case of investment companies, an alternative to the realized profits restriction is permitted. This allows them, under specified conditions, to make a distribution provided this does not reduce the company's assets below one and a half times the aggregate of its liabilities (sec. 265). The rules relating to insurance companies are modified by including any surplus or loss of their long-term business funds in realized profits.

An additional requirement is placed on public companies, which cannot make a distribution that would reduce their net assets below the sum of their share of capital and undistributable reserves. 'Undistributable reserves' includes share premiums, capital redemption reserves and revaluation reserves. The impact on public companies is to ensure that they have provided for unrealized losses before calculating profits available for distribution.

The Act does not directly interpret the term 'realized' but indicates that use should be made of generally accepted principles currently employed for accounting purposes. In order to clarify these requirements, the CCAB issued two technical releases, TR 481 and TR 482, in September 1982.[16] By way of guidance, profits computed 'in accordance with an accounting standard should normally be treated as a realised profit unless the accounting standard states otherwise'; other cases are to be determined by the application of the accruals and prudence concepts of SSAP 2. In addition to this general guidance, some areas will pose specific problems.

Development expenditure was considered in Chapter 4, where it was explained that under certain conditions this may be capitalized. However, for the purposes of calculating distributable profits, the expenditure capitalized must be treated as a realized loss unless directors are able to provide justification that, owing to special circumstances, treating as capital for these purposes is more appropriate.

Another intangible, goodwill, is the source of special reference in the corresponding standard. Appendix 2 to SSAP 22 recognizes that eliminating goodwill against reserves immediately on acquisition would reduce realizable profits, while capitalizing and amortizing would not.[17] It is suggested that, on the grounds on comparability, goodwill may be written off against reserves in the accounts, but distributable profits could be calculated on the less restricting basis as if goodwill had been capitalized and amortized. This appears to offer the best of both worlds, but by way of caution the appendix warns that legal advice should be sought in case of doubt.

Tangible assets have their own special aspects. For long-term contract work in progress, TR 481 suggests that profits recognized in accordance with SSAP 9 (see Chapter 3) should be treated as realized.[18] The exposure draft ED 40, released in June 1987, gave further attention to this issue.[19]

With fixed assets revaluation, gains are treated as unrealized and losses *normally* as realized. However, Section 275 of the Act indicates that a resulting loss on revaluation of all tangible fixed assets need not be treated as realized, although for a public company this is captured by the additional requirement to provide for unrealized losses.

Depreciation is a realized expense in calculating profit. However, depreciation is increased when an asset is revalued upwards, and the additional amount represents partial realization of the revaluation. As such, this additional amount may be transferred from unrealized to realized reserves. This has the effect of producing the same increase in realized reserves in a year as if the profit had been calculated by including depreciation based on historic cost but without tampering with the profit figure.

On disposal of an asset that has been realized, any surplus over depreciated cost becomes realized. In the case of a depreciating asset, the surplus is net of transfers to realized reserves in respect of depreciation.

For holding companies, it should be noted that distributions are made from the parent company and not the consolidated group. It follows that realized profits must be identified in the parent company's accounts. Group accounts are considered in Chapter 11. Foreign currency translation is another field with special considerations, given further attention in Chapter 12.

7.7 Summary

Although the topics considered in this chapter do not normally provide bookkeeping problems, they are of considerable importance for accounting. The law and accounting standards have had significant influence on the manner in which profit is identified to accounting periods, and on how it may be classified into realized, unrealized, exceptional and extraordinary elements. Taken with the need to make adequate disclosures, the treatment of these matters can be crucial in presenting the readers of financial statements with a true and fair view of the results and of the financial position at the balance sheet date.

Notes

1. IAS 8, 'Unusual and Prior-period Items and Changes in Accounting Policies', IASC, 1978.
2. SSAP 6, 'Extraordinary Items and Prior-year Adjustments', ASC, 1974, revised 1986.
3. SSAP 17, 'Accounting for Post-balance-sheet Events', ASC, 1980.
4. SSAP 18, 'Accounting for Contingencies', ASC, 1980.
5. Current examples include upward revaluations of fixed assets which must be taken to a revaluation reserve (Companies Act 1985, 4 sch. 34), certain exchange differences under SSAP 20, and the immediate write-off of goodwill permitted by SSAP 22.
6. ED 36, 'Extraordinary Items and Prior-year Adjustments', ASC, 1985.
7. APB 30, 'Reporting the Results of Operations—Reporting the Effects of Disposal of a Segment of a Business and Extraordinary, Unusual and Infrequently Occurring Events and Transactions', AICPA, June 1973.
8. B. A. Rutherford and R. T. Wearing, *Cases in Company Financial Reporting*, Harper & Row, New York, 1987.
9. D. J. Tonkin and L. C. L. Skerratt, *Financial Reporting 1987–88: A Survey of UK Reporting Practice*, ICAEW, 1987.
10. D. J. Tonkin and L. C. L. Skerratt, *Financial Reporting 1986–87: A Survey of UK Reporting Practice*, ICAEW, 1986.
11. Further explanation was given by the company in an accompanying publication. See Dee Corporation plc, *Some Questions Answered*, December 1987.
12. SSAP 2, 'Disclosure of Accounting Policies', ASC, 1971.
13. Department of Trade; reprinted as DOT statement on 'True and fair' in *Accountancy*, February 1982, p. 11. See also D. Keenan, 'Unfair accounts—Argyll directors summoned', *Accountancy*, August 1981, p. 19; and R. K. Ashton, 'The Argyll Foods case: a legal analysis', *Accounting and Business Research*, Winter 1986.
14. P. Bird, 'After Argyll Foods what is "a true and fair view"?' *Accountancy*, June 1982, pp. 80–1.
15. M. Dickson, 'Rescue from a financial minefield', *Financial Times*, 24 January 1986, p. 18.
16. TR 481, 'The Determination of Realised Profits and Disclosure of Distributable Profits in the Context of the Companies Acts 1948 to 1981'; and TR 482, 'The Determination of Distributable Profits in the Context of the Companies Acts 1948 to 1981', CCAB, September 1982.
17. SSAP 22, 'Accounting for Goodwill', ASC, 1984.
18. SSAP 9, 'Stocks and Work in Progress', ASC, 1975.
19. ED 40, 'Stocks and Work in Progress', ASC, 1986.

Further reading

Cabourn-Smith, A., 'A guide to accounting standards—accounting for post-balance-sheet events', *Accountant's Digest*, no. 101, ICAEW, 1981.

Hodgson, E., 'Extraordinary items', in D. J. Tonkin and L. C. L. Skerratt, *Financial Reporting 1987–88: A Survey of UK Reporting Practice*, ICAEW, 1987.

Keenan, D., 'The legal nature of contingent liabilities', *Accountancy*, January 1980, pp. 91–3.

Questions

1. Since SSAP 6 was originally published in 1974, there has been much discussion on the treatment of extraordinary items. Recently the Accounting Standards Committee has published a discussion paper

reviewing the working of this Standard. Set out below are details of events occurring in nine different companies. In each case, the financial effect is material in the context of the company's results.

(1) Redundancy and other costs relating to the closure of one of a manufacturing company's three factories.

(2) Amounts written off stock and additional depreciation following the removal of one shop of a chain of retail shops from one location to another.

(3) A substantial 'golden handshake' to a company's chief executive on his dismissal.

(4) Additional deferred taxation provision necessary following the acceptance that a company's profits would no longer fall within the small-company rate of corporation tax. The provision is made on the liability method.

(5) The 'profits' arising in a manufacturing company on the maturity of a sinking fund endowment policy for the repayment of a back-to-back loan. The sum assured is sufficient to meet the principal due.

(6) The gain made on the sale of a minority shareholding in a company engaged in a similar trade.

(7) The loss made on the sale of a building company's land bank in order to repay borrowings.

(8) The costs of a complete re-roofing of a leasehold office block held by a manufacturing company on a full repairing lease at a full rent.

(9) The deliberate suppression of creditors, discovered by new management of a company.

You are required to explain, with reasons, the accounting treatment you consider should be adopted in respect of each event by the relevant company. You are not required to draft extracts for the financial statements.

(18 marks)

ICAEW, PE II, FA II, July 1983

2. (a) How does SSAP 6 *Extraordinary items and prior-year adjustments* define a prior year adjustment?
(4 marks)

(b) Set out below is a draft statement of retained profits/reserves for Triathlon plc for the year ended 31 March 1986 and the comparative figures for the year ended 31 March 1985.

Statement of retained profits/reserves

	1986	1985
	£000	£000
Retained profit for the year	400	350
Retained profits at the beginning of the year	500	150
Retained profit at end of year	900	500

Two fundamental errors have just been discovered which consist of unreported profits that had been omitted from the above statement of retained profits/reserves. In the year ended 31 March 1984 there was an unreported profit before tax of £80,000 (tax £40,000) and in the year ended 31 March 1985 an unreported profit before tax of £100,000 (tax £45,000).

You are required to amend the above statement of retained profit/reserves in order to account for these two fundamental errors.   (6 marks)

(c) State, with reasons, whether you consider the following events, which are all material, should be accounted for as prior-year adjustments:

(i) A company changes its accounting policies in order to comply with a new SORP (Statement of Recommended Practice).

(ii) An error in the valuation of the closing stock in the financial statements issued two years previously has been discovered,

(iii) The directors of a company engaged in a long-term contract which had previously been valued in the financial statements at cost plus attributable profit (in accordance with SSAP 9, 'Stocks and work in progress') are now of the opinion that there will be a loss on the contract as a whole.

(iv) A computer, which had been purchased three years previously for £100,000 and was being depreciated at 15% per annum on the straight-line basis, has been sold for £15,000.

(v) A company has leased premises for five years and the terms of the lease state that the tenant is responsible for all the repairs during the lease. The lease has expired and the landlord has requested a sum of £1 million for repairs necessary to restore the property to its former condition. The company has agreed to pay this sum because it has failed to repair the property during the lease period.   (10 marks)

(20 marks)

ACCA, 2.8, RFA, June 1987

3. You are required to answer the following questions on distributable profits as defined by the Companies Act 1985.

    (a) What is the general rule for determining distributable profits?
        (Candidates are NOT required to discuss the special provisions relating to investment and insurance companies.)   (4 marks)

    (b) State whether each of the following are realised or unrealised profits or losses. Briefly explain the reason for your answer.
        (i)   A charge to the profit and loss account as a provision for bad debts.
        (ii)   The final dividend receivable from a subsidiary in respect of an accounting period ending before the end of the parent company's financial year.
        (iii) Foreign exchange gains or losses on unsettled short-term monetary items when the temporal method of foreign currency translation is used.
        (iv)   Surpluses arising on revaluation of assets (before sale).   (8 marks)

    (c) The summarised balance sheet at 30 September 1986 of Global Sports, a limited company, is set out below:

	£000
Authorised share capital	
250,000 ordinary shares of £1 each	250
Called up share capital	
200,000 ordinary shares of £1 each	200
Share premium account	175
Revaluation reserve (net deficit)	(175)
Other reserves	
Capital redemption reserve	125
General reserve	100
Profit and loss account	200
	625
Fixed assets	400
Net current assets	225
	625

Notes
1. The deficit on the revaluation reserve arose as a result of a revaluation of all the fixed assets.
2. The articles of association state that the general reserve is non-distributable.

What are the legally distributable profits of Global Sports if:
(i)   it is a private company?
(ii)   it is a public company?
(iii) what difference, if any, would it make to your answers in (c)(i) and (c)(ii) above if the deficit on the revaluation reserve had arisen on the revaluation of an individual asset?
Explain your workings.   (8 marks)
                                                                                                     (20 marks)
                                                                            ACCA, 2.8, RFA, June 1987

8. Accounting for taxation

Corporate activity in the UK is significantly affected by the existence of taxes, and it is not surprising that the accounting treatment given to taxation is an important factor in corporate reporting. If the treatment of government grants is included, no less than four statements of standard accounting practice currently in issue relate to taxation. For deferred tax a standard was issued, withdrawn, replaced following considerable public discussion and comment, and revised yet again following subsequent difficulties.

Taxation in the UK is a complex matter subject to regular modification,and only a few general features are relevant when considering accounting implications. Companies are liable to corporation tax at the rate determined by the government on taxable profits and chargeable gains, the gains arising from sale of long-term assets rather than trading profit. The same rate is applied to both taxable profits and chargeable gains. The calculation of taxable profits follows legal rules designed to implement government policies and to minimize any scope for varying the amount of taxable profit. As a result, taxable profits will not be identical to those contained in published financial accounts, i.e. reported profits. Two major differences exist. First, the depreciation charges used in calculating reported profits are not allowable in taxable profits, but deductions are made from profit for capital allowances calculated by highly specific rules. Second, some exceptions to the accruals approach exist. These include interest, which is treated on a cash basis, and provisions, which are disallowed for tax purposes.

In April 1973 the *imputation system* of taxation was introduced in the UK. The major feature of this system is that, when paying dividends, companies must pay advance corporation tax (ACT) representing the basic rate of income tax that would be payable by individuals on the dividend received grossed up by this tax. With the basic rate of tax set at 25 per cent, ACT is set at a third of the dividend paid, i.e. $25 \div (100 - 25)$ per cent. The system aids the collection of tax, since shareholders paying tax at the basic rate have no further tax to pay on dividends received. The ACT can be set off against the total corporation tax within limits designed to ensure that set-off is obtained only for ACT on dividends payable out of taxable profits net of corporation tax. If the ACT exceeds the limits, it may be set off against tax on future profits; when this is expected, it is known as 'recoverable' ACT; when future recovery is not expected, it is described as 'irrecoverable' ACT.

The balance of the total tax, net of the ACT already paid, is known as 'mainstream corporation tax'. Until 1990, the timing of the payment of the mainstream tax can vary, depending on the company's age and financial year-end. The tax may be payable from nine to 21 months after the corresponding year-end, i.e. in one of the following two financial years. However, starting with company financial periods ending 16 March 1987, there is a three-year transitional period which brings all companies in line with the tax being paid nine months after the corresponding year end. Tax losses may result in reductions in tax, but the timing and incidence of any reduction normally depends on the availability of profits in other years.

The imputation system ensures that dividends received from one UK company by another UK company have already borne corporation tax. They are exempt from further corporation tax and can be distributed without payment of ACT. This dividend income is known as 'franked investment income', and the ACT paid on it is similar to that paid directly by the company.

A final feature relevant to this initial overview arises in connection with income that is subject to overseas tax. The tax paid on this overseas income may be used to reduce the amount of corporation tax payable on that overseas income. Only payment of the mainstream element of corporation tax can be reduced in this way. It follows that, if the rate of overseas tax on the overseas income exceeds the rate of mainstream corporation tax, part of the overseas tax will be unrelieved. If all or a sufficiently large part of a company's dividends are paid out of its overseas income, then the ACT on the dividend paid out of overseas income cannot be used to reduce the corporation tax. Unrelieved tax may arise here which cannot be carried forward to be offset against other profits.

8.1 Corporation tax and the imputation system

The major matters of debate in accounting for taxation concern deferred taxation, which is examined in the next section. For other matters, requirements are laid down in paragraph 54 of the fourth schedule of the Companies Act 1985[1] and in SSAP 8, 'The Treatment of Taxation under the Imputation System in the Accounts of Companies'. This standard embodies the Companies Act requirements.

Both the Act and the standard require disclosure, in the profit and loss account, of the charge for UK corporation tax on the income for the year, before relief for overseas taxation. The basis of computation of the charge should be included together with the total overseas taxation charge, separating that relieved and specifying what part of the unrelieved overseas taxation arises from the payment or proposed payment of dividends. Disclosures must be made of the accumulated amounts set aside for deferred tax, showing any material transfers between the profit and loss account and deferred tax account in the current financial year. The Act calls for disclosure of any special circumstances affecting corporation tax in the current or future financial years. Guidance on what constitutes 'special circumstances' was given in the ICAEW recommendation, 'Treatment of Taxation in Accounts of Companies'. This is now withdrawn, but it specifically identified material distortion arising from expenses disallowed as a special circumstance. Tax losses and the adjustment of tax provisions in the light of updated information are other examples. The standard includes requirements that any tax attributable to franked investment income and irrecoverable ACT be shown. In addition to disclosing the balance on the deferred tax account, which must not be included among reserves, the standard includes requirements for disclosure in the balance sheet of corporation tax liabilities, ACT and dividends.

As indicated earlier, liabilities to corporation tax become payable in one of the following two financial years. For companies required to meet the liability in the following year, it is sufficient to show a single current liability to corporation tax. For other companies, the total tax liability comprises two elements, one relating to the current year and one to the previous year. The standard requires the two elements to be disclosed separately 'under current liabilities or otherwise as appropriate. If they are not shown under current liabilities the due date of payment should be stated.'[2]

The treatment of ACT in the profit and loss account is dependent upon whether it is treated as an appropriation or an expense. The former would suggest that the ACT should be shown as an additional cost of dividends; the latter would represent part of the total tax on the company's profits. Since the company must pay the ACT, and since this does not affect the amount paid to recipients, while it is intended to be an advance payment of the company's tax, SSAP 8 adopts the practice of treating it as an expense. As a result, dividends paid or payable should be shown excluding ACT even if the ACT is considered irrecoverable.

This approach to calculating earnings, which includes as an expense irrecoverable ACT and unrelieved overseas taxation, is known as 'the net basis'. Two other bases, the 'nil distribution' and 'full distribution', are sometimes used when evaluating the earnings performance of the company; SSAP 3 makes specific reference to the net and nil distribution bases (see Chapter 14). The full distribution basis calculates the maximum after-tax earnings that can be distributed and is relevant to an assessment of dividend cover. The nil distribution basis gives the after-tax earnings that would have arisen if no dividends were declared or paid. The disclosure of irrecoverable ACT and unrelieved overseas tax enables the nil distribution basis to be calculated by adding these disclosed amounts to the amount already disclosed on the net basis.

Dividends proposed or payable are to be treated in a similar manner, showing the cash amount payable to shareholders as a dividend liability, with the associated ACT liability being shown separately as a tax liability.

Franked investment income is shown including the attached tax credit. Although it can be distributed as dividends without paying any further tax, the case for grossing the income up by the full corporation tax rate is rejected by the standard, which considers the method adopted to be most consistent with the treatment of other elements of profits. As indicated earlier, the tax attributable to franked investment income is separately disclosed so the pre-tax and post-tax incomes can be identified.

Two aspects of calculation included in the standard are the tax rate and irrecoverable ACT. The tax rate should be disclosed, and, if it is not known for any part of the period covered by the accounts, the latest known rate should be employed.

ACT will be considered as recoverable only if recovery is reasonably certain and foreseeable. In interpeting this, the standard considers that treatment will depend on the existence of a deferred taxation account. If the ACT will not be recovered from the tax payments arising from the year under review or the two preceding years, recovery will depend either on having future income that sufficiently exceeds dividends or on a sufficiently large liability, represented by the deferred tax account, becoming payable. It is appropriate for reporting purposes to set off unrelieved ACT against the balance on the deferred tax account within the limits available for actual set-off. Deferred tax representing deferred chargeable gains is not included for set-off, so the remaining balance must represent taxable income out of which the ACT and associated dividend could have been paid. At a standard rate of taxation of 25 per cent, a quarter of the deferred taxation account relating to taxable profits can be used for set-off by ACT.

If there is no deferred tax account, or if it is too small to cover the unrelieved ACT, future income must be considered in establishing recoverability. The explanatory notes in the standard suggest, on the grounds of prudence, that the 'foreseeable future' in which future income can be considered should not normally extend beyond the next accounting period. Any unrelieved ACT not meeting the requirements for treatment as recoverable should be written off in the profit and loss account in which the related dividend is shown, as part of the net basis of calculation.

8.2 Deferred taxation

If taxation were calculated as a percentage of reported income, charging tax at that percentage of income would ensure that the matching process was being fulfilled, with tax expenses being reported in appropriate periods. Tax unpaid would represent a normal liability. However, taxation is based on taxable income, which is rarely (if ever) identical to the reported income. Two classes of difference can arise. The first represents *permanent differences*, which comprise items included in the calculation of reported profit but not taxable profit or vice versa. Disallowable expenses are the usual form of permanent difference, including certain entertainment expenses, fines and the amortization of goodwill. Tax-free income would be another example of a permanent difference. The treatment of permanent differences poses little problem, simply representing additional costs of the period. Permanent differences are not a concern for deferred taxation accounting.

The second class of difference consists of *reversing or timing differences*. As the names suggest, these differences occur when, for taxable income calculations, revenues or expenditures are recognized in different periods from those in which they are reported in financial accounts. The same values eventually are included in both taxable and reported income, but they differ in the year of inclusion; any difference is expected to cancel out or reverse over time. Deferred taxation arises in response to the differences. A good example of a timing difference is produced by the substitution of capital allowances for depreciation charges in adjusting reported income to taxable income. Since, in the period prior to the introduction of the Finance Act 1984, certain assets were entitled to 100 per cent first-year allowances, even though the asset would be depreciated over a life-span of many years, this was the cause of very substantial timing differences. Consider the purchase of a machine, which was eligible for 100 per cent first-year allowances, at a price of £20,000 when corporation tax rates were 50 per cent. If, for reporting purposes, it is depreciated over four years using the straight-line method, timing differences would have arisen as follows:

	Year 1	2	3	4	Total
	£	£	£	£	£
Depreciation charge	5,000	5,000	5,000	5,000	20,000
Capital allowance	20,000	—	—	—	20,000
Timing difference	(15,000)	5,000	5,000	5,000	—
Corporation tax at 50%	(7,500)	2,500	2,500	2,500	

As a result of the relief allowed on the purchase of this machine, the tax charge for the first year, calculated on the basis of reported profit, would overstate by £7,500 the liability to tax arising from the taxable income. However, in years 2, 3 and 4, calculating the tax charge on the basis of reported profit would understate the legal liability by amounts that sum to £7,500. The timing differences originate in the first period and would be reversed over the periods in which depreciation is charged. The size of these differences is significant and means that their treatment could have an important impact on reported results. The impact of the changes arising from the Finance Act 1984 are illustrated in the worked example in Section 8.2.4.

8.2.1 Sources of timing difference

Timing differences can arise as a result of many factors. It is useful to identify the following five categories.[3]

1. *Short-term timing differences* These arise mainly from the use of a receipts-and-payments basis for taxation purposes but an accruals basis for financial reporting. These differences normally reverse in the accounting period immediately following the period in which they originate. Examples of income taxed in a later period than that for which it is included in reported income are: interest receivable, which is accrued in the current accounting period for reported income purposes but is not taxed until received, and dividends from foreign subsidiaries, accrued in a period prior to that in which they arise for tax purposes. Examples of tax reductions that arise after the corresponding reduction in reported income are: a general provision for bad debts, which is allowable for tax purposes only when a specific bad debt is recognized; pension costs accrued but not allowable for tax purposes until funded; and interest or royalties payable but not allowed for tax until paid.

2. *Accelerated capital allowances* As illustrated above, when capital allowances differ from the depreciation charges included in financial accounts, timing differences occur. The Finance Act

1984 has removed almost all of the 100 per cent first-year allowances, and this has reduced the timing differences that arise as a result of this factor.

3 *Revaluation surpluses on fixed assets*   When fixed assets are revalued upwards, there is a potential taxation liability which will not arise until the gain is realized on disposal.

4. *Surpluses on disposal of fixed assets*   When these surpluses are subject to roll-over relief, no taxation liability arises. A reversal could occur on the subsequent sale of a replacement asset.

5. *Stock relief*   Although this was eliminated in relation to UK taxation as part of the changes introduced in the Finance Act 1984, it remains applicable in certain other countries. It usually takes the form of permitting a portion of increased stock values, particularly that due to price increases, to be deducted in calculating taxable profit.[4] Reversal could occur if ever stock values declined.

8.2.2   Accounting for timing differences

There are a number of ways of treating timing differences, the simplest of which is known as the flow-through method. This method shows, as an expense of a period, the actual liability arising in that period based on taxable profits. It effectively ignores timing differences, merely reflecting the legal liability to tax; the amount of tax is unlikely to relate closely to the reported income. As a result, fluctuations would be introduced in the trend of net-of-tax reported earnings even when the before-tax earnings contained no fluctuations.

This approach is consistent with the view that tax is an appropriation of profit rather than an expense. However, as with ACT, this view has not gained the support of standard-setters. Indeed, there is even less theoretical support for regarding tax on profits as an appropriation. A company cannot generally decide whether or not to pay taxes in the same way that it sets its dividend policy. It is under a legal obligation to pay taxes, and the obligation arises as part of its activity in producing profits. Another argument used to support a flow-through approach is that the tax obligation results not from accounting profit, but from taxable profits, and tax should be provided only on those taxable profits.

If profit is to be reported on the basis of applying the matching process to historical cost data, the flow-through method is inappropriate; taxation should be recognized as an expense and should be matched with the relevant revenue. In this case, tax expense should be matched with the period of reporting of the profit which leads to the expense. This means that not only must the legal liability to tax be recognized in a particular period, but allowance should be made for the tax on timing differences. This will produce a closer correspondence between the tax charged and the reported income.

Provided tax rates remain unchanged, the tax charge will be the ruling rate of tax applied to the reported income adjusted for any permanent differences. The differences between the legal liability to tax arising in the period and the tax charge based on the reported income (i.e. the tax on the timing differences) should be carried forward to future periods in anticipation of reversal. Early treatment was to create a tax equalization account in which the differences were accumulated. The balance on this account tends to represent a provision for a liability; indeed, it may be considered imprudent to carry forward a debit balance, representing future potential tax savings, as an asset. Modern terminology, adopted by the ASC, uses 'deferred tax' in place of 'tax equalization'.

An alternative approach to the treatment of timing differences is concerned with the balance sheet position as opposed to the matching process in the profit and loss account. One approach adopts the view that the existence of reported profit after adjusting for permanent differences will lead to the potential creation of a tax liability at some time. Although part of that potential takes the form of a legal liability immediately, part will become a liability only in the future; it is a deferred liability. An alternative form of this view is to consider, as a deferred liability, only those timing differences that are expected to reverse in the foreseeable future. This may be called the 'partial provision approach'. It is supported by two main arguments. The first is that, in the balance sheet, using the going concern principle if no liability is foreseen, no provision needs to be made since it would immensely reduce current profits. The second suggests that, in accordance with the matching approach, the tax charge in the profit and loss account should be that which is *expected* to become payable as a result of the period's transactions. It may be that, for a going concern, tax on some items strictly identified as reversing differences will be postponed indefinitely and would be more realistically treated as permanent differences.

A measurement problem arises if the rates of taxation change between the period in which the timing difference originated and its eventual reversal.

The *deferral method* adopts the view that deferred tax accounting is part of the matching process of the profit and loss calculation, so that timing differences should be calculated at the rate in force at the time the difference originates. This is consistent with the historic cost basis of accounting.

The *liability or accrual method* addresses itself to balance sheet values, regarding the credit balance on a deferred taxation account as a liability to pay tax in the future. This must be adjusted in response to changes in taxation rates or the imposition of new taxes. It may be viewed as the liability to tax which would arise if income represented by outstanding timing differences became liable to tax at the current rate.

8.2.3　Presentation of deferred taxation

There has been some disagreement about the meaning of the balance on a deferred taxation account. One view is that it represents a liability that must be met in the future, and therefore should be treated like long-term debt. Another view, which conflicts with the legal disclosure position, is that it represents a form of reserve included among shareholders' interests designed to smooth out reported after-tax profit and provide a closer link between before- and after-tax results. A third view, applicable to the timing differences resulting from accelerated capital allowances (and formerly to stock relief), is that it represents a tax incentive, lowering the after-tax cost of certain assets. Different affects would be produced in the reported gearing positions by the adoption of each of the three views:

View 1: Liability	£	View 2: Reserve	£	View 3: Reduction of cost	£
Assets (gross)	18,000	Assets (gross)	18,000	Assets (gross)	18,000
				less Deferred tax	6,000
	18,000		18,000		12,000
Equity	9,000	Equity	9,000	Equity	9,000
		Deferred tax	6,000		
Debt: Long-term	3,000		15,000	Debt	3,000
Deferred tax	6,000	Debt	3,000		
	18,000		18,000		12,000
Debt: equity ratio	1:1		1:5		1:3

View 2 conflicts with the Companies Act. View 1 is appropriate to the liability approach. View 3, which could be described as a 'dangling credit' approach, may be considered more consistent with deferral using the historic cost basis; although it recognizes that values of assets and liabilities are dependent on tax considerations, it is rejected by standard-setters on the grounds that assets are usually shown before tax. Had the flow-through method been used, no deduction from reported profit for timing differences would have been made. The result would be that the deferred tax would be included with retained profit and the gearing position would be as in view 2.

8.2.4   Development of standard practice

The ASC issued its first Exposure Draft on deferred taxation (ED 11) in May 1973. It proposed that deferred taxation should be provided on all material timing differences; the method of calculation to be used was the deferral method. The deferred tax account was to be described as 'deferred taxation' in the balance sheet and was not to be shown as part of shareholders' funds or included among current assets or current liabilities.

SSAP 11 was subsequently issued in August 1975. It no longer required that the deferral method should be used but permitted either the deferral or liability method. It continued to include all material timing differences in the calculation of deferred taxation. This standard was severely criticized, and its implementation was postponed from January until December 1976.

The managers of companies were concerned that the large deferred tax balances resulting from complying with SSAP 11 would make it appear that their companies had become grossly over-geared. The deferred tax included in the balance sheet was regarded as a form of liability, and yet corporate management considered it highly unlikely that any related tax payments would arise in the foreseeable future. A company regularly purchasing plant to maintain its physical capacity might expect to have first-year capital allowances each year which at least covered the depreciation charges on existing plant in that year. Assets may be revalued, but there may be no intention to sell them, and, even then, roll-over relief would probably ensure that no tax became payable. The partial provision approach was being supported in this way.

In response to the strong criticism, ED 19 was issued in May 1977. This proposed that, while deferred taxation should account for all short-term timing differences, other originating timing differences could be excluded if it could be shown that there was a reasonable probability that they would not reverse in the future. As a further move away from matching and the historical cost basis, ED 19 proposed that the liability method should be used to determine the appropriate tax rate.

SSAP 11 was withdrawn, and in October 1978 SSAP 15 was issued. It permitted either the deferral or the liability method and allowed the exclusion of timing differences that had a reasonable probability of continuing in the future. The demonstration of a reasonable probability of continuing requires that the going concern assumption is applicable and that there is evidence that no reversal of timing differences is likely in at least the next three years. Evidence could be provided by plans for asset purchases, producing new timing differences sufficient to cover any reversing differences up to the planning horizon of three years or more. In the case of revalued assets, the planned continued use or eligibility for roll-over relief would provide evidence. Any indication that, after the planning period of at least three years, the situation would change and liabilities crystallize is sufficient to reject the assumption that timing differences will continue. If only partial reversal of the timing differences is foreseeable, then it may be appropriate to provide only part of the full potential for deferred tax. This must be substantiated by calculations and assumptions explained in the financial statements.

The partial provision approach carries with it a danger. Circumstances can change so that the full potential can be seen to be reversing. A company whose lack of trading success leads them to cut back on fixed asset purchases may find that the added burden this causes in increasing deferred tax provisions may amplify any decline in their results.

A general change in circumstances was brought about by the Finance Act 1984. Not only did this eliminate stock relief, but, in conjunction with the progressive introduction of lower tax rates, it also reduced the timing advantages of capital allowances, bringing to an end 100 per cent first-year allowances for almost all assets (the only exception being plant and equipment for research and development). The effects may be usefully illustrated by the following worked example.

Worked example

Matchmakers Ltd have been formed to manufacture and market a range of products adopting a process that utilizes recently developed technology. Profits after depreciation but before tax for the foreseeable future are expected to be about £2 million per annum. Initial capital investment in machinery of £1 million is made in year 19–1. This machinery is expected to have a five-year life and will be depreciated on a straight-line basis over this life. The equipment will qualify for 100 per cent first-year capital allowances for tax purposes. In subsequent years, investment in similar equipment of about £0.5 million per year is anticipated.

If the corporation tax rate is 50 per cent, show the transfers to or from a deferred taxation account in respect of the initial investment for each year of the machinery's life
(a) on a full provision basis;
(b) on a partial provision basis.

(a) The originating timing difference arising from the excess of first-year capital allowance over that year's depreciation would reverse over the five-year life during which depreciation is charged. Applying the anticipated tax rate of 50 per cent gives the amounts to be entered in Matchmakers' accounts:

	19X1 £'000s	19X2 £'000s	19X3 £'000s	19X4 £'000s	19X5 £'000s	Total £'000s
Capital allowances	(1,000)					(1,000)
Depreciation charges	200	200	200	200	200	1,000
Timing differences	(800)	200	200	200	200	—
Debit (credit) to Deferred tax at 50% tax rates	(400)	100	100	100	100	—

(b) For the partial provision basis, timing difference reversals of £200,000 from the initial investment in the primary asset are reduced by the expected originating timing differences from subsequent years. Each year £500,000 capital allowances are to be available, and for the first five years of each asset's life £100,000 depreciation is charged. The initial provision is calculated by summing the tax impact of the reversals, taking into account only those that will relatively decrease net-of-tax profit (i.e. debit items)

	19X1 £'000s	19X2 £'000s	19X3 £'000s	19X4 £'000s	19X5 £'000s	Subsequent years £'000s
Timing differences on primary asset (as above)	(800)	200	200	200	200	—
Capital allowances on new items	—	(500)	(500)	(500)	(500)	(500)
Depreciation on new assets	—	100	200	300	400	500

	19X1	19X2	19X3	19X4	19X5	Subsequent years
	£'000s	£'000s	£'000s	£'000s	£'000s	£'000s
Expected reversals (debits only)	—	—	—	—	100	—
Debit to deferred tax at 50% rate					50	
Initial provision to deferred tax (=sum of debit to deferred tax)	(50)Cr					

A tax provision is made in the profit and loss account for 19X1 of £50,000 which will be used in 19X5, in addition to the charge on taxable profits.

Suppose it is announced in 19X2 that, for profits and capital expenditures in 19X2 and subsequent years, the corporation tax rate will fall to 40 per cent and first-year allowances to 25 per cent, with writing-down allowances of 25 per cent (straight-line) for subsequent years. Rework the calculations using
(a) the deferral method;
(b) the liability method.

   (a) Under the deferral method there will be no change in the earlier computations on the full provisions basis, since this method will apply the original tax rate to all entries relating directly to the primary asset. However, for the partial provision basis, it will be recognized during 19X2 that the offsetting effects of the subsequent asset purchases will have changed, owing to the reduction in capital allowances:

	19X1	19X2	19X3	19X4	19X5	Subsequent years
	£'000s	£'000s	£'000s	£'000s	£'000s	£'000s
Timing difference (on original asset)	(800)	200	200	200	200	—
Capital allowances on new items: 1st year		(125)	(125)	(125)	(125)	(125)
Writing-down allowances			(125)	(250)	(375)	(375)
Depreciation		100	200	300	400	500
Expected reversals		175	150	125	100	—
Debits to deferred tax at 50%		87.5	75	62.5	50	
Required provision (=sum of debits to deferred tax over foreseeable future)	(275)					

It can be seen that the partial provision of £50,000 calculated earlier, using 100 per cent allowances, would mean a £225,000 underprovision subsequent to the change in tax rules.

   (b) Since the liability method will take into account the reduction in tax rates accompanying the reduction in capital allowances, the impact of the change is diminished:

	19X1 £'000s	19X2 £'000s	19X3 £'000s	19X4 £'000s	19X5 £'000s
Expected reversals (as in (a) above)		175	150	125	100
Debits to deferred tax at 40%		70	60	50	40
Required provision	(220)				

Even here, the underprovision is over 300 per cent of the £50,000 provision made before new tax rules were known. Had a full provision under the liability method been made, the changes announced in 19X2 would have required a relatively small adjustment for an *overprovision*:

Timing difference on original asset	(800)	200	200	200	200
@ 50%	(400)				
@ 40%		80	80	80	80
Transfers to deferred tax		80	80	80	80
	(400)	+80 adjustment			

The adjustment represents only the direct effect of a change from 50 per cent of £800,000 to 40 per cent of £800,000.

8.2.5   The current position

Given that the standard in force at the time of the Finance Act 1984 advocated the partial provision approach, many companies found it necessary to substantially increase the deferred taxation provisions they had made. The size of these provisions was so large, in a number of instances, that inclusion of the additional provision would have had a very substantial effect on reported results. Companies could be expected to prefer to treat the adjustment as a prior-year item, arguing that it related to underprovision in earlier years. However, SSAP 6 indicates that, 'since a change in estimate arises from new information or developments, it should not be given retrospective effect by a restatement of prior years' (para. 16). The underprovision would appear to be exactly the type of change in estimate described. If the preparers of accounts had correctly anticipated the legislative change, there would have been no underprovision.

With prior-year treatment ruled out, a next preference might be treatment as an extraordinary item. Accounting for taxation is a perennial task, and changes in allowances and tax rates may not be considered to fall outside the normal commercial scope of business activity which would preclude utilization of the extraordinary classification. However, the problems of partial provision shown up by the Finance Act 1984 were taken on board by the Accounting Standards Committee, which set about revising SSAP 15.

Only two years earlier, Hope and Briggs had argued that the replacement of SSAP 11 by SSAP 15 in 1978 had been a political and social decision rather than one taken on purely technical grounds.[5] It should come as no surprise that a further revision of SSAP 15 was made and issued in May 1985. This offered the opportunity of treating the adjustment of the undeprovision as an extraordinary item, excluding it from ordinary profit: 'the effect of a change in the basis of taxation, or of a significant change in Government fiscal policy, should be treated as an extraordinary item where material' (para. 36).

The revised SSAP 15 also rejected the deferral method recommended in ED 11 in 1973, requiring only the liability method to be used. This is consistent with its adoption of a partial provision approach, representing a current estimate of the amount of tax payable or recoverable on the anticipated reversal of timing differences. The requirements for establishing which timing differences should be treated as reversing in a partial provision approach are less specific in the revised SSAP 15: the effects of timing differences should be included 'to the extent that it is probable that a liability or asset will crystallise' (para. 25). Some caution is added, requiring 'reasonable assumptions', ideally including financial plans, and a 'prudent view' responding to the level of uncertainty.

The original SSAP 15 was more specific in setting out a need for a horizon of at least three years with no foreseeable reversal, with no indication of subsequent change, and subject to the company being a going concern. However, the ASC did not include the words of caution in the revised SSAP 15 but instead indicated that what can be foreseen may be assumed to continue indefinitely, permitting appropriate elimination of provisions.

In the profit and loss account, in addition to deferred tax on ordinary activities, that relating to extraordinary items must be disclosed separately as part of the extraordinary items. In a recent survey of 300 companies, it was found that 22 per cent of companies provided in full for deferred taxation (the proportion being higher among large unlisted companies than among those listed). Some 13 per cent made no provision at all, and a further 14 per cent (28 per cent among large listed companies) provided for less than a fifth of the full potential.

Although a partial provisions approach is to be adopted in the preparation of accounts, disclosure, by way of note, of any unprovided deferred tax is required. This should include not only the position at the balance sheet date, but also movements in the accounting period; and both profit and loss and balance sheet notes should provide analysis into major components. These disclosures meet the need to report contingent liabilities.

Additionally, if the value of any asset is shown as a note, the tax implications of realization at that value should be given. This is an aspect of deferred tax arising from revaluation which receives further explicit attention in the 1985 standard. Roll-over relief may mean that, although the gain represented by a revaluation may be realized on the sale of the asset, because that asset is replaced by another on disposal at prices comparable to the revalued amount, no tax liability might arise and there would be no need to account for deferred tax given that a partial provisions approach was being followed.

The Companies Act 1985 includes a requirement for tax effects accounted for in relation to a revaluation reserve to be disclosed (4 sch. 34(4)); if there is no accounting for these tax effects, it would seem that there would not need to be any disclosure. The standard also suggests that no timing difference exists in this case of revaluation, but it does require that it should be stated in a note to the balance sheet that tax has not been quantified in relation to the revaluation(s).

It is of particular interest to note that the SSAP reveals that the ASC has sought legal advice indicating that 'unprovided deferred tax is a contingent liability except where the prospect of it becoming payable is so remote that it does not amount to a liability at all'. This would seem to justify a failure to quantify the deferred tax on revaluation, covered by roll-over relief so that the Companies Act was being complied with.

A further interpretation which may be put on this explanation is that any liability would be so far in the future that its value (perhaps on the basis of a discounted present value) is approximately zero. This would have provided some theoretical basis in support of the partial provision approach.

Prudence is also in evidence in the treatment of debit balances, requiring recovery to be 'assured beyond reasonable doubt', normally in the succeeding period, without being replaced by equivalent debit balances.

8.3 Other financial exchanges with government

In addition to statements relating to corporation tax, the ASC has issued two other standards that consider accounting for exchanges between companies and government. SSAP 4 considers the accounting treatment of government grants, and SSAP 5 deals with accounting for value added tax. Since, in addition to all the forms of exchange mentioned, companies collect income tax and national insurance contributions from employees, the exchanges with government represent a considerable part of the activities of companies. The production of a statement showing the cash exchanges with government would combine a variety of activities and might provide information of interest. 'The Corporate Report' recommended that such a statement be produced by companies.[7] However, very few UK companies have followed up this recommendation.[8]

8.3.1 The accounting treatment of government grants

Grants that relate to revenue expenditure, such as employment subsidies, do not create accounting problems, since matching clearly indicates that they should be included in the same period in which the revenue is reported. It may be necessary to estimate the amount of grant receivable when it is not known at the time of reporting.

When considering matching in relation to capital grants, a method that credits the grant to revenue over the useful life of the asset is required to match the amortization of the corresponding capital expenditure over its useful life. SSAP 4 accepts both the principal treatments that achieve this, i.e. either reducing the cost of the acquisition of the fixed asset by the amount of the grant, or treating the amount of the grant as a deferred credit, amortizing it over the estimated useful life of the asset. Acceptance of the former method contrasts with the rejection of showing the deferred tax balance as a reduction in the amount at which assets are reported. If a deferred credit is employed, this should be separately disclosed but not included as part of shareholders' funds.

8.3.2 Accounting for value added tax

The only significant accounting considerations arising from value added tax (VAT) concern the inclusion or exclusion of the tax from reported amounts. The relevant standard, SSAP 5, establishes uniformity with two requirements. The first is that turnover, shown in the profit and loss account, should exclude VAT on taxable outputs, although there is no restriction on disclosing turnover gross of VAT in addition to the required net amount. The other requirement is for irrecoverable VAT to be included in the cost of fixed assets or other items disclosed separately.

Notes

1. Companies Act 1985 (4 sch. 54).
2. SSAP 8, 'The Treatment of Taxation under the Imputation System in the Accounts of Companies', ASC, para. 14.
3. These categories are identified in SSAP 15, 'Accounting for Deferred Taxation', ASC, para. 6.
4. Technical and Research Committee, ICAEW, 'Accounting for stock relief: interim guidance', *Accountancy*, February 1981, pp. 108–9.
5. A. J. B. Hope and J. Briggs, 'Accounting policy-making—some lessons from the deferred taxation debate', *Accounting and Business Research*, Spring 1982, pp. 83–96.
6. D. J. Tonkin and L. I. Watson, 'Survey tables', in L. C. L. Skerratt and D. J. Tonkin (eds), *Financial Reporting 1986–87: A Survey of UK Published Accounts*, ICAEW, 1987.

7. 'The Corporate Report', a discussion paper published for comment by the Accounting Standards Steering Committee, July 1975, paras. 6.22–6.25.
8. See L. C. L. Skerratt and D. J. Tonkin (eds), *Financial Reporting 1982–83: A Survey of UK Published Accounts*, ICAEW, 1982. Out of 300 companies included in the survey, only 4 produced a statement of money exchanges with government. In later surveys in this series this statistic was not even considered worth providing.

Further reading

Munson, R. J., 'Deferred taxation', in L. C. L. Skerratt and D. J. Tonkin (eds), *Financial Reporting 1985–86: A Survey of UK Published Accounts*, ICAEW, 1986.
Nobes, C. W., 'Harmonisation of corporate accounting and taxation in the EEC', *Certified Accountant*, August 1978.
Watson, P. L., 'Accounting for deferred tax on depreciable assets', *Accounting and Business Research*, Autumn 1980.
Wolk, H. I. and M. G. Tearney, 'Discounting deferred tax liabilities: review and analysis', *Journal of Business Finance and Accounting*, Spring 1980.

Questions

1. With regard to SSAP 15, *Accounting for Deferred Taxation:*
   (a) Under what circumstances may a company assume that timing differences will not reverse and how might the existence of these circumstances be substantiated?   (8 marks)
   (b) What additional information must be disclosed in a note to the accounts with regard to deferred taxation?   (4 marks)
   (c) Comment on the possible justification for a note such as that in (b) above.   (8 marks)
                                                                                    (20 marks)
                                                                    ACCA, 2.8, RFA, December 1986
2. C-Fit Fuels Ltd have been formed to make and sell a new product, Superpower, which is expected to produce after-tax profits of one million pounds per annum for the foreseeable future. The operations require capital outlay in the first year of operations for the purchase of a processing machine at a price of £800,000 and outlays of £360,000 for auxiliary machines in each subsequent year. Each item of equipment is assumed to have a four-year life and will be depreciated using the straight-line method. Assume that 100% first-year capital allowances continue to be available.

   You are required to:
   (a) show in respect of the initial investment the transfer to or from a deferred taxation account for each year of the machine's life, given that the corporation tax rate is 50%, using
      (i) a full provisions basis
      (ii) a partial provisions basis; and
   (b) show how you would have to adjust your calculations under the liability method if the tax rate was reduced to 40% immediately after the first year of operations.   **(11 marks)**
3. How should you treat the following items when preparing financial statements in accordance with statements of standard accounting practice:
   (i)   franked investment income?   (3 marks)
   (ii)   proposed dividends and the related advance corporation tax?   (2 marks)
   (iii) recoverable advance corporation tax?   (2 marks)
   (iv)   irrecoverable advance corporation tax?   (2 marks)
   (v)   value added output tax on turnover for a VAT registered trader?   (2 marks)
   (vi)   irrecoverable value added input tax on a fixed asset, purchased
          by a VAT registered trader?   (2 marks)
   (vii) the receipt and payment of VAT to the Customs and Excise?   (2 marks)
                                                                                    (15 marks)
                                                                    ACCA, 2.8, RFA, December 1985

4. The 1985 revision of SSAP 15; *Accounting for deferred tax*, has made some changes in the criteria for making the relevant provisions in company accounts.

   Required:

   (a) Discuss the new criteria for determining the amount of the charge or credit for deferred tax in the profit and loss account, and that of the provision for it in the balance sheet.

   (15 marks)

   (b) Comment on the problems which SSAP 15 poses for the company accountant.

   (10 marks)

   (25 marks)

   ACCA, 3.1, AFA, December 1986

5. The following information is given in respect of Maharaja plc:

   (a) Fixed assets consist entirely of plant and machinery. The net book value of these assets as at 30 June 19–8 is £100,000 in excess of their tax written-down value.

   (b) The deferred tax provision (all relating to fixed asset timing differences) as at 30 June 19–7 was £21,000.

   (c) The company's capital expenditure forecasts indicate that capital allowances and depreciation in future years will be:

Year ended 30 June	Capital allowances	Depreciation
£	£	£
19–9	12,000	53,000
19–10	14,000	49,000
19–11	20,000	36,000
19–12	40,000	32,000
19–13	44,000	32,000
19–14	46,000	36,000

   From the year ended 30 June 19–15 onwards, capital allowances are likely to continue to be in excess of depreciation for the foreseeable future.

   (d) Corporation tax is to be taken as 35% for all years.

   You are required to:

   (a) Calculate the deferred tax charges or credits for the next seven years, commencing with the year ended 30 June 19–8, on the basis that the pattern of capital allowances and depreciation is as forecast.   (7 marks)

   (b) Calculate the deferred tax liability or asset at the end of each of the seven years.

   (4 marks)

   (c) Show how the deferred tax figures calculated in (a) and (b) would change if the net book value of the assets was only £70,000 in excess of their tax written down value as at 30 June 19–8. (10 marks)

   (21 marks)

   The authors wish to acknowledge Mr G. Loveday of Chart Foulks Lynch for providing this question.

9. Investment in other companies

9.1 Definitions

Modern business practice involves a considerable amount of inter-company investment. This can mean, at one extreme, a company with funds available deciding to purchase a few shares in another company, simply because it sees it as a profitable short-term use of funds. At the other extreme, it can mean a merger or takeover where the majority, possibly 100 per cent, of a company's shares are purchased, with the result that control of that company is obtained by the investing company. It is also quite common for a company to create a wholly owned subsidiary for some specific purpose, such as for the operation of its transport activities.

The accountant is therefore seldom called upon to prepare financial statements in which the question of ascertaining the value of an investment in another company does not arise. There are two sets of accounting problems that arise when a firm invests in other companies:

(a) the accounting entries to be made at the time of the investment, i.e. at the time of the acquisition of the shares;

(b) the accounting entries to be made at any time following the purchase of the shares, involving dividend payments, inter-company sales, indirect shareholdings and consolidation of assets.

This chapter begins by distinguishing between three classes of investment in other companies: investments in subsidiary companies, investments in associated/related companies, and what are referred to as 'other investments'. This distinction is important, as the accounting entries relating to investing in other companies depends on the classification of the investment. As companies grow, the group and financial structures can become more and more complex, and the accounting issues more involved.

A shareholder of a company needs to know where the company is making investments, whether it is in physical assets such as machinery or in financial assets such as shares of another company. The Companies Act 1985 requires a larger amount of information to be disclosed as the percentage of shares held in another company increases. The case requiring the least disclosure is that of a small shareholding in an unlisted company; the next level of disclosure is for a small shareholding in a listed company; we then move to shareholdings of more than 10 per cent, more than 20 per cent, to related or associated companies, and finally to subsidiaries.

Group accounts need to be prepared if a company owns one or more subsidiaries. The Act states that one company is deemed to be the subsidiary of another if (but only if)

(a) that other either

    (i) is a member of it and controls the composition of its board of directors, or

    (ii) holds more than half the nominal value of its equity share capital; or

(b) the first mentioned company is a subsidiary of any company which is that other's subsidiary. This definition is based on the concept of legally effective control, either through shareholding, or through control of the board of directors. This is referred to as the *de jure* approach, and it has been the basis of group accounting in the UK and the USA. In contrast, the definition of a subsidiary in West Germany and most other EEC countries is based on the concept of economic control, on the existence of a unified management which can influence the decisions made in a group of companies. The West German approach has had an influence on the wording in the EEC 7th Directive on Group Accounts, which will affect future UK legislation on the subject.

Group accounts mean that, although a shareholder owns shares in an individual company which is a holding company, when the accounts are prepared not only will the financial position of the individual company be reported, but so also will the aggregate financial position of all the companies legally controlled by the holding company. This is achieved by consolidating the assets and liabilities of the companies in the group.

The first part of this chapter is concerned with definitions and the classification of the investment, and also with the disclosure required in the financial accounts relating to such investments. Section 9.5 deals with the accounting entries to be made both at the time of the purchase of the shares and the recording of subsequent transactions. Chapter 10 covers the accounting position when subsidiary companies are acquired and when businesses are combined, and Chapter 11 deals with the preparation of group accounts.

It must be remembered that group accounts are normally required by law when an investing company owns subsidiaries. In such situations there are two sets of accounts to consider: the one being the accounts showing the state of affairs of the group, and the other the investing company's own accounts, that is, the accounts of the holding company, the parent company. Group accounts are not necessary when the investing company owns shares only in other companies that have associate/related status, i.e. where no subsidiary companies are involved.

It should be appreciated that the accounting entries relating to an investment in another company can affect the apparent performance of the acquiring company, not only during the year in which the investment is made but also in subsequent years. Such entries are therefore of considerable importance. Unfortunately, there is no single method of presenting an interest in another company in financial statements that is agreed upon as appropriate for all situations. Different accounting standards have had to be introduced to deal with the principles to be followed in different situations. For example, the presentation to be made when only a small proportion of shares of a company are purchased needs to be different from the presentation when, say, 30 per cent of the shares of a company are puchased. Again, a different presentation is necessary when a majority of the shares of a company are acquired. The important factor in deciding on the presentaton appropriate to the situation is the degree of control, the degree of influence, which the one company has over the decisions of the other company. The holding company is a legal entity. Accounting attempts to give the user information on all the assets and liabilities controlled by the entity from a legal point of view.

The reason why it is considered important to be able to classify investments in other companies is that the very nature of the investment can vary according to the degree of control. An inter-company transaction between an investing company and its associate companies can be different from that between a parent company and its subsidiary. For example, an investing company is thought to have no significant influence over the dividend decisions of a company classed as an 'other investment'; but it is thought to have some influence over the dividend decisions of an associate company, and could therefore influence the dividend that is paid by the associate company to itself. A parent company, clearly, controls not only the dividend decisions of a subsidiary company, but also all decisions relating to assets and liabilities. The nature of an investment in a subsidiary company is not so much an investment in shares, a monetary asset, as an investment in the real assets. Of course there are exceptions to this latter point, for example an investment in an overseas subsidiary in a country where there are restrictions on the movement of funds. This question will be returned to later.

In many ways it would be convenient if it were possible to classify an investment in another company on the basis of the percentage ownership of the shares. For example, owning 1 per cent of the shares would imply no influence over the decision of the company; 25 per cent would imply some influence but not control; 51 per cent would clearly imply control. If less than 20 per cent of the shares were owned, the holding could be regarded as a trade investment; if between 20 and 50 per cent of the shares were owned, it could be classed as an associate company, and over 50 per cent would imply subsidiary company status. Unfortunately, classifications based on percentages, although having an appealing simplicity, can lead to situations where the resulting accounts do not give a true and fair view. The percentage approach requires break-points, and, as with most areas of accounting, such arbitrary boundaries have been found in certain cases to be unsatisfactory. The UK is having to move away from a simple percentage definition of control.

9.2 Subsidiary companies

The practice of preparing group accounts was established in law in the UK and Northern Ireland by the Companies Act 1948, although several companies in the UK and elsewhere were producing such accounts very much earlier. Group accounts are therefore a familiar feature of financial reporting. Consolidated accounts are one form of group accounts. SSAP 14, issued in September 1978, required group accounts to be presented as consolidated accounts except in certain specific circumstances. 'It is generally accepted that consolidated financial statements are usually the best means of achieving the objective of group accounts which is to give a true and fair view of the profit or loss and the state of affairs of the group.'

There are therefore both statutory requirements and accounting standards concerning the preparation of group accounts and the disclosure of subsidiaries. The Companies Act 1985 requires certain particulars normally to be disclosed; these include the name of the subsidiary, the country in which it is incorporated and registered, and the proportion of the nominal value of the issued shares held by the investing company either directly or through another subsidiary

The balance sheet formats detailed in Schedule 4 to the Act specify the place where the aggregate amounts should be shown of any amounts owed to and from, and any interests in, any holding company, any subsidiary or any fellow subsidiary. Because amounts owed by and to group companies have to be shown in different positions in the formats, it is not acceptable for companies to net these balances off and to disclose the net balance in the balance sheet as 'Investment in subsidiaries'. This applies even where a note to the financial statements gives additional information that explains the net balance.

In addition, the Stock Exchange's Continuing Obligations and the USM's General Undertaking require listed companies and also companies that are traded on the USM to analyse amounts due to subsidiary companies on the basis of period until repayment. Group accounts need not be prepared if the holding company is itself, at the end of the financial year, a wholly owned subsidiary of another company incorporated in Great Britain.

Normally, a company that has invested in subsidiary companies needs to prepare group accounts. The Companies Act 1985 does however recognize situations in which the accounts of a particular subsidiary can be excluded. These occur, according to the Act, either when it is impracticable to do so, when it would be of no real value to shareholders to do so, when it would involve undue expense or delay, when it would be misleading or harmful to do so, or when the businesses of the companies concerned are so different that they cannot reasonably be treated as a single undertaking. If any subsidiaries' accounts are excluded from the group accounts, certain information nevertheless needs to be provided by way of statement. This information includes the reason for omission from the group accounts and the net aggregate amounts of any profits or losses attributable to the group.

The relevant accounting standard, SSAP 14, reduces the choice. The standard states that group accounts must be presented as consolidated statements except in certain specific circumstances. A subsidiary should be excluded from consolidation if

(a) its activities are so dissimilar from those of other companies within the group that consolidated financial statements would be misleading and that information for the holding company's shareholders and other users of the statements would be better provided by presenting separate financial statements for such a subsidiary; or

(b) the holding company, although owning directly or through other subsidiaries more than half the equity share capital of the subsidiary, either
  (i) does not own share capital carrying more than half the votes, or
  (ii) has contractual or other restrictions imposed on its ability to appoint the majority of the board of directors; or

(c) the subsidiary operates under severe restrictions which significantly impair control by the holding company over the subsidiary's assets and operations for the foreseeable future; or

(d) control is intended to be temporary.

Where a subsidiary is excluded from consolidation on the grounds of dissimilar activities, the group accounts should include separate financial statements for that subsidiary. They may be combined with the financial statements of other subsidiaries with similar operations, if appropriate.

The standard, apart from limiting the circumstances when exclusion is possible, requires consideration to be given to whether the resulting consolidated accounts, excluding a subsidiary, does in fact present a true and fair view.

The 1986 and 1987 financial accounts of a number of well-known companies revealed that neither the Act nor the standard was working satisfactorily. Companies were setting up new businesses which they effectively controlled but which did not come under the legal definition of a subsidiary. They were doing this to avoid the need to consolidate the accounts of what became known as 'controlled non-subsidiaries'. These 'non-subsidiaries' are discussed further in Chapter 16. The issue of principle involved is that, although the non-consolidation is allowed according to the law, it results in accounts that do not give a true and fair view of the state of affairs of the business. Which should take precedence, the legal position or the accounting concept of 'truth and fairness'?

The Accounting Standards Committee issued an exposure draft in 1988 on the subject of accounting for special-purpose transactions. One of the major issues discussed in this draft is controlled non-subsidiaries. If the proposals contained in the draft are accepted and the resulting standard is complied with, then the financial implications of these non-subsidiaries will be disclosed to users of the accounts. The UK Companies Act will need to change by 1990 to take in the requirements of the EEC 7th Directive. This should dramatically reduce the opportunity to exclude certain types of subsidiary from the consolidated accounts. The problem of non-consolidation of subsidiaries and controlled non-subsidiaries is discussed further in Chapter 11.

9.3 Other companies

A company might purchase shares for a variety of reasons. It might wish to exercise control over the other company or at last to exert influence on the decisions taken by the other company. If this is the reason, and if it intends to use its influence or control on a long-term basis, the investment is classed as being either a related, associated or subsidiary company.

On the other hand, a company may at a certain time have cash available and wish to earn a good return on that cash. One way to do this is to buy shares in another company, listed or otherwise. The investing company may even trade with the 'other' company, either buying goods from it or selling goods to it, and it may wish to own some shares in that company not to influence decisions but to show confidence in the company.

The Companies Act 1985 gives details of the disclosure required relating to the holding of shares in 'listed' or 'unlisted' companies. Certain information needs to be disclosed relating to all investment, whether it is 1 or 100 per cent of a company's shares that are held. The aggregate amount of the invesments at both the beginning and the end of the year must be disclosed, together with the amount of any acquisitions and any disposals during the year. For certain categories of investment further information is required. With regard to listed investments, the notes must disclose:

(a) the amount that relates to listed investments;
(b) the amount in (a) split between the investments listed on a recognized stock exchange and any other listed investments;
(c) the aggregate market value of listed investments, where it differs from the amount at which they are stated in the balance sheet;
(d) both the stock exchange value and the market value of any listed investments, where the latter value is taken as being higher than their stock exchange value. This disclosure is required because the market value and the stock exchange value may differ according to the size of the investment and its marketability.

'Listed investments' means an investment listed on a 'recognized' stock exchange or any other reputable stock exchange outside the UK. There is no definition of what is a reputable exchange. The only recognized exchange in the UK is 'the' Stock Exchange. For this purpose, the USM in London is not recognized, and so shares held in companies quoted on that market are unlisted. For unlisted investments, the information that needs to be shown is the aggregate amounts with movements during the year.

9.3.1 Shareholdings exceeding 10 per cent

Where a company holds shares of any class of equity capital in another company amounting to more than 10 per cent of the nominal value of all the issued shares, then further information is required to be disclosed. The notes must disclose:

(a) the name of the corporate body;
(b) its country of registration;
(c) its country of incorporation, where it is incorporated outside Great Britain;
(d) the identity of each class of shares the investing company holds;
(e) the proportion of the nominal value of the allotted shares of each class that the investing company holds.

There are situations where it is possible to disclose less information—for example where the directors believe that such disclosure would be harmful, and the Secretary of State agrees. A further case is where a company has a large number of such investments and the information normally to be disclosed would be excessively lengthy. In such a case, it is possible to disclose only the information that principally affects the company's profit performance and the amount of its assets.

9.3.2 Shareholdings exceeding 20 per cent

Where a company owns more than 20 per cent of the nominal value of the allotted shares of another company, information in addition to that required with a 10 per cent holding needs to be disclosed—that is, if it is material. This information covers the aggregate amount of the capital and the reserves and the profit or loss of the other company, taken from the most recent set of accounts. However, this information need not be given if the investment is accounted for in the holding company's financial statements according to the equity method.

The Stock Exchange's continuing obligations and the USM rules require that, when an equity holding in another company exceeds 20 per cent, and if it is not a subsidiary, that information must be given with respect to that company's principal country of operation, particulars of its issued capital and debt securities, and the percentage held. The USM also requires that, unless the interest in the other company is dealt with by consolidation, details of the other company's reserves must be disclosed. If the number of such investments by a listed company is large, then only details for the more material investments need be disclosed.

9.3.3 'Other investments'

The Companies Act 1985 also refers to the disclosure of 'other investments'. This covers investments in life assurance policies and partnerships as well as small holdings of shares. Even bank deposits and building society deposits can be classed as 'other investments', although it is more usual to regard these as 'cash at bank and in hand'.

'Other investments' can in some cases and in some situations be of a longer-term nature and so may be classed as a 'fixed asset', although it is more common for them to be regarded as a 'current asset'.

9.4   Related and associated companies

One special class of investment is referred to in the Companies Act 1985 as a 'related company', and in the accounting standard on the subject as an 'associated company'. An associated company is not always a related company, and vice versa, although in practice, in the vast majority of cases, if the company meets the one definition it meets the other.

Strictly, it is the term 'related company' that should be used in the financial statements, and a reference to the fact that the related company is an associated company should be made where appropriate. In practice, many companies use only the term 'associated company' in their financial statements. The Department of Trade and Industry (DTI) does not object to the use of this term.

The first accounting standard in the UK, SSAP 1, 'Accounting for Associated Companies', which was published in 1971, attempted to introduce a uniform treatment for the recording of investments in companies that were not subsidiaries. The standard met with a certain amount of opposition, and in 1982 was revised. SSAP 1 as revised defines an 'associated company' as

A company not being a subsidiary of the investing group or company in which:
(a) the interest of the investing group or company is effectively that of a partner in a joint venture or consortium and the investing group or company is in a position to exercise a significant influence over the company in which the investment is made; or
(b) *the interest* of the investing group or company is for the *long-term* and is *substantial* and, having regard to the disposition of the other shareholdings, the investing group or company is in a position to *exercise a significant influence* over the company in which the investment is made.

The revised definition is based not so much on the percentage holding as on significant influence. An associate company is defined as a company, not a subsidiary, in which the investing company or group is in a position to exercise a significant influence. In other words, in order to meet the definition, the percentage of shares owned by the investing group must be large enough to allow it to significantly influence the policies of the investee company.

It is the financial and operating policy decisions that constitute the areas where the influence of the investing group must be demonstrated. Significant influence does not mean having enough votes to have a power of veto: it means having enough influence to allow a meaningful participation in the policy decisions. Representation on the board of directors is indicative of such participation, but it is not a sufficient condition to indicate participation. After all, one director can be a paper tiger. Other evidence of participation is necessary.

How large the percentage holding has to be for the investing company to have a significant influence is a question of fact. If the investing company owns 15 per cent of the shares and there is one other shareholder in the joint venture owning the remaining 85 per cent of the shares, then the fact would suggest that the influence was not significant. On the othe hand, if the investing company owns 15 per cent of the shares and there are hundreds of other shareholders, each owning less than 1 per cent of the shares, the fact would suggest that the investing company did have a significant influence. However, both cases would need to be looked at for evidence of influence, for the percentage ownership figures cannot be relied upon.

The definition of an associated company given above is based on a 'qualitative' criteria. It does not state a pecentage holding above which a company is an associate and below which it is not. Such a clear dividing line would give an opportunity for creative accountants. The investing company could sell or buy shares to get just below or above the limit, at or near the end of the accounting period, to achieve the status required. The difference in status is important, because as an associated company the equity method of accounting has to be followed as opposed to the cost method.

The standard does not depart completely from a percentage guideline. It indicates that the 'quantitative' criteria can be used to give guidance as to the status of the shareholding. A holding of 20 per cent or more of the equity voting rights of a company leads to a presumption that it is an associated company; a holding of less than 20 per cent leads to the presumption that it is not an associated company—that is, unless evidence to the contrary can be demonstrated and the investing company and the so-called associate company agree that significant influence does exist. The SSAP definition is therefore a 'qualitative' criteria.

The definition is similar to that used in the International Standard on the subject, IAS 3, and to the appropriate US standard, APB 18. It differs from the first version of SSAP 1, which kept more closely to the percentage definition of an associate company.

The Companies Act 1985 refers to 'related companies'; these are not quite the same as associated companies as discussed in the standard. A 'related company' is defined as

> Any body corporate (other than one which is a group company in relation to that company) in which that company holds on a *long-term basis* a *qualifying capital interest* for the purpose of securing a contribution to that company's own activities by the *exercise of any control or influence* arising from that interest.

A 'qualifying capital interest' is an interest in a class of the equity share capital of that body corporate that *carries rights to vote in all circumstaces at general meetings* of that body corporate. Unless the contrary can be shown, a body corporate will be presumed to be a related company if the investing company has a qualifying capital interest of 20 per cent or more in that body corporate.

The definition of a related company is in most respects wider than that of an associated company, although it is possible for an associated company not to be a related company. For example, if a company has a substantial interest in an associated company, but that interest does *not carry rights to vote in all circumstances at general meetings*, then that associated company is not a related company.

The definitions of 'related company' and 'associated company' contain several points of difference. For instance, under SSAP 1, where the investing company's interest is not that of a partner, for it to be an associate company that interest has to be substantial. In contrast, it is sufficient, for the purposes of the definition of 'related company', that the investing company has an interest in those equity shares that carry voting rights 'for the purpose of securing a contribution to that company's own activities by the exercise of any control or influence arising from that interest'.

The aggregate of parent company and subsidiary company holding is defined as follows.

Where different companies in a group hold shares in a company, for the purposes of establishing whether or not significant influence is presumed to exist, the invesment of that company should be taken as the aggregate of the holdings of the investing company together with those of its subsidiaries but not its associates.

This is an important point, as it means that, even though an investing company, call it Lowerline Ltd, may only own, say, 10 per cent of the shares of a company named Decatur Ltd, it could well be that it needs to regard Decatur as an associated company. If a subsidiary of Lowerline owns, say, 12 per cent of the shares of Decatur, then it might be presumed that the group has a significant influence over the company.

One question that still needs to be considered is whether the relevant pecentage is the total holding of the group, or the adjusted holding after allowing for minority interests. If, in the above example, the subsidiary owns 12 per cent of the shares of Decatur but the parent company, Lowerline, owns only 60 per cent of the shares of the subsidiary, then it could be argued that the group owns or controls less than the 20 per cent of Decatur at which significant influence is presumed: it owns the 10 plus 60 per cent of the 12 per cent (i.e. 17.2 per cent altogether). Nevertheless, significant influence could well still exist.

Another difficult situation that could arise is where the parent company, Lowerline, owns no shares itself in another company, let us say once again Decatur, but has to regard this company as an associate company within the group. This arises when the subsidiary companies of Lowerline, looked at together own a sufficient number of shares in Decatur for the group to be presumed to have a significant influence. Then, even though the parent company owns no such shares, Decatur becomes an associate company.

A minimum level of disclosure is sometimes permitted even when the investing company owns more than 20 per cent of another company. One such situation is where a parent company owns more than 50 per cent of another company but is permitted not to consolidate, because to do so would mislead. The activities of the second company have little in common with those of the parent, and it could give the wrong impression if one set of assets were simply added to the other set. In such a situation the investment would be treated in the group accounts as an 'other' investment. Similarly, an associated company may be so different from the investing company that to add respective earnings figures together would mislead.

Immateriality is another reason that has been used to avoid associate or subsidiary company accounting. If associate or subsidiary treatment were avoided, then such holdings would be entered in the accounts as if they were 'other' investments, but the fact that this has been done must be drawn to shareholders' attention, together with the reasons for so doing.

9.4.1 Information to be disclosed

Information about related companies additional to that required for 'other company' investments needs to be disclosed in an investing company's financial statements. 'Shares in related companies' and 'Loans to related companies' appear as separate subheadings under the fixed asset main heading of 'Investments', in the balance sheet. Also, the balance sheet requires the disclosure of 'Amounts owed by related companies' under the current asset main heading of 'Debtors', and the disclosure of 'Amounts owed to related companies' under the liabilities main heading of 'Creditors'. In addition, amounts owed by and to related companies that are due for payment within one year must be shown separately from amounts due after one year. These requirements of the formats effectively prohibit companies from showing investments in associated companies as one figure, including the cost of the shares in the associates and loans to them, and after deducting loans from them.

It is necessary to show the division of the accumulated reserves of the group between profits retained by the group and profits retained by associated companies. If any profits retained overseas are subject to further taxation when they are distributed to the investing company, this must be drawn to shareholders' attention, along with any problems of repatriating profits arising from statutory, contractual or exchange control regulations. Clearly, it is important for shareholders of the investing company to know whether or not any of the net assets of the group are in fact tied up in a country and not likely to be available in the UK, should they be needed.

When an investing company does not need to prepare group accounts, it must disclose its share of the annual earnings of an associate company, and also the balance sheet information relating to its associate, by way of a note in its accounts or by preparing a separate balance sheet. This is clearly necessary, otherwise the shareholders of such an investing company would be ill-informed about the activities of any associate companies.

In a situation where an investing company or group holds 20 per cent or more of the equity voting rights of a company, and does not treat that company as an associate or subsidiary, details of the accounting treatment that has been followed should be shown as a note, together with the reasons why this 'unusual' practice has been adopted. Similarly, an investing company that owns less than 20 per cent of the equity voting rights of a company and nevetheless treats that company as an associate has to disclose the basis on which the significant influence is exercised.

9.4.2 Worked example: related companies

The above discussion relates to the classification of investments in other companies and the information that needs to be disclosed. A worked example will help to demonstrate the points involved.

The following question is adapted from an ICAEW question set in the Financial Accounting II paper in July 1984. In no way is the solution given below an official answer.

Question

Alderbrook plc is the listed parent company of a group engaged mainly in the engineering industry. At 31 December 1987 its share investments were:

	Holding	Cost	Market value	Directors valuation
	%	£000s	£000s	£000s
Alderbrook Manufacturing	100	3	—	53
Barston Grinding plc	45	47	96	—
Barston Jobbing Ltd	24	18	—	18
Barston Property plc	1	6	7	—
10% Treasury stock		150	152	—
Selly Oak Enterprises Ltd	2	2	—	100
Edgbaston Engineering Ltd	12	10	—	40

The following additional information is given.
(a) Barston Grinding is a listed company. There are no other holders of more than 5 per cent of the issued capital. Alderbrook plc has three nominees on the seven-man board of directors and has a significant interest in the day-to-day management. Shares purchased on 1 January 1987.
(b) With Barston Jobbing the shares are not listed, and the remainder of the shares are held by one other public company which effectively controls the company.
(c) Barston Property plc has a full listing, as has the Treasury stock.

(d) The profit and loss accounts for the year ended 31 December 1987 of Barston Grinding and Barston Jobbing are:

	Barston Grinding £'000s	Barston Jobbing £'000s
Profit for the year	33	76
Dividends	8	26
	25	50
Retained profit brought forward	96	124
Retained profit carried forward	121	174
Excess of cost of shares over net assets acquired	13	10

(e) With the exception of the Treasury stock, all holdings are of ordinary shares and there are no other classes of capital.

(f) The net assets of Barston Grinding plc as at 31 December 1986 were £200,000. There were no revaluations during 1987.

Required

Show the Balance Sheet figures and the notes relating to these investments as they would appear in the accounts of Alderbrook plc for the year ending 31 December 1987.

Solution

Barston Jobbing will not be treated as a related company, as Alderbrook has no influence over its activities and it cannot be said to be able to influence dividend decisions, or the use of its share of retained earnings.

Extracts from notes to the accounts

1. *Holding company accounts: investments in subsidiary companies in balance sheet*

	£'000s
Shares at cost	3

2. *Group accounts: other investments in balance sheet*

	1/1/87 £'000s	Share of retained profit £'000s	31/12/87 £'000s
Related companies (listed)	47	11	58
Related companies (unlisted)	—	—	—
Listed securities	156	—	156
Other investments	30	—	30

The interest in related companies are valued on the equity basis. The remaining other investments are held at cost.

The shares in the related company are listed on the Stock Exchange and as at 31 December 1987 have a market value of £96,000. The listed securities have an aggregate market value of £159,000.

3. *Particulars of investments*   *Proportion of ordinary*
                                            shares held

Subsidiary company
   Alderbrook Manufacturing   100%
Related company
   Barston Grinding plc   45%

Other investments The following investments represent more than 10 per cent of the equity share capital of the relevant company.

                                            Proportion of ordinary
                                            shares held

Barston Jobbing Ltd   24%
Edgbaston Engineering Ltd   12%

The investment in Barston Jobbing is stated at cost. It has not been treated as a related company since the group does not exercise any influence over it. Its aggregate reserves as at 31 December 1987 were £174,000, and its profit for the 1987 financial year was £76,000.

9.5 Equity accounting

SSAP 1 requires associated companies to be accounted for using the equity method. It is necessary to distinguish the equity method from the cost method. This distinction can also be important when accounting for interests in subsidiary companies.

There are two possible ways of recording an investment in the accounts of an investing company. With the equity approach, the initial investment is recorded in the balance sheet at the cost of purchase, and each year this figure is adjusted to reflect the investing company's share of the post-acquisition retained profits or losses of the company whose shares have been purchased. The value of the investment in the balance sheet is intended to reflect the share of the total equity of the associate or subsidiary company. It is the share of the annual profits or losses of the associate that is taken to the investing company's profit and loss account. With the cost method at the date of acquisition, the investment is again recorded at total purchase cost, but this value is not adjusted up or down each year to reflect the share in the associated or subsidiary's retained profits or losses. Only dividends paid by the associate or subsidiary to the investing company are taken to the profit and loss account. Associate or subsidiary company profits are not recorded by the investing company; only dividends paid or to be paid are so recorded.

The entries in the books of the investing company will illustrate the difference. The following example is based on transactions between an investing company and its associate. It is equally relevant to transactions between a parent company and its subsidiary.

	Cost method		Equity method	
Initial entry				
		£		£
1/1/88				
40% of A Ltd shares are purchased for £100,000	Dr Investment in associate	100,000	Dr Investment in associate	100,000
	Cr Cash	100,000	Cr Cash	100,000
Subsequent entries				
31/12/88				
A Ltd reports profits for the year of £10,000	No entry		Dr Investment in associate	4,000
			Cr Earnings of associate	4,000
31/12/88				
A Ltd declared dividends of £6,000	Dr Dividends receivable	2,400	Dr Dividends receivable	2,400
	Cr Dividend income	2,400	Cr Investment in associate	2,400

The entries shown above record the initial investment and the subsequent earnings and distribution of the associate company. As can be seen under the equity method, the resulting balance at 31 December 1988 on the 'investment in associate company's' account is £101,600 which represents not only the cost of the investment but also a proportion of the retained profits of the associate company. It includes the investing company's share of the post-acquisition profits retained by the associate in reserves. It has been argued by the opponents of this method that the investing company technically has no control over these reserves.

The credit to the profit and loss account of the investing company under the equity method is £4,000, the earnings of the associate. Under the cost method, the credit to the profit and loss account is only £2,400, these being the dividends to be received.

The equity method reflects, in the books of the investing company, changes in the book value of the investment in the period in which the changes take place. If the associate makes a loss in a year, the relevant share of this is shown in the accounts of the investing company in the same year. Recording only dividends received does not reflect changes in the book value of the investment.

In the UK, if group accounts are prepared, the method of recording an investment in the shares of another company varies according to the degree of influence. As explained above, influence and ownership are not the same thing. Normally, however, less than 20 per cent ownership means that the investment is recorded using the cost method; between 20 and 50 per cent, using the equity method; and over 50 per cent, using a consolidation technique. In fact, there is a connection between the equity method and consolidation: the equity method has been called 'one-line consolidation'.

We will illustrate the different approaches by means of an example.

9.5.1 Worked example

Question

Pine plc purchased 50 per cent of the ordinary shares of Oak plc on 1 January 1987 for £4 million when the reserves of Oak plc were £3.8 million.

The balance sheets of the two companies as at 31 December 1987 were as follows:

	Pine £'000s	Oak £'000s
Ordinary share capital	4,000	2,000
Reserves	6,900	4,000
Loans	4,000	3,000
Current liabilities	9,100	5,000
	24,000	14,000
Fixed assets	13,000	8,000
Investment in Oak plc at cost	4,000	—
Current assets	7,000	6,000
	24,000	14,000

You are required to prepare the group balance sheet on three different bases:
(a) when Oak is treated as a subsidiary;
(b) when Oak is treated as an associated/related company;
(c) when Oak is treated as an investment in an unrelated company.

First we will look at full consolidation. The resulting group balance sheet is:

	Pine plc £'000s	Oak plc £'000s	Minority interest £'000s	Elimination £'000s	Group b/s £'000s
Share capital	(4,000)	(2,000)	1,000	1,000	(4,000)
Reserves	(6,900)	(4,000)	2,000	1,900	(7,000)
Loans	(4,000)	(3,000)			(7,000)
Current liabilities	(9,100)	(5,000)			(14,100)
Minority interests			(3,000)		(3,000)
					(35,100)
Fixed assets	13,000	8,000			21,000
Investment	4,000			(4,000)	
Current assets	7,000	6,000			13,000
Difference on consolidation				1,100	1,100
					35,100

With Oak being treated as an associate company, there would be no need for group accounts unless there were subsidiary companies that we had not been told about. There would therefore be only one change from the balance sheet of Pine as shown in the question. The undistributed profits of Oak earned post-acquisition are £200,000, half of which belong to Pine. Therefore Pine's reserves would be increased by £100,000, as would the investment in Oak.

The resulting balance sheet is:

	£'000s
Share capital	4,000
Reserves	7,000
Loans	4,000
Current liabilities	9,100
	24,100
Fixed assets	13,000
Investment in Oak	4,100
Current assets	7,000
	24,100

SSAP 1 recommends that the 'investment in associated companies' figure shown in the group accounts be broken into two components, the attributable net assets and the goodwill. In this example the attributable net assets of Oak are £3,000,000 and the goodwill £1,000,000. The attributable net assets are 50 per cent of the total assets less the loans and current liabilities.

The balance sheet, treating the shareholding as an 'other investment'—recording it at cost—would be the same as in the question.

This example brings out an interesting point. As mentioned above, in the UK group accounts have to record investments in related/associated companies using the equity method. In individual company accounts, in this case those of the holding company Pine, the method of recording an investment does not vary according to the degree of ownership: in all cases, the investment is recorded at cost. SSAP 1 makes clear that, unless it is shown at a valuation, the interest in associated companies should be shown at the cost of investment, less any amounts written off.

A shareholder in a company that has subsidiaries will see group accounts where the associated companies will be recorded on an equity basis. A shareholder in a company that does not have subsidiaries will not see group accounts; the associate company investment will only be shown in the balance sheet at cost. One can ask why it is possible that the method of recording the peformance of an associated company should depend on whether or not the investing company has subsidiary companies. Only one set of accounts needs to be prepared, and in these accounts the investing company has only to record the actual dividends received or to be received from the associate. The standard does however make the point that in such cases, where the investing company does not have to prepare consolidated accounts, it should nevertheless disclose the relevant information, either in a separate balance sheet and profit and loss account or by adding the information in a supplementay form to its own balance sheet, with the share of profits given in notes to the financial statement.

If group accounts have to be prepared, then it is the percentage share of the earnings of the associate company that is recorded as earnings of the group. In the accounts of the individual holding company, it need be only the dividends received that are recorded. The reason why it is the percentage share of the group in the profits less losses of the associated company, rather than the dividends received, that is considered the significant figure for disclosure is that, by definition, the investing company can influence the dividend policy of the associated company. The shareholders of the investing company should be kept informed, and it would not be acceptable if the situation developed where large earnings were being accumulated in an associate company and were being hidden from the shareholders of the investing company because only small dividends were being distributed.

The standard recommends that the group profit and loss account, in addition to disclosing the appropriate share of the profits before tax for the year, and of the taxation of the associate companies, should also disclose the share of any extraordinary items. Further, it is recommended that the group's share of the annual retained profits or losses of the associated companies needs to be shown. This latter point means that the years retained profits figure for the group would need to be divided into three parts: the retained profits of the individual investing company, those of the subsidiaries and those of the associated companies.

Equity accounting has been referred to as one-line consolidation. Alternatively, consolidation can be seen as an extention of equity accounting. With equity accounting the net value of the investment, including any goodwill purchased, is recorded in the group accounts and is adjusted each year to reflect the latest changes in value resulting from the associate company's trading and from any dividend and loan transactions with the investing company. In a set of consolidated accounts, the total value of each category of asset and liability of a subsidiary company is combined with the assets and liabilities of the parent company, and any assets and liabilities that cannot be claimed by the group are deducted as minority interests. In 'equity' accounting a single figure, representing the investing company share of the assets and liabilities of the associate company, is brought into the group accounts. Rather than bringing into the group accounts 100 per cent of the assets and liabilities and deducting as minority interests the percentage not owned, only the actual share that is owned is recorded.

In the above example, with full consolidation all the assets and liabilities of Oak plc are aggregated with those of Pine, and the minority interests in the net assets of Pine are shown as a claim on the net assets. The book value of the assets is £14,000,000, and the liabilities £8,000,000. This means that Pine's share of the attributable assets amounts to £3,000,000. Pine paid £1,000,000 above book value for these net assets, and this is shown as an intangible asset, goodwill. The one-line consolidation in the case where equity accounting is used shows the assets, the investment in the associate, as the same £4,100,000. SSAP 1, in fact, requires this £4,100,000 to be divided into two components in the notes to the accounts. It could be further disaggregated if so required, so approaching line-by-line consolidation.

The purchase price is divided between the value of assets acquired and any payment for goodwill to help investors. A problem arises, however, where the shares in an associate company are not acquired all at one time but are built up over a period of time. When the percentage shareholding of a company is small, the investments will just be recorded in the books of the investing company as an 'other investment', being shown at cost or market value whichever is lower. When this initial shareholding has been added to, and the company eventually becomes an associate, then it will be difficult to go back to the times of the early investments and determine how much of the price paid was to acquire the net tangible assets and how much for the goodwill. Only the purchase (which itself may be small) that led to the presumption of significant influence, and any subsequent purchases, can be divided into the two constituent parts.

A problem arises in connection with any purchases of shares in the associate by the investing company beyond the stage where associate company status comes into being. Each purchase will result in a division of the price between the payment for net assets and goodwill. The resulting figures to be shown in a note to the balance sheet for any one associate company could be aggregates of net assets and goodwill acquired at different points in time.

In addition to the figure in the balance sheet showing 'interest in related/associated companies' (with its supporting footnote), details of any balances included in debtors or creditors that relate to normal trading between the investing company and its associate have to be shown.

9.5.2 Entity accounting

The above example of Pine plc can be used to illustrate an alternative method of accounting for invesment in other companies. This approach, the entity approach, is not in practice used, but it does have theoretical support. In accounting for the purchase of shares by Pine in Oak, it will have been noticed that Pine paid goodwill of £1,100,000 in purchasing half of the net assets of Oak. The investment by Pine is being valued in its accounts at £4,100,000, whereas the other 50 per cent of the share ownership, the minority interest, is being valued at only £3,000,000. If Pine owns half of the business of Oak, it could be argued that the total business should be valued at £8,200,000. This is treating the 'minority interests' in the same way as the majority; in our example the two halves are being treated equally. It can be argued that such treatment is justified if one considers Pine and Oak as a single entity. It means in this case that the total goodwill shown in the group consolidated accounts should be £2,200,000, and the minority interest should be increased by £1,100,000.

9.5.3 Profit and loss account

We have shown why equity accounting can be seen as one-line consolidation from the point of view of the balance sheet. In fact, it can be regarded similarly in its treatment in the profit and loss account. With full consolidation, each item of income and expenditure of the subsidiaries in the group are aggregated with those of the parent company. With equity accounting, the profit or loss of the associated company is brought into the group accounts in a single line.

SSAP 1, in fact, requires a limited breakdown of the profit and loss account of the associated company, the items to be disclosed being:
(a) profits attributable to associates before tax;
(b) attributable tax charges of the associate;
(c) extraordinary items of the associate, attributable to investing company.

A note to the accounts should show the attributable retained earnings of the associate.

In the Pine case discussed above, let us assume the profit and loss accounts of the two companies as at 31 December 1987 were:

	£'000s	£'000s
Profit before tax	2,200	1,000
Dividend from Oak (net)	200	—
Taxation	(1,200)	(400)
	1,200	600
Dividends paid	(600)	(400)
Retained profits	600	200

The group profit and loss account, treating Oak as an associated company, will be:

	£'000s	
Profit before tax	2,700	(2,200 + 500)
Taxation	(1,400)	(1,200 + 200)
	1,300	
Dividends paid	(600)	
Retained profits	700	

The retained profits figure consists of £600,000 with Pine and £100,000 with Oak, which is attributable to Pine.

The dividend received by Pine from Oak will be credited to the 'Investment in Oak' account, not the profit and loss account, as this is in fact reducing the value of the investment in the associate company.

The journal entries affecting the 'Investment in associate' account are:

Dr	Investment in Oak	£500,000	
Cr	Earnings of associate (P & L a/c)		£500,000
Dr	Taxation of associate (P & L a/c)	200,000	
	Investment in Oak		200,000
Dr	Cash	200,000	
Cr	Investment in Oak,		200,000
	being the receipt of the dividends		

The balance at the beginning of the year on the 'Investment in associate' account was £4,000,000; the balance following these adjustments and transactions is £4,100,000, which is the balance shown in the 'group' balance sheet as at 31 December 1987.

9.5.4 Adjusting entries

When shares in an associated company are purchased during that company's accounting year, it is necessary to divide the associates' profits for that year between those earned before acquisition and those earned after acquisition. The pre-acquisition profits can in no way be regarded as being part of the earnings for the year of the investing company. They were earned before the investing company had any influence, and in fact were represented by a share of the assets and liabilities that were purchased.

Similarly, a dividend payment by the associate company to the investing company can consist of two parts, a distribution of earnings earned before acquisition and a distribution of earnings earned after acquisition. The way in which earnings and dividends can be divided between their pre- and post-acquisition component will be dealt with in Chapter 11, when an identical problem is discussed in relation to subsidiary companies' earnings.

Another problem that needs to be resolved is the possibility of inter-company profits arising on any trading that takes place between the investing company and the associate company, or between the associate company and any other company in the group. This is an important issue in the preparation of consolidated accounts when subsidiary companies are involved, but it also arises in connection with associate companies.

SSAP 1 expresses the view that, 'wherever the effect is material, adjustments similar to those adopted for the purpose of presenting consolidated accounts should be made to exclude from the investing groups' consolidated accounts such items as unrealized profits on stocks transferred to or from associated companies. ...' The procedure for adjusting for intercompany transactions in consolidated accounts will be covered in Chapter 11.

The question of which transactions between an investing company and an associate should be adjusted is still not resolved, and, of course, the question of whether a particular transaction is large enough to be judged material is a matter of opinion. If the equity method of accounting is considered to be 'one-line consolidation', all inter-company transactions need to be taken into account in determining the single figure representing the value of the investment in the associate. This approach, however, can be criticized on the grounds that the investing company and the associate do not constitute a single business, and so transactions between the two can take place on an arm's length basis. A company is required to consolidate other companies only if it controls them, and significant influence is not the same as control. It can be argued therefore that, if transactions between companies are at arm's length, there should be no need to eliminate all unrealized inter-company profits.

Further reading

See Chapter 11.

Questions

1. The equity method of valuing certain forms of investment made by one company in another has been in common use since the early 1970s.

    Required:
    (a) Define concisely the term 'equity method' and outline the accounting procedures by which it is applied.   (5 marks)
    (b) Describe the present position regarding the use of the method, as referred to in the law and in SSAPs 1 and 14.   (10 marks)
    (c) Assess the validity of the equity method as an alternative to other modes of accounting for the relevant investments.   (10 marks)
    (25 marks)
    ACCA, 3.1, AFA, December 1985

2. The accountancy profession has developed a range of techniques to measure and present the effects of one company owning shares in another company.

    Briefly describe each of these techniques and how the resulting information might best be presented.

    (The Companies Act 1985 disclosure requirements are NOT required.)

    (20 marks)
    ACCA, 2.8, RFA, December 1986

3. Public consideration has recently been given to the composition of a group for the purpose of presenting the group accounts for a commercial organization. Consider the following data relating to the year ended 31 August 1981 of Octopus Ltd and Uncertain Ltd.

Balance sheet (£'000)	Octopus	Uncertain
Issued ordinary share capital	2,000	1,000
Reserves	3,450	2,000
Debentures	2,000	1,500
Current liabilities	4,550	2,500
	12,000	7,000
Fixed assets (net)	6,500	4,000
Investment in Uncertain Ltd at cost	2,000	—
Current assets	3,500	3,000
	12,000	7,000

Profit and loss account (£'000)		
Trading profit before tax	1,100	500
Dividend from Uncertain Ltd including tax credit	130	—
Taxation	(630)	(200)
Profit after tax	600	300
Dividends paid	(300)	(200)
Retained	300	100

Octopus Ltd acquired 50 per cent of the ordinary share capital of Uncertain Ltd on 1 September 1980 for £2,000,000 when its reserves were £1,900,000 and sold this holding on 3 September 1981 for £2,050,000.

You are required to:
(a) prepare the 'group' profit and loss account and balance sheet on three bases:
    (i)   when Uncertain Ltd is treated as a subsidiary;
    (ii) when Uncertain is treated as an associated company;
    (iii) when Uncertain is treated as an investment;   (9 marks)
(b) calculate relevant financial ratios from the financial data produced by these three bases;
                                                                          (4 marks)
(c) comment on the validity of these three alternative bases.   (7 marks)
                                                      (20 marks)
                                    ICAEW, PE II, December 1981

4. In the early days of group accounting (up to about 1929), the consolidation and equity methods were regarded as alternative accounting treatments for invesments in subsidiaries and for the profits/losses generated by them. Since then the consolidated method has prevailed in this field.

You are required:
(a) to outline the similarities, and differences, between the two methods;   (5 marks)
(b) to explain the conventional present-day uses of the two methods;   (5 marks)
(c) to argue for *or* against the general use of the equity method, in accounting for investments in subsidiaries.   (6 marks)
                                                      (16 marks)
                                    ACCA, 3.1 AFA December 1983

10. Group accounts: accounting at time of acquisition

10.1 Business combinations

The previous chapter was concerned with the situation when one company acquires less than 50 per cent of the shares of another company. This chapter deals with the accounting entries necessary to record the position where one company acquires 50 per cent or more of the shares of another company.

When two or more companies come together under common ownership, this is referred to as a 'business combination'. Not all combinations are similar in nature. For business, legal and accounting purposes it has become necessary to differentiate between different forms of combination. Two of the most common are what are known as 'mergers' and 'takeovers'.

At the extremes, it is easy to decide what is a merger and what is a takeover. When two more or less equal-sized companies come together, with the shareholders and directors of the two companies supporting the union and continuing to have an interest in the combined business, it is a merger. On the other hand, when a large company makes a cash bid for the shares of a smaller company, the directors of the small company advice their shareholders not to sell but the shares are sold anyway, and neither the old shareholders nor the directors of the purchased company have any continuing interest in the enlarged business, it is clearly an acquisition or takeover.

In the first situation, what is known as *merger accounting* is considered to be appropriate, and in the second situation the *acquisition accounting* method would be used. Unfortunately, few cases are as clear-cut as the two described.

Before considering the legal position, the relevant accounting standard and the pros and cons of the two principle accounting approaches to handling the coming together of two (or more) companies, we shall briefly consider the main differences between the two accounting techniques.

With the merger accounting approach, the purchase of shares in one company by the other is seen as a coming together of two businesses, the creation of a single group. The emphasis is on the continuity of ownership, the continuing interest in the business of both sets of shareholders. In the USA this is referred to as a 'pooling of interests'.

With the acquisition accounting approach the one business is seen as having been purchased by the other, just as if a set of assets and liabilities had been purchased, with the previous owners—the selling shareholders—giving up their interest in the business. This approach stresses the lack of continuity in ownership, with the one group of shareholders ceasing to have an interest and the other group taking over their interests.

The main differences resulting from the two accounting techniques arise over the treatment of (a) goodwill, (b) the value of the shares exchanged and (c) any pre-acquisition profits. Ignoring possible complications, the differences can be summarized as follows.

(a) *Acquisition*: Goodwill must be disclosed if acquired.

    Merger: As no real change in ownership occurs, the merger should produce consolidated accounts that do no more than combine the existing balance sheets; i.e., assets remain at the values at which they appear in the separate company accounts and goodwill is not recognized since none is effectively acquired.

(b) *Acquisition*: Shares issued to acquire another company are recorded at market value.

Merger: Shares issued to acquire another company are recorded at nominal value; i.e., no share premium is recognized.

(c) *Acquisition*: Distributable profits of any acquired company are frozen, and are not normally available for distribution by the group.

Merger: Reserves of each company are merged; i.e., those that were distributable before the merger may be distributable after the merger.

The differences in the accounting treatment are therefore important and significant. If the preparer of accounts wishes to create a favourable impression, merger accounting offers considerable advantages.

There are, again, two sets of financial statements to consider: those of
(a) the purchasing company, being the individual holding company; and
(b) the consolidated accounts of the holding company and its subsidiaries.

10.2 Accounts of holding company

It must be remembered that, in the UK, company law requires a holding company to present both its own accounts and a set of consolidated accounts. Unfortunately, the rules and guidance on the treatment of a business combination appear in two different places. Company law deals with the holding company's accounts, whereas SSAP 23, which is concerned with mergers and takeovers, deals with their treatment in the consolidated accounts. The interaction between the two sets of accounts is referred to in the appendix to SSAP 23, which is for guidance only.

The Companies Act 1985 requires an investment in another company to be stated at 'fair value' and the excess over nominal value to be credited to a 'share premium account', unless 'merger relief' applies. If the conditions for merger relief do apply, the company has the option of recording the investment at nominal value or fair value. This, it is emphasized, applies to the holding company accounts.

The 'merger relief' conditions of the Act are in fact, less strict than the merger accounting conditions of SSAP 23, which apply to the group accounts. It is possible, therefore, for some companies to satisfy the merger conditions for holding company accounts and not satisfy the conditions necessary to use merger accounting in their consolidated accounts. It is possible for a business to be in a position where it must use a fair value approach in its group accounts but can use the nominal value approach in the holding company accounts. Where this situation arises, it is recommended in the appendix to the standard that the holding company record its investment at the fair value, not the nominal value. The difference between the nominal value and the fair value of the consideration need not, however, be credited to a share premium account; instead, it can be credited to a special merger reserve. The advantage of this is that the merger reserve can be treated in a different way to a share premium account. As well as appearing in the holding company's account, the merger reserve can appear in the consolidated accounts. Goodwill arising on consolidation can be written off against this merger reserve. An example illustrating this treatment appears later in the chapter.

Under the Companies Act, but not under SSAP 23, a 'merger reserve' account can be created, instead of a share premium account, when a combination is eligible for merger relief. If the merger reserve is established in the group accounts, it can be used to write off any goodwill that arises on the consolidation. The group would not generally be able to do this against the share premium account, which, apart from specific uses, has to be treated like paid-up capital, and can be reduced only with court permission for a capital reduction.

The merger reserve can also be regarded in certain circumstances as realized and so as available for distribution. It can do this, according to the appendix to the standard, when the subsidiary makes a distribution to the holding company from pre-acquisition profits. This will be discussed later. A share premium account could not be used for this purpose. The recommendations in the appendix to SSAP 23 are designed to reconcile problems that will arise with the different treatments possible in the two sets of accounts.

This approach of SSAP 23 tries to ensure consistency between the two sets of accounts. If a company is eligible and chooses merger accounting in the consolidated accounts, then it should record the investment at nominal value in the holding company accounts. If a company uses acquisition accounting in the consolidated accounts, it should record the investment at fair value in the holding company accounts, even though under the Companies Act it is eligible for merger relief. SSAP 23 is, of course, only optional; a business does not have to follow this recommendation.

As explained, merger accounting is available in the UK as an option. The *Survey of UK Published Account 1986–87* reports that, when a combination satisfies the criteria for merger accounting, in most cases this is the technique used. The fact that in some cases one technique is used and in another case the other does not help the users of the accounts. The situation is made worse by the fact that no explanation needs to be given as to why merger accounting has been chosen or, alternatively, ignored.

An example of a combination that met merger accounting criteria but was accounted for in the consolidated accounts as an acquisition was the purchase by the Ladbroke group of Comfort Hotels International. The note in the 1985 group accounts explaining the merger reserve shows:

	£m
Merger reserves net of goodwill arising on the acquisition of Comfort Hotels	29.2
Goodwill in respect of the acquisitions during the year	(11.8)
Balance as at (31/12/85)	17.4

We begin considering the accounting entries by looking at a straightforward situation. The normal method of recording the acquisition of the shares in the financial accounts of the purchasing company—the holding company—is at the fair value of the consideration given. This value is usually either the agreed cash price or the market value of the shares issued, or some combination of the two. A cash purchase for £1 million of a majority shareholding in another company would be recorded in the purchaser's accounts with the following entries:

Dr Investment in subsidiary	£1,000,000	
Cr Cash		£1,000,000

In a share-for-share exchange, if the fair value of the acquired shares exceeds the nominal value of the shares given in exchange (as normally it will), the difference is normally entered in the holding company's accounts as share premium. The entries to record the purchase of shares having a fair value of £1 million, the consideration being a new issue of 625,000 shares each of £1 nominal value, would be:

Dr Investment in subsidiary	£1,000,000	
Cr Share capital		£625,000
Share premium		375,000

The above practice is the normal treatment. However, as mentioned above, the Companies Act

1985 does allow for an alternative treatment. 'Merger relief' is available when certain conditions are met, the details of which are contained in Section 131(2) of the Act. These conditions are as follows.

(a) A company (which is known as either the 'issue company' or the 'acquiring company') secures at least 90 per cent of the nominal value of each class of the equity share capital of another company (the acquired company) as a result of an arrangement.

(b) The arrangement provides for the allotment of equity shares in the issuing company. (Such allotment will normally be made to the acquired company's shareholders.)

(c) The consideration for the shares so allotted is either the issue, or the transfer to the issuing company, of equity shares in the acquired company, or the cancellation of those equity shares in the acquired company that the issuing company does not already hold.

In determining whether a particular combination satisfies the conditions under which the merger accounting technique can be adopted, the following rules apply.

(a) Any shares in the acquired company that are held by other companies in the same group (other than associates) as the issuing company, or their nominees, should be treated as being held by the issuing company.

(b) A company will be treated as having secured a 90 per cent holding in another company as part of the arrangement, irrespective of whether or not it actually acquired, under that arrangement, all the equity shares that it holds. This rule means that, in determining whether or not a company has obtained a 90 per cent holding in another company, prior holdings can be taken into account.

(c) 'Equity share capital' is a company's issued share capital, excluding any part that (as regards both dividends and capital) does not carry a right to participate beyond a specified amount in a distribution. 'Non-equity shares' are all other shares. In particular, preference shares do not form part of a company's equity share capital.

It should be noted that in this Companies Act definition of a merger there is no 'cash limit criterion'. It is not stated that a certain percentage of the consideration must be satisfied by the issue of equity shares, only that the arrangement provides for the allotment of some equity shares to the selling shareholders. The merger relief provisions can therefore be satisfied by any combination of cash and equity consideration. This is perhaps surprising, as one of the characteristics of a merger is the continuity in ownership. The accounting standard does have a cash limit constraint.

The difference in the accounting treatment of a merger and a takeover has been briefly mentioned above. One important relief is that in a merger situation a share premium account does not have to be created. The transfer of the shares can be recorded at nominal value rather than 'a fair value'. In the above example, with 625,000 shares being exchanged, each with a nominal value of £1, the journal entry would be:

$$\text{Dr Investment in subsidiary} \quad £625,000$$
$$\text{Cr Share capital} \quad\quad\quad\quad\quad\quad\quad £625,000$$

The Companies Act 1985 makes it necessary, however, for a holding company that adopts the merger accounting approach, with the difference between fair value and nominal value not having been shown on the face of the accounts, to disclose certain relevant information by way of a note. This includes the number and nominal value of any shares issued, details of the accounting treatment adopted with respect to the merged company, and details of the extent to which the group's profit or loss for the year is affected by the other company's pre-merger profit or loss.

It is necessary for the holding company to give details of any profit or loss realized on the disposal of shares or fixed assets of the merged company during the financial year of the merger. Any such profit or loss that arises within the two years following the merger also has to be disclosed. The reason for this is to enable shareholders to observe whether the merger accounting approach is being used as a cloak for an 'asset-stripping' exercise. This term will be explained and the arguments for and against merger accounting discussed in Section 10.4.

If in the above example the holding company is eligible for merger relief in its holding company accounts but according to SSAP 23 it should follow acquisition accounting in its consolidated accounts, then the recommendation is that a merger reserve be created. The journal entries would then be:

Dr	Investment in subsidiary	£1,000,000	
Cr	Merger reserve		£375,000
	Share capital		625,000

This point will be returned to in the following section.

10.3 Group accounts

When two companies come together as an economic unit, either willingly or as a result of a contested takeover, it is necessary to produce consolidated accounts, which means combining the assets and liabilities of the two companies. In a way this is misleading; the acquiring company has technically purchased *shares* in the other company, not its individual assets and liabilities. Nevertheless, for consolidation purposes it is the assets and liabilities of the two companies that are added together. This is because, with the parent company owning more than 50 per cent of the shares, it effectively controls these assets and liabilities; it should be remembered however that it is the shares that have been purchased.

The acquired company will have purchased its assets over a period of time prior to the takeover or merger, and the parent company will be obtaining the use of these assets. Their value at the date of the acquisition might be more than the price originally paid for them by the acquired company. How is this difference to be treated? Is it goodwill or not?

A problem also arises with regard to profits that the acquired company earned and has taken to reserves before it was taken over or merged. Do these represent profits that the newly combined business can distribute, or are they part of the net assets that the parent company has purchased?

The first attempt in the UK at a standard on this subject, ED 3 (published in 1971), proposed a distinction between an acquisition and a merger. According to the standard, an *acquisition* takes place when one company takes over another; the one company is in effect absorbing the other one. A *merger* occurs when two or more companies come together and each continues to have some identity: neither has absorbed the other. The distinction was to be important, as different accounting methods were proposed for the two situations. Normally acquisition accounting procedures would be followed, but in certain circumstances merger accounting would be allowed. The difference was to be crucial, for as previously mentioned, under acquisition accounting the subsidiary company's assets were to be restated to their value at the time of acquisition, but not under merger accounting. Under acquisition accounting pre-acquisition profits could not be distributed, but they could be under merger accounting. Under acquisition accounting, if shares were issued at a premium as part of the purchase consideration, then a share premium account would be created, but this would not apply under merger accounting. Finally, under merger accounting the profits earned by the subsidiary during the year of acquisition but prior to the date of acquisition could be added to the consolidated annual profits of the group, to boost apparent performance: this would not be possible with acquisition accounting.

The definition proposed in ED 3 was somewhat arbitrary, as it must be with all definitions in which percentages are used to decide which treatment is appropriate. For example, one of the conditions that was required to be met for the business combination to be classed as a merger was that 'the equity voting rights of the amalgamated undertaking to be held by the shareholders of any one of the constituent companies is not more than three times the equity voting rights to be held by the shareholders of any of the other constituent companies'. One could ask, why should it be a merger when the voting shares are divided three-quarters to one group of shareholders and one-quarter to the other group? Why not, say, five-eighths and three-eighths? This particular requirement with regard to voting rights was completely changed in the standard that was eventually introduced. The exposure draft itself never resulted in a standard.

Both methods of accounting were still being practised in 1980, when a decision was made in a tax case, Shearer (Inspector of Taxes) v. Bercain Ltd, which appeared effectively to outlaw merger accounting. In this case it was held that, when shares are issued at a premium, this premium must be held in a share premium account as per section 56 of the Companies Act 1948. The decision meant that this section of the Act was mandatory and not, as had previously been thought, optional. The decision was interpreted by legal counsel to mean that the pre-acquisition reserves of an acquired company were to be capitalized and therefore were not available for distribution. The difference between the market value of shares issued and the nominal value of shares issued had to be credited to a share premium account.

The decision created a great deal of anxiety. It led to the accounting bodies making representation to have Section 56 of the Companies Act 1948 amended to allow for the non-recognition of share premiums in certain cases. It was proposed that merger accounting be allowed in the case of mergers between non-independent parties in particular intragroup reorganizations. Another worry about the Shearer v. Bercain decision was that it meant that companies that came together before the decision, and had used merger accounting to record the amalgamation, had not been free to distribute pre-acquisition profits to shareholders. Indeed, past transactions involving the distribution of pre-acquisition profits could be challenged.

As a result of the concern expressed, the Companies Act 1981 included provision to allow merger accounting in certain cases. This relief from the need to set up a share premium account in a situation that could be described as a merger is now contained in Section 131 of the Companies Act 1985. This means that it is not always necessary for the holding company to place in a share premium account any excess of the fair value of assets acquired over the nominal value of shares issued in exchange. If the holding company issues shares at a premium and the new subsidiary has pre-acquisition profits, then it is possible for the holding company to distribute part of the pre-acquisition profits as dividends. The holding company is allowed to transfer a specified amount of the premium to a 'share premium pre-acquisition profits reserve'. It is this reserve that is available for distribution.

Group reconstructions can also follow merger accounting rules in certain cases—for example, when the issuing company is itself a 100 per cent owned subsidiary and allots shares at a premium to its own parent company or to a fellow 100 per cent subsidiary in exchange for shares in the other subsidiary. Where this happens, provided the nominal value of shares allotted equals the original cost of the shares allotted, no share premium will arise. Pre-acquisition profits will be available for distribution by the holding company.

The 1981 Act recognized that companies might have used merger accounting before the Shearer v. Bercain decision, believing the practice to be legal, and they were not required to account for such past mergers on a fair value basis. The Act ended some of the confusion caused by the legal decision. Merger accounting was to be allowed in limited cases. The 1985 Act continued this principle.

The Companies Act's provisions relate only to the accounts of individual companies, not to groups. The Accounting profession was left to decide when the purchase of the shares of one company by another could be classified as a merger for consolidation purposes. The ASC issued a statement on accounting for acquisition and mergers, SSAP 23, which became effective in 1985. It specifies the circumstances in which merger accounting can be used, and it lists a number of criteria, all of which must be met before merger accounting can be applied.

(a) The business combination must result from an offer to the holders of all equity shares and the holders of all voting shares not already held by the offeror.

(b) The offeror must have secured, as a result of the offer, a holding of (i) at least 90 per cent of all equity shares (taking each class of equity separately) and (ii) the shares carrying at least 90 per cent of the votes of the offeree.

(c) Immediately prior to the offer, the offeror must not hold (i) 20 per cent or more of all equity shares of the offeree (taking each class of equity separately), or (ii) shares carrying 20 per cent or more of the votes of the offeree.

(d) Not less than 90 per cent of the fair value of the total consideration given for the equity share capital (including that given for shares already held) can be in the form of equity share capital; not less than 90 per cent of the fair value of the total consideration given for voting non-equity share capital (including that given for shares already held) can be in the form of equity and/or voting non-equity share capital.

When merger accounting is adopted in a company's consolidated accounts, the following information needs to be disclosed.

(a) the fair value of the consideration given by the issuing company;

(b) an analysis of the current year's attributable profit before extraordinary items, comparing the profit before with that after the effective date of the merger;

(c) an analysis of the attributable profit before extraordinary items of the current year up to the effective date of the merger, and that of the previous year, between that of the issuing company and that of the subsidiary;

(d) an analysis of extraordinary items so as to indicate whether each individual extraordinary item relates to pre- or post-merger events, and to which party to the merger the item relates.

Unfortunately, SSAP 23 has not ended the controversy on this important area of financial accounting. The standard still allows a choice of treatment by companies. If all the criteria are met, merger accounting is available as an option, but it is not compulsory. SSAP 23 is what is referred to as an 'optional' standard: it allows companies a choice. One of the main reasons for introducing accounting standards was to reduce the range of choice open to preparers of accounts, to make it easier for users of accounts to understand the basis on which the accounts have been prepared.

In the USA the standard on acquisition and mergers makes it compulsory for merger accounting to be followed if certain conditions apply. The US criteria are designed to ensure that merger accounting is adopted if the shareholding groups exchange voting shares in a ratio that reflects their respective interests. They exclude from merger accounting those situations in which the intention is either to sell off assets in the future at a book profit, to distribute pre-acquisition profits, or to boost the group profits during the year of acquisition.

10.3.1   The acquisition accounting technique

The essential features of acquisition accounting in the consolidated accounts are as follows.

(a) The underlying net assets of the company being acquired are valued at their 'fair value' as at the date of the transaction.

(b) Any excess of the fair value of the consideration over the net assets of the company acquired is regarded in the consolidated accounts as goodwill arising on consolidation.

(c) Pre-acquisition profits of the company being acquired do not normally appear as part of the distributable reserves of the group.

Example 10.1

To illustrate acquisition accounts, we will use a simple example in which the purchase is recorded at its full market price and a share premium account and goodwill account are created. Suppose there are two companies, A and B; their balance sheets at the year-end are as follows:

Company A

	£		£
Share capital 16,000 shares,		Fixed assets	5,000
each of £0.50	8,000		
Reserves	2,000		
Current liabilities	5,000	Current assets	10,000
	15,000		15,000

Company B

	£		£
Share capital 5,000 shares,		Fixed assets	4,000
each of £1	5,000		
Reserves	1,000		
Current liabilities	5,000	Current assets	7,000
	11,000		11,000

A Company purchases all the shares in company B by exchanging two shares in A for every one in B. The market price of company A shares is currently £1. The acquisition would be reflected in the consolidated accounts of company A as below. (It is assumed that the directors of company A, having considered the matter, have decided not to revalue the assets of company B.)

Company A and its subsidiaries

	£		£
Share capital 26,000 shares,		Fixed assets	9,000
each of £0.50	13,000		
Share premium account	5,000	Goodwill	4,000
Reserves	2,000		
Current liabilities	10,000	Current assets	17,000
	30,000		30,000

The goodwill arising on consolidation is simply the cost of the acquisition less the fair value of the net assets, which in this case is £[10,000 – (11,000 – 5,000)]. The share premium is the difference between the market price of the shares and their nominal value: £(1.00 – 0.50) on 10,000 shares.

If the fair value of the fixed assets acquired is estimated to be £8,000 (rather than £6,000) then the goodwill figure will be shown as £2,000. There will be a two-stage division of the difference between the price paid for the purchase and the book value of the assets: first the revaluation of the assets by £2,000, then goodwill, being deemed the remainder.

The resulting balance sheet would be:

Share capital	13,000	Fixed assets	11,000
Share premium account	5,000	Goodwill	2,000
Reserves	2,000	Current assets	17,000
Current liabilities	10,000		
	30,000		30,000

The goodwill will probably not stay for long in the accounts. As we explained in Chapter 4, the majority of companies write it off against reserves as quickly as possible. One reason why this policy is adopted by many companies is because there is some uncertainty as to the amount of goodwill that should be entered in the accounts. This depends on how the cost of the acquisition is calculated, which is discussed below. Another reason is that many companies just do not like keeping an intangible asset in the accounts.

Cost of acquired shares

One problem with acquisition accounting is that the amount entered in the accounts as goodwill can depend upon the acquiring company's share price on one day. It could be argued that this dependence on the price on one day is not important, because even if the share price were at a lower level on that one day, more shares would have to be issued in exchange and the total purchase price and the size of the goodwill would be the same. This implies that a value is attached to the company to be purchased and the size of the goodwill depends on this valuation; if the purchasing company's share price rises and falls, this merely affects the number of shares that have to be issued in exchange. Usually, however, the number of shares to be issued will have been determined well in advance of knowledge of the price movements, and will have been decided on the basis of long-term considerations.

There is a legal dispute on the question of the value of acquired shares. The one side of the argument favours using market value, thus supporting acquisition accounting; the other argument favours nominal value, which in fact supports merger accounting.

There is legal authority for the approach whereby shares issued for a consideration other than cash—to acquire, for example, the assets of a business—are considered to be issued at a premium if the value of the assets acquired is more than the nominal value of the shares (Henry Head & Co Ltd v. Ropner Holdings Ltd (1952)). The people who oppose this approach argue that the Companies Act does not require a company to value the shares of a subsidiary by any prescribed method. They explain the decision in the Head v. Ropner case by the fact that the directors had chosen to value shares on the underlying asset basis, arguing that the directors could have valued the shares on a different basis.

It is quite clear, however, that the accounting standard bodies both here and in the USA intend the acquired shares of a subsidiary to be valued on the basis of the fair value of the consideration that is given in exchange. If shares are issued in consideration, they are valued at a fair price.

Discount on acquisition

In the majority of cases, the purchase consideration will be greater than the book value or revaluation on acquisition of the net tangible assets and identifiable intangible assets acquired. However, in a few cases the purchaser may be paying less than the apparent value of the net assets acquired. This could happen if, for some reason, the vendor's shareholders were eager to dispose of the company. In such cases the difference between the purchase price and the net assets acquired is a 'discount on acquisition'. If the purchase consideration is an issue of shares, the assets are debited to their respective accounts and the credits are to the share capital account—where appropriate the share premium account—with the discount being credited to reserves.

It must be emphasized that the calculation of the premium or discount should be after a fair valuation has been made of the net assets acquired. In practice, in may cases no revaluation takes place and it is assumed that the net book value represents the fair value.

What the 'fair price' is is not always easy to decide. Unfortunately, SSAP 23 does not define what it means by fair value. This is surprising. The term is mentioned numerous times in the standard, for example in paragraph 16, which explains acquisition accounting and how goodwill should be calculated:

> Where a business combination is accounted for as an acquisition, the fair value of the purchase consideration should, for the purpose of consolidated financial statements, be allocated between the underlying net tangible and intangible assets other than goodwill on the basis of the fair value to the acquiring company in accordance with the requirements of SSAP 14. Any difference between the fair value of the consideration and the aggregate of the fair values of the separable net assets including identifiable intangibles such as patents, licences and trade marks will represent goodwill, which should be accounted for in accordance with the provisions of SSAP 22.

In a statement attached to the standard, the ASC explains that

> Acquisition accounting involves the concept of 'fair value'. A number of commentators on ED 31 (and on ED 30 'Accounting for goodwill') requested that guidance should be provided on the determination of the fair value of various assets and liabilities. The ASC has set up a working party to develop such guidance.

In practice, of course, if shares are exchanged and there is a market price for the shares, then this is taken as the 'fair value'.

10.3.2 Merger accounting

The alternative method of recording the purchase of shares in another company, where over 90 per cent of the shares are acquired, is to adopt the merger accounting approach. This involves recording the shares issued in exchange at their nominal value.

Example 10.2
To illustrate the approach, the same companies as in Example 10.1 will be used. The shareholders in company B accept the offer of two shares in company A in exchange for one of their shares. The fair value of the shares issued to company B shareholders does not matter; in this case the amalgamation will be treated as a merger. With merger accounting there is no requirement to open a share premium account. The combined group balance sheet would appear as:

	£		£
Share capital	13,000	Fixed assets	9,000
Reserves	3,000	Current assets	17,000
Current liabilities	10,000		
	26,000		26,000

This is a simple form of merger accounting. Because the pooling does not involve writing up the assets acquired to their current value, it is possible for a book profit to be made on any future sale of the assets. There are built-in profits. Pooling also enables a company to maintain the depreciation charge at the aggregate of the separate companies. It enables a company, by keeping its asset values at the levels they were before the pooling of interests, to show a good profit/asset ratio, which is the weighted average of the separate companies. The position with respect to any book profit on future sales of assets, to the annual depreciation charge and to the profit/asset ratio is not as favourable, following the accounting entries for an acquisition, as it is for a merger. It can be seen how, with merger accounting, the reserve accounts of the two companies are simply added together, which, as will be explained later, has advantages from a distribution-of-dividends point of view.

There are two obvious differences between the balance sheet shown above and that produced after using the acquisition method. With the merger method no goodwill is created and the reserves are enlarged, which may be useful if the company is short of profits to distribute.

Example 10.3

An example will now be given which shows the entries both in the books of the holding company and in the consolidated accounts. Company Q acquires all of the shares of company W. The nominal value of the share capital acquired is £500,000. The purchase consideration is an issue of new shares in company Q, shares that have a nominal value of £400,000 but a market value of £750,000. The group and the parent company decide to use merger accounting. The respective balance sheets (in £000s) after the merger will be:

	Company Q	Company W	Elimination column	Group
Net tangible assets	1,000	500		1,500
Investment in subsidary	400		(400)	
	1,400	500	(400)	1,500
Share capital: Old	400	500	(500)	400⎫
New	400			400⎭
Profit & loss account	600			600
Reserve on consolidation			100	100
	1,400	500	(400)	1,500

This time the nominal value of the shares acquired by the holding company (i.e. £500,000) is greater than the carrying value of the investment in the holding company's accounts (i.e. £400,000). When such excesses or shortages arise, SSAP 23 says that the reserves of the group should be adjusted for the difference. When, as in this example, the carrying value is less than the nominal value, this should be treated as a reserve on consolidation.

When the difference goes the other way, that is when the nominal value of the shares acquired is less than the carrying value, the difference represents the extent to which the group has capitalized its reserves as a result of the merger. Because of this, the group should reduce its reserves by this amount. If, in the above example, the purchase consideration had been shares with a nominal value of £600,000, such a situation would have arisen. The balance sheets after the merger would then be:

	Company Q	Company W	Elimination column	Group
Net tangible assets	1,000	500		1,500
Investment in subsidiary	600		(600)	
	1,600	500	(600)	1,500
Share capital: Old	400	500	(500)	400
New	600			600
Profit and loss account	600			600
Difference on consolidation			(100)	(100)
	1,600	500	(600)	1,500

The difference on consolidation is:

Nominal value of shares acquired	500
less Holding company's carrying value	600
	(100)

In this case the difference on consolidation would be written off against the profit and loss account reserve. If by any chance this particular reserve, resulting from retained earnings, was not large enough for the difference to be written off, it is not clear which other reserves could be used for that purpose. The Companies Act 1985 (4 sch. 61) allows directors, when preparing consolidated accounts, to make what adjustments they think necessary. The Act does however place restrictions on the way in which share premium accounts and revaluation reserves can be used in the accounts of individual companies. Most writers on the subject believe that there is freedom to use the reserves to eliminate the consolidation differences in the group accounts.

Example 10.4

One further example of merger accounting will be given. This is based on the bringing together of company A and company B, referred to above. Both companies are now quoted on the Stock Exchange, and company B is being valued at its market valuation. Shares in company A will be given in exchange for shares in company B. Although company B is being valued at market price, from the point of view of the exchange of shares, it will be treated as a merger, for accounting purposes. The relevant data for determining the pooling (the merger arrangements) are:

	Company A	Company B
Number of shares	16,000	5,000
Book value per share	£0.625	£1.20
Profit available to ordinary shareholders	£800	£665
Earnings per share	£0.05	£0.133
Market price of share	£0.60	£1.50
Market value of company	£9,600	£7,500
Nominal value per share	£0.50	£1.00

The share price of A is £0.60, which means that 12,500 shares in company A will be given in exchange for 5,000 shares in company B. With acquisition accounting this would result in a share premium account of £1,250 (12,500 × £0.10) but with merger accounting no share premium account needs to be opened.

The merger accounting approach takes the view that shares with a nominal value of £6,250 have been given in exchange for shares with a nominal value of £5,000. The carrying value of the holding company's investment, £6,250, is greater than the nominal value of the shares acquired, £5,000. This could be regarded as company A having paid a sum of money for the reserves of company B.

The issue of shares will be recorded at their nominal value, that is 12,500 shares each of £0.50. The resulting balance sheet is:

	£		£
Share capital 28,500 shares			
at £0.50	14,250		
Reserves	3,000		
Difference on consolidation	(1,250)	Net assets	16,000
	16,000		16,000

It should be noted that the reserves have been pooled. The difference on consolidation can be written off against these reserves.

The result of this approach is to retain the value of the assets of the separate companies. There is no recognition of the real value, as represented by the real worth of the securities being exchanged. This is one of the criticisms of merger accounting.

The emphasis in this section has been on the balance sheet; it must be remembered that the two accounting methods lead to a difference in the profit and loss account. All the profits of the merged company for the year of the merger can be consolidated in the group profit and loss account, irrespective of when in the year the profits were earned, and when in the year the merger took place. This is not the case with acquisition accounting.

When Dixons tried to take over Woolworth in 1986, part of Woolworth's defence was based on the way Dixons had assimilated the profits of Curry's, which it had acquired the previous year. Acquisition-oriented companies need to be able to show a high growth rate in earnings. It is possible for earnings records to be boosted by merger accounting.

Coats Viyella, in their accounts for the year ending 30 November 1985, included the full year's profits of a company with which they 'merged', the Nottingham Manufacturing Company—despite the fact that the merger was completed only on 5 August 1985, just four months before the end of the Nottingham Manufacturing Company's accounting year.

10.4 SSAP 23

It has proved very difficult to produce a satisfactory standard on merger and acquisition accounting in the UK. In 1987, only two years after it was issued, the ASC announced that it was to review SSAP 23. This followed much criticism of the standard, along three main lines. First, there are those who believe that merger accounting should not be allowed under any circumstances; second, there are those who think that it does have a place but that SSAP 23 allows it to be inappropriately used; finally, there are those who argue that the ways that have been devised by companies for avoiding the restrictions on the use of merger accounting should be closed. We shall look at each of these categories of criticism, beginning with a brief summary of the arguments for and against merger accounting.

10.4.1 Merger accounting: for and against

The advocates of merger accounting make the following points.
(a) It recognizes substance over form. Two businesses come together for their mutual benefit. Why should restrictions be placed on them? Why should they have to behave differently after the merger from the way they behaved before? Why should goodwill need to be created? Why should pre-acquisition profits not be available for distribution? Mergers emphasise the continuity of interest by the shareholders.
(b) The alternative, acquisition accounting, is itself illogical. The acquired company effectively has its assets revalued to current values, but the parent company does not have to revalue *its* assets. You are therefore not consolidating like with like. How goodwill should be treated in accounts is itself the subject of controversy, so why should the creation of goodwill be seen as logical?
(c) Acquisition accounting can be shown to be illogical if you consider the reverse takeover situation. If company A takes over company B and consolidates, you will have one set of figures. If however B is said to take over A, you will have a different set of figures in the consolidated accounts. Why should this be so? It is in effect the same business combination, whichever company is said to acquire the other.

A major reason for the above problem is that most companies' accounts are based on historical cost figures with periodic revaluation. If current value accounting were being used, then the assets of both the acquired and the acquirer would be valued on the same basis.

The main arguments against merger accounting are as follows.

(a) It understates true asset values, which results in unrealistic future depreciation charges, which in turn give a misleading impression of the group's performance. It means that the merged company is in a position to sell assets and gives the impression of having made a profit. This argument is that merger accounting can be used as a cloak for 'asset-stripping'. ED 3 tried to guard against this by making it a necessary condition that before merger accounting could be introduced the intention of the combined business should be to continue in the existing lines of operation.

The EEC 7th Directive on group accounts also makes it a necessary condition for the use of merger accounting that no significant economic resources leave the group. This directive will have to be enacted into UK company law by 1990. SSAP 23 does not contain this provision. There is not even a requirement that 'profits' resulting from selling merged assets at the market price be separately disclosed in the accounts to enable shareholders to ascertain how post-merger profits have been achieved.

(b) With merger accounting, profits of the acquired company earned before the date of the acquisition can be added to the profits of the group in the year of the acquisition, so giving a misleading impression.

10.4.2 Criticisms of the wording of the standard

SSAP 23 is itself subject to much criticism. First, it does not define 'fair value'. Two types of fair value are referred to: the value of the shares given in consideration, and the value of the assets acquired. Second, it is an optional standard; a combination may satisfy the conditions that would enable it to adopt merger accounting, but it does not have to adopt this technique. This makes a comparison of company accounts more difficult.

Third, a problem arises in that the requirements that need to be met in order to obtain merger relief in the Companies Act 1985 (S.131) are different from those in the relevant accounting standard, SSAP 23.

(a) Under SSAP 23, the offeror must secure a holding of at least 90 per cent of each class of equity shares, and it must also secure a holding of the shares that carry at least 90 per cent of the offeree's votes. To qualify for merger relief under the Act, the issuing company must secure a holding of at least 90 per cent of each class of equity shares, but the issuing company does not need to secure shares that carry at least 90 per cent of the offeree's votes.

(b) Under SSAP 23, at least 90 per cent of the fair value of the total consideration that the issuing company gives for equity shares must itself be in the form of equity shares. The Act only requires that some of the consideration be equity shares.

(c) SSAP 23 stipulates that the offeror's prior holding in the offeree must not exceed 20 per cent. Again, the Act imposes no such condition.

A further problem arises because the UK is subject to EEC directives. The provisions of the 7th Directive on consolidated accounts will have to be enacted into law. When this happens merger accounting will be available on a more limited basis than allowed under SSAP 23 and the Companies Act 1985.

The 7th Directive requires acquisition accounting rules to be followed in all but a few cases. It refers to a set-off of the values of the shares issued against the fair value of the net assets acquired. It is a two-stage set-off, first recognizing the difference between the book value of the net assets of the subsidiary and the fair value of these assets, and then recognizing the difference between the value of the shares issued to acquire the subsidiary and the fair value of the assets. The first difference is a type of asset revaluation; the second, a difference arising on consolidation.

At one stage of drafting, the EEC directive did not contain any provision for merger accounting. At a later stage, largely owing to pressure from the British representatives, limited provision was introduced. The directive allows member states the option to require or permit the book values of shares to be used in the set-off, provided that the shares held represent at least 90 per cent of the nominal value of the acquired business, and that these have been obtained under an arrangement providing that at least 90 per cent of the purchase consideration given is in the form of shares with therefore not more that 10 per cent in the form of cash.

It should be noted that, to qualify as a merger under the directive, not more than 10 per cent of the nominal value of the total consideration can be paid for in cash, whereas SSAP 23 only requires that not more than 10 per cent of the fair value of the total consideration should be in the form of cash. The nominal value will usually be much less than the fair value, which means that more equity will need to be offered to qualify under the directive rules than to qualify under the standard. When the directive becomes incorporated in law in the UK, some combinations that at present qualify for merger relief will cease to do so.

The wording of the EEC directive is more precise than that used in the Companies Act 1985 with regard to the 'cash' constraint. But there are still difficulties in interpreting the EEC definition. It is, for example, unclear whether loan stock is acceptable as the non-cash element of the consideration.

10.4.3   Avoiding the restrictions

Although the conditions for merger accounting under SSAP 23 are more restrictive than those required by the Companies Act 1985, companies have found ways around the restrictions.

Vendor placing and vendor rights

For a merger to take place, the shares in one company have to be exchanged for the shares in the other company. On occasions, however, the shareholders in the company to be purchased do not want shares in the acquiring company: they want cash. This should mean that a merger is not possible, although an acquisition is.

The wording of the standard is such as to provide a loophole. 'Merger accounting is considered to be an appropriate method of accounting when two groups of shareholders continue, or are in a position to continue, their shareholding as before but on a combined basis.'

The words 'or are in a position to' have permitted a technique to develop whereby the selling shareholders (the vendors) can receive cash for their shares, but still be in a position to continue their shareholding as before. This is made possible by vendor placing and vendor rights. A share-for-share exchange takes place between the shareholders of the company being purchased and those of the acquiring company, but arrangements are made for the shares received by the vendor to be placed with institutional investors, if this is what the vendor wants. The shareholders in the company being acquired are therefore in a position to receive cash in payment for their shares in the acquired company. The scheme is usually set up by the acquiring company's merchant bank, which arranges for the shares to be placed with a third party. Merger accounting conditions have thereby been met, and the shareholders of the acquired company are in a position to continue their shareholding if they so wish; they do not have to sell for cash. If, however, they do not want to continue to be shareholders in the new 'merged' business, they have a guarantee that they can sell their shares for cash at a price known by them.

Vendor rights are a variation on vendor placing. With vendor placing the shares received by those selling off their business are placed, usually with institutional shareholders. This means that the shares of the acquiring company can become widely dispersed. With vendor rights, if the shareholders of the target company do not want to retain the shares they receive in consideration, then the acquiring company, again, will arrange through its brokers to have them placed. With this approach, however, the shares will first be offered to other shareholders of the acquiring company, who will have a right to buy them before they are placed with institutions. From the point of view of the acquiring company's shareholders, it is like a rights issue. But with vendor rights, the existing shareholders pay out cash not to the acquiring company, but rather to those who were once shareholders of the company that has been purchased.

The buy-back scheme

One of the requirements of SSAP 23 that needs to be met before merger accounting can be used is that 'Immediately prior to the offer, the offeror [must] not hold (i) 20% or more of all equity shares of the offeree (taking each class separately) or (ii) shares carrying 20% or more of the votes of the offeree.' The intention of this restriction is to ensure that a merger is a genuine coming together of two independent companies, not an arrangement whereby one company, which has a considerable influence over another, carries out a takeover. Companies have, however, found ways around this restriction; they meet the 'form' of the wording but not the spirit.

The standard says 'immediately prior to the offer'. It is possible, therefore, by making certain arrangements with regard to the shares held in the company to be acquired, to reduce the shareholding immediately prior to the offer. British Syphon Industries, on the day before it made an offer for the shares of Marshalls Universal, reduced its shareholding in the target company from 25.6 to 13.6 per cent. If the offer was to prove successful, British Syphon would therefore be able, as far as this criterion was concerned, to adopt merger accounting. The sale of the 12 per cent was reported to be to a friendly purchaser, the firm's financial advisers.

Preference share issues

For the purposes of SSAP 23, when equity shares are referred to, they exclude preference shares. One severe restriction in the use of merger accounting is that, in order to qualify, a large amount of the purchase consideration has to be in the form of equity shares. If the selling shareholders want cash, and/or if the acquiring company wishes to use more cash than allowed for in the restrictions, it can overcome the problem by using cash to buy the preference shares of the company to be acquired, and using equity to acquire the equity share.

Even if the target company does not have many preference shares when negotiations begin, it can issue them to all its equity holders just before the planned date of the acquisition. The acquiring company then pays however much cash it wants for the preference shares, with the balance of the consideration being a nominal amount of equity shares from the equity of the acquired company.

Those who support merger accounting argue that it can be justified when the two sets of shareholders come together and continue to have an interest in the new group. When a high percentage of cash is included in the purchase consideration, it effectively means that one group of shareholders is selling out. They can hardly be said to have a continuing interest. In the situation just described, where preference shares are bought for cash, it can be argued that the shareholders of the acquired company still have an equity interest, but only a nominal one. The acceptance of the cash offer reduces the continuing interest.

All these techniques to find ways around the wording of the standard are artificial. They permit merger accounting to be used in cases where there is little or no justification for claiming that a merger has taken place.

In the conglomerate merger boom in the USA in the 1960s, the merger accounting technique developed a bad name for itself. When in the UK an accounting standard was being prepared on this topic, there were many who argued that the technique of merger accounting should not be allowed in any circumstances. There were others, however, who were strong advocates of the technique, and with accounting standard-setting being a political process, a compromise was reached. Merger accounting was to be allowed in certain circumstances; but, as has been shown, when the rewards are thought to be great enough, there are those who find ways of getting round arbitrary criteria introduced into company law and 'optional' accounting standards.

If merger accounting is to be allowed, it is not possible to introduce 'hard' accounting measures. Unfortunately measures can always be manipulated if they are not hard. Some managers and shareholders benefit from the application of merger accounting techniques; therefore it is not surprising that the vested interests continue to argue for as much choice for the preparers of accounts as possible. The user of accounts has to be aware.

The accounts of the Dee Corporation for the period ended 25 April 1987 provided a very interesting supplement. It was entitled 'Some questions answered'. One of the questions answered was on the company's policy on the use of merger and acquisition accounting.

Dee has always applied the following tests before merger accounting for any acquisition:
1. Is there a true merger of the managements, identities and physical assets of the two business in the layman's sense, and is there a clear trading benefit?
2. What is the size of the transaction relative to the existing business?
3. Will the management materially impact the trading and management of the acquired business before the next report and accounts?
4. How can the presentation to shareholders best depict the company's future trading base?
The accounting treatment of Dee's major acquisitions was as follows:

Acquisition	Date	Form of consideration	Accounting basis adopted	Principal reasons
Key Markets	June 83	Cash	Acquisition	No choice
F. A. Wellworth	Dec. 83	Shares	Merger	Scale—business impacted in 1983/84. Expansion of existing business
Lennons	Oct. 84	Shares	Acquisition	Small— substantial part of business sold within 1984/85 year
International Stores	Dec. 84	Shares	Merger	Scale—business totally integrated
Herman's	April 86	Shares	Acquisition	New stand alone business: management not impacted in 1985/86 year
Fine Fare	June 86	Shares	Merger	Scale—business totally integrated
M & H Sporting Goods	Aug. 86	Cash	Acquisition	No choice
Medicare	Dec. 86	Cash & shares	Acquisition	No choice

Dee has treated its acquisitions consistently by applying the tests mentioned above. This has not always given the highest immediate reported results. For instance, if Fine Fare had been acquisition-accounted, then Dee's earnings per share for the year to 25 April 1987 would have been marginally higher than the 17.7 pence per share reported.

10.5 Using both acquisition accounting and merger accounting

A holding company may decide to claim merger relief under the Companies Act in its own accounts, but either is not eligible or does not want to use merger accounting in its group accounts. In this situation the parent company should show the investment in the subsidiary at the fair value of the consideration given, not the nominal value. However, SSAP 23 states that it is not necessary in such a situation to create a share premium account; the difference between the fair value and the nominal value can be taken to a separate 'merger reserve'. The merger reserve will appear in the holding company accounts and the group accounts.

As mentioned earlier, it is unclear whether this merger reserve is to be classed as realized or unrealized, and so whether or not it is available for distribution. The appendix to the standard suggests that in certain situations most of the reserve can be distributed. This is discussed further in Section 10.6 below.

Example 10.5
An example will illustrate a situation in which merger accounting is adopted in one set of accounts and acquisition accounting in the other. A holding company (J) purchases all the shares of a subsidiary (S). The pre-combination balance sheets are:

	Company J £'000s	Company S £'000
Net tangible assets	100	50
Share capital	70	40
Profit and loss account	30	10
	£100	£50

The consideration given to the shareholders of company S is new shares in company J having a nominal value of £45,000 and a fair value of £70,000. The holding company decides to adopt merger accounting in its own books and acquisition accounting in the group accounts. The fair value of company S's net tangible assets is £50,000. After the acquisition, the accounts would appear as follows:

	Company J £'000	Company S £'000	Group £'000
Net tangible assets	100	50	150
Goodwill			20
Investment in subsidiary	70		
	170	50	170
Share capital	115	40	115
Profit and loss account	30	10	30
Merger reserve	25		25
	170	50	170

The difference between the fair value of the shares issued (£70,000) and the nominal value (£45,000) has been taken to a merger reserve account. In the group accounts, the goodwill arising on consolidation reflects the difference between the fair value of the consideration given (£70,000) and the value of the net tangible assets acquired (£50,000).

SSAP 23 requires companies to provide an explanation of the basis adopted when combining the accounts of two businesses. The *Survey of UK Published Accounts* for 1986–87 reveals that most of them in fact do so. Typically, they disclose information on the time period for which the profits of the acquired company have been included in the consolidated profit and loss account, the market value and the nominal value of the shares issued to the shareholders of the acquired company, and details of any merger reserve.

10.6   Pre-acquisition profits

The Companies Act 1948 stated that the pre-acquisition profits of a subsidiary may not normally be distributed by the holding company. The profits of a purchased company made prior to the date of acquisition of the company were not deemed to be trading profits for the purpose of consolidation. The purchasing company could not, therefore, add to its own revenue reserves or profit and loss account any balance of profit already earned by the subsidiary at the date of acquisition. The profits earned by the acquired company up to its last balance sheet date that have been retained would have been accumulating in the revenue reserve, and these have been purchased. Profits earned by the acquired company between its last balance sheet date and the date of acquisition are also reflected in the price that has to be paid for the shares. The profits are reflected in the assets that have been purchased. To let a company distribute profits that it has purchased as part of a capital transaction could be seen as allowing it to distribute its capital as dividends. This is not allowed.

When a merger takes place, the transaction can be interpreted somewhat differently. It can be argued that it is not so much one company purchasing another as two companies coming together: there is no acquirer, no predator. It could well be that the transaction is handled administratively by one company becoming the subsidiary of the other one, but it is still a merger. If this happens, why should it not be possible for the pre-acquisition profits of both companies to be available for distribution to the shareholders of the parent company, who will include the shareholders of both companies in the merger? Although the Companies Act 1948 indicated in an accompanying schedule that pre-acquisition profits should be regarded as a partial realization of an asset and should not be available for distribution by the holding company, there is a legal case which suggests that a dividend may be paid out of those profits, provided that the book value of the holding company's fixed assets have been maintained following a general revaluation of assets (Lubbock *v.* British Bank of South Africa (1892)). In fact, the practice developed in the UK with regard to pre-acquisition profits is that such profits of a purchased company following an acquisition cannot be used by the acquiring company or the group for distribution purposes; however, following a merger, if merger accounting principals are adopted, then the pre-acquisition profits of all the companies involved would be available for distribution. Therefore, when the conditions permitting merger accounting are present, the purchased company's profits can be distributed to the shareholders of the new group, which would include those of the purchasing company.

Clearly, there was confusion.

Paragraph 15(5) of Schedule 8 to the Companies Act 1948 implied that a subsidiary's pre-acquisition profits were not to be treated as the holding company's profits. However, the

Companies Act 1981 specifically amended this requirement so that a company wishing to claim the benefit of the merger relief provisions is able to distribute to its shareholders the subsidiary's pre-combinaton profits. If the 1981 Act had not included this amendment, one of the principal advantages of merger relief would have been lost, because the distributability of the subsidiary's pre-combination profits would still have been restricted.

The merger accounting approach is normally regarded as a technique for allowing pre-acquisition profits to be distributed. The acquisition approach is the technique for freezing profits; that is, they are not available for eventual distribution to the holding company's shareholders. This is the position in most cases, but there are some exceptions and some uncertainties.

There is confusion in the wording of the relevant parts of the Companies Act 1985 and SSAP 23 as to whether distribution from pre-acquisition profits can be treated as income by the parent company. The Companies Act 1985 appears to allow in certain circumstances a dividend to be paid to the acquiring company out of the pre-acquisition (combination) profits of the acquired company, without the amount involved needing to be applied to reduce the carrying value in the parent company accounts of the investment in the subsidiary. This would mean that it is available for distribution to the parent company's shareholders.

It might have been thought that such a dividend payment would in fact reduce the value of the investment in the subsidiary and so should be used to write down the value of that investment in the books of the parent company. This indeed would seem to be the prudent treatment, and was the position under the Companies Act 1948. The position now is not quite so clear.

A situation in which it may be possible to distribute pre-acquisition profits even though acquisition accounting is involved arises when the holding company is treating a combination as a merger in its own accounts,but as an acquisition in the group accounts. As explained above, this gives rise to a 'merger reserve', and part of this reserve may be distributed to shareholders following a payment of dividends from the subsidiary.

With merger accounting, the subsidiaries' pre-combination profits are normally available for distribution to the shareholders of the holding company. This is not always the case, however. When the investment carrying value in the holding company accounts exceeds the nominal value of the shares that the holding company acquired, some pre-acquisition profits may effectively be frozen, even with merger accounting. The dividends should be used to reduce the carrying value of the investment to the extent necessary in order to provide for a diminution in that carrying value.

If, for example, the carrying value of a subsidiary is £100,000, this being the nominal value of the shares issued in consideration, and the subsidiary, with net assets of £150,000, paid a very large dividend of, say, £125,000 to the parent, it would be incorrect to pay all of this dividend out to the parent company shareholders. The value of the subsidiary has in fact been very much reduced from the £100,000. There are few assets left in the subsidiary; the carrying value should be written down to reflect the new situation. It is only the balance between the amount written off (say, £75,000) and the £125,000 that could be distributed.

Some worked examples follow the next section, in which this problem is further discussed.

10.7 Date of acquisition

SSAP 14 (para. 32) defines the effective date for accounting for acquisitions as the earliest of
(a) the date on which consideration passes, or
(b) the date on which an offer becomes or is declared unconditional.

This definition, and that in the Companies Act 1985 as to when a company is and is not a subsidiary, appears straightforward enough, but it has led to problems. It is only when a company is a subsidiary that its accounts can be consolidated in the group accounts. An interesting case on this point was the Argyll merger with Morgan Edwards.

At 31 December 1979 Argyll Foods Ltd was discussing a merger with another company, Morgan Edwards Ltd. In March 1980 Argyll made an offer for the shares of Morgan which was accepted. Argyll produced group accounts as at 31 December 1979, and included in the consolidation the figures for Morgan Edwards.

The Department of Trade then took the directors of Argyll to court for consolidating the accounts of a company that was not legally a subsidiary at the date of the accounts. It was claimed that the financial accounts did not comply with the relevant sections of the Companies Act and SSAP 14. As a result of this breach, it was claimed that the accounts were misleading. Argyll's defence was that, despite the breach of the Companies Act and SSAP 14, the accounts showed a true and fair view in terms of generally accepted accounting principles, and were not misleading.

The defence was based on the fact that, as at 31 December 1979, both companies were managed and effectively controlled by the same group of people. Gulliver Foods Ltd owned 100 per cent of a company Avonmiles Ltd, which owned 29.9 per cent of Morgan Edwards. Gulliver Foods owned 16.7 per cent of the shares of Argyll. In addition, Avonmiles had options to acquire a further 8.3 per cent of Argyll and effectively controlled the voting power of another block of 13 per cent. It can be seen therefore that, although at 31 December 1979 no offer had been made formally, there was reason to believe that the two companies were far from being independent. Merger talks were taking place, and it was claimed that the consolidated accounts reflected the economic reality of the situation; they gave a true and fair view.

It was decided by the court that the accounts did not in fact show a true and fair view, and so contravened the Companies Act. Although the notes to the accounts explained that Morgan was not a subsidiary, it was decided that the naïve investor might not read the notes and so could be misled by the consolidation.

There are a number of implications of this decision, one being that companies could subsequently be reluctant to consolidate the accounts of companies that were 'legally' not subsidiaries although from the point of view of economic reality they were controlled. These controlled non-subsidiaries are a problem, and the issue is discussed further in Chapter 16.

10.8 Worked example

The worked example is concerned with merger accounting and the profits available for distribution. It is a question devised by Chart Foulks Lynch.

Cowan Gate plc

Cowan Gate plc (a company with no subsidiaries) wanted to acquire Cart plc (a service company worth substantially more than its net asset value), and its offer of five new £1 shares for every four existing Cart plc £1 shares was accepted by all the shareholders of Cart plc. On the day the new shares were issued, the market price of Cowan Gate plc's shares was £4 each.

The balance sheets of Cowan Gate plc and Cart plc before accounting for the exchange of shares were as follows:

	Cowan Gate plc £'000s	Cart plc £'000s
£1 ordinary shares	1,500	1,000
Profit and loss reserves	1,500	2,000
Share premium	800	—
Capital redemption reserve	1,200	—
	5,000	3,000
Net assets (at fair value)	5,000	3,000

The financial director of Cowan Gate plc, Mr Dairy, has written to you, his auditor, saying:

I think that we shall have to merger account for Cart plc since, if we use acquisition accounting, goodwill of some £2 million will arise and cancel out all of the group reserves leaving nothing left for distribution to our shareholders this year. Also, I understand that we can treat some of Cart plc's profits as distributable as well if we use merger accounting.

You are required to write Mr Dairy and advise him of what factors he should bear in mind when considering how to account for this business combination. You should include *pro forma* accounts in the letter to illustrate your points, and you should consider the impact on distributable profits of the alternative methods of accounting available to this company.

We shall first give the answer to the numerical part of the question and then consider the issue of the distributable profits.

We shall start by examining the balance sheet of the holding company with acquisition accounting. The holding company issues 1,250,000 shares, each with a nominal value of £1 and a market value of £4. The fair value of the acquisition is therefore £5 million, and this is shown as the investment in Cart. The amount to be credited to the share premium account in accordance with Section 130 of the 1985 Act is £3,750,000, (that is, 1,250,000 shares at £3).

The journal entry in the holding company books recording the acquisition is therefore

Dr Investment in Cart	£5,000,000	
Cr Ordinary shares		£1,250,000
Share premium		3,750,000

When shares are issued at a value above nominal, company law requires a share premium account to be utilized, unless the combination qualifies as a merger. In this case, the coming together of Cowan Gate and Cart can be classed as a merger, as more than 90 per cent of the shares in Cart have been purchased, and some equity shares have been included in the consideration. In such a situation, Cowan Gate has the option of recording the investment in the holding company accounts at either a nominal value or a fair value. If the directors elect to use fair value, they do not have to create a share premium account, but can instead open a 'merger reserve'. As explained above, there are advantages in creating such an 'unrealized' reserve, as there is greater freedom in the way in which it can be used. This alternative treatment is shown as solution B in the acquisition accounting balance sheet shown below.

Now to consider the position with merger accounting. The entry is recorded by Cowan Gate in the holding company accounts at the nominal value of the shares issued, the entry being

Dr Investment in Cart	£1,250,000	
Cr Ordinary shares		£1,250,000

Turning now to the consolidated accounts. First, there is the journal entry with the acquisition accounting approach:

Dr Goodwill	£2,000,000	
Net assets	3,000,000	
Cr Ordinary shares		£1,250,000
Share premium		3,750,000

The goodwill, or 'excess arising on consolidation', can be shown as an asset in the balance sheet (as in solution A below). There is an accounting standard on the treatment of goodwill (SSAP 22), and the recommendations contained therein could be followed with respect to this amount. The current recommendation is that, preferably, the goodwill is written off immediately against reserves; as a 'second-best' solution, it could be written off over its estimated useful life. In solution B to the problem, the goodwill is written off immediately against the profit and loss account reserves, reducing the credit balance of £1.5 million to a debit balance of £0.5 million. Not all would agree with this treatment, however.

Now with the merger accounting approach, to consolidate the accounts of Cart plc we have

Dr Net assets	£3,000,000	
Cr Ordinary shares		£1,250,000
Cr Reserves		2,000,000
Dr Difference on consolidation	250,000	

Nominal value of shares acquired	1,000,000
Holding company's carrying value of investment	1,250,000
Difference on consolidation	(250,000)

Following the recommendations in SSAP 23, Cowan Gate need to reduce their reserves by this amount of £250,000.

Pro forma balance sheet of holding company: Cowan Gate plc (in £000s)

	Acquisition accounting		Merger accounting
	(A)	(B)	
Ordinary £1 shares	2,750	2,750	2,750
Profit and loss account	1,500	1,500	1,500
Share premium	4,550	800	800
Capital redemption	1,200	1,200	1,200
Merger reserve	—	3,750	—
	10,000	10,000	6,250

	Acquisition accounting		Merger accounting
	(A)	(B)	
Investment in Cart	5,000	5,000	1,250
Other net assets	5,000	5,000	5,000
	10,000	10,000	6,250

Pro forma consolidated balance sheet (in £000s)

	Acquisition accounting Solution		Merger accounting
	(A)	(B)	
Ordinary £1 shares	2,750	2,750	2,750
Profit and loss reserves	1,500	(500)	3,500
Less difference on consolidation			(250)
Share premium reserve	4,550	800	800
Merger reserve		3,750	
Capital redemption reserve	1,200	1,200	1,200
	10,000	8,000	8,000
Goodwill	2,000		
Net assets	8,000	8,000	8,000
	10,000	8,000	8,000

The question raises the issue of whether the choice of accounting methods affects the level of distributable profits. It must be remembered that distributions are made by individual companies, not by the groups. As the balance sheets for the holding company stand with the present information, the amount of distributable profits is the same whichever method of accounting is used.

The position could, however, be changed if Cart plc declared a dividend of £2 million (or up to that amount) out of its accumulated profit and loss reserves. If this happened, in a merger accounting situation Cowan Gate could distribute to its shareholders a part of the subsidiaries' £2 million of pre-acquisition profits.

As was explained on page 173, there is not an overriding requirement in company law for a dividend received out of pre-acquisition profits to be credited against the cost of the investment. The dividends only have to be credited against the cost to the extent that the distribution has caused an impairment in the value of the investment. This normally means that with merger accounting all or most of the dividend received will be available for distribution to the holding company's shareholders, whereas with acquisition accounting normally none or very little of the dividends will be available for distribution.

Let us consider the position first under merger accounting. The investment is recorded by Cowan Gate at £1.25 million. The tangible net assets (at book value) of Cart after the £2 million dividend would be reduced from £3 million to £1 million. Therefore the value of the investment has been impaired by £0.25 million. Of the £2 million dividend, it would appear that £1.75 million could be seen as distributable profits that could be paid to the shareholders of Cowan Gate. The entry recording the receipt of dividends by the holding company would be:

Dr Cash	£2,000,000	
Cr Investment in Cart		£ 250,000
Profit and loss reserve		1,750,000

There is a question of whether or not the net assets of Cart before the distribution should be regarded as £3 million or £5 million, the latter figure taking into account the price Cowan Gate was prepared to pay. If this latter figure is used, the distribution of the dividend does not reduce the value of the assets to below the carrying value in the books of Cowan Gate (£1.25 million). It can be regarded as unjust, however, to use this argument, as one of the main points about merger accounting is that the goodwill element can be ignored. One cannot ignore it from the point of view of valuing assets, and hence the write-down of assets against reserves and profits, and then take it into account because it helps in distributing profits.

The position with acquisition accounting is a little more confused. First, the normal position will be explained. By this is meant the situation where a combination does not qualify for 'merger relief', but has to be treated as an acquisition. With acquisition accounting pre-acquisition profits are not, in most cases, available for distribution to the holding company's shareholders. In some circumstances, however, they may be. When a subsidiary pays dividends to the holding company out of pre-acquisition profits, the holding company must first apply the dividend to reduce the investment carrying value. But it need do this only in so far as it is necessary to allow for the diminution in that carrying value.

Let us look at the situation in this case. The dividend is paid by Cart plc. The value of the investment in the holding company accounts before the distribution is £5 million. What are the value of the net assets of Cart after the distribution?

The holding company originally paid £5 million for the net assets, by definition a 'fair value'. £2 million has been paid out, so the fair value of the assets remaining is now £3 million. The whole of the £2 million dividend received will have to be credited against the cost of the investment so as to reduce it to its new value of £3 million.

Dr Cash	£2,000,000	
Cr Investment in Cart		£2,000,000

This would imply that none of the pre-acquisition profit of the acquired company can be paid out to the shareholders of Cowan Gate.

The confusion arises if the holding company, instead of crediting the share premium account with £3,750,000 (as in solution A), instead credits it to a 'merger reserve' (as with solution B). The circumstances under which this can be done arise where the combination is eligible for merger relief, and the purchasing company decides to record the investment in its own books at the fair value rather than the nominal value.

In the case being considered, with such circumstances applying, the value of the investment in Cart is reduced by £2 million, and the value of the merger reserve by a similar amount. This is accomplished by transferring the £2 million from the 'merger reserve' to the 'profit and loss account reserve', which means that it would be available for distribution. It should be explained that SSAP 23 does point out that, at the time the standard was written, it was unclear whether such action had legal justification.

The adjusting entry would be:

Dr Cash	£2,000,000	
Cr Investment in Cart		£2,000,000
Dr Merger reserve	2,000,000	
Cr Profit and loss a/c reserve		2,000,000

Further reading

See Chapter 11.

Questions

1. On 1 January 1987, Wigan Industries plc announced that they had obtained 90% of the shares of Barr Ltd in exchange for 200,000 of their own ordinary shares whose stock market price stood at £3.75 per share at the close of trading on 31 December 1986.

Balance sheets for the two companies were drawn up on 31 December 1986 and are summarised below:

	Wigan		Barr	
	£'000s	£'000s	£'000s	£'000s
Ordinary shares of £1 each		400		200
Share premium		250		100
General reserves		600		250
Profit and loss account		150		150
		1,400		700
Loan Stock	400		140	
Current liabilities	200	600	160	300
		2,000		1,000
Fixed assets at cost	2,300		900	
less Depreciation	800	1,500	250	650
Goodwill		—		150
Current assets		500		200
		2,000		1,000

You are required to:
(a) prepare a consolidated balance sheet for Wigan Industries plc immediately following the combination and treating it as
  (i) an acquisition   (10 marks)
  (ii) a merger   (10 marks)
(b) set out the arguments which suppose the use of merger, explaining how these are reflected by the requirements of SSAP 23 ('Accounting for acquisitions and mergers')   (7 marks)
                                                                                         (27 marks)

2. Accountants in the United Kingdom/Ireland have been trying for some twenty years to determine the appropriate respective uses of the acquisition (purchase) and merger (pooling) methods of preparing group accounts.

Required:
(a) Explain (*without* numerical illustrations) the objectives of the two methods, and the ways in which the said objectives are attained.   (10 marks)
(b) Give your opinion of the success or otherwise of SSAP 23: *Accounting for acquisitions and mergers* (1985) in assigning each of the two methods of group accounting to its proper sphere. (15 marks)
                                                                                         (25 marks)
                                                              ACCA, 3.1, AFA, December 1986.

3. Consolidated Furniture Group plc wishes to adopt the merger accounting principles in ED 31, 'Accounting for acquisitions and mergers', in respect of its combination with Tables & Chairs Ltd on 30 September 1983.
On 1 August 1983 Consolidated Furniture Group plc acquired 5% of the issued share capital of Tables & Chairs Ltd for a consideration of 80,000 shares of 25p each at an agreed value of 125p each.
The terms of the merger on 30 September 1983, which were accepted by all shareholders and declared unconditional on the same day, were that, for every 8 shares held in Tables and Chairs Ltd, a holder received 20 shares of 25p each at an agreed value of 135p each in Consolidated Furniture Group plc plus £3 nominal of 13% Unsecured Loan Stock 2002.
All the shares issued were credited as fully paid and ranked *pari passu* with existing shares in issue, except

that those issued on 30 September 1983 were not to rank for the final dividend in respect of the year ended 30 November 1983.

The draft summarised balance sheet and profit and loss account of the companies for the year ended 30 November 1983, the accounting reference date for Consolidated Furniture Group plc were:

	Consolidated Furniture Group plc	Tables & Chairs Ltd
Balance sheet:	£'000s	£'000s
Fixed assets	4,563	3,092
Goodwill at cost	—	800
Investments	175	—
Current assets	2,369	3,626
Current liabilities	(2,286)	(4,207)
	4,821	3,311
Share capital	3,000	1,600
Reserves	1,821	1,711
	4,821	3,311
Profit and loss account:		
Turnover	36,873	25,003
Profit before tax	1,151	127
Taxation	260	—
Profit after tax	891	127
Dividends paid	288	—
Profits retained	603	127

Additional information is given as follows:
(1) The reserves of Consolidated Furniture Group plc at 30 November 1983 consisted of a share premium account of £140,000 and revenue reserves of £1,681,000. The reserves in Tables & Chairs Ltd are undistributed revenue reserves.
(2) The issue of the shares made on 1 August 1983 is reflected in the draft financial statements.
(3) It is the policy of Consolidated Furniture Group plc to write off goodwill in equal instalments over 5 years.
(4) It is considered that the market value of the 13% loan stock issued is par.
(5) The share capitals of the companies are:
    Consolidated Furniture Group plc—ordinary 25p each
    Tables & Chairs Ltd   —ordinary £1 each
(6) The directors of Consolidated Furniture Group plc resolve to propose a final dividend of 1p per share. This is not yet reflected in the draft financial statements.

You are required to:
(a) prepare a consolidated balance sheet and profit and loss account, in summary form, of Consolidated Furniture Group plc at 30 November 1983;   (14 marks)
(b) give the revised analysis of reserves of Consolidated Furniture Group plc at 30 November 1983 suitable for inclusion in the published financial statements;   (5 marks)
(c) comment whether you consider merger accounting to be appropriate in the above example, giving an indication of advantages which may arise.   (5 marks)

Note: Make calculations to nearest £'000 and ignore the costs of the merger and advance corporation tax.
                                                                                             (24 marks)
                                                              ICAEW, PEII, FAII, December 1983
4. The managing director of Holdings plc is considering with his merchant bankers the mix of the

consideration in formulating the proposals to make an offer for all the ordinary shares in Sitting Duck plc. He is concerned about the effect on the consolidated accounts of Holdings plc of the various offers the company could make in the light of the principles for acounting for acquisitions and mergers now embodied in SSAP23, and the two different methods of accounting dependent upon the circumstances of the business combinations.

Requirement

Write a report to the managing director stating:

(a) what conditions are required to be met if merger accounting is to be used;   (3 marks)

(b) what are the differences in principle between acquisition accounting and merger accounting;

(3 marks)

(c) how the difference on consolidation is calculated under merger accounting and how it is reflected in financial statements;   (3 marks)

(d) the advantages and disadvantages of using each method of accounting so that he can structure a proposed deal using the appropriate method.   (12 marks)

(21 marks)

ICAEW, PEII, FAII, July 1986

5. With regard to SSAP 23, *Accounting for acquisitions and mergers:*

(a) What are the conditions that must be met if a business combination is to be accounted for as a merger?

(8 marks)

(b) Give *four* examples of items in a group balance sheet that may alter when merger rather than acquisition accounting is used and briefly explain why.   (8 marks)

(c) Give *two* examples of items in a group profit and loss account that may alter when merger rather than acquisition accounting is used and briefly explain why.   (4 marks)

(20 marks)

ACCA, 2.8, RFA June 1987

11. Consolidated statements: post-acquisition

As has been explained in the two previous chapters, it is necessary for a company that owns subsidiary companies to prepare group accounts. The group accounts show the state of affairs, the profit and loss account, and the sources and application of funds statement of a holding company and its subsidiaries. It is recognized that the most useful way of presenting the financial position of a group is by consolidating the accounts of the separate companies. The assets and liabilities of the separate companies that belong to the group are added together, with intragroup transactions eliminated. It should be recognized that consolidated accounts are in a certain sense a fiction. The group is not a legal entity: it is the individual holding company and each of its subsidiaries that are legal entities. Nevertheless, if all the companies in the group operate as one, although the group is not a legal entity, it is an economic entity. It is therefore meaningful to require this economic unit to report its state of affairs and its trading position.

This is the EEC approach; the 7th Directive on group accounts states that a group exists not only in the situation of dependency, where one undertaking exercises directly or indirectly a dominant influence over another undertaking, but also if 'undertakings operate in a concerted manner and in a common interest on a long-term basis as regards their assets or management'.[1] This latter definition is of an economic unit rather than a legal unit.

The purpose of consolidation is to bring together the accounts of the different companies in the group, and to present them as if they were the accounts of a single entity. To achieve this aim,

Uniform group accounting policies should be followed by a holding company in preparing its consolidated financial statements. Where such group accounting policies are not adopted in the financial statements of a subsidiary, appropriate adjustments should be made in the consolidated financial statements. In exceptional cases where this is impracticable, different accounting policies may be used provided they are generally acceptable and there is disclosure of:
(a) the different accounting policies used;
(b) an indication of the amounts of the assets and liabilities involved and, where practicable, an indication of the effect on results and net assets of the adoption of policies different from those of the group;
(c) the reasons for the different treatment.[2]

In order to present a set of financial statements for a diverse group of companies as if they were a single entity, not only is it necessary to adopt similar accounting policies, but it is also necessary for the subsidiaries, wherever practicable, to prepare their accounts to the same accounting date as the holding company and for identical accounting periods:

If a subsidiary does not prepare its formal financial statements to the same date as the holding company, and if it is not practicable to use for consolidation purposes special financial statements drawn up to the same date as those of the holding company (Department of Trade or other Government consent having been obtained, as necessary), appropriate adjustments should be made for any abnormal transactions in the intervening period and the following additional information should be given for each principal subsidiary with a different accounting date:
(a) its name; and
(b) its acounting date; and
(c) the reason for using a different accounting date.

Where the accounting period of a principal subsidiary is of a different length from that of the holding company, the accounting period involved should be stated.[3]

The chapter now considers in detail the accounting entries necessary to consolidate the financial statements of a group of companies.

11.1 Consolidating profits

The object of the consolidated profit and loss account is to show the profit or loss for the group. The approach adopted is to calculate the aggregate profit or loss for all companies in the group, after eliminating any profits or losses on inter-company transactions in goods or assets. All other intragroup transactions need to be eliminated, such as, for example, interest charges on any loans within the group.

Example 11.1

To begin with, a simple example will be considered. Company P owns 100 per cent of the shares of company S. The purchase price was £10,000. The respective balance sheets, in a summarized form, of the two separate companies as at 31 December 19X0 are as follows:

	Company P £	Company S £
Share capital	20,000	5,000
Reserves	20,000	8,000
Current liabilities	20,000	7,000
	60,000	20,000
Fixed assets	30,000	13,000
Investment in subsdiary	15,000	
Current liabilities	15,000	7,000
	60,000	20,000

Company S has made after-tax profits in the year of £5,000. It is assumed that company P is using the equity method of accounting in its own books, and so the balance of £15,000 in the 'investment in subsidiary account' includes the £5,000 profit of company S. In the consolidated accounts this balance needs to be eliminated, as the share capital and profits of the subsidiary are in fact represented by assets in the subsidiary company which are combined in the consolidation process with those of the parent company.

It is necessary to be able to distinguish between pre-acquisition profits and post-acquisition profits. To do this, one needs to know the reserves of the subsidiary at the time it was purchased by the parent company. In the above example such reserves equalled £3,000. The eliminating entries and the resulting consolidated figures are as follows:

	Company P £	Company S £	Eliminations Dr £	Cr £	Consolidated £
Sales	200,000	80,000			280,000
Earnings from subsidiary	5,000		5,000 (2)		
	205,000	80,000			280,000

	Company P	Company S	Eliminations		Consoli-dated
			Dr	Cr	
	£	£	£	£	£
Cost of sales	165,000	35,000			200,000
Other expenses	30,000	40,000			70,000
Profits	10,000	5,000		5,000 (2)	10,000
	205,000	80,000			280,000
Share capital	20,000	5,000	5,000 (1)		20,000
Reserves: opening	10,000	3,000	3,000 (1)		
additions	10,000	5,000	5,000 (3)		20,000
Current liabilities	20,000	7,000			27,000
	60,000	20,000			67,000
Fixed assets	30,000	13,000			43,000
Investment in subsidiary	15,000		$\begin{cases} 10,000\ (1) \\ 5,000\ (3) \end{cases}$		
Current assets	15,000	7,000			22,000
Goodwill on consolidation			2,000 (1)		2,000
	60,000	20,000	20,000	20,000	67,000

It has been assumed that all profits have been retained. For illustrative purposes, the reserves of the two companies have been divided between their pre- and post-acquisition elements. The eliminating entries will now be explained.

Entry (1) As explained in the previous chapter, upon consolidation the assets and liabilities of the parent company and subsidiary are added together. To avoid double-counting, certain items are eliminated. This initial investment in the subsidiary of £10,000 by the parent company is balanced against the share capital and reserves (equivalent to the net assets) that were purchased. The excess of the purchase price over the book value of the net assets acquired is referred to as 'goodwill arising on consolidation': £10,000 − (£5,000 + £3,000).

Entry (2) With the equity method of accounting, the earnings of the subsidiary are included as earnings in the profit and loss account of the parent company. This entry avoids double-counting the £5,000.

Entry (3) The earnings of the subsidiary are included as reserves of both the parent and the subsidiary. The entry avoids double-counting.

Example 11.2

The next situation that will be considered is one where company P purchases only 80 per cent of the shares of company S. The same companies are being used as in the previous example, but this time the £50,000 purchases only 4,000 shares of company S. The profits from the investment to be brought into the parent company books, again assuming equity accounting, by the parent company is now only £4,000 (i.e., 80 per cent of £5,000). The relevant journal entry is:

Dr Investment in subsidiary   £4,000
Cr Earnings from subsidiary   £4,000

A consolidated profit and loss account will be prepared as well as a consolidated balance sheet.

	Company P	Company S	Eliminations Dr	Cr	Consoli- dated
	£	£	£	£	£
Sales	200,000	80,000			280,000
Earnings from subsidiary	4,000		4,000 (1)		
	204,000	80,000			280,000
Cost of sales	165,000	35,000			200,000
Other expenses	30,000	40,000			70,000
Minority interests			1,000 (2)		1,000
Profits	9,000	5,000		4,000 (1) 1,000 (2)	9,000
	204,000	80,000			280,000
Share capital	20,000	5,000	4,000 (6) 1,000 (7)		20,000
Reserves: opening	10,000	3,000	2,400 (6) 600 (5)		10,000
additions	9,000	5,000	4,000 (3) 1,000 (4)		9,000
Current liabilities	20,000	7,000			27,000
Minority interests				1,000 (4) 600 (5) 1,000 (7)	2,600
	59,000	20,000			68,600
Fixed assets	30,000	13,000			43,000
Investment in subsidiary	14,000			10,000 (6) 4,000 (3)	
Current assets	15,000	7,000			22,000
Goodwill on consolidation			3,600 (6)		3,600
	59,000	20,000	21,600	21,600	68,600

Entry (1) Eliminates earnings of S that appear in the parent company profit and loss account and the profit and loss account of S.
Entry (2) The minority interest's share of the earnings of S.
Entry (3) Eliminates earnings of S that have already been taken to reserves of P.
Entry (4) The minority interest's share of this year's retained earings of S.
Entry (5) The minority interest's share of the reserves of S at the time P acquired its interest.
Entry (6) The purchase by P of its interest in S. The creation of the goodwill on consolidation account (see explanation of entry (1) in Example 11.1): £10,000 − (£5,000 + £3,000) × 0.8.
Entry (7) The share capital of S that was not purchased by P.

The earnings of the subsidiary attributable to the parent have been taken to the parent company's own accounts. They are included in the profits figure which is taken to reserves. The addition to reserves in the consolidated balance sheet represents £5,000 earned by the parent company and £4,000 earned by the subsidiary. This £4,000 is post-acquisition profits and so can be included in the consolidated balance sheet. The funds, or investments, represented by the reserves are at the moment still with the subsidiary. Nothing has been said at this stage of the analysis about a distribution of these profits to shareholders.

The appropriate share of post-acquisition reserves of subsidiaries should be included in the group's reserves in the consolidated accounts. The issue of whether they should be included in the reserves of the parent company depends upon whether the company is following the equity or the cost method. The method that will be followed in most cases in this chapter is the equity method. This means that a share of the post-acquisition reserves of the subsidiary is already reflected in the parent company's balances and so it is necessary, to avoid double-counting, to eliminate the subsidiary company's reserves. For comparative purposes, one or two examples in the chapter will show the alternative cost method, and it will be seen that a part of the subsidiary's reserves need to be added to the parent company's reserves to arrive at the consolidated figure. Such an example follows.

In both of the above examples, with 100 per cent ownership and 80 per cent ownership, the equity method of recording the investment in the books of the parent company has been followed. The following example will show the 100 per cent situation where the investment is being entered in the books of company P using the cost method. The balance sheets at the end of the year, the eliminating entries and the consolidated figures are as follows:

Example 11.3

	Company P	Company S	Eliminations Dr	Cr	Consolidation
	£	£	£	£	£
Share capital	20,000	5,000	5,000		20,000
Reserves	15,000	8,000	3,000		20,000
Current liabilities	20,000	7,000			27,000
	55,000	20,000			67,000
Fixed assets	30,000	13,000			43,000
Investment in subsidiary	10,000			10,000	
Current assets	15,000	7,000			22,000
Goodwill on consolidation			2,000		2,000
	55,000	20,000			67,000

The amounts appearing in the consolidated balance sheet are the same as in Example 11.1, but the parent company's balance sheet is different. It has been necessary to add the £5,000 reserves of company S to the parent company's reserves in order to obtain the consolidated reserves of £20,000.

11.2 Inter-company dividends

Continuing with Example 11.2, in which company P purchased 80 per cent of the shares of company S, it is now assumed that company S proposes to distribute one-half of its £5,000 profits for the year as dividends. The investor company P will therefore receive £2,000 (i.e. 80 per cent of

£2,500). In the books of S, the intended distribution would be reflected by the following entry:

>Dr Proposed dividends   £2,500
>Cr Dividends payable   £2,500

the dividends being declared but not distributed.

   In the parent company's books, the entry to record the earnings and intended distribution would be:

>Dr Dividends receivable from subsidiary   £2,000
>Dr Investment in subsidiary   2,000
>Cr Earnings of subsidiary   £4,000

This entry replaces the one where all the £4,000 is debited to investment in subsidiary. It should be remembered that these are the entries under the equity method of recording transactions in the parent company's books. With the cost method, the only entry in the parent company's books would be:

>Dr Dividends receivable   £2,000
>Cr Dividends from subsidiary   £2,000

The eliminations necessary to arrive at the figures for the consolidated profit and loss account are as shown in the following example.

Example 11.4

	Company P	Company S	Eliminations Dr	Cr	Consolidation
	£	£	£	£	£
Sales	200,000	80,000			280,000
Earnings of subsidiary	4,000		4,000 (1)		
	204,000	80,000			280,000
Cost of sales	165,000	35,000			200,000
Other expenses	30,000	40,000			70,000
Dividend proposed		2,500		2,000 (1)	500
Minority interests			500 (2)		500
Profits retained	9,000	2,500		500 (2) 2,000 (1)	9,000
	204,000	80,000			280,000

The only difference between this and the consolidated profit and loans account in Example 11.2 is that the minority interest's £1,000 is now split between £500 as the dividends that it is proposed they should receive, and £500 representing their share of retained profits. To illustrate what has happened in the example these two items have been shown separately, but a more usual presentation would be to add the two figures together and show minority interests as £1,000. Entry (1) divides P's share of the earnings between the amount to be distributed as dividends to P and the amount to be retained in S. Entry (2) represents the minority interest's share of the retained earnings. The eliminations in the balance sheet would be as follows:

	Company P	Company S	Eliminations Dr	Cr	Consoli- dation
	£	£	£	£	£
Share capital	20,000	5,000	4,000 (6) 1,000 (7)		20,000
Reserves					
—P	19,000				19,000
—S pre-acquisition		3,000	2,400 (6) 600 (5)		
—S post-acquisition		2,500	2,000 (3) 500 (4)		
Dividends payable		2,500		2,000 (8)	500
Minority interests				500 (4) 600 (5) 1,000 (7)	2,100
Current liabilities	20,000	7,000			27,000
	59,000	20,000			68,600
Fixed assets	30,000	13,000			43,000
Investment in subsidiary	12,000			10,000 (6) 2,000 (3)	
Dividends receivable from subsidiary	2,000		2,000 (8)		
Current assets	15,000	7,000			22,000
Goodwill on consolidation			3,600 (6)		3,600
	59,000	20,000			68,600

Entry (3)   Eliminates the retained earnings of S, as they have already been taken to reserves of P.
Entry (4)   As per (4) in Example 11.2.
Entry (5)   As per (5) in Example 11.2.
Entry (6)   As per (6) in Example 11.2.
Entry (7)   As per (7) in Example 11.2.
Entry (8)   Eliminates inter-company payment of dividends.

The only difference between this balance sheet and the one in Example 11.2 is that the involvement of the minority interest is now reflected in the £500 dividend payable, which is a current liability, and the £2,100 longer-term claim of the minority interest. The usual presentation is to present these two items as one, namely 'minority interests £2,600'. The inter-company liability and claim with respect to dividends has been eliminated. When the dividends are actually paid, the entry in the parent company's books is:

Dr Cash	£2,000	
Cr Dividends receivable		£2,000

and in the books of the subsidiary company:

> Dr Dividends payable £2,500
> Cr Cash £2,500

The net result in the consolidated balance sheet is that on the asset side cash is reduced by £500, and on the liabilities side the dividends payable (to minority shareholders) is eliminated.

11.2.1 Dividends paid out of pre-acquisition profits

The next situation that will be considered is where dividends are paid out of pre-acquisition profits. In this case, the acquired company is paying out cash which was part of the net assets that the parent company purchased. What is happening, in effect, is that part of the assets purchased on acquisition are being returned so the purchase price is being reduced. Such dividends received by the parent company are not profits available for distribution, as they are not profits that have been earned.

In Example 11.2, company P pays £10,000 for 80 per cent of company S. It will now be assumed that at the time of acquisition company S has announced that it is to make a distribution of £1,500. This appears as dividends payable in its year-end balance sheet. Company P purchases the shares cum dividend and anticipates that it will receive the dividend from S; the two balance sheets at the time of acquisition and the necessary eliminations are shown in the following example.

Example 11.5

	Company P	Company S	Eliminations Dr	Eliminations Cr	Consoli- dated
	£	£	£	£	£
Share capital	20,000	5,000	4,000 (1) 1,000 (2)		20,000
Reserves	10,000	1,500	1,200 (1) 300 (2)		10,000
Dividend payable		1,500	1,200 (3)		300
Current liabilities	20,000	7,000			27,000
Minority interests				1,300 (2)	1,300
	50,000	15,000			58,600
Fixed assets	25,000	8,000			33,000
Investment in subsidiary	8,800			8,800 (1)	—
Dividends receivable	1,200			1,200 (3)	—
Current assets	15,000	7,000			22,000
Goodwill on consolidation			3,600 (1)		3,600
	50,000	15,000			58,600

Entry (1) The purchase by P of an interest in S. The entry necessary to prepare the consolidated accounts is:

> Dr Share capital £4,000
>   Reserves 1,200
>   Goodwill 3,600
> Cr Investment in subsidiary £8,800

Entry (2) The minority interest's share of share capital and reserves.
Entry (3) Eliminates inter-company element of dividends to be paid.

Company P has anticipated its share of the dividend (80 per cent of £1,500) and this amount has been used in its own accounts to reduce the cost of its investment in S from £10,000 to £8,800. In the consolidated accounts, the goodwill figure remains unaltered from Example 11.2, as the same quantity of assets have been purchased for the same price. The inter-company dividend payments are eliminated, but the dividends to be received by minority shareholders are shown as a current liability.

When the dividends are paid, the entries are similar to those for post-acquisition profits. Company S credits cash and debits dividend payable. Company P, in its own books, debits cash and credits dividend receivable. The net result in the consolidated accounts is that current assets are reduced by £300 and the dividends payable are eliminated.

11.3   Aquisition of subsidiary during accounting year

The examples up to now have assumed that the company has been purchased on the date at which its accounts are prepared. In reality this is most unlikely to happen. If, as is normal, the shares of the purchased company are acquired *during* its accounting period, one has the problem of deciding what proportion of its annual profits are pre-acquisition and what proportion are post-acquisition. In fact, it is necessary to apportion the profits on a time basis.

There is also the problem of dividends to consider. The acquired company may have paid out interim dividends before the holding company purchased shares.

Example 11.6

P acquired 80 per cent of the equity shares of S Ltd on 1 July 19X0 for £100,000. S Ltd made profits after tax of £10,000 during 19X0. The reserves of S Ltd at 1 January 19X0 were £32,000. S Ltd paid an interim dividend of £2,000 on 30 June 19X0, and declared a final dividend of £5,000. In preparing its final accounts P Ltd has anticipated the dividend to be received, but has made no adjustments for the pre-acquisition element.

When the acquisition is made on 1 July 19X0, the entry in the books of P Ltd is as follows:

> Dr Investment in subsidiary   £100,000
> Cr Cash   £100,000

When the earnings of S Ltd are determined for the year, P Ltd, using the equity method of accounting, takes credit for its share of these earnings in its accounts. The profits for the second half of the year were £5,000, and 80 per cent of these relate to the shares acquired by P. The entry in P's books are:

> Dr Investment in subsidiary   £4,000
> Cr Earnings of subsidiary   £4,000

When the final dividend is announced, it is necessary to make another entry:

> Dr Dividend receivable   £4,000
> Cr Investment in subsidiary   £4,000

In order to make the eliminating entries needed to arrive at the figures for the consolidated balance sheet, it is necessary to calculate the pre-acquisition profits, the goodwill and the minority interests. These calculations are shown in three stages as follows.

Step 1
Ascertain pre-acquisition reserves of S Ltd

	£
Reserves balance at 1/1/19X0	32,000
add profit earned up to date of acquisition	
($\frac{1}{2} \times$ £10,000)	5,000
	37,000
less Pre-acquisition dividends	2,000
	35,000 × 80% = £28,000

Step 2
Having established that P Ltd purchased £28,000 of the reserves of S Ltd, it is possible to calculate whether or not there was any goodwill purchased at the time of acquisition. The purchase price has to be adjusted for repayment of part of the price in the form of dividends. It is the amount of dividends that has been received by the purchasing company that is a distribution of pre-acquisition profits, that needs to be deducted from the price. It is only the dividends actually received by the purchasing company that matter; any interim dividends paid before the shares were acquired are not relevant.

	£
Share capital of S Ltd acquired	
(80% of £50,000)	40,000
Reserves of S Ltd acquired	28,000
	68,000
Price paid	100,000
Goodwill arising on consolidation	32,000

Of the total dividend for the year of £7,000, apportionment on a time basis would mean that £3,500 relates to the pre-acquisition situation. The interim dividend of £2,000 was paid out of pre-acquisition profits, but P Ltd received none of this. Of the final dividend of £5,000, the amount that would be payment from pre-acquisition profits is £1,500. P Ltd would receive £1,200 of this distribution of pre-acquisition profits. However, it can be approached by treating the £5,000 post-acquisition dividend as paid entirely out of the £5,000 post-acquisition earnings, requiring no further adjustment.

Step 3
The minority interest as at 31 December 19X0 consists of:

Share capital (20% of £50,000)	£10,000	
Reserves (20% of (£32,000 + £3,000 retained profits))	7,000	£17,000

These three steps enable the necessary adjustments to be made, and the balance sheets of the two separate companies and the resulting consolidated balance sheet are as follows:

Balance sheets as at 31 December 19X0

	Company P	Company S	Eliminations Dr	Eliminations Cr	Consolidated
	£	£	£	£	£
Share capital	140,000	50,000	40,000 (1) 10,000 (2)		140,000
Reserves	74,000	35,000	28,000 (1) 7,000 (2)		74,000
Dividends payable to minorities		5,000	4,000 (3)		1,000
Current liabilities	30,000	20,000			50,000
Minority interest				17,000 (2)	17,000
	244,000	110,000			282,000
Goodwill on consolidation			32,000 (1)		32,000
Fixed assets	74,000	80,000			154,000
Dividends receivable	4,000			4,000 (3)	
Current assets	66,000	30,000			96,000
Investment in subsidiary	100,000			100,000 (1)	
	244,000	110,000			282,000

Entry (1)   This covers steps 1 and 2 referred to above, eliminating the pre-acquisition profits and recording the goodwill. It covers the purchase by P of its interest in S.

Dr Share capital—S	£40,000	
Reserves—S	28,000	
Goodwill on consolidation	32,000	
Cr Investment in subsidiary		£100,000

Entry (2)   Minority interests in share capital and reserves.
Entry (3)   Elimination of inter-company dividend: 80% of £5,000.

11.4 Taxation

An added complication is now introduced. Normally when a company pays dividends it also has to make a payment to the Inland Revenue in respect of ACT which was discussed in Chapter 8. It would be illogical to make such ACT payments to the Inland Revenue in respect of dividends passing from one company in a group to another company in the group. Companies in a group are, therefore, allowed to select not to account for ACT on inter-company dividends. Such dividends are known as 'group income'. Dividends paid by a subsidiary to minority shareholders are not group income and so have to be treated in the same way as any dividend payment to outsiders.

SSAP 8 establishes a standard treatment of ACT and mainstream corporation tax.[4] Dividends received from UK resident companies should be included at the amount of cash received or receivable plus the related tax credit. Outgoing dividends should not include the related ACT. We have a situation, therefore, where SSAP 8 requires a company to disclose dividends received as gross of ACT, and dividends paid as net of ACT. The way in which such adjustments can be handled to arrive at consolidated figures is shown in Example 11.7 below. As well as introducing the treatment of tax, this example also introduces inter-company holdings of loan stock, and inter-company directors' emoluments.

Example 11.7

	Company P	Company S	Eliminations Dr	Eliminations Cr	Consolidated
	£	£	£	£	£
Turnover	100,000	40,000			140,000
Trading profit	26,738	8,962			35,700
Dividends recd—outside	1,000			333 (5)	1,333
Dividends recd—S Ltd	800		800 (1)		
Debenture interest—S Ltd	1,000		1,000 (4)		
	29,538	8,962			37,033
less					
Depreciation	10,000	1,000			11,000
Interest paid		2,000		1,000 (4)	1,000
Directors' emoluments	10,000	2,000			12,000
Audit fees	2,000	500			2,500
	22,000	5,000			26,500
Profit before tax	7,538	3,462			10,533
Tax	2,638	1,212	333 (5)		4,183
Profit after tax	4,900	2,250			6,350
Minority interests			200 (2) / 250 (3)		450
Dividends paid	3,000	1,000	800 (1) / 200 (2)		3,000
Transfer to reserves	1,900	1,250	250(3)		2,900

Entry (1) Eliminate inter-company dividends.
Entry (2) Minority interest's share of S Ltd's dividends.
Entry (3) Minority interest's share of S Ltd's retained profits.
Entry (4) Eliminate inter-company interest payment.
Entry (5) Tax paid on dividends received.

The profit and loss accounts of P Ltd and S Ltd given above are for the year ending 31 December 19X1. P Ltd owns 80 per cent of the equity shares of S Ltd and 50 per cent of the loan stock of S. P Ltd prepares its individual company accounts on the cost basis. At the date the shares were acquired, the revenue reserves of S Ltd amounted to £20,000. Included in the emoluments of the directors of S Ltd is £1,000 paid to a director of P Ltd.

The total emoluments paid to the directors of P Ltd are £11,000, that is the £10,000 paid by P Ltd plus the £1,000 paid by S Ltd. The amount of directors' remuneration to be disclosed in the consolidated accounts is £11,000, the amount paid to directors of the holding company. In calculating the operating profit, however, it is necessary to deduct the total directors' remuneration, that is the £12,000.

The amount to be transferred to the consolidated reserve is the £1,900 retained by P Ltd plus 80 per cent of the balance of £1,250 in S Ltd, that is a total of £2,900. This figure is arrived at after transferring 20 per cent of the £1,250 from reserves to minority interests. In the above accounts, S Ltd pays £800 dividends to P Ltd. As explained, this is group income and so no ACT is payable. S Ltd pays £200 of dividends to minority shareholders. These are recorded in the accounts of the paying company net of ACT; it is the receiving shareholders who, if they are companies, will have to gross up these amounts. The £1,000 of dividends received from investments outside the group do need to be adjusted. It is assumed that the base rate of income tax is 25 per cent, which means that the investment income figure to be shown in the consolidated accounts will be £1,333 (i.e., £1,000 × 100/75). The taxation charge for the group is the combined corporation tax £3,850 plus the tax already paid on dividends received of £333.

The minority interest consists of 20 per cent of the after-tax profits, that is £450. This figure is made up of £200 dividends and £250 retained earnings. The appropriate eliminating entries can be seen above.

The resulting consolidated profit and loss account, in the form in which it can be published, will be:

	£
Turnover	140,000
Operating profit (i)	9,200
Investment income	1,333
Profit before taxation	10,533
Taxation	4,183
Profit after taxation	6,350
Minority shareholders' interest	450
Profit attributable to group	5,900
Dividends	3,000
Transfer to reserves	2,900

Note (i)   The operating profit is arrived at after taking into account the following amounts:

Depreciation	£11,000
Debenture interest	1,000
Director's emoluments	11,000
Audit fees	2,500

11.5   Inter-company sales

Another form of inter-company transaction is where one company in a group sells goods to another company in the group. To illustrate the preparation of consolidated statements in such situations an example will be used. P Ltd owns 80 per cent of S Ltd, and half of the goods produced by S Ltd are 'sold' to P Ltd. The goods are transferred to P Ltd at cost. All the goods transferred have been sold by P Ltd by the year-end. There is one other inter-company transaction: S Ltd leases its factory from P Ltd, at an annual rental of £10,000. The eliminations necessary to arrive at the consolidated figure are shown in Example 11.8.

Example 11.8

Profit and loss accounts

	P Ltd	S Ltd	Eliminations Dr	Cr	Consoli-dated
	£	£	£	£	£
Sales	200,000	80,000	40,000 (2)		240,000
Earnings from subsidiary	4,000		4,000 (3)		—
Other revenue	10,000		10,000 (1)		—
	214,000	80,000			240,000
Cost of sales	165,000	60,000		40,000 (2)	185,000
Other costs	30,000	15,000		10,000 (1)	35,000
Minority interests			1,000 (4)		1,000
Profits	19,000	5,000		4,000 (3) 1,000 (4)	19,000
	214,000	80,000			240,000

Entry (1) Elimination of inter-company rental transactions.
Entry (2) Elimination of inter-company sales. The sales revenue to S Ltd is the same as the cost to P Ltd (£40,000), and it is this that is being eliminated.
Entry (3) P Ltd is keeping its accounts according to the equity principle and so has taken credit for its share of the profits of S Ltd.
Entry (4) Minority interest's share of profit of S Ltd.

Balance sheets

	P Ltd	S Ltd	Eliminations Dr	Cr	Consoli-dated
	£	£	£	£	£
Share capital	20,000	5,000	4,000 (8) 1,000 (7)		20,000
Reserves—opening	10,000	3,000	2,400 (8) 600 (5)		10,000
—additions	19,000	5,000	4,000 (9) 1,000 (6)		19,000
Current liabilities	20,000	7,000			27,000
Minority interests				600 (5) 1,000 (6) 1,000 (7)	2,600
	69,000	20,000			78,600

	Balance sheets				
	P Ltd	S Ltd	Eliminations		Consoli-
			Dr	Cr	dated
	£	£	£	£	£
Fixed assets	40,000	13,000			53,000
Investment in subsidiary	14,000			{ 4,000 (9) { 10,000 (8)	
Current assets	15,000	7,000			22,000
Goodwill on consolidation			3,600 (8)		3,600
	69,000	20,000			78,600

Entry (5)   Minority interest's share of opening reserve of S Ltd.
Entry (6)   Minority interest's share of additions to reserve of S Ltd.
Entry (7)   Minority interest's share of share capital of S Ltd.
Entry (8)   Elimination of initial investment of P Ltd in S Ltd.

            Dr Share capital   £4,000
                Reserves   2,400
                Goodwill   3,600
            Cr Investment in subsidiary   £10,000

Entry (9)   As per 3, but in the balance sheet.

11.5.1   Unrealized profit on inter-company stock transactions

In the previous example, the transfer was made at cost; often a profit element is included in the transfer prices, and if any of the goods remain unsold at the year-end, there will be unrealized profit from the viewpoint of the group. When P Ltd sells to S Ltd for, say, £5,000, goods that cost £3,000, and S Ltd sells to outsiders those same goods for £6,000, there is not much of a problem. P Ltd is showing £2,000 profit in its own books, S Ltd is showing £1,000 profit, and the group is sharing £3,000 profit on the transaction. Minority shareholders of the group might argue that P Ltd is claiming too large a proportion of the profits in the transaction, but that is a matter of inter-company pricing, a policy decision and not an accounting problem.

However, when S Ltd does not sell the goods that have been transferred within the accounting period, and they are consequently shown as stock in the balance sheet of S Ltd valued at the cost to S Ltd, then it becomes an accounting problem. Unrealized intragroup profit has to be eliminated. The explanatory notes in SSAP 14 optimistically state that 'The method of... eliminating intragroup balances and transactions and unrealized intragroup profit is well understood in the UK and Ireland.'[5]

The profit must be eliminated on items that have not been sold outside the group so as to avoid overstating profits. The profit has not yet been realized and a company could give a false impression of its position if it recognized, in group accounts, the profit on sales by one company in the group to another company in the group. Hopefully, the stock concerned will one day be sold at a profit, but this has not yet happened.

The basic accounting technique for eliminating such profit is to reduce the value of the stock in the consolidated balance sheet and to reduce the profit by the same amount. A decision has to be made as to the amount of profits to be eliminated. There are three possibilities:

(a) One hundred per cent of the profits on the goods in stock are deducted from the interests of the majority shareholders and from the stock value.

(b) One hundred per cent of the profits on the goods in stock are deducted from the interests of the majority and minority shareholders in proportion to their respective interests and from the stock value.

(c) The proportion of the profits accruing to the majority shareholders is deducted from the majority shareholders' interests, but the profits belonging to the minority shareholders are still credited to them. The effect on stock valuation is shown below.

These three methods will be illustrated. P Ltd purchased 75 per cent of the shares of S Ltd for £4,500 on 1 January 19X0. There were no pre-acquisition profits. During 19X0 S Ltd purchased £5,000 of goods from P Ltd, resulting in P Ltd showing a profit of £2,000 on the deal. All these goods were in stock at the year-end. The balance sheets of the two separate companies as at 31 December 19X0 are as shown in Example 11.9. So that the intra-company profit eliminations are easier to identify, it is assumed that neither company made any profits on any other transactions.

As can be seen, all three methods show slightly different results. It could be argued that, in the case of a parent selling to a subsidiary, method 1 is the more logical: the minority shareholders have not been able to influence the transaction, so why should their position be affected by dealings and pricing which were not negotiated at arm's length? Method 3 includes an element of profit in the stock valuation, the profit realized on the sale to the minority interests. All three methods of elimination have their supporters, but the Accountants International Study Group (AISG) found that the usual practice, where the sale is from the parent to a partially owned subsidiary or from a wholly owned subsidiary to a partially owned subsidiary, is to eliminate 100 per cent of the inter-company profits from the interests of the majority of shareholders.[6] Such 100 per cent elimination is often made on the basis of conservatism and simplicity, especially when the amounts applicable to the minority interests are not material.

The use of method 2 can be criticized in the case of a sale from a parent to a subsidiary. As can be seen, the result in this somewhat extreme case is that the minority interest is shown as £1,000, which is less than the minority interest in the share capital.

11.5.2 Subsidiary company sells to parent company

The direction of the intra-company transfer is now changed. The position of minority interests needs to be reconsidered. Example 11.9 will again be used, but this time it is S Ltd that sells £5,000 of goods to P Ltd and makes £2,000 profit on the transaction. At the end of the accounting period, these goods have not been sold and remain in the stocks of P Ltd. We have therefore to eliminate the intra-company profit.

The problem of whether to eliminate the profit that belongs to the minority shareholders of S Ltd has to be resolved. It could be argued in this case that, as far as the minority shareholders are concerned, a sale has been made and they should obtain credit for this. Such a line of reasoning would suggest that 100 per cent of the profit on the transaction should be deducted from the majority shareholders of S Ltd, that is, method 1 in Example 11.9. On the other hand, method 2 seems logical in this case, with both groups of shareholders sharing in the elimination. The minority shareholders will receive financial statements from the subsidiary, which will show the position, including the profit on the transaction. The group itself has not made a profit, as no sale has been made. The different methods are illustrated in Example 11.10.

The AISG found that the usual practice, where a partially owned subsidiary sells to the parent company or to another subsidiary, is again to eliminate 100 per cent of the profit from the interests of the majority shareholders. Method 1 in Example 11.10 is again justified on the grounds of simplicity and conservatism. There was, however, in these circumstances found to be some support for simply eliminating the parent company's proportion of the profit, this being method 3. Undoubtedly, the simplest treatment is method 1, where the entire profit is charged against the

Example 11.9

	P Ltd £	S Ltd £	Method 1 Eliminations Dr £	Method 1 Eliminations Cr £	Method 1 Consolidated £	Method 2 Eliminations Dr £	Method 2 Eliminations Cr £	Method 2 Consolidated £	Method 3 Eliminations Dr £	Method 3 Eliminations Cr £	Method 3 Consolidated £
Share capital	10,000	6,000	4,500 (2) 1,500 (3)		10,000	4,500 (2) 1,500 (3)		10,000	4,500 (2) 1,500 (3)		10,000
Profit retained	2,000		2,000 (1)			1,500 (1)		500	1,500 (1)		500
Minority interest	–	–		1,500 (3)	1,500	500 (1)	1,500 (3)	1,000		1,500 (3)	1,500
	12,000	6,000			11,500			11,500			12,000
Fixed assets	7,500				7,500			7,500			7,500
Investment in S (75% of shares)	4,500	–		4,500 (2) 2,000 (1)			4,500 (2) 2,000 (1)			4,500 (2) 1,500 (1)	
Stock		5,000			3,000			3,000			3,500
Cash		1,000			1,000			1,000			1,000
	12,000	6,000			11,500			11,500			12,000

Entry (1)   Refers to the elimination of the profit on the goods in stock. With methods 1 and 2 all of the profit is eliminated; with method 3 only 75 per cent is eliminated.

Entry (2)   Is the elimination of the shares purchased by P Ltd.

Entry (3)   Is the minority interest in the share capital of S Ltd.

Example 11.10

	P Ltd £	S Ltd £	Method 1 Eliminations Dr £	Method 1 Eliminations Cr £	Method 1 Consolidated £	Method 2 Eliminations Dr £	Method 2 Eliminations Cr £	Method 2 Consolidated £	Method 3 Eliminations Dr £	Method 3 Eliminations Cr £	Method 3 Consolidated £
Share capital	10,000	6,000	{ 4,500(2) 1,500(3)		10,000	{ 4,500(2) 1,500(3) 500(5)		10,000	{ 4,500(2) 1,500(3) 500(5)		10,000
Profit retained	1,500	2,000	2,000(1) { 1,500(4) 500(5)	1,500(3) 500(5)	(500)Dr	{ 1,500(1) 1,500(4)	1,500(3) 500(5)	—	{ 1,500(1) 1,500(4)	1,500(3) 500(5)	—
Minority interest					2,000	500(1)		1,500			2,000
	11,500	8,000			11,500			11,500			12,000
Fixed assets	500	7,000			7,500			7,500			7,500
Investment in S											
(75% of shares)	4,500			4,500(2)			4,500(2)			4,500(2)	
(75% of profits)	1,500			1,500(4)			1,500(4)			1,500(4)	
Stock	5,000			2,000(1)	3,000		2,000(1)	3,000		1,500(1)	3,500
Cash		1,000			1,000			1,000			1,000
	11,500	8,000			11,500			11,500			12,000

Entry (1) Elimination of profit on the goods in stock.
Entry (2) Elimination of shares purchased by P Ltd.
Entry (3) Minority interest in share capital of S Ltd.
Entry (4) Elimination of double-counting of 75 per cent of S Ltd's profit. As can be seen, equity accounting is being used. P Ltd has taken credit for the profits of S Ltd.
Entry (5) Minority interest in profits of S Ltd.

interests of the majority shareholders. The position with regard to a uniform treatment is somewhat unsatisfactory. Undoubtedly, this area of consolidation accounting is neglected.

It will be seen that with methods 1 and 2 the stock in the consolidated balance sheet is valued at the cost to S Ltd, whereas in method 3 the stock is being valued at the cost to S Ltd plus the share of the profit on the sale accruing to minority interests.

There is still one problem, concerned with the amount of profit to eliminate, that has not been mentioned. It is usually the gross profit on the item sold that is eliminated. This means that no part of the selling or administration expenses of the selling company is regarded as part of the cost of the item. A justification for this approach is that intra-company transactions are often marginal in nature and do not incur selling and administrative costs. Another argument is that capitalizing selling and administrative expenses by including them in stock values is improper accounting. The weight of opinion seems to be in favour of eliminating the gross profit margin, although there are those who argue in favour of eliminating net profit. The normal practice of the company in valuing stock is obviously of importance. Similar arguments and eliminations should be considered in relation to trade between associate and other group companies.

11.5.3 Taxation

The company in the group that has sold the item to another company in the group will show in its accounts the profit on the transaction. That company will be taxed on the profit. If we are eliminating the profit on the transaction, we have to consider what to do with the tax. The simplest approach is to ignore it, rationalizing such an approach by arguing that the amount of tax involved is small and immaterial. In fact, it is tax that has been allowed for in advance of the sale to a third party. Following this approach, either the deferred tax account or an account for tax paid in advance would be debited with the amount involved and the taxation charge for the year in the consolidated profit and loss account would be credited. The deferred tax account is supposed to be there to take account of timing differences with tax payments.

To illustrate the approach, it is asumed that P Ltd sells £10,000 worth of goods to S Ltd, its subsidiary, and its gross profit on this transaction is £5,000. The goods have not been resold by the end of the accounting period. P Ltd has been taxed at a rate which for simplicity will be taken to be 35 per cent on its profits. In this case the profits of S Ltd will not be affected. The cost of the goods was £10,000 and is shown at this amount in its stock. The profits belonging to any minority interests in S Ltd are not affected, therefore. In the consolidated accounts of the P Ltd group, stock is reduced by the £5,000 profit, the eliminating entry being

Dr	Deferred tax	£1,650	
Dr	Retained profits	£3,350	
Cr	Stock on hand		£5,000

11.6 Fixed asset transfers

Again we have a situation where there are a number of possible treatments. If an asset is transferred from one company in the group to another company in the group at the net book value, there is no problem. The asset is simply transferred from the books of one company to those of another, and there is no question of a profit on the deal. There would be no need for an adjustment upon consolidation.

If the disposing company makes a profit on the transfer, as it might do if the transfer is at current market value, then it is necessary to make an adjustment to eliminate the profit on the inter-company transaction. To illustrate the problem it is assumed that S Ltd, the subsidiary, transfers assets to H Ltd, the parent company, at a value of £10,000. The net book value of the assets in the accounts of S Ltd at the time of the transfer was £7,500. A profit of £2,500 appears therefore in the individual company accounts of S. On consolidation to eliminate the profit, the value of the asset in the books of H Ltd needs to be reduced, as does the profit of S Ltd. The eliminating entry is

Dr Profits (S Ltd)	£2,500	
Cr Fixed assets (H Ltd)		£2,500

As with inter-company profits on the transfer of goods, one has to consider the position of the minority interests. It could be argued in the above example that minority interests in S Ltd should be allowed their share of the profits on the transaction. In fact, the same alternative accounting treatments are available in this case as with unrealized profits on inter-company trading discussed above. The techniques and arguments will not be repeated.

No recommendation is provided by SSAP 14 and the guidance provided by professional bodies has been withdrawn. The Chartered Accountants Members' Handbook included under the heading 'Transfers of Fixed Assets' the statement 'Any profit arising should be eliminated from the consolidated accounts except that part of it which is attributable to minority share-holders.'[7] The Handbook referred to the necessity to eliminate inter-company profits or losses on such transfers, but states 'where minority interests are involved it may not be appropriate to eliminate their proportion of the profit or loss'.[8] This is in fact suggesting that method 3 above should be used, but it does not say that this method *must* be used, merely that it *may* be used. This means that, where they are considered the more appropriate, methods 1 or 2 will be used instead.

There is a complication in the case of transfer of fixed assets that does not arise in the case of the transfer of goods. The difficulty arises over depreciation. The ICAEW Handbook states: 'Fixed assets transferred within a group should normally be shown in the consolidated balance sheet as though there had been no transfer.'

If the purchasing company within the group treats the transfer price as the cost of the asset, and the disposing company has made a profit on the transaction, then, if an adjustment is not made, the total depreciation charge of the group may well have increased as a result of the transfer. The purchasing company will base its depreciation charge on the 'transfer price' of the asset, which will be different from the value the disposing company was using as a base for its depreciation charge. It is quite clear that the consolidated accounts should be prepared as if there has been no transfer. The depreciation charge in the consolidated accounts should be based on the 'cost to the group'. An adjustment is therefore required.

Using the earlier example, where S Ltd sells an asset to H Ltd on 1 January 19X8 at £10,000 and makes a £2,500 profit on the transfer, it will be assumed that both companies have a similar straight-line depreciation policy. When the asset was purchased by S Ltd it was estimated to have a four-year life. The asset cost S Ltd £15,000 on 1 January 19X6. Two years' depreciation at £3,750 per annum means that the net book value at the time of the transfer was £7,500. H Ltd obtains the asset, and the depreciation charge in its accounts for the year ending 31 December 19X8 is £5,000, that is, based on straight-line depreciation over the remaining two-year life. An adjustment is required in the consolidated accounts to bring the situation to what it would have been if the transfer had not taken place. As the transfer has occurred, the asset appears in the books of H Ltd at 31 December 19X8 as:

Cost	£10,000	
less Accumulated depreciation	5,000	£5,000

If the transfer had not occurred on 31 December 19X8, the asset would have appeared in S Ltd's books, and in the consolidated accounts, as:

Cost	£15,000	
less Accumulated depreciation	11,250	£3,750

The eliminating entries in the consolidated accounts need to be:

Dr	P & L a/c—Eliminate profit on transfer	£2,500	
Cr	P & L a/c—depreciation		£1,250
Cr	Fixed assets		1,250

Without these eliminations, the profits of S Ltd coming into the consolidated accounts would include the £2,500 on the inter-company transaction, the assets of H Ltd to be consolidated would include this asset valued at £5,000 instead of £3,750, and the depreciation charged against the consolidated profit would be £5,000 instead of £3,750.

This is just one example of a situation that can arise. It is possible to think of different situations, with, for instance, different depreciation policies in the two companies, but the principle remains the same. To prepare the consolidated accounts, the eliminating entries needed are those that result in the same consolidated figure as those that would have appeared if the asset transfer had not taken place.

A similar situation arises where one company in the group manufactures assets that it then transfers to other companies in the group. The transfer price might include a profit element which would appear in the accounts of the manufacturing company. The purchasing company will base its depreciation charge on the price it has paid. For consolidation purposes it is necessary to eliminate this inter-company profit, and to base the depreciation charge on the 'cost to the group', this latter cost being the transfer price less the inter-company profit.

11.7 Multiple holdings

Consolidation can become very much more difficult when there are more than two companies in the group. In the following example company B is both a parent company and a subsidiary. It is the parent of company C, and the subsidiary of company A. Company A's control over company C is indirect, through company B.

Company B purchased 60 per cent of the shares of company C on 1 January 19X2 for a price of £8,800; the reserves of C at the time of acquisition were £1,000. Company A purchased 90 per cent of the shares of company B on 1 January 19X3 for a price of £12,850; the reserves in the consolidated accounts of company B were at the time £4,000. Company C has not paid any dividends to company B since the shares were acquired, nor has company B paid any dividends to company A.

The earnings for the three companies exclusive of any earnings of subsidiaries are as follows: for the years ending 31 December 19X2 and 31 December 19X3, company C made £1,000 profit each year. For the year ending 31 December 19X3, company B made £2,900 profits and company A £2,350. For the year ending 31 December 19X2, company B made £2,000 profits. These profits were all after tax, and no dividends were declared. As at 31 December 19X3 the balance sheets of the three separate companies are as shown below. The investment accounts are carried under the equity method.

Example 11.11

	Company A £	Company B £	Company C £
Share capital	10,000	10,000	10,000
Reserves	10,000	7,500	3,000
Current liabilities	3,000	3,000	5,000
	23,000	20,500	18,000
Fixed assets	5,000	8,000	10,000
Investment in company B	16,000		
Investment in company C		10,000	
Current assets	2,000	2,500	8,000
	23,000	20,500	18,000

Two-stage method

One method of preparing consolidated accounts for a group involving multiple holdings is by a two-stage process. The first stage in this example is to consolidate company C with company B. To do so, it is necessary to analyse the reserve account of company C:

	Company C reserves	of which	Minority interest
Profits pre-acquisitioned by B	£1,000		£400
Profits post-acquisitioned by B	2,000		800
			£1,200

The goodwill arising on consolidation calculated at the time of acquisition was as follows:

Share capital (60%)	£6,000	
Reserves	600	
		£6,600
Price paid		8,800
Goodwill		£2,200

The consolidated accounts of Company B as at 31 December 19X3 are therefore arrived at as follows:

	Company B £	Company C £	Eliminations Dr £	Cr £	Consoli- dated £
Share capital	10,000	10,000	4,000 (5) 6,000 (1)		10,000
Reserves	7,500	3,000	600 (1) 400 (3) 1,200 (2) 800 (4)		7,500
Minority interest				4,000 (5) 400 (3) 800 (4)	5,200
Current liabilities	3,000	5,000			8,000
	20,500	18,000			30,700

	Company B	Company C	Eliminations		Consolidated
			Dr	Cr	dated
	£	£	£	£	£
Fixed assets	8,000	10,000			18,000
Goodwill on consolidation			2,200 (1)		2,200
Investment in subsidiary	10,000			1,200 (2) 8,800 (1)	
Current assets	2,500	8,000			10,500
	20,500	18,000			30,700

The profits of company C that had been entered in the individual accounts of company B were £600 in 19X2 and £600 in 19X3. These had been debited to 'Investment in subsidiary' and credited to 'Earnings of subsidiary'. It is adjustment (2) that eliminates these entries for consolidation purposes.

An explanation of the eliminations is as follows.

Entry (1) Investment by company B in shares of company C.

Dr Share capital   £6,000
   Reserves—pre-acquisition 600
   Goodwill on consolidation 2,200
   Investment in subsidiary   £8,800

Entry (2) B's share of post-acquisition reserves of C.
Entry (3) Minority interest's share of reserves of C, at time of purchase of control by B.
Entry (4) Minority interest's share of reserves of C, subsequent to control by B.
Entry (5) Minority interest in share capital of C.

The second stage in the preparation of the group accounts is to combine the accounts of the parent company A with the consolidated accounts of its subsidiary B:

	Company A	Group B	Eliminations		Consolidated
			Dr	Cr	dated
	£	£	£	£	£
Share capital	10,000	10,000	1,000 (4) 9,000 (1)		10,000
Reserves	10,000	7,500	750 (3) 3,600 (1) 3,150 (2)		10,000
Minority interest		5,200		1,000 (4) 750 (3)	6,950
Current liabilities	3,000	8,000			11,000
	23,000	30,700			37,950
Goodwill on consolidation		2,200	250 (1)		2,450
Fixed assets	5,000	18,000			23,000
Investment in subsidiary	16,000			3,150 (2) 12,850 (1)	
Current assets	2,000	10,500			12,500
	23,000	30,700			37,950

Entry (1)   Investment by company A in shares of group B, the eliminating entries being:

Dr Share capital	£9,000	
Reserves—pre-acquisition	3,600	
Goodwill on consolidation	250	
Cr Investment in subsidiary		£12,850

Entry (2)   A's share of post-acquisition profits of group B. This includes 90 per cent of the £2,900 profits of company B for the year ending 31 December 19X3 and 54 per cent (i.e. 90% × 60%) of the £1,000 profits of company C for the same year.

Entry (3)   Minority interest's share of reserves of group B, this being 10 per cent of the £6,300 reserves of company B exclusive of subsidiary earnings (i.e. 10 per cent of £7,500 – £1,200), plus 10 per cent of the post-acquisition profits from company C.

Entry (4)   Minority interest in share capital of company B.

One-stage method

In this example, it is possible to prepare a set of consolidated accounts for A Ltd and its subsidiaries without needing to go through the intermediate stage of preparing the consolidated accounts of group B. It is also possible to prepare the consolidated accounts from individual company accounts where the investments are recorded on the cost basis rather than the equity basis. This alternative approach is illustrated below. First, it is necessary to consider the reserve accounts of each of the three companies in order to ascertain the amount of the reserves that arose from the activities of the individual company and the amount that was credited as the earnings of subsidiaries. From the information given the reserve accounts can be broken down as follows:

	Company A £	Company B £	Company C £
Total			
Reserve: balance as at 31/12/X1	2,500	1,400	1,000
Individual company profits for 19X2	2,000	2,000	1,000
Share of earnings of subsidiary 19X2		600	
Reserve: balance at 31/12/X2	4,500	4,000	2,000
Individual company profits for 19X3	2,350	2,900	1,000
Share of earnings of subsidiary 19X3	3,150*	600	
Reserve: balance at 31/12/X3	10,000	7,500	3,000
Ignoring earnings of subsidiaries			
Reserve: balance at 31/12/X3	6,850	6,300	3,000

*90% of £3,500 earnings of company B.

Company B acquired 60 per cent of company C on 1 January 19X2, since that date there has been two years' trading resulting in £2,000 of profits, of which £800 belongs to minority interests in company C. The £1,200 belonging to company B is transferred to the reserves of company B. However, not all this £1,200 is post-acquisition profits from company A's point of view, as A did not purchase its shares in company B until 1 January 19X3. From company A's point of view, and it is the consolidated account of the 'A' group we are considering, post-acquisition profits are only 90 per cent of £3,500 (the £600 from company C and the £2,900 earned by company B). It is this £3,150 of post-acquisition reserves of B, which is added to the reserves of company A (ignoring subsidiaries) to give the £10,000 consolidated figure.

The single stage worksheet is as follows.

	Company A	Company B	Company C	Eliminations		Consoli-
				Dr	Cr	dated
	£	£	£	£	£	£
Share capital	10,000	10,000	10,000	4,000 (3) 6,000 (1) 9,000 (2) 1,000 (4)		10,000
Reserves (exclusive of earnings of subsidiaries)	6,850	6,300	3,000	800 (5) 400 (3) 600 (1) 3,600 (2) 400 (6) 350 (7)		10,000
Minority interests in Company B					1,000 (4) 400 (6) 350 (7)	1,750
Company C					4,000 (3) 400 (3) 800 (5)	5,200
Current liabilities	3,000	3,000	5,000			11,000
	19,850	19,300	18,000			37,950
Fixed assets	5,000	8,000	10,000			23,000
Goodwill on consolidation				2,200 (1) 250 (2)		2,450
Investment in subsidiaries (exclusive of earnings of subsidiaries)						
Company B	12,850				12,850 (2)	
Company C		8,800			8,800 (1)	
Current assets	2,000	2,500	8,000			12,500
	19,850	19,300	18,000			37,950

Entry (1) Investment of company B in company C (see entry (1) in first stage of two-stage approach).

Entry (2) Investment of company A in company B (see entry (1) in second stage of two-stage approach).

Entry (3) Minority interest in share capital and pre-acquisition reserves of C (see entries (3) and (5) in first stage).

Entry (4) Minority interest in share capital of company B (see entry (4) in second stage).

Entry (5) Minority interest in those reserves of C accumulated after share purchase by company B (see entry (4) in first stage).

Entries (6) and (7) Minority interest in reserves of group B (see entry (3) in second stage).

11.7.1 Direct and indirect holdings

Example 11.11 will now be slightly altered to bring in an added complication. It is now assumed that, not only did A purchase 90 per cent of the shares of company B on 1 January 19X3, but it also purchased 20 per cent of the shares of company C on the same date for a price of £3,000. All other facts in the example remain unchanged. Both companies A and B now own shares in company C.

The balance sheets of the three separate companies as at 31 December 19X3 prepared according to the equity method are shown in Example 11.12. The balances in the reserve accounts and the investment accounts are arrived at as follows:

		Reserves	
	Company A £	Company B £	Company C £
Balance as at 31/12/X2	2,500	1,400	1,000
Individual company profits for 19X2	2,000	2,000	1,000
Earnings of subsidiary		600	
Balance as at 31/12/X2	4,500	4,000	2,000
Individual company profits for 19X3	2,350	2,900	1,000
Earnings of subsidiary C	200	600	
Earnings of subsidiary B	3,150		
Balance as at 31/12/X3	10,200	7,500	3,000

The investment account of company A in company C is £3,200 as at 31 December 19X3, which is £200 higher than the price paid for the shares: this reflects the earnings from the investment in company C during 19X3. In fact, company A directly owns only 20 per cent of C, and so it may not be thought to be an associate company, but it does exercise a significant influence on company C, through its shareholding in company B. It is therefore being shown in the individual accounts of company A as an associate company, its earnings being treated on an equity basis.

Example 11.12

	Balance sheets as at 31 December 19X3		
	Company A £	Company B £	Company C £
Share capital	10,000	10,000	10,000
Reserves	10,200	7,500	3,000
Current liabilities	4,000	3,000	5,000
	24,200	20,500	18,000
Fixed assets	5,000	8,000	10,000
Investment			
A in B	16,000		
A in C	3,200		
B in C		10,000	
Current assets		2,500	8,000
	24,200	20,500	18,000

The consolidated accounts of group B are exactly as in the above example. From company B's point of view, it owns 60 per cent of company C, and it will treat the other 40 per cent as minority interests. The fact that company A, who is B's parent, owns 20 per cent of C will affect the next stage of the preparation.

Moving now to the preparation of the consolidated accounts for the A Group, we have

	Company A	Company B	Company C	Eliminations Dr	Eliminations Cr	Consolidated
	£	£	£	£	£	£
Share capital	10,000	10,000	10,000	9,000 (2) 1,000 (5) 2,000 (3) 2,000 (4) 6,000 (1)		10,000
Reserves (equity method)	10,200	7,500	3,000	750 (7) 600 (6) 1,200 (9) 600 (1) 400 (3) 200 (10) 3,600 (2) 3,150 (8)		10,200
Current liabilities	4,000	3,000	5,000			12,000
Minority interests					750 (7) 1,000 (5) 600 (6) 2,000 (4)	4,350
	24,200	20,500	18,000			36,550
Fixed assets investment:	5,000	8,000	10,000			23,000
A in B	16,000				12,850 (2) 3,150 (5)	
A in C	3,200				3,000 (3) 200 (10)	
B in C		10,000			8,800 (1) 1,200 (9)	
Current assets		2,500	8,000			10,500
Goodwill					250 (2) 2,200 (1) 600 (3)	3,050
	24,200	20,500	18,000			36,550

Entry (1) Investment by company B in company C (see entry (1), first stage, Example 11.11).
Entry (2) Investment by company A in company B (see entry (1), second stage, Example 11.11).

Entry (3) Investment by company A in company C, the eliminating entries being:

Dr	Share capital	£2,000	
	Reserves—pre-acquisition		
	(20% × £2,000)	400	
	Goodwill on consolidation	600	
Cr	Investment in subsidiary		£3,000

Entry (4) Minority interest in share capital of company C.
Entry (5) Minority interest in share capital of company B.
Entry (6) Minority interest in reserves of company C (20 per cent of £3,000).
Entry (7) Minority interest in reserves of company B (10 per cent of £7,500).
Entry (8) Company A's share of post-acquisition profits of group B (see Entry (2), second stage, Example 11.11).
Entry (9) Company B's share of post-acquisition profits of company C (see Entry (2), first stage, Example 11.11).
Entry (10) Company A's share of post-acquisition profits of company C.
Company C's reserves are divided as follows:

	£
Minority interest (20%)	600
To company B:	
Pre-acquisition	600
Post-acquisition	1,200
To company A:	
Pre-acquisition	400
Post-acquisition	200

Of course, company A has a larger claim overall to company C's reserves than this £600, as it can claim 60 per cent of company B's share. Company A directly and indirectly owns 74 per cent of company C. That is,

Direct	20%
Indirect (90% × 60%)	54%

A owns 74 per cent of C. The minority shareholders of C own 20 per cent, and the minority shareholders of B own 6 per cent (i.e. 10% × 60%). There are other methods of consolidation. For example, it is possible to prepare the consolidated accounts from investment and reserve accounts kept on the cost basis. It is possible to ignore the intermediate stage of group B's consolidated accounts.

11.7.2 Chain control

Situations can develop where the parent company P owns shares in the subsidiary S, and the subsidiary owns shares in another company Z, but the percentage holdings are such that P does not apparently exercise control over Z; that is, it controls less than 50 per cent of Z's shares. For example, P may own 60 per cent of the shares of S, and S may own 60 per cent of the shares of Z.

In this situation, although P only has a 36 per cent indirect interest in Z, the consolidated statements should be prepared consolidating Z. This is because P controls S, having 60 per cent of the voting power, and in turn S controls Z, again having a majority of the votes. This constitutes effective control.

11.8 Preference shares

If a parent company owns preference shares of a subsidiary, then it is necessary to eliminate the amounts involved when consolidated accounts are being prepared. The cost of the preference shares acquired by the parent has to be cancelled against the nominal value of the preference shares appearing in the subsidiary's accounts. Any difference between cost and nominal value affects the balance sheet item 'goodwill arising on consolidation'.

If all the preference shares of the subsidiary have not been acquired, then the interests of the independent preference shareholders has to be credited to the minority interest account. In fact, the parent company may have acquired less than 50 per cent of the preference shares, but this does not affect the issue. The interests of the independent preference shareholders are still credited to minority interest. The size of the holding of preference shares is not taken into account in determining whether or not a controlling interest exists unless there are arrears of dividends or other provisions which could give preference shareholders votes.

The balance sheets of company P and company S as at 31 December 19X0 are as shown in Example 11.13. It will be assumed in this case that company P records its investment in company S according to the cost basis.

Example 11.13

	Company P	Company S	Eliminations Dr	Eliminations Cr	Consolidated
	£	£	£	£	£
Share capital					
Ordinary shares	100,000	50,000	30,000 (2) 20,000 (3)		100,000
Preference shares		20,000	5,000 (1) 15,000 (5)		
Reserves	50,000	50,000	18,000 (2) 20,000 (4)		62,000
Minority interest				20,000 (3) 20,000 (4) 15,000 (5)	55,000
	150,000	120,000			217,000
Fixed assets	60,000	100,000			160,000
Investments in subsidiary					
30,000 ordinary shares	50,000			50,000 (2)	
5,000 preference shares	7,500			7,500 (1)	
Goodwill on consolidation			2,500 (1) 2,000 (2)		4,500
Net current assets	32,500	200,00			52,500
	150,000	120,000			217,000

Company P acquired 60 per cent of the ordinary shares and 25 per cent of the preference shares of company S, when the reserves of company S were £30,000.

Entry (1) Eliminates the investment of P in the preference shares, the adjustments being:

Dr	Preference shares	£5,000	
	Goodwill on consolidation	2,500	
Cr	Investment in subsidiary		£7,500

Goodwill arising on consolidation is the result of P paying more for these shares than their nominal value. There is no question of the size of the reserves affecting this entry: the reserves belong to the ordinary shareholders (unless there are some special terms to the contrary).

Entry (2) The investment of P in the ordinary shares of S, the elimination being:

Dr	Ordinary shares	£30,000	
	Reserves	18,000	
	Goodwill on consolidation	2,000	
Cr	Investment in subsidiary		£50,000

Entry (3) Minority interest in share capital of company S.
Entry (4) Minority interest in reserves of company S (i.e., 40 per cent of £50,000).
Entry (5) Minority interest in the preference shares of company S.

Dividends on preference shares are treated in exactly the same way as dividends on ordinary shares. Any dividends paid on the preference shares held by company P are taken as dividends received into the individual company accounts of P. In the consolidation process these have to be eliminated. In the above example, assume they are 10 per cent preference shares, which means that £2,000 will have been distributed as preference dividends, £500 being received by company P. The example is simplified, with taxation ignored. The profit and loss account of the two companies and the consolidated profit and loss account are:

	Company P	Company S	Eliminations Dr	Cr	Consolidated
	£	£	£	£	£
Profits	5,000	3,000			8,000
Preference dividend paid		2,000		500 (1)	1,500
Preference dividend received	500		500 (1)		
Minority interests (40% of £1,000)			400 (2)		400
Retained profits	5,500	1,000		400 (2)	6,100

Entry (1) Eliminates the payment by S, and the receipt by P, of the £500.
Entry (2) Transfers the appropriate share of the retained profits to the minority shareholders.

11.9 Changes in parent company's equity

11.9.1 Piecemeal acquisition

Where control of another company already exists, and additional shares are purchased, the consolidation process is comparatively simple. For example, say a holding company already owns 60 per cent of the subsidiary (S) and now buys another 20 per cent. The 20 per cent of the reserves of S at the time of the latest acquisition are treated as pre-acquisition reserves. The reserves attached to the 60 per cent holding will already have been included in the consolidated accounts, some being treated as pre-acquisition reserves and some as post-acquisition reserves.

The situation is more complicated when shares in another company are being accumulated over time, and it is one of the later purchases that makes the other company a subsidiary. By way of example, assume that P Ltd buys shares in S Ltd during 19X0 and 19X1. The number of shares purchased, the acquisition cost and the reserves of S Ltd at the date of purchase are:

Date of purchase	Cost £	No. of shares purchased	Balance on S Ltd reserve account (£)
1/1/X0	30,000	20,000	5,000
30/6/X0	17,000	10,000	7,000
31/12/X1	75,000	40,000	10,000

The share capital of S Ltd during the two-year period was 100,000 shares, each of £1 nominal value. The necessity to consolidate does not legally arise until 31 December 19X1, for it is only at that date that S Ltd becomes a subsidiary. The pre-acquisition reserves of S Ltd that P purchases at the date it obtains control are 70 per cent of £10,000. The remaining £3,000 belongs to minority interests. The position is, however, complicated by the earlier purchases of P Ltd; some of the £7,000 pre-acquisition reserves, although being pre-subsidiary status, were in fact earned on shares belonging to P in 19X0.

The situation can be treated in one of two ways. Either a step-by-step approach can be followed, or an approach which follows the letter of the law can be employed: namely, the company is not consolidated until it becomes a subsidiary. With this latter approach, there is one computation of pre-acquisition profits at the date of control.

First, the step-by-step approach: in 19X0 S Ltd is an associate of P Ltd. If P Ltd needs to prepare group accounts, because of other subsidiaries, and keeps its own individual accounts based on the equity accounting method, the appropriate journal entries would be:

1/1/X0	Dr	Investment in associate	£30,000	
	Cr	Cash		£30,000
30/6/X0	Dr	Investment in associate	17,000	
	Cr	Cash		17,000
31/12/X0	Dr	Investment in associate	1,000	
	Cr	Earnings of associate		1,000

(Assuming that profits for the year of S Ltd equal £4,000, all being retained, P Ltd can claim 20/100 of the full year's £4,000, and 10/100 of the second half of the year's profits, £2,000.)

31/12/X1	Dr	Investment in associate	£300	
	Cr	Earnings of associate		£300

(being 30 per cent of the profits of S Ltd for 19X1 of £1,000).

The balance on the investment in associate company account at the date of purchase of control is, therefore, £48,300. The entry when the controlling purchase is made would be:

Dr Investment in subsidiary	£75,000	
Cr Cash		£75,000

The balance on this invesment in associate/subsidiary account is now £123,300.

It is necessary to consolidate S in the group accounts for the year ending 31 December 19X1. This means that the net assets of S Ltd are now brought into the consolidated accounts together with any goodwill arising on consolidation. To ascertain the goodwill, we follow the step-by-step approach:

	First purchase (20%)		Second purchase (10%)		Third purchase (40%)	
	£	£	£	£	£	£
Investment cost		30,000		17,000		75,000
Net assets purchased						
Share capital	20,000		10,000		40,000	
Reserves	1,000		700		4,000	
		21,000		10,700		44,000
Goodwill arising on consolidation		9,000		6,300		31,000
			Total = £46,300			

It is possible to illustrate the adjustments required for consolidation using a very simplified balance sheet (Example 11.14). It is assumed that the only asset of P is the investment in its subsidiary.

Example 11.14

Balance sheet as at 31 December 19X1

	Company P	Company S	Eliminations Dr	Cr	Consoli- dated
	£	£	£	£	£
Share capital—S		100,000	70,000 (1) 30,000 (3)		
Reserves—S		10,000	3,000 (3) 5,700 (1) 1,300 (2)		
Share capital and reserves—P	123,300				123,300
Minority interest				33,000 (3)	33,000
	123,300	110,000			156,300
Net assets—S		110,000			110,000
Investment in subsidiary	123,300			1,300 (2) 122,000 (1)	
Goodwill on consolidation —			46,300 (1)		46,300
	123,300	110,000			156,300

Entry (1)   Investment by company P in shares of company S, the eliminating entries being

Dr	Share capital—S	£70,000	
	Reserves—S		
	Pre-acquisition profits (i.e., £4,000 +		
	£700 + £1,000)	5,700	
	Goodwill on consolidation	46,300	
Cr	Investment in S Ltd		£122,000

Entry (2)   Company P's share of post-acquisition profits of company S, the eliminating entry being:

Dr	Reserves—S	£1,300	
Cr	Investment in S Ltd		£1,300

Entry (3)   The minority interests share in the capital and reserves of company S.

The above step-by-step approach can be contrasted with the one-computation approach. If the individual books of P Ltd are being kept on a cost basis, then the investment in the associate subsidiary account will show a balance after the third purchase of £122,000. The consolidated balance sheet would be arrived at as follows:

Balance sheet as at 31 December 19X1

	Company P	Company S	Eliminations Dr	Eliminations Cr	Consolidated
	£	£	£	£	£
Share capital		100,000	⎰70,000 (1) ⎱30,000 (3)		
Reserves		10,000	⎰ 7,000 (1) ⎱ 3,000 (1)		
Share capital plus reserves	122,000				122,000
Minority interests	—			33,000 (2)	33,000
	122,000	110,000			155,000
Net assets		110,000			110,000
Investment in subsidiary	122,000			122,000 (1)	
Goodwill on consolidation			45,000 (1)		45,000
	122,000	110,000			155,000

The goodwill is the difference between the purchase price (being a total of £122,000 for the three purchases) and the net assets acquired (being 70 per cent of £110,000). This is shown in elimination (1). The elimination entry (2) represents the minority interest in the share capital and reserves of company S. As can be seen, the step-by-step method results in the post-acquisition reserves of P Ltd and the P Group being larger than under the alternative method. More reserves are therefore available for distribution under the step-by-step approach.

Which method is best? Technically, the step-by-step method is correct. SSAP 14 does not make clear which method should be followed. One thing to be said for the one-computation approach is that it is quicker. This point has been recognized in the USA. The APB has stated: 'If small purchases are made over a period of time and then a purchase is made which results in control, the date of the latest purchase, as a matter of convenience may be considered as the date of acquisition.'[9] It should be emphasized that this is done only for convenience; it is not strictly correct, it is just practical.

11.9.2 Effective date of acquisition of subsidiary

The actual date at which the shares in another company are acquired is sometimes unclear. It was therefore necessary for the standard to clarify the point. SSAP 14 states:

> the effective date for accounting for both acquisition and disposal of a subsidiary should be the earlier of
> (a) the date on which consideration passes; or
> (b) the date on which an offer becomes or is declared unconditional.
> This applies even if the acquiring company has the right under the agreement to share in the profits of the acquired business from an earlier date.[10]

11.9.3 Disposal of shares

SSAP 14 states:

> where there is a material disposal, the consolidated profit and loss account should include:
> (a) the subsidiary's results up to the date of disposal; and
> (b) the gain or loss on the sale of the investment, being the difference at the time of the sale between
>   (i) the proceeds of the sale and
>   (ii) the holding company's share of its net assets together with any premium (less any amounts written off) or discount on acquisition.[11]

It is therefore necessary to calculate the value to the holding company of the shares being sold, that is, the value in the books of the holding company. This value will depend on whether the investment is being valued on an equity or a cost basis. SSAP 1 makes it clear that equity accounting principles should apply in valuing investments in the consolidated accounts. In the holding company's own accounts, the valuation may be based on cost. Thus, it is possible on disposal of shares to show a different profit or loss in the holding company's accounts from that in the consolidated accounts.

The difference will be illustrated. To begin with, it will be assumed that all the shares held in the subsidiary are being sold. Taking Example 11.14, all the 70,000 shares owned in company S are sold on 28 February 19X2. The price received is £130,000. No profits were earned by S between the end of 19X1 and the date of sale. No goodwill has been written off.

It was shown that, when equity accounting principles were followed, the book value of the investment was £123,300. This is the cost of £122,000 plus earnings of £1,300. It represents P Ltd's share of the net assets (£110,000 × 70% = £77,000) plus the goodwill premium of £46,300 paid on acquisition. There is therefore a profit on sale of £6,700, being the difference between the sale proceeds of £130,000 and the value of £123,300. This is the profit that will be shown in the consolidated profit and loss account, and in the parent company's accounts if equity accounting is being followed.

Now we consider the position when the value is based on cost accounting. The cost to the holding company was £122,000 and its share of the net assets of S Ltd is £122,000. The profit on sale is, therefore, £8,000. This is equivalent to the £6,700 profit shown above plus the realization of the share of the post-acquisition reserves of S, namely £1,300. This £8,000 would be the figure appearing in a parent company's profit and loss account, based on cost principles. It can be justified on the basis that it is not until realization (in this case by the sale) that the earnings should be credited. The earnings however will have been included in the consolidated profit and loss account year by year, so if a profit on disposal of £8,000 is shown in P's accounts, this will need to be reduced to £6,700 in the consolidated accounts.

When only a part of the shareholding of the subsidiary is sold, the treatment is slightly different. Again, the profit or loss to be shown in the profit and loss account is the difference between the proceeds of the sale and the value of the shares sold as shown in the accounts of the holding company. There are a number of different ways of arriving at the 'carrying value' of the shares being sold. The strongest conceptual case is to use the average value of the shares being held at the time of the disposal. It might be thought possible to trace the individual shares being sold, and calculate their cost plus (where using the equity method) the share of earnings. However, it can be argued that all shares are interchangeable and of equal value. When a share is sold in the market, the purchaser does not mind which actual share is being sold. Would it be correct to allow a company to determine the profit or loss which appears in the profit and loss account by deciding which actual share, which piece of paper, it was selling to the purchaser?

To illustrate the value, based on the average carrying value, the earlier example will again be used. Let us say that 15 per cent of the shares in S are sold on 28 February 19X2 for a price of £25,000. The average book value of the shares being held at that date, under the equity accounting procedure, is £1.76 (i.e., £123,300/70,000), and so the average carrying value of the shares being sold is £26,400. The loss on the sale, based on equity principles, is therefore £1,400. The average carrying value based on cost principles is £1.743 per share, which means a value of the shares being sold of £26,145, and a loss of £1,145.

Notes

1. European Economic Community, 7th Directive, 'Group Accounts', 1983.
2. SSAP 14, 'Group Accounts', ASC, para. 16, 1978.
3. Ibid., para. 18.
4. SSAP 8, 'The Treatment of Taxation under the Imputation System in the Accounts of Companies', ASC, 1974.
5. SSAP 14, para. 3.
6. Accountants International Study Group, *Consolidated Financial Statements*, AISG, 1973.
7. Chartered Accountants Members' Handbook, *P5 Group Accounts*, 1978.
8. Institute of Chartered Accountants in England and Wales, *Handbook*, ICAEW, section S1.
9. Accounting Principles Board, *Accounting Research Bulletin 51*, para. 10, 1959.
10. SSAP 14, para. 32.
11. Ibid., para. 31.

Further reading

Ashton, R. K., 'The Argyll Foods case: a legal analysis', *Accounting and Business Research*, Winter 1986.

Cooke, T. E., *Mergers and Acquisitions*, Basil Blackwell, Oxford, 1986.

Griffin, C. H., T. H. Williams and K. D. Larson, *Advanced Accounting*, 4th edn., Richard Irwin, Homewood, Ill., 1980.

Holgate, P. A., 'A Guide to Accounting Standards. SSAP 23: "Accounting for Acquisitions and Mergers"', *Accountants Digest*, no. 189, ICAEW, 1986.

IAS 3, 'Consolidated Financial Statements', IASC, 1976.

IAS 22, 'Accounting for Business Combinations', IASC, 1983.

Nobes, C., *Some Practical and Theoretical Problems of Group Accounting*, Deloittes, London, 1986.

Parker, R. H., 'The Seventh Directive: some first impressions', *Accountant's Magazine*, October 1983.

Parker, R. H., 'Consolidation accounting', in C. W. Nobes and R. H. Parker (eds), *Comparative International Accounting*, 2nd edn, Philip Allan, Oxford, 1985.

Shaw, J. C. (ed.), *Bogie on Group Accounts*, Jordan, London, 1973.

Taylor, P. A., *Consolidated Financial Statements: Concepts, Issues and Techniques*, Harper & Row, New York, 1987.

Walker, R. G., 'Consolidated statements: a history and analysis', Arno Press, New York, 1978.

Whittaker, J. and T. E. Cooke, 'Accounting for goodwill and business combinations: has the ASC got it right', *Accountant's Magazine*, February 1983.

Wilkins, R. M., *Group Accounts*, 2nd edn, ICAEW, 1979.

Wilkins, R. M., 'Takeovers', in L. C. L. Skerratt and D. J. Tonkin (eds), *Financial Reporting 1985–86: A Survey of UK Published Accounts*, ICAEW, 1986.

Questions

1. The following figures for the year to 30 April 1986 have been extracted from the books and records of three companies which forme a group:

	Old plc £	Field Ltd £	Lodge Ltd £
Revenue reserves at 1 May 1985	30,000	40,000	50,000
Stocks at 1 May 1985	90,000	150,000	80,000
Sales	1,250,000	875,000	650,000
Purchases	780,000	555,000	475,000
Distribution expenses	125,000	85,000	60,000
Administration expenses	28,000	40,000	72,000
Interim dividends:			
Paid 31 July 1985, ordinary	45,000	35,000	15,000
Paid 31 October 1985, preference		4,000	
Share capital—fully paid			
ordinary shares of £1 each	450,000	350,000	200,000
8% preference shares of £1 each		100,000	
Stocks at 30 April 1986	110,000	135,000	85,000

Profits are deemed to accrue evenly throughout the year.

Other information:
(a) Corporation tax of the following amounts is to be provided on the profits of the year:

       Old plc   £125,000
       Field Ltd   75,000
       Lodge Ltd   20,000

(b) Final dividends proposed are:

       Old plc   15p per share
       Field Ltd   12.5p per share on the ordinary shares and a half-year's
                         dividend on the preference shares
       Lodge Ltd   7.5p per share

(c) Field Ltd sells goods for resale to both Old plc and Lodge Ltd. At 30 April 1986, stocks of goods purchased from Field Ltd are:

       in Old plc   £40,000
       in Lodge Ltd 28,000

The net profit percentage for Field Ltd on sales of these goods is 25%.
Old plc had £36,000 of these goods in stock at 1 May 1985.
Total sales in the year by Field Ltd to Old plc were £150,000 and to Lodge Ltd £120,000.

(d) Old plc acquired the whole of the ordinary shares in Field Ltd many years ago. 50,000 of the preference shares were acquired on 1 August 1985.

Old plc acquired 120,000 shares in Lodge Ltd on 1 August 1985.

Required:

A consolidated profit and loss account for Old plc and its subsidiaries for the year ended 30 April 1986, together with any relevant notes. **(30 marks)**

ACCA, 2.9, AAP 2, June 1986

2.   Bryon Ltd has held 1,500,000 shares in Carlyle Ltd for many years. At the date of acquisition, the reserves of Carlyle Ltd amounted to £800,000. On 31 March 1986 Carlyle Ltd bought 400,000 shares in Doyle Ltd for £600,000 and a further 400,000 shares were purchased on 30 June 1986 for £650,000.

At 30 September 1986 the balance sheets of the three companies were:

	Bryon Ltd		*Carlyle Ltd*		*Doyle Ltd*	
	£	£	£	£	£	£
Freehold land and buildings—cost		950,000		1,375,000		300,000
Plant and equipment						
Cost	500,000		10,000,000		750,000	
Depreciation	280,000		7,500,000		500,000	
		220,000		2,500,000		250,000
		1,170,000		3,875,000		550,000
Investments						
1,500,000 shares in Carlyle Ltd		1,600,000				
800,000 shares in Doyle Ltd				1,250,000		
Stocks	50,000		2,050,000		850,500	
Debtors	325,000		2,675,000		1,700,000	
Cash at bank	25,500		—		16,500	
		400,500		4,725,000		2,567,000
		3,170,500		9,850,000		3,117,000
Creditors under 1 year	91,500		2,385,750		1,395,800	
Proposed dividend	200,000					
Bank overdraft	—		1,450,850		—	
		291,500		3,836,600		1,395,800
		2,879,000		6,013,400		1,721,200
10% Debenture		—		2,000,000		—
		2,879,000		4,013,400		1,721,200
Ordinary shares of £1 each		2,000,000				1,200,000
50p each				1,000,000		
8% Redeemable preference shares of £1 each				2,000,000		
Reserves		879,000		1,013,400		521,200
		2,879,000		4,013,400		1,721,200

Proposed dividends have not yet been provided for on the shares in Carlyle Ltd and Doyle Ltd although Bryon Ltd has included dividends of 5p per share as receivable from Carlyle Ltd in debtors. Dividends on the preference shares were paid for one half-year on 1 April 1986; the next payment date was 1 October 1986. Dividends on the ordinary shares in Doyle Ltd are proposed at the rate of 10p per share and on Carlyle's shares as anticipated by Bryon.

Profits for the year in Doyle Ltd were £310,000, before making any adjustments for consolidation, accruing evenly through the year.

The directors of Bryon Ltd consider that the assets and liabilities of Carlyle Ltd are shown at fair values but fair values for Doyle Ltd for the purposes of consolidation are:

		£
Freehold land and building		500,000
Plant and equipment—Valuation	968,400	
—Depreciation	639,600	328,800

Other assets and liabilities are considered to be at fair values in the balance sheet.

Additional depreciation due to the revaluation of the plant and equipment in Doyle Ltd amounts to £40,000 for the year to 30 September 1986.

Included in stocks in Carlyle Ltd are items purchased from Doyle Ltd during the last three months of the year, on which Doyle Ltd recorded a profit of £80,000.

On 30 September 1986 Carlyle Ltd drew a cheque for £100,000 and sent it to Doyle Ltd to clear the current account. As this cheque was not received by Doyle Ltd until 3 October, no account was taken of it in the Doyle Ltd balance sheet.

Required:

Prepare a balance sheet as at 30 September 1986 for Bryon Ltd and its subsidiaries, conforming with the Companies Act 1985, so far as the information given will permit. Ignore taxation.   **(30 marks)**

ACCA, 2.9, AAP. 2, December 1986.

3. Summarised accounts for three private companies are given below:

Summarised balance sheets on 30th June 1986

	Cruet Ltd £'000s	Salt Ltd £'000s	Pepper Ltd £'000s
Goodwill	—	—	160
Tangible fixed assets	2,675	1,925	1,180
Investments (note 2)	1,980	60	—
Intercompany loans	100	—	(100)
Net current assets (liabilities)	930	1,743	(620)
Loans from third parties	(500)	—	—
	5,185	3,728	620
Ordinary shares of £1 each	3,000	1,000	400
Preference shares of £1 each	1,000	1,200	—
Reserves	1,185	1,528	220
	5,185	3,728	620

Summarised profit and loss accounts for the year to 30th June 1986

	Cruet Ltd £'000s	Salt Ltd £'000s	Pepper Ltd £'000s
Profit after taxation	600	360	200
Extraordinary items	(100)	40	—
	500	400	200
Preference dividends—paid	(30)	(30)	—
—payable	(30)	(30)	—
Ordinary dividends—paid	(100)	(60)	(40)
—proposed	(200)	(80)	(80)
Retained for year	140	200	80
Reserves brought forward	1,045	1,328	140
Reserves carried forward	1,185	1,528	220

The following additional information is given:

(1) All shares are fully paid. Preference shares carry a vote only when their dividends are in arrears. The preference dividends are payable on 1st January and 1st July each year.

(2) Investments comprise:

	Cost £'000s
Cruet Ltd	
900,000 Ordinary shares in Salt Ltd	1,500
400,000 Preference shares in Salt Ltd	400
46,000 Ordinary shares in Pepper Ltd	80
	1,980
Salt Ltd	
60,000 Ordinary shares in Pepper Ltd	60

Cruet Ltd exercises a significant influence over Salt Ltd and Pepper Ltd.

(3) When Cruet acquired its investments in Salt and Pepper during 1983 those companies had reserves of £400,000 and £100,000 respectively. Salt acquired its holding on the incorporation of Pepper in 1980. Fair values should be assumed to be balance sheet values in 1983 other than for Salt's investment in Pepper.

(4) The summarised profit and loss accounts include only those dividends which have been received. No accruals or provisions which may be required have been made for dividends receivable.

Requirement

Prepare a summarised consolidated balance sheet and summarised profit and loss account with full working and supporting schedules, showing clearly consolidation adjustments, movements in reserves, minority interests and the carrying value of investments.

Note: Ignore taxation.

(25 marks)

ICAEW, PEII, FAII, July 1986.

12. Accounting for foreign activities

An organization may be involved with transactions expressed in foreign currency in various ways:

(a) by a simple sale or purchase expressed in a foreign currency;
(b) by the ownership of assets in an overseas country, or long-term obligations expressed in a foreign currency;
(c) by the operation of a branch in a foreign country with day-to-day transactions in a local currency;
(d) by the ownership, complete or partial, of shares in a company registered overseas which expressed its own accounts in a currency different from that of the parent company.

The effect of transactions in groups (a) and (b) will have been recorded in sterling in the normal course of events and at each periodic balancing date will be valued in accordance with the normal principles. This is historic cost or market value, whichever is the lower for assets and whichever is the higher for liabilities. These 'normal' rules will provide an acceptable result (or at least no less acceptable than the results arising under the historical basis for UK transactions) in all situations except those in which an overseas-currency-denominated loan has been raised and used to buy a fixed asset in the same country. If the rate of exchange between that currency and sterling were to rise, then the liability would increase, but the fixed assets would, unless revalued, still be translated at the lower historical rate, thereby producing an exchange loss. This would not be in agreement with the most likely economic facts, which would suggest that the earnings from the use of the asset would continue at the same rate in the foreign currency. At the new rate of exchange these would be worth more in terms of sterling, so it is unrealistic to say that a loss has arisen. It is this 'related transaction' aspect that caused the long gestation period for the production of a standard on foreign currency. ED 27 was issued by the ASC in October 1980 following earlier drafts, ED 16 in 1975, and ED 21 in 1977, neither of which became a standard. However, SSAP 20, 'Foreign Currency Translation', was issued in April 1983.[1]

The point concerning loans and fixed assets raised earlier applies similarly when consolidated accounts are prepared for a group that contains an overseas subsidiary.

12.1 Definitions and approaches

It is useful to define a number of terms in the present context, and the following are particularly relevant.

● *Conversion* The actual exchanging of one currency for another.
● *Translation* This is the process whereby financial data denominated in one currency are expressed in terms of another currency. It includes both the expression of individual transactions in terms of another currency and the expression of a complete set of financial statements prepared in one currency in terms of another currency.
● *Local currency* This refers to the currency of the primary economic environment in which an entity operates and generates net cash flows.

● *Current/non-current method*   Generally, this translates current assets and liabilities at the current rate and non-current assets and liabilities at applicable historical rates.

● *Monetary/non-monetary method*   Generally, this refers to the translation of monetary assets and liabilities at the current rate and non-monetary assets and liabilities at applicable historical rates. For translation purposes, assets and liabilities are monetary if they are expressed in terms of a fixed number of foreign currency units; all other balance sheet items are classified as non-monetary.

● *Temporal method*   Under this method, assets, liabilities, revenues and expenses are translated at the rate of exchange ruling at the date on which the amount recorded in the financial statements was established. At the balance sheet date, any assets or liabilities that are carried at current values are retranslated at the closing rate.

● *Closing rate method*   Under this method, assets and liabilities denominated in foreign currencies are translated using the closing rate. Revenue items are translated using either an average or the closing rate of exchange for the period.

● *Net investment*   The net investment that a company has in a foreign enterprise is its effective equity stake and comprises its proportion of such a foreign enterprise's net assets; in appropriate circumstances, intragroup loans and other deferred balances may be regarded as part of the effective equity stake.

● *Closing rate/net investment method*   This recognizes that the investment of a company is in the net worth of its foreign enterprise rather than as a direct investment in the individual assets and liabilities of that enterprise. The amounts in the balance sheet of the foreign enterprise should be translated into the reporting currency of the investing company using the closing rate, i.e. the rate at the balance sheet date. Exchange differences will arise if this rate differs from that at the previous balance sheet date or at the date of any subsequent capital injection (or reduction) and should be dealt with in the reserves. Revenue items should be translated at an average rate for the year or closing rate. Where an average rate is used which differs from the closing rate, the difference should also be dealt with in the reserves.

12.1.1   Conversion

When conversion takes place, there will be a difference if the rate of exchange used at the time of conversion is different from the rate when the transaction was recorded. It is a realized difference, and there is no dispute that when it relates to a trading item it should be reflected in the trading profit. There might have been some argument in the past that the differences relating to the repayment of a loan and the sale of fixed assets should be taken through the reserves, but this is now unlikely. The current practice (following SSAP 12) would be to deal with the deficit or surplus in the profit and loss account.

12.1.2   Translation

It is where consolidated accounts are prepared for a group that contains an overseas subsidiary that most discussion on accounting for foreign currencies and variety of treatment has occurred.

The questions are (1) What rate should be used for translating the financial statements of the subsidiary company before they are aggregated with those of the other members of the group? and (2) If differences between translation at the date of the transaction and date of the balance sheet arise, how should they be treated? Assets and liabilities were translated in the first half of the century using the current/non-current basis to ensure a similar basis to that used in the parent company accounts—which were, of course, on the historical cost basis. Fixed-asset accounts were, therefore, translated either at the rate ruling at the date of acquisition, or, after it became customary in the UK accounts to revalue fixed assets, at the date of revaluation and long-term debt at historical rates. Other assets and liabilities, i.e. current ones, were translated at the closing, i.e. current, rates of exchange.

The exchange rates in those early days were usually reflecting a strong pound; i.e., liabilities expressed in foreign currencies were diminishing, if there was any change at all. The monetary/non-monetary basis, as its name implies, states that monetary items were to be translated at the closing rate and non-monetary ones at the historical rate. Under this method there could be some discussion about the appropriate rate for some investments and stock, so the temporal method was formulated, which uses the rate applicable to the time of the actual measurement basis that is used, i.e. historical for asset items at historical cost and closing for items at a current cost or value. Items expected to be realized in the future should be translated (using the temporal method) by the use of a future rate, but it has been accepted that the present rate is the best predictor of future rates.

12.2   Pronouncements

12.2.1   SFAS 8 and 52

The USA was the first in this area with a standard, SFAS 8,[2] which required the use of the temporal method. This follows theoretically from historical cost accounting and the proprietary theory of consolidation. The latter was probably more appropriate in the early days of group accounting, when the overseas subsidiary represented an extension of the parent company activity which it was convenient to pursue through a company structure instead of a branch. Nowadays, it is much more likely that the subsidiary is an economic entity with a life of its own, independent of the parent company. It is this independence that may support the view that it is only the net asset position that is at risk and all assets and liabilities should be translated at the same rate, which inevitably means the closing rate. A further development, however, could suggest that this independence may mean that the company is not a subsidiary but merely another investment; if this were so, then perhaps consolidation is inappropriate.

The discussion about translation, and the subsequent amendment to SFAS 8, i.e. SFAS 52, and the issue of SSAP 20 based on ED 27, are notable as the first major attempts by the national bodies of accountants in the UK, Canada, the USA and the IASC to produce a comparable standard.

12.2.2   ED 27 and SSAP 20

The exposure draft and the standard recognize both the temporal and closing rate methods and distinguish between the position of an individual company and a group. The standard, in so far as it relates to individual companies, states:

Individual companies
46   Subject to the provisions of paragraphs 48 and 51, each asset, liability, revenue or cost arising from a transaction denominated in a foreign currency should be translated into the local currency at the exchange rate in operation on the date on which the transaction occurred; ... Where a trading transaction is covered by a related or matching forward contract, the rate of exchange specified in that contract may be used.
47   Subject to the special provisions of paragraph 51, which relate to the treatment of foreign equity investments financed by foreign currency borrowings, no subsequent translations should normally be made once non-monetary assets have been translated and recorded.

48   At each balance sheet date, monetary assets and liabilities denominated in a foreign currency should be translated by using the closing rate or, where appropriate, the rates of exchange fixed under the terms of the relevant transactions. . . .

49   All exchange gains or losses on settled transactions and unsettled short-term monetary items should be reported as part of the profit or loss for the year from ordinary activities (unless they result from transactions which themselves would fall to be treated as extraordinary items, in which case the exchange gains or losses should be included as part of such items).

50   Exchange gains and losses on long-term monetary items should also be recognised in the profit and loss account; however, it is necessary to consider on the grounds of prudence whether, in the exceptional cases outlined in paragraph 11 [doubts as to convertibility or marketability], the amount of the gain, or the amount by which exchange gains exceed past exchange losses on the same items to be recognised in the profit and loss account, should be restricted.

51   Where a company has used foreign currency borrowings to finance, or provide a hedge against, its foreign equity investments and the conditions set out in this paragraph apply, the equity investments may be denominated in the appropriate foreign currencies and the carrying amounts translated at the end of each accounting period at closing rates for inclusion in the investing company's financial statements. Where investments are treated in this way, any exchange differences arising should be taken to reserves and the exchange gains or losses on the foreign currency borrowings should then be offset as a reserve movement, against these exchange differences. The conditions which must apply are as follows:

(a) in any accounting period, exchange gains or losses arising on the borrowings may be offset only to the extent of exchange differences arising on the equity investments;
(b) the foreign currency borrowings, whose exchange gains or losses are used in the offset process, should not exceed, in the aggregate, the total amount of cash that the investments are expected to be able to generate, whether from profits or otherwise; and
(c) the accounting treatment adopted should be applied consistently from period to period.[3]

There is no difference in principle between the accounting records necessary for a home and those for an overseas branch. However, because the value of some assets or liabilities of an overseas branch may have changed owing to changes in the exchange rate between the date of the transaction and the date of the statement, there will be a need to consider more carefully the values to be recorded at the end of the period.

If, during the normal course of events, an overseas branch grants credit to local customers, these sales will probably be translated at the average rate of the period. The value of the debtors at the year-end will be at the closing rate of exchange, which will produce a translation difference.

There is no dispute that these differences should be dealt with in the profit and loss account.

It is worthwhile reading the exposure draft as well as the standard, as the draft shows the development of the standard, and the changing and developing approach to the standard-setting process. Although there are only two extra paragraphs for the individual company in the standard, there is one extra important principle: the matching or hedging process, which is described in paragraph 51 above.

Most of the controvesy has concerned the translation of financial statements prepared by a subsidiary company in a different currency, so that the assets, liabilities and results can be aggregated with those of the parent company or other subsidiaries to prepare consolidated statements. The standard makes the following requirements.

Consolidated financial statements

52   When preparing group accounts for a company and its foreign enterprises, which includes the incorporation of the results of associated companies or foreign branches into those of an investing company, the closing rate/net investment method of translating the local currency financial statements should normally be used.

53   Exchange differences arising from the retranslation of the opening net investment in a foreign enterprise at the closing rate should be recorded as a movement on reserves.

54   The profit and loss account of a foreign enterprise accounted for under the closing rate/net investment method should be translated at the closing rate or at an average rate for the period. . . .

55   In those circumstances where the trade of the foreign enterprise is more dependent on the economic environment of the investing company's currency than that of its own reporting currency, the temporal method should be used.

56   Where foreign currency borrowings have been used to finance, or provide a hedge against, group equity investments in foreign enterprises, exchange gains or losses on the borrowings, which would otherwise have been taken to the profit and loss account, may be offset as reserve movements against exchange differences arising on the retranslation of the net investments, provided that:

(a) the relationships between the investing company and the foreign enterprises concerned justify the use of the closing rate method for consolidation purposes; ... (b), (c) and (d) detail further restrictions.

Disclosure

57   The methods used in the translation of the financial statements of foreign enterprises and the treatment accorded to exchange differences should be disclosed in the financial statements.

58   The following information should also be disclosed in the financial statements:

(a) for all companies, or groups of companies, which are not exempt companies, the net amount of exchange gains and losses on foreign currency borrowing less deposits, identifying separately:

 (i)   the amount offset in reserves under the provisions of paragraphs 51, 57 and 58; and

 (ii) the net amount charged/credited to the profit and loss account;

(b) for all companies, or groups of companies, the net movement on reserves arising from exchange differences.[4]

The standard adopted the proposal in the exposure draft that normally the closing rate method should be used for the balance sheet. Whereas the exposure draft proposed the use of an average rate for the profit and loss account, the standard gives an unrestricted choice. The annual surveys show significant movement from the use of the closing rate to an average rate over recent years. Clearly, the latter is justified on a day-by-day view of the results for the period, but the standard accepts that the normal view is a net investment view of the subsidiary. On this view, some would argue that the closing rate is more appropriate. Using an average rate for the profit and loss account and a closing rate for the balance sheet inevitably produces a further difference on translation. The translation method used for the profit and loss account is shown below.

% *for 300 companies*	1982/3	1983/4	1984/5	1985/6	1986/7
Closing rate	48	49	43	46	33
Average rate	24	21	29	31	40
Other method	3	1	—	—	—
Not disclosed	12	12	16	13	16
No evidence of foreign operations	13	17	12	10	11
	100	100	100	100	100

Note: The sample companies changes from year to year.

12.3   Illustrations

Apart from representing international collaboration, the exposure draft was innovatory in several other respects—it included numerous examples and explained the options considered by ASC in more detail than usual. These were not repeated in the standard, but the following examples cover the same points.

Example 12.1

This concerns the individual company engaging in foreign activities. A UK company, keeping its books in sterling, bought plant and machinery from France for Ffr250,000 when the exchange rate was £1 = Ffr10.50 and paid for it immediately. The company also purchased raw materials from France for Ffr130,000 (£1 = Ffr10.60) on credit, which had not been paid at the year-end. Similarly, sales to a French customer expressed in francs amounted to Ffr90,000 when £1 = Ffr10.75 and were unpaid at the year-end. At the year-end the rate of exchange was £1 = Ffr10.90.

(a) The purchase of plant would be recorded as 'Dr Plant, Cr Cash', with the cost in sterling of £23,810 (being 250,000 ÷ 10.50). Thereafter, the fact that the machinery cost Ffr250,000 is immaterial: it cost £23,810, and this amount will be used in subsequent statements. If credit terms had been agreed so that there was a delay between the agreement to buy and payment, there would be the possibility of a change in the exchange rate between these two dates. Some accountants would use the rate of exchange at the date of payment in the calculation of the cost of the plant, but theoretically the appropriate rate is that ruling at the date of the agreement. The subsequent change in the rate causes a difference which will be written off as part of the expenses (or income) of the year.

(b) The purchase of the raw materials would require 'Dr Raw materials, Cr Sundry suppliers £12,264' (being 130,000 ÷ 10.60), with a note that the liability is in French francs. At the year-end, this note will draw attention to the need to consider the valuation of the liability. This will be calculated at the closing rate of £1 = Ffr10.90 and produces a liability of £11,927. Assuming that the difference between £12,264 and £11,927 is material, or that in total similar differences are material, there will be a 'Dr Sundry suppliers' and 'Cr Differences on exchange of £337', the net difference on this account, in so far as it represents differences of a revenue nature, being written off.

(c) The sale would be recorded as 'Cr Sales, Dr Sundry debtors £8,372' (being 90,000 ÷ 10.75). Again at the year-end this will be valued by reference to the year-end rate of exchange, i.e. at £8,257 (being 90,000 ÷ 10.90) with the difference of £115 being written off.

(d) *Supplementary remarks* The wide fluctuations in exchange rates have led to many papers indicating the need for more planning and control in this area.[5] The current trend appears to be for the emergence of a new area within the finance function.[6] In these examples the year-end position is a net liability expressed in Ffr40,000 or at the year-end rate £3,670. Modern management would expect this net position to be calculated on a frequent, regular basis in respect of each different currency.

Example 12.2

A wholly-owned subsidiary of a UK company is registered in a foreign country and prepares its accounts in accordance with UK standards, but they are expressed in the local monetary unit, Zs. The shares were acquired by the parent company at a nominal value of Z1,500 when the rate of exchange was £1 = Z3. The financial statements recently prepared are summarized as:

Balance sheet				
	Z'000s		Z'000s	Z'000s
Share capital	1,500	Fixed assets net		1,620
Unappropriated profit	30	Long-term advance		300
	1,530	Current assets		
Long-term liability	900	Stock	450	
Current liabilities	360	Debtors	420	870
	2,790			2,790

Profit and loss account

	Z'000s
Sales	720
Cost of sales	690
Profit	30

The rate of exchange at the end of the year on the balance sheet date was £1 = Z5. These statements need to be translated into pounds sterling so that they can be incorporated into the group accounts.

To begin with, use the closing rate method. This example, in which there is no unappropriated profit at the beginning of the year, requires that all items in the balance sheet, apart from the share capital (for which the historical rate is used), should be translated to sterling using the ratio 5:1. This gives:

	£'000s		£'000s	£'000s
Share capital	500	Fixed assets net		324
Loss on translation	(200)	Long-term advance		60
Unappropriated profit	6	Current assets		
	306	Stock	90	
Long-term liability	180	Debtors	84	
Current liabilities	72			174
	558			558

For the profit and loss account we have, using either (a) closing rate or (b) average rate (say, £1 = Z4):

	(a) £'000s		(b) £'000s
Sales	144	Sales	180
Cost of sales	138	Cost of sales	172.5
Profit	6	Profit	7.5

If the average rate is used for translating the profit and loss account, then the unappropriated profit of £7,500 has to be retranslated using the closing rate before incorporation in the balance sheet, the difference of £1,500 being deducted from reserves. The advantage of the closing rate method is that the traditional ratios from the accounts are unaltered; profit is still 4.2 per cent of sales, current assets are still 2.42 times current liabilities, and this stability is considered useful. As far as the parent company is concerned, the net asset value of the subsidiary is now £306,000 compared with £500,000. The profit of £6,000 (or £7,500) has been more than offset by the loss arising on the translation of the share capital, Z1,500,000 (the net assets at the beginning of the year), at £1 = Z5 instead of £1 = Z3. The standard requires that these two components of the result for the year should be treated differently, the trading result being part of the normal trading and the exchange difference arising from the retranslation of the opening net investment dealt with through reserves.

If the temporal method is implemented, then further information is needed. It is necessary to determine the rate of exchange appropriate to the date inherent in the basis of measurement used to determine the value of particular assets and liabilities. These rates will be those appropriate to the historical cost for fixed assets—long-term advances and stock valued at cost—and the closing rate for all other items. The practical implication of this method is that fixed assets are translated by reference to the rate of exchange when they were acquired, which retains their effective historical cost in terms of sterling. Automatically, the depreciation charge would be based on this historical translated amount. In times of relative rising prices (declining value of Z in relation to £) in the overseas country, the historical-cost-based depreciation charge represents a higher proportionate expense; e.g., if the fixed assets costing Z1,800,000 had been acquired when £1 = Z3, they would be translated to £600,000 less depreciation for one year of Z180,000 (or £60,000) to net £540,000 instead of the £360,000 less £36,000, net £324,000, when using the closing rate of £1 = Z5. The difference in the depreciation charge would be reflected in the profit for the year: £24,00 higher when using the closing rate. The stock aspect can be significant in particular cases (and examination problems), but in most practical situations the rate of stock turnover in relation to changes in exchange rates means that there is only a small difference between stock translated at the closing rate and stock translated at the historical rate.

The closing rate/net investment method should normally be used. The temporal rate is required in the circumstances described in paragraph 55 of the standard (see above). The corresponding paragraph in the exposure draft was more explicit:

54   In those circumstances where the trade of the subsidiary is a direct extension of the trade of the holding company, the temporal method should be used.

The original phrase clearly indicated that, where the trade of the subsidiary 'was an extension of the parent', it should be treated as part of the parent and the transaction accounted for as if it were part of the parent, i.e. on the historical cost basis. The wording of paragraph 55 in the standard has rarely led to companies in the annual survey using the temporal method.

Where the subsidiary has unappropriated profits at the beginning of the year, these will be either pre-acquisition profits or profits earned since acquisition and not distributed. They will be translated as follows:

Pre-acquisition   — just like share capital, at the rate pertaining at the date of acquisition
Post acquisition — a balancing figure reflecting aggregate exchange differences since acquisition, as well as translated profit for each year.

12.4 Treatment of the difference and disclosure

There is little disagreement that the policy used should be disclosed. There is more disagreement about what figures should be disclosed and where they should be debited or credited.

The differences arising on normal trading transactions clearly belong to the trading profit. If exceptional, perhaps, the amount should be disclosed, but a counter-argument that has some weight is that companies may avoid exchange gains or losses in many ways, e.g. by entering into forward contracts, or arranging the transactions at fixed exchange rates, or using a currency that is expected to be more stable. The costs associated with these alternative arrangements are difficult to quantify, but they are as much part of the cost associated with foreign transactions as a difference on foreign currency transactions. It is therefore suggested that the disclosure of the differences associated with normal trading transactions is not necessary, although others[7] argue for full disclosure.

The alternative treatments of the differences arising from the translation using the net investment method, or that arising in respect of fixed assets using the closing rate method, or of loans payable whenever the rate changes, are less easily resolved. UK practice has allowed the revaluation of fixed assets and the crediting of the surplus to reserves. The difference arising on translation of the investment or fixed assets is very similar, and the UK financial community has no difficulty in accepting a transfer through reserves. The use of the closing rate provides an automatic matching of loans and fixed assets (at least initially, when the loan was used to buy fixed assets), and the net difference is in most cases not significant. If the loan proceeds are not invested to produce an income stream in the same currency as the loan itself, there is the possibility of a large difference which, even in the UK, would have to be written off through the profit and loss account if it is adverse. Some UK companies were tempted to borrow from Switzerland or Germany in the late 1960s and early 1970s at much lower interest rates than were quoted in the UK. The proceeds were then used to finance investment in the UK or elsewhere in the world. The problem arose when the loans were repaid, or at an earlier date, as far as the accounting problem was concerned, as the rate of exchange changed between the date of borrowing and the year-end or the repayment date. Then it became apparent that these were very costly loans. A rate of interest of 7 per cent on a Deutschmark loan seems a bargain compared with 12 per cent for a UK-sterling-based one, but if the original Dm40 million (i.e. £10 million) raised when £1 = Dm4.00 had to be repaid a year later when the rate of exchange was £1 = Dm3.50, then the Dm40 million will cost £11,428,571, so the 'saving' of gross interest of initially £500,000 p.a. (but now less, as the interest will have increased with the change in the exchange rate) has cost £1,428,571, or a net deficit of £928,571. In practice, it was often worse than this, as the lower interest would have increased taxable profit and the extra cost of the loan resulting from the currency rate change did not represent an expense on which tax relief was available. After much pressure, tax relief is now obtainable.

The accounting problem is one of presentation. The interest is charged against profit which will benefit from the lower nominal rate. The loss on the loan, it was argued, was extraordinary. Theoretically, it is possible to envisage an equalization arrangement whereby the borrowing organization recognizes that the 'cheap' interest on the loan will be offset by the extra cost of repaying the principal. In accordance with the accrual concept, this extra cost should be built up over the life of loan by an additional debit to the profit and loss account. A similar argument is advanced for amortizing over the remaining life a difference that has arisen at a particular year-end. There is no need to provide in full for the loss this year; the exchange rate may change next year in the opposite direction, and by the time the loan is due to be repaid it could be a different rate again. In other words, there could be very large fluctuations, and with the fluctuating exchange rates of recent years this has been very significant. If this difference could be dealt with through reserves, it would not affect the bottom line, or earnings per share. If it is required to go through the profit and loss account not merely at the year-end but also for interim financial statements, it would produce results that were fluctuating 'too much' and in some circumstances in the opposite direction to the most likely economic effect. The 'matching' allowed in the current standards enables the usual major fluctuations to be absorbed in the reserves rather than in the profit and loss account when the loan has been invested in appropriate assets.[8]

The movement on reserves will appear in the notes to the balance sheet, but there is less agreement on the disclosure in the profit and loss account. The requirements of the EEC 4th Directive and the Companies Act 1985 mean that it is necessary to distinguish between operating and other income and expense. A translation difference relating to an extraordinary item should be included in that part of the account (as is the tax effect), and similarly with exceptional items and interest payable or receivable. An illustration is provided by Unilever.

In the consolidated profit and loss account for the year ended 31 December 1985 (and similarly for 1986), there are references to the notes, as follows:

		£ million	
	1984	1985	1986
5. *Other interest receivable and similar income*			
Interest receivable	113	119	160
Exchange difference	(2)	5	19
	111	124	179
6. *Interest payable and similar charges*			
Interest on borrowings	(152)	(157)	(193)
Other interest payable	(26)	(32)	(25)
Exchange differences	(8)	(6)	7
	186	195	211

There has been considerable argument (e.g. SFAS 52, para. 144) about the disclosure of the effect of changes in the rates used for translation. It is possible to make a simple mathematical calculation of using the old rate of, say $1.45 to £1 and comparing the result with that obtained by using the current rate of $1.76 to £1 and describing the difference as being 'due to the change in exchange rates'. But what was the effect of this change on the underlying economic transactions? In the case of import/export activities it could be significant: when the subsidiary has its own separate economic environment, exchange rates may have no effect on the economic reality and the calculated difference will be an appropriate explanation of change in the reported results. There is no legal or standard requirement for the disclosure of this difference.

Examples of the accounting policy statements from published accounts illustrate the previous discussion.

Britoil plc, for the year ended 31 December 1986 (*xiv*) *Foreign currency transactions*
Income and expenditure is translated into sterling at the exchange rate prevailing at the date of the transaction. Monetary items are retranslated at the balance sheet date at the then prevailing exchange rate. Exchange gains or losses are taken to the profit and loss account except that:
   (a) Gains or losses relating to the acquisition of fixed assets are credited or debited to fixed assets.
   (b) Unrealised currency gains on long-term debt can be taken to the profit and loss account subject to two limitations. Firstly, they are limited to the extent that they relate to the level of debt in respect of which unrealised currency losses had occurred in the past. Secondly, they are limited to the extent of the amount of those unrealised losses.
   (c) Gains or losses arising on foreign borrowings used to finance or hedge foreign currency investments are shown as a movement in reserves.
Overseas equity investments are translated at the balance sheet date using the then prevailing exchange rate. Exchange gains or losses arising on the retranslation of the opening net investment are taken to reserves.

This note reflects the relatively strong pound sterling, at least in relation to the US dollar, during the year.

The policy statement from Grand Metropolitan Group for the year ended 30 September 1986 is typical of many that comply with the bare essentials of the standard:

Foreign Currencies
Transactions in foreign currencies are recorded at the rates of exchange ruling at the date of the transaction. Assets and liabilities in foreign currencies, including the group's interest in the underlying net assets of related companies, are translated into sterling at the balance sheet exchange rates.

Profits and losses of overseas subsidiaries and related companies are translated into sterling at weighted average rates of exchange during the year with the year-end adjustment to closing rates being taken to reserves.

Gains or losses arising on the translation of the net assets of overseas group companies are taken to reserves, net of exchange differences arising on related foreign currency borrowings. Other exchange differences are taken to the profit and loss account.

Several companies expand the basic disclosure in the directors' report, notes to the accounts or elsewhere in the substantial 'Annual report and accounts'.

Redland PLC, in the accounts for the year ended 28 March 1987, includes the more important exchange rates in its accounting policy note:

(c)   Foreign currencies
Assets and liabilities denominated in foreign currencies are translated into £ sterling at the exchange rates ruling at the year end. Profits and losses of overseas companies are translated in £ sterling at average rates of exchange.

The more important rates of exchange are:

		Rate to the pound		
		1986/7		1985/6
	28/3/87	ave. rate	29/3/86	ave. rate
Australian dollar	2.30	2.25	2.08	2.00
US dollar	1.60	1.49	1.48	1.38
Deutschmark	2.92	3.04	3.45	3.72

Differences arising out of the translation of foreign currencies, except those arising on current transactions which are dealt with in the profit and loss account, are taken to reserves.

The financial review includes a separate section concerning exchange rates:

Exchange Rates
The sterling value of profits in Europe benefited from the movement of the Deutschmark from an average rate of 3.72 to 3.04 (with a corresponding strengthening of the Dutch guilder). Profits from North America suffered from a 7% decline in the average United States dollar rate, and those from Australia by a decline of 11% in the Australian dollar.

The overall effect of exchange rate movements was to enhance profit before tax by approximately £6 million.

Profit before tax was £130.7 million, so it can be calculated that the £6 million represents 4.6 per cent of that total or, more significantly, 33 per cent of the overall increase in profit before tax of £17.9 million compared with the preceding year. The analysis of reserves shows an increase of £1.8 million in the revaluation reserve but a reduction of £19.1 million (for Redland plc) and a reduction of £15.6 million for the group. There is a foreign currency adjustment, an increase of £6.7 million in the provision for liabilities and charges in connection with the group pensions. A note relates this to a German subsidiary. The use of the rates given above and the opening balance of £36.4 million confirms that the movement in the Deutschmark exchange rate from 3.45 to 2.92 to the pound sterling does have this significant effect. Foreign currency adjustments also appear in the schedule of fixed assets.

The annual survey for 1985/86 illustrated the additional analysis provided by Redland for 30 March 1985 of 'net assets by currency' and 'loans and bank overdrafts'. Using the accounts for several years, it is possible to build up a picture of the results of the financing activities, at least on one particular date in the year.

Loans and bank overdrafts

	£ million			
	1983/4	*1984/5*	*1985/6*	*1986/7*
Sterling	(16.8)	9.5	70.3	(28.4)
US dollar	(99.1)	101.2	62.1	149.3
Other currencies	6.9	7.8	10.7	82.2
Total	89.2	118.5	143.1	203.1

Net assets (i.e. total assets less current liabilities)

Sterling	164.4	176.2	200.4	224.2
European	117.4	146.3	174.0	276.0
US dollar	110.7	135.7	141.3	346.4
Australian dollar	38.1	36.6	32.2	36.5
Other countries	7.7	9.8	6.6	5.6
	438.3	504.6	554.5	888.7

This is the type of information that management should be providing. Given the magnitude of exchange rate changes, the analysts will be, or should be, looking for disclosures of this type of data.

The net asset analysis was provided as part of the more usual geographical analysis of turnover and operating profit (CA 1985, 4 sch.55(2), and Stock Exchange). The geographical analysis of turnover, operating profit and net assets is shown below.

	Turnover	1986/7 operating profit	Net assets	Turnover	1985/6 operating profit	Net assets
	£m	£m	£m	£m	£m	£m
UK	600.2	69.0	224.2	652.3	61.4	200.4
Continental Europe	357.9	44.2	276.0	288.4	30.8	174.0
USA	224.6	22.4	346.4	209.3	20.1	141.3
Australia and Far East	101.5	7.4	36.5	120.1	10.7	32.2
Other	15.8	0.8	5.6	21.5	1.7	6.6
	1,300.0	143.8	888.7	1,291.6	124.7	554.5

An illustration of the disclosure required by the standard in respect of foreign currency borrowings is provided by Thorn EMI plc in the annual report for the year ended 31 March 1987:

Accounting Policy
Foreign currencies   The trading results of overseas subsidiaries and related companies are translated into sterling at year-end rates.

Assets and liabilities denominated in foreign currencies are translated into sterling either at year-end rates or, where there are related forward foreign exchange contracts, at contract rates.

Exchange differences arising from the retranslation of the opening net investments in overseas subsidiaries and related companies and from foreign currency borrowings, in so far as they are matched, are dealt with in group reserves:

Note to Profit and Loss Account

4. *Finance charges*

	1987 £m	1986 £m
Interest payable:		
on bank overdrafts and loans repayable within 5 years	(51.9)	(48.3)
on other loans	(2.2)	(17.0)
	(54.1)	(65.3)
Bank and other interest receivable	33.9	12.4
Exchange gain on foreign currency borrowing	—	3.6
	(20.2)	(49.3)
Net interest receivable by financing subsidiary, included in other operating income (note 2)	(12.1)	—
	(32.3)	(49.3)

Note to Balance Sheet

22. *Reserves*

	Company £m	Subsidiaries £m	Sub-total £m	Related companies £m	Total £m
Profit and loss account:					
At 31 March 1986	122.7	42.8	165.5	22.1	187.6
Currency retranslation	—	5.9	5.9	2.1	8.0
Gains on foreign currency borrowings	—	6.4	6.4	—	6.4
Goodwill written off	—	(13.1)	(13.1)	(1.5)	(14.6)
Retained profit for year	2.9	27.4	30.3	1.4	31.7
At 31 March 1987	125.6	69.4	195.0	24.1	219.1

12.5 Conclusion

The theoretical basis of translation in the historical cost context requires the use of an exchange rate appropriate to the date at which the value of an asset was originally determined—the temporal basis. It is justified to use the current rate, but it should be applied to a current valuation. If equity accounting has been followed, then the stated amount in the investing company books will be cost plus retained profits. If prices were stable (i.e. if there were no inflation or price changes for other reasons), this book amount would be an accurate measure of current value. The use of a current exchange rate for the net investment would be theoretically justified—but this would not necessarily imply its use for the separable assets and liabilities. While there is the requirement to translate the separable items for consolidation purposes, the use of the 'easy' closing rate/net investment method will continue to be widely accepted. Conceptually, the use of a current exchange rate applied to an historical cost is ridiculous, and the subsequent aggregation has no real economic value. This is recognized in the extreme case of hyperinflation, when the local currency statements should be adjusted to current price levels before translation.

Notes

1. ED 27, 'Accounting for Foreign Currency Translations', ASC, 1980; SSAP 20, 'Foreign Currency Translation', ASC, 1983.
2. Financial Accounting Standards Board, 'Statement of Financial Accounting Standards'; SFAS 8, 'Accounting for the Translation of Foreign Currency Transactions and Foreign Currency Financial Statements', FASB, 1975.
3. SSAP 20, paras. 46–51.
4. Ibid., paras. 52–60.
5. For example, 'Exposed assets', *Management Accounting*, June 1980, p. 27; M. Earl and D. Paxson, 'Value accounting for currency transactions', *Accounting and Business Research*, Spring 1978; see also Further Reading list below.
6. Statement by the Organization of Corporate Financial Directors.
7. J. K. Shank and G. S. Shamis, 'Reporting foreign currency adjustments: a disclosure perspective', *Journal of Accountancy*, April 1979.
8. SSAP 20, para. 57.

Further reading

Accounting Standards Committee, ED 27: 'Accounting for Foreign Currency Translation', 1980.

American Accounting Association (selected by), *Notable Contributions to the Periodic International Accounting Literature 1975–1978*, AAA, 1979.

Briggs, P. W., *Foreign Currency Exposure Management*, Butterworth, London, 1986.

Choi, F. and G. Mueller (eds), *Essentials of Multinational Accounting*, University Microfilms International, Ann Arbor, 1979.

Clay, M., 'Exchange rates: cause of problems, or just an excuse?' *Accountancy*, May 1986.

Demiray, I. S., 'How UK companies account for foreign exchange', *Accountancy*, April 1987.

Financial Accounting Standards Board, SFAS 8: 'Accounting for the Translation of Foreign Currency Transactions and Foreign Currency Financial Statements', FASB, 1975.

Financial Accounting Standards Board, ED 'Foreign Currency Translation', Proposed statement of financial accounting standards, FASB, 1980.

Financial Accounting Standards Board, SFAS 52: 'Foreign Currency Translation', FASB, 1981.

Lorenson, L., Accounting Research Study 12, 'Reporting foreign operations of US Companies in dollars', AICPA, New York 1972.

McMonnies, P. and B. Rankin. 'Accounting for foreign currency translations', *Accountants Magazine*, November 1980.

Nobes, C. W., 'A review of the translation debate', *Accounting and Business Research*, ICAEW, Autumn 1980.

Watt, G., R. Hammer and M. Binge, *Accounting for the Multinational Corporation*, Financial Executives Research Foundation, 1977.

Westwick, C., *Accounting for Overseas Operations*; Gower Press, Farnborough, Hants, 1986; *Certified Accountant*, May 1986.

Questions

1. Describe and identify the major differences between
   — the closing rate/net investment method;
   — the current/non-current method;
   — the monetary/non-monetary method;
   — the temporal method.

2. SSAP 20 states that in some circumstances the closing rate/net investment method should be used and in other circumstances the temporal method. Describe the appropriate circumstances and the justification for the use of the particular method.

3. Explain why there was so much concern over the appropriate rate for translating the profit and loss account, and justify the proposal in the exposure draft and the change made in the standard.

4. Justify the proposal that exchange differences resulting from translating the net investment in a foreign subsidiary should be dealt with as adjustments to reserves.

5. Explain and justify the circumstances in which it may be appropriate to allow differences on foreign loans to be offset against differences on the translation of the net investment in a subsidiary.

6. Set out below are the balances as on 30th June 1985 in the books of Box Ltd, incorporated in England, and Carton, its unincorporated branch in West Germany. Carton manufactures parts mainly for Box Ltd which are shipped direct to England.

	Box Ltd £	Carton DM
Share capital	(12,000)	—
Share premium account	(2,000)	—
Profit and loss account	(12,280)	—
Head office account	(22,600)	93,420
Fixed assets—cost	24,000	141,710
Depreciation on fixed assets	(12,800)	(63,720)
Stock	37,220	14,930
Debtors	37,000	890
Cash	960	2,960
Current liabilities	(14,880)	(12,680)
Loan from US bank	—	(60,000)
Turnover	(308,530)	(275,650)
Overheads	26,420	67,490
Manufacturing cost including wages	259,490	90,650
	—	—

The following information is supplied:

(1) The loan was raised by Carton from a US bank on the guarantee of Box Ltd for a total of $22,500 on 1st July 1984.

(2) Cash remitted by Box Ltd of £4,300 has not yet been recorded in the books of Carton at 30th June 1985. In addition, goods in transit from Carton invoiced at DM 10,000 have not been included in the books or closing stock of Box Ltd. These transactions may be taken as occurring at the year end.

(3) No depreciation has yet been provided by either Box Ltd or Carton. This will be uniformly calculated at the rate of 10% on cost.

(4) The fixed assets of Carton were purchased at an average rate of exchange of £1 = 4.5 DM before 1st July 1983. Stock was all purchased within 4 months of the balance sheet date. Closing physical stock amounts to £32,490 for Box Ltd and DM 26,710 for Carton.

(5) The rates of exchange were:

1st July 1983	£1 = 4.5 DM	1st July 1984	£1 = 4.0 DM = $1.5
28th February 1984	£1 = 4.3 DM	28th February 1985	£1 = 3.6 DM
30th April 1984	£1 = 4.2 DM	30th April 1985	£1 = 3.4 DM
		30th June 1985	£1 = 3.0 DM = $1.0

Average year to 30th June 1984   £1 = 4.4 DM
Average year to 30th June 1985   £1 = 3.6 DM

Requirements

(a) State briefly the factors which should be taken into account when determining which method of accounting for overseas entities as recommended by SSAP 20 should be applied by Box Ltd.

(5 marks)

(b) Produce the balance sheet on 30th June 1985 of Box Ltd incorporating the German branch.

(16 marks)

(21 marks)

Note: Make all calculations to the nearest £ and ignore taxation and the elimination of any inter branch profit.

ICAEW, PEII, FAII, December 1985

7. Westerby Vision plc acquired an 80% interest in the share capital of Cassock Corporation which manufactures video accessories. The consideration was £5.2 million. At the date of acquisition the reserves of Cassock were Ą7.5 million and the exchange rate was £1 = Ą2.5. No further shares have been issued and no fixed assets have been acquired by Cassock since the acquisition. Cassock Corporation's profit and loss account for the year ended 31/3/88 can be summarised as:

	Ą'000s
Profit before depreciation	4,200
Depreciation	1,000
	3,200
Taxation	1,600
Transferred to reserves	1,600

The balance sheet at 31/3/88 showed:

	Ą'000s	Ą'000s
Fixed assets at cost	10,000	
less depreciation	4,000	6,000
Net current assets		20,000
		26,000
Share capital		6,000
Reserves		15,000
Debentures		5,000
		26,000

Exchange rates to £1 are given as follows:

31/3/88	31/3/87	Ave. for year ended 31/3/88
1.25	1.6	1.4

You are required to:

(a) show the amounts to be included in respect to Cassock Corporation in the consolidated accounts of Westerby Vision Group for the year ending 31/3/88 using
   (i) the closing rate method
   (ii) the temporal rate method.

(19 marks)

(b) discuss the view that, while the temporal method can be supported theoretically, it does not possess the practical advantages of the closing rate method, the latter producing results which fit better the business realities.

(6 marks)

(25 marks)

8. SSAP 20 deals with foreign currency translation. The overseas activities of two UK-based companies are as follows:

(1) Terrier Ltd has two overseas branches as follows:
   (i) One branch in South America is concerned with buying raw materials for use in the company's UK manufacturing operation. The branch will arrange purchases from local suppliers settling

the payments either on monthly accounts or on three-month bills. The funds will be remitted from the UK on a monthly imprest system. The rates of exchange in the South American country have been volatile and local inflation has averaged 120% for the past three years. There are also restrictions on the export of currency. The branch's fixed assets consist of office equipment and motor vehicles and specific currency has been remitted from the UK for each item.

(ii) The other branch is based in West Germany. It assembles local components which are shipped back to the company in the UK for inclusion in its own products. All purchases are made locally with funds remitted from the UK. The expatriate manager is paid directly from the UK. A Swiss franc loan is outstanding from a bank in Switzerland which was used to purchase the factory in West Germany. The rates of exchange have been fairly constant but there has been some variation in the exchange rate between the franc and the mark.

(2) Spaniel plc has several subsidiaries. The following are its overseas subsidiaries.

(i)   Alsatian is concerned with the manufacture of chains in Italy and was purchased four years ago. It is run by local management and all transactions take place in Italy.

(ii) Boxer is based in the Cayman Islands and is a captive insurance company for the UK parts of the group. In the UK companies' accounting records insurance premiums are credited in sterling to a current account with Boxer at the beginning of the financial year. Claims are debited to this current account as they arise and the resultant balance paid at the year end. When a premium is credited, the appropriate foreign currency is bought forward at the year-end rate and used to settle the balance due. Boxer, which carries on no business outside the UK group, enters each credit or debit in its accounting records in local currency translated at the daily spot rate.

You are required to:

(a) give the details of the two alternative treatments set out for the translation of financial statements in SSAP 20 and explain the circumstances in which they should be applied;   (9 marks)

(b) state briefly how you would deal with the translation of foreign currencies arising in the cases of Terrier Ltd and Spaniel plc stating specifically the accounting treatment of any profit or loss arising.

(9 marks)

(18 marks)

ICAEW, PEII, FAII, July 1984

13. Accounting for changing price levels

The historical cost basis for accounting was described in Chapter 1, but not without some reservations. Difficulties arise from aggregating values obtained using a mixture of money values. Reference was made to a bias in times of rising prices which distorts asset values and leads to an overstatement of profit; it affects expenses more than revenue since expenses are generally made in advance of the resulting revenues. Criticism can be directed at the failure of the historical cost basis to respond to a variety of changes in prices including a change in the purchasing power of money.

The realizaton approach is a relevant consideration here. This has been explained in terms of the accountants' assumption that the original acquisition price was somehow attached to an item as its 'cost' until realization is achieved and the original cost 'expired'. Realization can arise from the usage of current assets and from the depreciation or amortization charges that relate to long-term fixed assets. While this may have conservative properties, it may be considered ostrich-like, since the upward movements in values of items still held may be considered essential in a full description of the economic changes a business undergoes.

The realization rule for recognizing value change has not been strictly adhered to. Prudence has prevailed at times, requiring downward movements to be recorded when identified, as in the case of the 'lower of cost or market' rule for valuing stocks. Sale is not always required before realization; revaluations for land and buildings have been incorporated subject to certification by an appropriately qualified valuer.

It can be seen that the historical cost basis does not provide entirely satisfactory solutions to setting the three basic dimensions (i.e., the units of measurement, the valuation model and the concept of capital maintenance). The valuation model is ossified, frozen in time; the unit of measurement requires aggregation of figures expressed in an unstable unit of value. The concept of capital maintenance becomes increasingly divorced from current economic reality. However, the historical cost basis has continued to dominate practice, with some modification, supported by its relative objectivity, low cost and familiarity.

Although alternatives have been discussed by academics throughout the last half-century,[1] it is only in recent years that there have been efforts by professional bodies in the UK to make a substantial departure from the traditional basis. Cash flow accounting has been advocated, with notable support from Professors Lawson and Lee, but it has been given little attention by standard-setting bodies.[2] It was May 1974 when a provisional standard was issued proposing that the historical-cost-based accounts should be adjusted for changes in the purchasing power of money, and not until 1980 that a standard appeared temporarily giving some consideration to incorporating the different price changes that occur for different products.

This chapter gives some attention to the history of UK pronouncements on price change and accounting, but precedes this with a view of the theoretical considerations. To provide some understanding of the various methods suggested, it is necessary to be aware of what price change means and what effects it has on accounting numbers. A general solution to the price change problem is introduced to provide some perspective on specific recommendations and explanation. In giving specific attention to alternative methods for valuing assets, relevant recommendations included in the 1980 SSAP standard are considered, as they recognize a variety of problems of financial accounting practice that should be of interest to preparers and users of accounts.

13.1 Price change: its form and impact

It may be noticeable that the word 'inflation' has been given little usage in this book so far, despite the regularity of its use in everyday conversation concerning accounting. It is a word that has acquired a number of meanings, perhaps familiar to the non-accountant or non-economist but differing in ways that would interfere with the understanding of accounting for price change. For these purposes, two types of price change need to be considered and distinguished.

The first type, *specific price change*, is probably the most straightforward. It refers to the price change, measured in money terms, of a specific item or class of items. If the price of a packet of your favourite cereal goes up from 50 to 53, this would be a specific price increase of 6 per cent ($3 \div 50$). For a class of items, a 5 per cent increase in the price of all air fares would be a suitable example.

By contrast, *general price change* is used to describe an average change in the prices of all goods. An alternative way of viewing a general price increase is as a decrease in the purchasing power of money. Although not the original meaning, in economics, of 'inflation', the word is so commonly used to describe general price change that this meaning will be accepted here, particularly since this will not cause any interference with the present discussion.

In computing an 'average' change, weights must be given to the specific price changes entering these calculations. Setting the weights is not without its hazards, owing to the fluctuations in weights over time or from varying points of view. An individual would want to measure changes in the purchasing power of money by evaluating how it affected him. He would want the specific price changes to be weighted in the proportions in which he purchased the specific items or classes of goods and services. However, these proportions are not constant but will change as his tastes change, and maybe as his income and the specific prices themselves change. Different individuals will have different sets of weights, so deciding how an index of general price change can be calculated for a group of individuals is at least as complex. There are different indices for different groups; a retail price index considers 'consumers'; an index of factor prices takes the purchasers of factors of production as its interest group.

Having distinguished between these two types of price change, it is a small step to introduce the concept of *relative price change*. This is not a third type of price change, but merely an alternative way of describing specific price change; it is the change of a specific commodity or class of items relative to the price of goods in general. If, during a given period, the general price index shows an increase of 10 per cent while the price of electronic calculators remains stable, the relative price of electronic calculators can be described as falling by 10 per cent.

13.1.1 The time-lag error and operating profit

In understanding how both types of price change affect the measurement of income, a most useful insight is given by considering the time lag error.[3] Chapter 2 showed that the accounting approach to calculating income made particular use of the matching process. The profit and loss account is produced by matching debits and credits representing expenses and revenues, but what are the effects of price change?

If the historical cost basis is being used, then, for a typical business, the time lag between acquiring the factors of production and selling the resulting product will cause out-of-date expenditures to be matched with current revenues. Raw material values will be expressed at prices and in units of purchasing power that were current when they were purchased, while the associated revenues will be based on prices and money values current when the final product incorporating the material is sold. Since production normally takes a finite time, the profit and loss account will be combining figures measured on different bases. It is like deducting inches from centimetres; the answer is confused and disobeys the conventions of mathematics. This is the time-lag error.

During periods of general price increase, the time-lag error will tend to distort profit in an upward direction; a trader can report a profit when he pays £1,000 for goods from a wholesaler, even though the retail price is just £1,000 at that time and all prices increase in line with inflation. With a 10 per cent increase in all prices between his purchase and selling date, he could sell the goods for £1,100 and show a 'profit' of £100 caused only from the change in the meaning of the money units used to measure the payment and receipt. If a correction is made for the time lag error, then it will lead to a reduction in realized profit during times of price rise.

It is possible to view the time-lag error in terms of a general price change or specific price changes. This will depend on the manner in which the three basic dimensions are selected. When it is decided to calculate income by comparing the revenue with the current purchasing price of the inputs embodied in the product being sold, specific price change is being used and a concept of physical capital maintenance is implied; profit is the excess of revenue over that sum required to purchase the inputs so that the stock of inputs could be maintained. A general price change approach is consistent with economic capital maintenance, profit being the excess of revenue over the general purchasing power of the money that acquired the inputs.

The effect of the time lag error is most easily seen in the costs of stock, raw materials, direct labour and other direct costs. The time lag error may be even greater in the case of depreciating assets. A depreciation charge may relate to an asset purchased years before the charge and yet, using the historical cost basis, that charge is based on the prices prevailing when the asset was purchased. The error clearly reduces comparability. The depreciation charge for a building based on the price paid a decade ago will be incomparable with that for an identical building, built at the same time but acquired only a year ago.

These items are concerned with the normal trading activities of a business and are of direct relevance to any attempt to isolate current cost operating profit, i.e. selling items for more than the current cost of producing them, current cost reflecting the concept of either physical or economic capital maintenance. Current cost operating profit provides a measure which can help in assessing a company's performance in producing and selling its output.

A further situation in which the time-lag error can arise is in the sale of fixed assets. The disposal of land may produce a gain, using the historical cost basis, that would be considerably reduced or would even disappear if the cost were updated for either the general increase in prices or the increase in the price of land. Once the time-lag error is eliminated, it may be acceptable to include any remaining gain with current cost operating profit.

Recommendations for coping with price change make regular reference to 'cost of sales adjustment', 'depreciation adjustment' and other terms which can be seen now as attempts to deal with the time-lag error.

13.1.2 Holding gains

Current-cost operating profit provided a useful focus in the last section, but it ignores an important aspect of business performance. Buying inputs when prices are low and selling after prices have risen, produces gains which, it has been suggested, should be eliminated as time-lag errors in calculating operating profit. The gains are described as holding gains; they arise from holding an asset during a period when the price increases. To understand the appropriate treatment of these gains, it is necessary to classify and analyse types of holding gains.

As might be expected, a distinction is made between *realized holding gains* and *unrealized holding gains*. The former will relate both to current items and to the depreciation element of fixed assets, since both provide elements of expense in the matching process. Unrealized holding gains arise when the prices of items still held have increased. The distinction is important both because only realized gains have been verified by the evidence of the sale and because dividend law gives different treatment to the two gains, as discussed in Chapter 7.

A holding gain measured in money terms can be divided into two components. Part of the total gain might arise simply because prices in general have risen. This is the first component. However, where the specific price rise exceeds the general increase in prices, the total gain will exceed that arising from the general price change. The excess is described as *a real holding gain* and is the second component.

This can be illustrated by the price change effects on an asset purchased for £1,000. Assume that, in a given period, there is a general rise in prices of 10 per cent while the specific index for the particular asset rises by 15 per cent. At the end of the period, the asset will have a current price of £1,150; the original purchase price of £1,000 becomes £1,100 when restated in terms of constant general purchasing power, indicating a real holding gain of £50 (i.e., £1,150 − £1,100).

If the concept of maintenance of economic capital is adopted, then real holding gains form part of profit; the gain exceeds that needed to maintain the economic purchasing power used in the purchase that resulted in the gain. However, when the concept of maintenance of physical capital is applied, no part of the holding gain can be regarded as profit. To pay a dividend from an unrealized holding gain would require the sale of an asset and, consequently, a reduction in physical capital. Using the above example as an illustration, if the asset considered were the only investment, not even the £50 could be withdrawn without disposing of at least part of the asset.

Even a realized holding gain does not provide a source for dividends if physical capital is to be maintained, but the gain must be retained to permit replacement. In the example, if the asset had been sold for £1,150, the whole of this sum would be required to replace that asset, as an item of physical capital. Under a physical capital maintenance approach to calculating profit, an appropriate accounting treatment for such gains would be to create a revaluation reserve which would be credited with an amount equal to the total gain; the corresponding debit is made to the asset account until realization, when it would be included as an expense in the profit and loss account. This would ensure that the gain was not included in profit.

Holding gains and operating profits have been introduced as complementary measures of business performance. Their identification provides some explanation for the view that assets should be depreciated if they have a finite life even though the specific price increase for the asset offsets the depreciation write-down. The depreciation charge enters the operating profit and loss calculation, representing a realization of the cost of the asset; the specific price rise produces holding gains that are not operating profit and are not realized, except to the extent that they represent additional depreciation.

13.1.3   Monetary assets and liabilities

The previous paragraph indicated that real holding gains that arise when the specific price increase exceeds the general price index are an element of profit under the concept of economic capital maintenance. Monetary assets and liabilities are those having values that are constant when measured in terms of money. Cash is probably the most obvious example; no matter how much price change occurs, £1 sterling is always currently worth £1, even if its purchasing power has undergone considerable decline. This means that the specific index for monetary items is always unity and their relative price index is equal in size but opposite in sign to the general price index.

During periods of inflation, there will be real losses arising from holding a monetary asset owing to its decline in purchasing power. There is a loss in economic capital from holding monetary assets and a real gain from holding monetary liabilities. Consider money borrowed to purchase assets whose price changes in line with inflation. If the assets are sold at their current price after some time has elapsed, this would provide sufficient money to repay the borrowing and provide a surplus. It would certainly be a real gain.

When the concept of maintenance of physical capital is adopted, gearing can also result in an additional element of profit. This is true if the maintenance of shareholders' interest in physical capital is considered, since then the gains outlined above could all be paid out to the shareholders without affecting any physical capital they had financed. From the point of view of the company as a whole, there would not be any additional profit, since this approach to the concept requires that all physical assets, whether financed by equity or by debt, be maintained.

13.2 Asset valuation

The value of an asset not only varies over time but is different from different points of view. Market value is not an unambiguous description, since the price of a replacement (or entry price) may be considerably higher than the price for which the item could be sold (the exit price). In addition to entry and exit values, this chapter considers one other basic approach, that of economic or net present value, which attempts to evaluate the future value of an asset. A value that combines all three basic approaches is then considered. This is known as 'deprival value', although current terminology uses 'value to the owner' or 'value to the business'.

The application of this approach to specific assets introduces further considerations, and these are given attention utilizing some of the views found in the development of SSAP 16[4] and its associated guidelines.

13.2.1 Net realizable value

One approach to providing asset values that are up to date is to measure what would be received for the asset if it is sold. Chambers argues that only selling price 'is uniformly relevant at a point of time for all possible future actions in markets'; it indicates the 'current cash equivalent . . . the capacity on the basis of present holdings, to go into a market with cash for the purpose of adapting oneself to contemporary conditions'.[5] He calls this approach 'Continuously Contemporary Accounting' or 'CoCoA'. In calculating the current cash equivalent, the full selling price must be reduced by the costs of selling the asset. The reduced selling price is known as the *net realizable value*.

A common criticism of this approach argues that establishing the net realizable value offers too much scope for subjectivity. The costs of selling must be estimated; selling prices are usually less from a forced sale than sales in the normal course of business; the selling prices will depend on the degree of disaggregation adopted. This last consideration recognizes that, for interdependent items, selling a number of items as a unit produces a different value from selling them individually. Selling a car as a whole or as dismantled parts is unlikely to produce the same sales value. The disaggregation problem is common to most of the approaches to establishing a current value. A suitable rule of thumb might be to disaggregate to the level that is usually traded. In establishing exit values, selling would be the obvious trading activity considered. If the firm concerned usually trades in whole cars, then whole cars would be the appropriate basis for valuation. A similar argument would support the use of normal trading conditions rather than forced sale prices.

Semi-finished goods also provide problems for this and other valuation methods. There is no absolute answer to the question of whether to value in terms of the inputs or the completed output less the costs of completion. When nearing completion, the latter becomes more appropriate; when barely started, the former would seem to warrant more attention.

A more fundamental criticism of the use of net realizable value considers the purpose of financial accounts. Although the liquidation value is of interest, giving an indication of the cash potentially available for alternative use, this does not provide information on the major aspects of business performance. Businesses do not continue principally to improve their break-up value; assets are not only acquired to sell. Purchasing an oil rig and towing it out into the North Sea is carried out with the final intention not of selling the rig but of operating it. When judging the performance of the business that carries out such actions, the resale value of such assets will not be the relevant data. The net realizable value approach abandons the convention of a going concern.

13.2.2   Replacement cost

If the above arguments lead to dissatisfaction with net realizable value, replacement cost offers an alternative market price which appears to be less vulnerable to these considerations. It can be given substantial support. From the point of view of measuring realized expenses, it provides a measure of the sacrifice that is made when the item is used, provided the organization expects to continue to use items of its type. The item must be replaced if the firm is to be as well stocked before the sale as after. Considering the balance sheet, the sum of replacement cost valuations is a measure of how much it would cost to achieve the extant position from nothing. This could be envisaged as a measure of competitive advantage and as particularly relevant to business performance. In fact, Edwards and Bell describe the profit measure resulting from the use of replacement costs as 'business profit'.[6]

The measure is not without its problems. In addition to the problems of disaggregation and of semi-finished goods, technological change may mean that identical replacement will not represent sound business behaviour. A more modern asset may fulfil the function better and cheaper. Calculation of the cost of replacement by an updated version of the asset requires adjustment for differences in capacity, life, operating costs and functions performed. The problem is concerned with establishing a cost for the *modern equivalent asset*, and suggestions for the calculation are given in Section 13.2.7. However, the solution offered by the modern equivalent asset may be unsuitable in many cases. For some assets, replacement even by a modern asset may not be worthwhile or possible if there is no replacement. Replacement cost becomes inappropriate. (This is considered further in Section 13.2.4.)

Another consideration in establishing a replacement cost for assets that have a life of a number of years is how an old asset should be valued. Two alternatives are available; the replacement cost in the second-hand markets, and the buying price of a new asset suitably adjusted by depreciation. If the firm owning the asset buys only new assets, the use of second-hand values bears only a limited relationship to the position of the business; second-hand goods may have entirely different properties to new items and the markets may differ substantially. On condition that depreciation is calculated in an appropriate manner, the depreciated replacement cost can produce a measure consistent with the view that assets are owned to supply production capacity rather than to accommodate second-hand dealings. The former view would be applicable to most items of machinery and plant.

13.2.3   Economic value or net present value

A good deal of attention is given in the literature of the theory of finance to discounting future cash flows in order to produce an economic value or net present value. This approach to valuation is consistent with theoretical models of income introduced in Chapter 1. Its use could introduce anticipations of future elements of income, producing smoothed income results over time. However, this approach depends entirely on future predictions, and therefore will not perform well in terms of objectivity, verifiability, bias and consistency. By anticipating the results of future business activity, this may not be a suitable measure for business performance purposes.

Disaggregation provides a particular problem for this method, since the sum of the net present values of each of a set of mutually dependent assets can exceed the net present value of the set, taken as a unit, considerable amounts. This method may not offer much potential as an accounting measure, but it will assist in considering the valuation approach that follows.

13.2.4 Deprival value or value to the business

In the above discussion on asset valuation, it was indicated that, where replacement of an item or its continued use was anticipated, the replacement cost basis could be employed in the production of meaningful accounting reports; some adjustment may be necessary in response to technological change. However, since replacement is not always anticipated, circumstances do arise in which this basis is inappropriate. The requirement is for a valuation approach that utilizes the replacement cost in all situations in which replacement is anticipated, but adopts a more suitable basis under other conditions. A measure that meets these needs is *value to the business*. Although this title for the measure is to be found in much of the recent professional literature, it was known to academics for a considerable time before its current popularity as 'deprival value'.[7] Both titles are useful in understanding the approach.

In deciding whether or not to replace an asset, an individual would attempt to compare the cost of replacement with the value of the future benefits he expected if he did replace. In quantifying these future benefits, he might make use of the economic value or net present value concept, and a useful shorthand is provided by describing the value of future benefits as the economic value. It would be rational not to replace only if the replacement cost exceeded the economic value, so a rule that would meet the needs outlined in the previous paragraph would be: use replacement cost if it is lower than economic value.

The description 'deprival value' can be useful here. Consider the position of the owner of an asset, for example a car. If he is suddenly deprived of that asset (say it is stolen), he will replace it only if he considers it worthwhile to spend the amount of the replacement cost. This illustration can provide more insight by considering the amount needed to compensate him for the sudden deprival. If he lives in a remote location, so that his very existence depends on having a car, the economic value to him will be very high. However, the most any insurer could be expected to pay in compensation for his loss would be the cost of a replacement. If the car were replaced, he could not be worse off.

Now consider the opposite position. Suppose that, as a result of serious traffic offences, the owner had been banned from using the car. In this case, the economic value would be relatively low. Although an insurer might argue that, because the owner cannot use the asset, virtually no compensation is required, it can be argued that the car is worth at least what would be raised if it were sold.

Deprival value sets replacement cost as an upper limit to value and net realizable value as a lower limit. There are some assets that would not be worth replacing if lost, but are not worth selling because their selling price is too low. In this case the economic value will represent the deprival value. An alternative to calculating value in terms of the compensation for loss is to consider the value of owning rather than not owning. The two are equivalent, and 'value to the owner' or 'value to the business' are alternatives to 'deprival value'.

Deprival value makes use of all three basic approaches to valuation discussed in this chapter, the appropriate basic value depending on the ranking of the three values. It may be useful to indicate which value to select given any ranking:

Rank	Case 1	Case 2	Case 3	Case 4	Case 5	Case 6
1st	EV	RC	RC	NRV	NRV	EV
2nd	RC=DV	NRV=DV	EV=DV	RC=DV	EV	NRV
3rd	NRV	EV	NRV	EV	RC=DV	RC=DV

where RC = replacement cost; NRV = net realizable value; EV = economic value and DV = deprival value.

● *Case 1*   This represents the position that hopefully would apply to most assets. The decision to acquire them continues to appear correct since the economic value exceeds the replacement cost. This should apply to most of the assets of a successful enterprise. If the asset is lost, a replacement would be worth purchasing.

● *Case 2*   Since the economic value is less than the net realizable value, the best course is to sell the asset. This illustrates a further feature of this approach. Consideration of the relationship of the three values is a valuable guide to ownership policy.

● *Case 3*   Here, the asset is neither worth replacing nor worth selling. The major drawback in this case is that the deprival value is the highly subjective economic value. The two other basic values do place limits on the extremes that this could take, but these can be very wide in the case of some assets. If the asset is irreplaceable the replacement cost becomes infinitely large, and yet it may raise very little if sold.

● *Cases 4, 5 and 6*   In all these cases net realizable value exceeds replacement costs. An obvious opportunity for profit exists by trading in these assets, and it is always worthwhile replacing. The replacement cost upper limit is normally taken to predominate, possibly as an application of the prudence convention.

The link between deprival value and economic value introduces not only the use of a subjective value on occasions but also the possibility that the sum of separate deprival values might exceed the deprival value of the combination. Using maximum compensation for loss as an approach to valuation indicates that the deprival value of a whole business should be adopted if it is lower than the sums of individual deprival values. The manner in which this may be applied to the major classes of assets can be considered in greater detail.

13.2.5 Land and buildings

The valuation of land at its net current replacement cost should employ open market value for the existing use of the land. If the land is surplus to requirements, it should be valued at its open market value less any costs of disposal; this is its net realizable value.

Buildings might be divided into two classes, specialized and non-specialized. They would be regarded as specialized if they, 'because of their location or arrangement, the form of their construction, or perhaps their size, are rarely sold except by way of sale of the business in which they are used'.[8] Typically, many industrial buildings on works sites come into this category. Their value is the net current replacement cost, or, if there has been a recognized permanent fall in the value of the asset, the net realizable value. Because they are specialized, there is no market for such assets; there is no readily obtainable second-hand value. An appropriate method of calculating the net current replacement cost is first to calculate the gross replacement cost through the application of relevant indices to existing gross book value, and then to depreciate this adjusted gross cost.

In the case of non-specialized buildings, such as offices, shops and general-purpose industrial sites, the valuation should be based on the open market value of such properties for existing use. The value is determined by such factors as the regional position, and (if material) acquisition costs should be included in the valuation. If land and such properties are sold together, they can be valued together on the same basis, although for depreciation purposes an estimate of the value of the building will be needed. There are certain types of building that can be classed as non-specialized, for example hotels, public houses, cinemas and petrol-filling stations, which should be valued at their open market values. These should not necessarily be their value as in present use; the inherent trading potential of such properties should be taken into account. Buildings such as cinemas can be converted for other uses, and often in recent years their value in the alternative uses has exceeded their value as a cinema. Clearly, the categorization of buildings between specialized and non-specialized is not exact. On occasions it needs to be decided upon according to the circumstances.

To obtain the open market valuation, it is normally necessary to use the services of a recognized professionally qualified person. The business is allowed either to use a qualified valuer employed on its own staff or to engage the services of an external valuer. If internal valuers are used, it is desirable that on occasions the values attached to significant properties be corroborated with evidence from an outside valuer. The frequency of valuations should be decided upon, 'having regard to such factors as the extent to which property values generally have changed since the last valuation. It is unlikely that valuations at intervals of more than five years will be sufficient.'[9]

13.2.6 Plant and machinery

The value to the business of plant and machinery is its net current replacement cost or, if lower, its recoverable amount. As with specialized buildings, this involves calculating the gross replacement cost, and then depreciating this amount.

A business has to decide how to calculate the gross replacement costs, the lives of its assets, and the depreciation method to be used. Again, the most convenient method of arriving at the gross replacement cost is to multiply the existing historical gross book values by relevant indices. Index numbers can give an approximation of the effect of price changes in replacement costs. Index numbers representing movements in the general price level would give only a rough approximation; index numbers representing particular classes of assets, specific price indices, are likely to give a more accurate estimate. However, it was acknowledged in SSAP 16 that special circumstances and problems relating to asset purchases can always arise, and the ASC commented that this may happen

(a) if there has been substantial technological change [this subject is discussed later];
(b) when changes in the costs of specific assets are known to have been significantly different from the changes in the index appropriate to that group of assets; or
(c) when the historical purchase cost of the asset to which the index is to be applied was affected by special circumstances which are unlikely to be repeated and for which allowance cannot accurately be made.

To use index numbers, it is necessary to be able to date an asset and then apply the relevant index number to the year in which the asset was acquired. In most cases there will be no problem in deciding on the age of the asset — a plant register could be used, or it may be possible to identify its age physically. In cases where difficulties arise, an estimate of the age will be sufficient, since with old assets the amounts involved are not likely to be significant.

Other information which may be helpful in arriving at a current replacement cost include suppliers' official price lists, trade catalogues and insurance values. Technological change means that fixed assets are seldom replaced by identical assets. This creates a problem in arriving at replacement costs, which will be discussed next.

13.2.7 Technological change

In fields involving fast-moving technology, it is possible that a business will need to be replacing its machines quite frequently in order to remain competitive. The new machines could well look very different and give different levels of output from the machines being replaced. An obvious example that comes to mind is computers, but there are many other less well-known areas where similar rapid technological change is taking place.

In such situations it is obviously not appropriate to find the value to the business of an existing machine by multiplying its original cost by an index number, or by reference to the price of new machines now available. Allowance must be made for the differences in performance between the existing machine being used and that of new machines available in the market. The allowance for price change should take account of technological change.

It is stated in the 'Guidance notes to SSAP 16' that the use of 'broadly based indices' may allow for some of the effects on current costs of gradual technological change. It is however recognized that it may sometimes be necessary to 'derive the equivalent current cost of an existing fixed asset from the cost of a modern asset'. The important word is 'derive'. There is no perfect way of doing this, but the ASC stuck its neck out by showing in the 'Guidance notes' a technique for how this 'may' be achieved. It was only a suggestion, however, and was heavily criticized.

The 'modern equivalent asset' is a guide to the current cost of the existing asset being used. No such equivalent asset actually exists. The business could not obtain a similar asset to the one being used, so an attempt is made to derive its value in relation to the performance that could be achieved from the newer machines now available. To be able to do this, it is necessary to have detailed information about the costs and performance of the newer machines.

Let us begin with a simple example, with the same assumption that was made in the 'Guidance notes'; that the operating costs per unit, and the asset lives from now, of the existing machine and the new more modern machine are identical. Let us say that the net current cost of the existing machine is £50,000, this being based on movements in a relevant price index. The current cost of a modern machine is £100,000. The existing machine has an output of 10,000 units per annum, and the new machine an output of 40,000 units per annum.

The current cost of the existing output potential is

$$\frac{10,000}{40,000} \times £100,000 = £25,000.$$

The existing asset would be over-valued if it were shown in the current cost balance sheet at £50,000. It is suggested that it be shown at its modern equivalent value of £25,000.

This approach is based on the idea that the value of the existing asset should be such that it gives the same total cost per unit of output as the modern equivalent asset. It has been assumed above that operating costs are the same for the new machine as for the old one. If it is also assumed that both machines have a five-year life, the capital cost per unit of output of the new machine is £100,000/(40,000 × 5) = £0.50. The existing machine, over its five years of remaining life, can produce 50,000 units which, with the same cost per unit as the new machine of £0.50, gives the modern equivalent value of £25,000.

The example can be made more complicated by assuming that the running costs of the new machine are £0.25 per unit and those of the existing machine £0.15 per unit. The total cost per unit of the output of the new machine would be £0.70 (i.e., £0.50 + £0.20). The total running cost of the existing machine, in producing 50,000 units, would be £7,500. The value of the modern equivalent asset equals x where $(£7,500 + x)/50,000 = £0.70$.

The modern equivalent asset value (x) equals £27,500. The example can be further complicated by assuming that the future lives for the machines are different. The same principle can be followed to derive an estimate, namely, valuing the existing asset such that it gives the same total cost per unit of output as a new machine. A problem arises with different lives in respect of whether the time value of money should be taken into account in the calculation, and this could be incorporated although it would make computation more involved.

13.2.8 Backlog depreciation

When discussing the use of current values for depreciable assets, it was argued that a depreciated replacement cost of a new asset was often more suitable than a second-hand replacement price. The same considerations do not apply, of course, to net realizable value and economic value. Accounting for depreciation under conditions of price change requires special attention.

A difficulty arises because, in the accumulated provision for depreciation, charges from different years are aggregated. Some adjustment is necessary, although the implications of this adjustment are not necessarily as significant as they may first appear. Consider the following example of an asset for which the replacement cost is selected as the basis of valuation and straight line depreciation is considered appropriate:

$$\text{Original buying price} = £4,000$$
$$\text{Scrap value} = \text{zero at the end of 4-year life}$$

	Year 1	Year 2	Year 3	Year 4
Replacement cost (new)				
Mid-year	£4,400	£6,000	£6,800	£7,600
End-year	£5,000	£6,400	£7,200	£8,000

$$\text{Straight-line depreciation (historical cost basis)} = \frac{£4,000}{4} = £1,000.$$

Examine the results of basing the depreciation charge on year-end values. (Note that the accumulated depreciation balance is found by simply aggregating charges to date; the required provision is found by finding that proportion of the replacement cost which represents the fraction of the total life expired to date.)

End of year of life	(a) Depreciation charge	(b) Accumulated depreciation	(c) Required depreciation provision	(d) Backlog, i.e., (c) less (d)
	£	£	£	£
Year 1	$1,000 \times \dfrac{5,000}{4,000} = 1,250$	1,250	$\frac{1}{4} \times 5,000 = 1,250$	nil
Year 2	$1,000 \times \dfrac{6,400}{4,000} = 1,600$	2,850	$\frac{1}{2} \times 6,400 = 3,200$	350
Year 3	$1,000 \times \dfrac{7,200}{4,000} = 1,800$	4,650	$\frac{3}{4} \times 7,200 = 5,400$	750
Year 4	$1,000 \times \dfrac{8,000}{4,000} = 2,000$	6,650	$1 \times 8,000 = 8,000$	1,350

Adopting the concept of maintenance of physical capital, it can be seen that, if cash were set aside equal to the provision for depreciation, a shortfall would build up over the life of the asset so that, by the end of the life, this cash sum would be insufficient to pay for the replacement. In this case, funds of only £6,650 would be accumulated to replace an asset costing £8,000.

The backlog element can be calculated by a method other than that used above. If the 'accumulated provision' had grown in value in line with the increase in the specific price of the asset, the growth would exactly offset the backlog. The £1,250 at the end of year 1 would grow to £1,600 (£1,250 × £6,400 ÷ £5,000), the growth being £350 (£1,600–£1,250), and the accumulated depreciation adjusted for such growth would be £3,200. Similarly, for year 2 the balance carried forward to year 3 must be increased from £3,200 to £3,600 (£3,200 × £7,200 ÷ £6,400), the increase of £400 being the backlog adjustment for the year. The total backlog for years 1 and 2 amounts to £750 (£400 + £350), which is identical to the required amount shown in the above schedule.

Before examining the impact of the backlog problem under the concept of economic capital maintenance, let us consider what happens if depreciation charges are based on mid-year replacement values. Mid-year values are employed to avoid over-compensating for the time-lag error. Using physical capital maintenance and measuring in money terms, a year's revenue is, effectively, being measured at the average date of sale. If sales occur evenly throughout the year, this can be taken as the middle of the year; if most sales occur at the start of the year the average date of sale will be in the first half of the year. To match the revenue and depreciation charge, the depreciation is taken at a mid-year value.

For the present example, the result would be:

End of year of life	Depreciation charge	Accumulated depreciation provision	Required depreciation (as before)	Backlog
	£	£	£	£
Year 1	$1,000 \times \dfrac{4,400}{4,000} = 1,100$	1,100	1,250	150
Year 2	$1,000 \times \dfrac{6,000}{4,000} = 1,500$	2,600	3,200	600
Year 3	$1,000 \times \dfrac{6,800}{4,000} = 1,700$	4,300	5,400	1,100
Year 4	$1,000 \times \dfrac{7,600}{4,000} = 1,900$	6,200	8,000	1,800

Not unexpectedly, the backlog figures are greater than when a year-end basis is used. These figures can be calculated by adjusting the accumulated provision as before. In effect, the provision is being restated by adjusting the charges from their original value to values current at the year-end concerned. For year 1, the charge of £1,100 is current at the mid-point of that year (when the replacement cost is £4,000). At the year-end the current replacement cost is £5,000, so the charge must be increased in the ratio 5,000/4,000 to adjust it to year-end values. This would produce a provision of £1,250 as required.

Why does a backlog discrepancy arise under this concept? Because the value of the money unit at the appropriate time for the matching of revenue and expense is different from that at successive year-ends when it is used to calculate asset values. In Chapter 1, two approaches to income accounting were outlined; one where the profit calculation was the primary account, with the balance sheet a residual, and another in which the balance sheet was the primary account. Concern with obtaining a desired entry in the profit and loss account and a desired value in the balance sheet leads one to attempt to adopt both approaches at the same time.

However, recognizing this cause makes it clear that the depreciation charge, unadjusted for backlog, is the desired expense in the profit and loss account. Backlog depreciation should not be an additional charge but rather a reserve adjustment needed to achieve the capital maintenance approach adopted.

If economic capital maintenance and a stable unit of value representing constant purchasing power are the dimensions adopted, the backlog problem becomes trivial. The adjustment to the accumulated provision balance is made when it is updated by restating it in units of constant purchasing power. This does not mean that it no longer matters that, if an amount equal to the depreciation charge is set aside in cash, the total set aside will not keep up with price increases. Under the dimensions being considered, holding such monetary sums will produce a loss on holding a monetary asset. It is the storing in cash, not the size of the sum set aside, that creates the problem. Provided the sum set aside is invested in assets that maintain their real value, the real value of the capital is maintained, which fully reflects the concept adopted.

13.3 History of early recommendations in the UK

The problems facing the implementation of the theoretical solutions to accounting under conditions of price change are considerable. The difficulties of measurement of general indices have been discussed earlier in this chapter. Establishing a specific price change cannot be achieved without cost, and the variety of assets to be considered makes this potentially very expensive. Handling the many detailed changes creates a significant workload. The major implementation requirement is to determine a method of accounting which recognizes the effects of price change and provides an improvement in the usefulness of the resulting reports that exceeds the additional effort required to provide it. A series of attempts has been made to design procedures that can be carried out without excessive cost.

A more fundamental problem concerns the usefulness of the reports. The familiarity to users of accounts produced from a version of the historical cost basis may inhibit change. The users themselves will need to adapt to the changing nature of accounting information. The adaptation involved in responding to price change can be particularly severe.

In this section the development of the relevant recommendations is outlined, illustrating the major procedures and interpreting the resulting accounts in terms of the theoretical framework already discussed.

13.3.1 Current purchasing power accounting

After the publication of ED 8 on 17 January 1973, a provisional standard, PSSAP 7, was issued in May 1974. The provisional standard proposed that companies should disclose, in addition to accounts produced under existing conventions, a supplementary statement prepared under the current purchasing power method. This method was designed to make adjustments for inflation using the retail price index as an index of general price change.

The procedure is to restate opening and closing balance sheets in units of purchasing power, current at the year-end. All items in the opening balance sheet and all non-monetary items including equity in the closing balance sheet are adjusted using general indices. Monetary items in the closing balance sheet require no conversion as they are already stated in units of current purchasing power. No allowance is made in this procedure for specific price change. The difference between the restated balance sheets is the current purchasing power profit. This is analysed into two components: the historical cost profit, which is adjusted by general indexation to produce the current purchasing power operating profit, and a loss (or gain) on holding net monetary assets, which is calculated by reconciling current purchasing power operating profit and total current purchasing power profit.

Example 13.1

The following balance sheet has been prepared using the historical cost basis:

Chester Illustrations Ltd

	Opening at 1/1/X1 £	Closing at 31/12/X1 £
Fixed assets		
Cost	—	4,000
less Depreciation	—	400
WDV	—	3,600
Stock	—	2,250
Cash	5,000	100
	5,000	5,950
Ordinary share capital	4,000	4,000
Revenue reserves	—	950
Shareholders' interest	4,000	4,950
Long-term debt (15%)	1,000	1,000
	5,000	5,950

The transactions that occurred during the year were:

		£
1/1/X1	Purchased fixed assets	4,000
31/3/X1	Purchased 500 units for stock	3,600
30/6/X1	Sold 500 units	5,100
30/9/X1	Purchased 270 units for stock	2,250
30/12/X1	Paid interest	150

Indices	RPI	Stock	Fixed assets
1/1/X1	100	100	100
31/3/X1	106	108	103
30/6/X1	112	117	107
30/9/X1	118	125	112
31/12/X1	124	130	120

Current purchasing power accounts can be prepared as follows.

(a) Restate the opening balance sheet in units of current purchasing power at 31/12/X1 using the retail price index; the units change from historical pounds (£H) to pounds of current purchasing power at the year-end (£CPP):

	£H	Conversion factor	£CPP
Cash	5,000		6,200
Ordinary share capital	4,000		4,960
		124/100	
Long-term debt	1,000		1,240
	5,000		6,200

(b) Restate the closing balance sheet:

	£H	Conversion factor	£CPP
Fixed assets	3,600	124/100	4,464
Stock	2,250	124/118	2,365
Cash	100		100
	5,950		6,929
Long-term debt	1,000	—	1,000
Shareholders' interest	4,950	(balancing figure)	5,929
	5,950		6,929

(c) Total current purchasing power profit is indicated by the increase in the shareholders' interest over the year; i.e., £5,929 − £4,960 = £969.

(d) This can be analysed finding first the current purchasing power operating profit:

	£CPP	£CPP
Sales (5,100 × 124/112)		5,647
Less cost of goods sold (3,600 × 124/106)	4,211	
Depreciation (400 × 124/100)	496	
Interest	150	4,857
		790

(e) Finally, the difference between total current purchasing power profit (£969) and current purchasing power operating profit (£790), i.e. £179, is explained by examining the effect of the general index on the cash flow:

	£CPP	£CPP
Opening net monetary items (cash less debt):		
4,000 × 124/100		4,960
add Sales: 5,100 × 124/112		5,647
		10,607
less Purchases:		
fixed assets: 4,000 × 124/100	4,960	
stock: 3,600 × 124/106	4,211	
2,250 × 124/118	2,365	
Interest	150	
		11,686
CPP adjusted closing net monetary items		(1,079)
Actual closing net monetary items (cash less debt)		(900)
Gain from holding monetary items		179

Had the liability and cash balances maintained constant purchasing power, the net closing balance would have been a liability of £1,079. Since it is only £900, a gain of £179 has been made.

The current purchasing power approach can be described in terms of the three basic dimensions. The unit of measurement employed is the pound of purchasing power current at the year-end, and the concept of capital maintenance adopted is that of maintaining shareholder purchasing power calculated using the retail price index. The valuation model adjusts historical costs for the general change in prices. With the exception of monetary assets, and to the extent that the specific price change for assets is not in line with general price change, the resulting asset values will not represent a current value.

The method has the advantage of requiring only limited, relatively objective, adjustments from historical cost and consequently has similar properties regarding objectivity, reliability and verifiability. The lack of response to specific price change and substantial dependence of the retail price index are obvious weaknesses.

12.3.2 The Sandilands Report

Before PSSAP 7 had been issued, the British government had set up the Inflation Accounting Committee, chaired by Mr (later Sir) Francis Sandilands, which published its findings in a report in September 1975.[10] The report changed the direction of price level accounting from the use of general indices to the recognition of specific price change. This approach has come to be known as 'current cost accounting', and pronouncements subsequent to 1975 proceeded along similar lines to those indicated in the report.

Three major recommendations are found in the report. First, the adjustment for inflation itself by the use of general indices and a current unit of measurement was rejected in favour of the use of specific indices for non-monetary asset valuation and of ignoring inflationary effects on the unit of measurement. This means that losses or gains on holding monetary items, which arise from the change in the value of the money unit, are not recognized. Second, the report indicated the importance of allowing for the time-lag error from operating profit by adjusting for the realized holding gains included in expense items. The source of a time-lag error in both the cost-of-goods-sold expense and the depreciation expense were recognized. These lead to two adjustments in calculating a current operating profit: a *cost of sales adjustment* and a *depreciation adjustment*. Finally, the report provides the opportunity for the adoption of the concept of physical capital maintenance. It creates a *revaluation reserve*, into which are made entries equal and opposite to the realized holding gain adjustments in the operating profit calculation and the unrealized holding gains arising from the revaluation of the assets contained in the closing balance sheet.

The Sandilands Report recommended that value to the business (deprival value) should be used as the valuation model, and uses the historically based money unit of measurement. The suggestion in the report that the revaluation reserve should be non-distributable is clear support for the concept of maintenance of physical capital.

13.3.3 Developments leading to current-cost accounting requirements

The task of applying the recommendations of the Inflation Accounting Committee was taken up by the ASC. A number of difficulties were considered. The need to take account of the many specific price changes created a requirement for the data to provide both the sources of valuation and the capacity to handle that data so that valuation could become a less variable, more subjective, process.

Although the physical capital maintenance concept was incorporated into subsequent pronouncements, by the mid-1980s there was some concern to slightly modify this. The concept employed by the Sandilands Report is of maintenance of the physical capital of the business as a whole. This ignores the position of the shareholders, since the distribution of holding gains financed by debt does not conflict with the maintenance of the shareholders' physical capital. This led to the introduction of a modification known as the 'financial capital maintenance concept'. Of course, by not making any adjustment to the shareholders' capital for general price change, no attempt is made to assess whether or not the shareholders' interest is being maintained in real (purchasing power) terms.

The first response by the ASC to Sandilands was to publish an exposure draft, ED 18, issued in November 1976.[11] In recommending the production of a supplementary current cost accounting statement, it modified the Sandilands proposals by introducing a *'statement of change in shareholders' Net Equity Interest after allowing for the change in the value of money'*. This adjusts the opening shareholders' interest for general price change. The adjustment becomes the revaluation reserve and reflects the concept of maintenance of the shareholders' economic capital. Any net amount that arises from the substitution of this value in the revaluation reserve for the amount produced under Sandilands is combined with general reserves.

Although this offered a compromise between the current purchasing power and current cost accounting proposals, apart from making no allowance for the effects of holding monetary items, it was rejected. On 6 July 1977 a special meeting of members of the ICAEW passed a resolution opposing any compulsory systems of current cost accounting. A major concern was the apparent complexity of the ED 18 proposals. The draft, including preface, covered over 100 pages in itself and over 400 pages with the accompanying guidance manual.

Despite the rejection of compulsory current cost accounting, an attempt was made to achieve the production of some current cost information when the *Hyde Guidelines* were issued.[12] These were an interim recommendation to prepare a single supplementary current cost statement, which was a restatement of the profit and loss and appropriation account after adjusting for current cost. The only adjustments were the cost of sales adjustment and the depreciation adjustment introduced in the Sandilands Report, plus a gearing adjustment which has been modified in later pronouncements.

ED 24[13] and the corresponding standard, SSAP 16, were issued in April 1979 and October 1980, respectively. They retained the cost of sales and depreciation adjustments and added two more: a monetary working capital adjustment, to allow for the time-lag error resulting from credit transactions rather than immediate cash, and a gearing adjustment. The gearing adjustment attempts to recognize that there is no need to create a reserve for holding gains financed by debt in order to maintain shareholders' interest in physical capital. The attempt is somewhat incomplete, since the gearing adjustment is applied only to realized holding gains.

Omitting to apply the gearing adjustment to unrealized holding gains prevents a clear interpretation of the resulting profit figure. The capital maintenance concept relates to neither the shareholders' capital nor the capital of all long-term investors; it does relate more closely to a physical maintenance concept than the one employed in ED 18, but it fails to maintain any identifiable operating capacity. The effects of the gearing adjustment are eventually included in an account known as the 'current cost reserve', in which the corresponding entries for realized and unrealized holding gains are also included. As a result, this account becomes something of a hotch-potch and the whole procedure defies the identification of a sound theoretical basis.

However, SSAP 16 was employed widely in company accounts in the period 1982–85 and was given continuing support by the ASC. The standard put forward requirements for a comprehensive technical approach to accounting for price change, and, as such, held a special position in financial accounting practice which makes it worthy of further attention here.

13.4   SSAP 16

The particular version of current cost accounting that was introduced in the UK for a trial period of three years has evolved from a series of contributions on the subject in the form of both theories and proposals.

The standard, SSAP 16, became operative for accounting periods commencing on or after 1 January 1980. It applied to all listed companies and all large non-listed companies, but it did not apply to insurance or property companies, investment or unit trusts or non-profit organizations. The following sections will closely follow SSAP 16 and the techniques outlined in the 'Guidance notes' issued to assist in implementing the standard. To illustrate these techniques, inflation-adjusted accounts will be prepared for Comus Ltd. Details of the company's accounts prepared on an historical cost basis and other relevant information are as follows:

Balance sheets as at 31 December

	19X8	19X9		19X8	19X9
	£	£		£	£
Share capital	5,000	5,000	Fixed assets (net)	12,500	20,000
Reserves	10,000	12,000	Stock	12,000	14,000
Loan	7,000	8,000	Debtors	6,500	6,000
Creditors	4,000	5,000	Cash	6,000	5,000
Overdraft	3,000	6,000			
Taxation	8,000	9,000			
	37,000	45,000		37,000	45,000

Profit and loss account for the year ended 31 December 19X9

	£	£
Sales		100,000
Cost of sales		70,000
		30,000
Interest	1,000	
Depreciation	7,500	
		8,500
		21,500
Taxation		10,750
After-tax profit		10,750
Dividends paid		8,750

The following information is also given:
(a) £10,000 of fixed assets were purchased on 1 January 19X7, £10,000 on 1 January 19X8 and £20,000 on 1 January 19X9. The assets all have a four-year life and are being depreciated on a straight-line basis. The asset that was purchased on 1 January 19X7 was sold for £5,000 on 1 January 19X9.
(b) Sales are made evenly over the year.
(c) The inventory at 31 December 19X8 and 19X9 had been purchased evenly over the previous four-month period.
(d) Relevant price indices are given below; all prices increased evenly throughout the year:
   (i) Sales and cost of goods sold

1/1/X7	100		
1/1/X8	125	1/11/X8	146
1/1/X9	150	1/11/X9	167.5
31/12/X9	170	Average for the year to 31/12/X9	160

   (ii) The current replacement cost of the type of fixed asset held by this business has been increasing at a rate of 20 per cent per annum.

The adjustments that affect the profit and loss account will be the first to be considered. These are the cost of sales adjustment, the monetary working capital adjustment, the depreciation adjustment and the gearing adjustment. In calculating these adjustments, certain of the items to appear in the current cost balance sheet will need to be valued.

The double entry relating to the adjustments is normally completed by using an account called the 'current cost reserve'. Since the adjustments generally reflect specific price changes and the reserve is not to be considered available for distribution, this is in line with the concept of physical capital maintenance. Further attention will be given to the nature of the current cost reserve after considering the adjustments themselves.

13.4.1   The cost of sales adjustment

This adjustment is one of the three designed to allow for the impact of price changes on the net operating assets. The cost of sales adjustment takes into account price changes affecting stock (inventory); the monetary working capital adjustment allows for price changes in other short-term assets and liabilities, for example debtors and creditors. Changes in medium- and long-term assets affect the depreciation adjustment.

The cost of sales adjustment aims to reflect the difference between the real value of the stock used up or sold during the accounting period and the charge that appears in the historical cost accounts as stock having been used up or sold. It represents the price change, on the items of stock consumed, during the time-lag between purchase and sale. Ideally, it would be the sum of the differences between the historical cost and the replacement cost, at the time of sale, of each unit of stock that has been consumed. This, however, would involve either the company keeping very detailed records or computational problems, and so the averaging method can be used as an approximation. The objective is to calculate the cost of sales adjustment at the average point of sale.

Prices

The first question that needs to be decided upon is how the replacement costs at the time of sale are to be determined. To prepare a cost of sales adjustment, the company needs details of the price movement relating to its items of stock. This might be based on details of the actual cost incurred at the date of purchase of the materials and services, and of the labour and overhead costs that together make up the value of stock, together with details of the replacement cost of the items at the time the stock is sold. Alternatively, the price movements might be based on either an external price index or a company-compiled index for each type of stock. Index numbers are produced by the Department of Industry for a number of classes of asset and stock and are published three times per year as *Price Index Numbers for Current Cost Accounting.*[14] In addition to this publication, there are others prepared by government agencies as well as by private agencies.[15] It is very much easier and less expensive to use index numbers relating to the assets and goods of the company, but produced externally, than to use those produced by the company and based on its own purchasing experience.

The adjustment

Having obtained details on the movement of prices, or the movement of index numbers relating to prices, the next stage of the analysis is to determine how these price movements affect the cost of sales. As mentioned, the cost of sales adjustment can be based on the 'averaging method'. This assumes that both the quality and the price of the stock rises or falls evenly throughout the year, or that they are stable. The method assumes that the stocks held at the beginning and end of the accounting period are representative of the levels of stock throughout the period. In certain cases this approach may not be appropriate—for example, where there are seasonal purchases of stock or non-repetitive contracts, where dealing stock has been purchased and where there are special purchases of commodities or metals.

To begin with, the averaging method will be explained. To illustrate the technique, the entries will be calculated appropriate to Comus Ltd. It is assumed that the stock has been purchased evenly during the last four months of the year. The value of the stock, based on historical prices, was £14,000 at the end of the year and £12,000 at the beginning of the year. This increase of £2,000 could be based on price changes, volume changes or a combination of the two. The cost of sales adjustment represents the price change. To obtain this using the averaging method, we deduct the volume change from the total change, and are left with the price change.

The average current cost of the closing stock is

$$£14,000 \times \frac{160}{167.5} = £13,373.$$

The adjustment factor is

$$\frac{\text{Average index number for the period (denote by } I_a)}{\text{Index number appropriate to closing stock (i.e. when purchased) } (I_c)}.$$

The average current cost of the *opening* stock is

$$£12,000 \times \frac{160}{146} = £13,150.$$

The adjustment factor is

$$\frac{\text{Average index number for the period } (I_a)}{\text{Index number appropriate to opening stock } (I_o)}.$$

The difference between these two adjusted stock figures, the closing minus the opening, gives us the volume change. In this example it shows a volume increase of £233 (i.e. £13,373 − £13,150).

To obtain the change in the historical value of the stock that was due to price changes, simply deduct the volume change from the total change; that is, £2,000 − £233 = £1,677. It is this price change, £1,677, that is the cost of sales adjustment (COSA).

In this example there was a volume increase over the period, and so this increase was deducted from the total change to give the cost of sales adjustment. It should be appreciated that in some cases the volume change may turn out to be a reduction; that is, the adjusted closing stock may be less than the adjusted opening stock. In this case the volume decrease is added on to the total change in the historical figures to give the cost of sales adjustment.

The appropriate formula for calculating the adjustment is

$$\text{COSA} = \Delta HC_s - \left[\left(C_s \times \frac{I_a}{I_c} \right) - \left(O_s \times \frac{I_a}{I_o} \right) \right] = £2,000 - (£13,373 - £13,150) = £1,677$$

where ΔHC_s = closing stock − opening stock (both taken from historical cost balance sheets),
O_s = historical cost of opening stock,
C_s = historical cost of closing stock

and the symbols for the index numbers are as shown above.

The entry for this cost of sales adjustment is

Dr	Current cost profit and loss account	£1,677
Cr	Current cost reserve	£1,677

As explained, the averaging method would be applied only if there are no major fluctuations in stock levels during the year. If there have been such fluctuations, then it is not possible to adopt the averaging method to give the required estimate of the cost of sales adjustment. One technique to adopt in such cases would be to subdivide the year into suitable periods and determine an adjustment for each period, the adjustments being added together to give the figure for the year. The periods would run from, let us say, a low point in the level of the stock at the beginning of the year to a high point in the middle of year, and then from this high point in the middle to the year-end level.

One problem area that can arise involves seasonal purchases, i.e. where items are purchased in a particular season. At the time the company that purchased them sells them to a consumer or another company, it may not be possible to replace them, as they are, by definition, out of season. It would be misleading to think of replacement at an estimated purchase price for next season. All that is possible is to estimate the replacement price based on a price index which corresponds to the long-term trend. A similar difficulty would arise with purchases of seasonal agricultural produce.

Where fashion goods are involved, not only may there not be a suitable replacement price, but it may be that the manufacturing company never intends to replace the items. In this case stock should be treated as monetary working capital. The adjustment required for this is shown below. Another situation where stock should be treated as part of the monetary working capital is where dealing stock is involved. This is stock that is deliberately purchased with the intention of gaining in value from expected future increased prices. The stock is not purchased to be worked upon or to be sold in the short term.

13.4.2   The monetary working capital adjustment

The objective of the monetary working capital adjustment is that, together with the cost of sales adjustment, it will 'allow for the impact of price changes on the total amount of working capital used by the business in its day to day operations'.

The monetary working capital adjustment is based on changes in certain items normally used in the day-to-day operating activities of the business. These items would include: trade debtors and trade creditors; cash or overdrafts, to the extent that they have fluctuated with the level of debtors, creditors and stock; cash floats required to support the day-to-day operations of the business; and stocks not subject to the cost of sales adjustment. The last of these has already been explained. The standard recognized that it can sometimes be difficult to decide whether an item should be included in the cost of sales adjustment or the monetary working capital adjustment, and so it was permitted to combine the two adjustments.

One item that can give problems is the extent to which cash and overdrafts should be included in the monetary working capital adjustment rather than in the gearing adjustment. Including these items in the one adjustment rather than the other can have a significant affect on the reported current cost profit. It is necessary to understand more about the respective adjustments before this point can be appreciated, and so the issue will be returned to later in the chapter.

To estimate the fluctuating element of cash, or overdrafts, involves a degree of estimation. The base level of cash or overdraft needs to be included in the gearing adjustment. In the Comus example that is being followed, it will be assumed that both the cash and the overdraft reflect the long-term position, and that at no time during the year have the levels fluctuated significantly about the long-term trend in order to finance short-term items such as debtors, creditors and stock. The standard appreciated that 'there can be difficulties in practice in identifying, on an objective basis, those monetary assets and liabilities which are part of the net operating assets of the business'. The standard went on to state that 'reasonable accuracy and objectivity may usually be achieved by including only trade debtors and trade creditors within monetary working capital, with an extension in the case of financial institutions'.[16]

Having decided upon the items to be included in the monetary working capital adjustment, and on whether one wishes to calculate a single figure for the whole year or to subdivide the year as has been shown for the cost of sales adjustment, the next stage is to choose the appropriate index numbers.

The monetary working capital adjustment is supposed to represent the fact that, if the funds invested in the debtors less the creditors of a business were £10,000 at the beginning of the year, and then were still only £10,000 at the end of the year, then with inflation, the company has in real terms reduced the funds invested in working capital. The index to use is the one most appropriate to the business. It could be that a separate index is needed for debtors to 'reflect changes in the current cost of goods and services sold attributable to changes in input prices over the period the debt is outstanding'. It could be that an index is needed for creditors to 'reflect changes in the cost of the items which have been financed by those creditors'. On the other hand, a single index could be used to cover both debtors and creditors; and as an approximation of the appropriate index, certainly the easiest approach is to use the same index as that used for the cost of sales adjustment. If no other suitable index is available, even the retail price index could be used, as this, of course, reflects general movements in the price of goods and services.

Having decided on suitable index numbers, the business is now in a position to calculate its monetary working capital adjustment. It is possible, indeed usual, to use the averaging method.

The technique to achieve the adjustment is very similar to that for the cost of sales adjustment. The logic is the same; over the year there has been a change in the level of working capital employed in the business; this change has been caused by two factors, the volume change and the price change. As the volume of business expands, or contracts, the volume of working capital it needs will rise or fall, and a certain level of working capital will be needed to maintain a level of activity. On top of this there are price effects. With inflation the monetary level of activity will increase, even though in one sense the volume of business may not have changed. The monetary working capital adjustment (MWCA) is designed to isolate the price change from the volume change. It signifies that part of the change in the monetary working capital that represents the price change. In the Comus example, the opening working capital is £2,500 (that is, the debtors less the creditors) and the closing working capital is £1,000. The items, cash and bank overdraft are dealt with in other adjustments. The formula to use is:

$$MWCA = \Delta MWC - \left[\left(C_{wc} \times \frac{I_a}{I_c} \right) - \left(O_{wc} \times \frac{I_a}{I_o} \right) \right].$$

Substituting in the equation,

$$MWCA = -1,500 - \left[\left(1,000 \times \frac{160}{170} \right) - \left(2,500 \times \frac{160}{150} \right) \right]$$
$$= -1,500 - [941 - 2,666]$$
$$= -1,500 - [-1,725]$$
$$= £225.$$

This amount is debited to the current cost profit and loss account and credited to the current cost reserve.

13.4.3 Depreciation adjustment

SSAP 16 required that the fixed assets included in the historical cost balance sheet be restated at their value to the business by reference to current costs. In the normal case this is the net current cost of a replacement asset that has a similar useful output or service capacity. One problem immediately arises: what happens if the business has excess capacity and would not want to replace the existing asset with one that had as large a capacity? This is referred to as 'permanent excess capacity'. It arises from over-investing in the past. A business would not wish to aggravate the problem by revaluing its assets on the basis of providing capacity that it knows it will no longer need. The standard recognized this point, and where there is permanent diminution to below the net current replacement cost, the value to the business was defined as the 'recoverable amount'.

This is the greater of the net realizable value of the asset and, where applicable, the amount recoverable from its further use. The net realizable value is the amount that could be obtained if the asset were sold or scrapped, less any realization expenses, and the amount recoverable from its further use is the sum of the discounted future cash flows arising from the use of the asset including its ultimate disposal.

This problem exists with historical cost accounting; it is, however, more likely to be highlighted with current cost accounting, where revaluations are required. It is possible that it is a group of assets, comprising, say, a particular factory site, with all its machinery, that has suffered permanent diminution, and it would then be the recoverable amount of the group of assets that is required.

The total depreciation charge for current cost accounting will represent the estimated consumption of the value of assets by the business during the period. In many cases this will simply mean using the normal depreciation policy of the business to write down the gross replacement cost figures. Similarly, in most cases there will be no need to change the life of the asset for current cost accounting purposes from that used for historical cost purposes.

Situations can arise in which the business may wish to use different asset lives in current cost accounting from those used in the traditional historical-cost-based accounts. 'It may happen that conservative asset lives or rates of depreciation have been used in historic cost accounts, perhaps in order to make some allowance for inflation.' This is suggesting that an artificially fast write-off policy has been used. With the introduction of current cost accounting, the depreciation figures will automatically be raised to take account of inflation, and so it was suggested in the 'Guidance notes' that the business may wish to move back to more realistic assumption about the asset life. It is possible, therefore, that the asset life employed for current cost accounting purposes would be different from that for historical cost accounting purposes. Any adjustment to the net replacement cost resulting from changes in assumptions about asset lives should be adjusted through the current cost reserve.

In preparing current cost accounts, assets that have already been fully depreciated for historical cost purposes but are still being used may need to be brought back into the accounts. The assets are being used and will have a replacement value. It is clearly important, on introducing current cost accounting, that 'the existing asset lives and rates of depreciation should be reviewed in order to ensure that the CCA asset values and depreciation changes are realistic for all group assets'.

To illustrate the techniques, the earlier example will be returned to.

Gross current cost of fixed assets at 1 January 19X9

Purchased	Cost	Index	
	£		£
1/1/X7	10,000	144/100	14,400
1/1/X8	10,000	120/100	12,000
			26,400
1/1/X9	20,000		20,000
			46,400

It should be noted that the index numbers used are those relevant to the replacement cost of the fixed assets, and are different from the index numbers used to represent the price changes of sales, purchases and monetary assets.

Accumulated depreciation as at 1 January 19X9

Purchased	Historical cost depreciation	Index	£
1/1/X7	5,000	144/100	7,200
1/1/X8	2,500	120/100	3,000
			10,200

	£
Gross current cost at 1/1/X9	46,400
less Disposals at gross current cost at 1/1/X9	14,400
	32,000

	£
Adjusted to the average current cost value during the year	
(£32,000 × 1.10)	£35,200
Additions during year	0

The depreciation charge in the historical cost profit and loss account is based on asset values in the balance sheet prepared mainly on historical cost principles. (It is possible that there have already been some revaluations.) The total depreciation charge in the current cost accounts is based on the assets valued according to the current cost approach. The difference between the two depreciation charges, the total historic cost charge and the total current cost charge, is the depreciation adjustment.

The depreciation charge in the current cost profit and loss account is based on the average value of the assets during the year. Assuming an even rate of price increase, this is the mid-year value. In the example in this chapter, it is assumed for ease of calculation that the price increase over the first six months has been 10 per cent. Any additions during the first half of the year have to be multiplied by the appropriate index to get them to their mid-year value. There is a choice as to which procedure to follow with the assets purchased between the mid-year and year-end; probably the most sensible solution is to base the depreciation on their actual purchase price. The company does not wish to alter its depreciation policy, or change its assumption on the life of the assets as a result of introducing current cost accounting. Therefore the depreciation adjustment in the current cost profit and loss account is:

	£
Current cost depreciation	
(£35,200 × 25%)	£8,800
Historic cost depreciation	7,500
Depreciation adjustment	£1,300

A pro forma balance sheet can now be prepared.

Value of fixed assets

Opening valuation (as at 31/12/X8)

		£
Gross current cost (as shown above)		26,400
Gross historic cost		20,000
Revaluation surplus (gross)		6,400
less Depreciation: current cost	£10,200	
historic cost	7,500	
		2,700
To opening current cost reserve—net		3,700

Closing valuation

	Gross	Current cost Accumulated depreciation
	£	£
Current cost values as at 31/12/X8	26,400	10,200
Additions (1/1/X9)	20,000	
	46,400	10,200
less Disposals	14,400	7,200
	32,000	3,000
Increase in value during 19X9 with 20% price increase	6,400	600
Year's depreciation charge in current cost profit and loss account		8,800
Effect of price change from mid-year to year-end on depreciation charge [£8,800 × (120 − 110)/110]		800
Total value as at 31/12/X9	38,400	13,200

It is these figures of £38,400 and £13,200 that appear in the closing current cost balance sheet as the gross fixed assets and accumulated depreciation. It should be noted that the £8,800 depreciation charge appearing in the profit and loss account was based on mid-year (average) values of the assets; to obtain the appropriate current cost accumulated depreciation charge for the year-end, an additional £800 depreciation has had to be introduced. The £600 depreciation was reflecting the indexation of the opening accumulated depreciation provision to year-end values. Both the £600 and the £800 represent different aspects of backlog depreciation, introduced earlier in the chapter. An entry needs to be made in the current cost reserve for the £6,400 revaluation surplus for the year and the £600 and £800 depreciation adjustments, representing backlog and revalued depreciation.

To summarize, the above calculations with respect to fixed assets mean that the following adjustments need to be made to the accounts prepared on the historical cost basis in order to produce current cost accounts:

31/12/X8	Dr	Fixed assets	£6,400	
	Cr	Current cost reserve		£6,400
	Dr	Current cost reserve	2,700	
	Cr	Accumulated depreciation		2,700
31/12/X9	Dr	Fixed assets	6,400	
	Cr	Current cost reserve		6,400
		(being adjustment of figures at beginning of year for price change over the year)		
	Dr	Current cost reserve	600	
	Cr	Accumulated depreciation		600
		(being adjustment of figures at beginning of year for price change over the year — backlog depreciation)		
	Dr	Profit and loss account	1,300	
	Cr	Accumulated depreciation		1,300
		(being adjustment to year's depreciation charge)		

Dr	Profit and loss account	2,200	
	Accumulated depreciation	2,200	
Cr	Fixed assets		4,400
	(adjustment on sale of asset)		
Dr	Current cost reserve	800	
Cr	Accumulated depreciation		800
	(adjustment of depreciation from mid-year to year-end)		

13.4.4   Loss/gain on sale of fixed asset

One of the current cost account adjustments that may need to be made is for a gain or loss on the sale of an asset. With historical cost-based accounts, a gain or loss that may arise on the sale of an asset is either credited or debited to the profit and loss account. The gain or loss will be different if based on current cost figures, and it is the difference between the two calculations that is the current cost adjustment.

In the Comus example, it has been shown that the gross current cost of the asset sold was, at the time of its sale (1 January 19X9), £14,400. Comus had used the asset for half of its life, so the inflation-adjusted depreciation figure at the time of its sale should be £7,200. The current cost net book value is therefore £7,200 (the historical cost value being £5,000); with the asset being sold for £5,000, there is a resulting loss on sale, according to current cost principles, of £2,200. With historical cost values, there was neither a profit nor a loss on the sale, and so it is the difference of £2,200 between current cost and historical cost calculations that needs to be charged as an adjustment against the current cost profit and loss account.

13.4.5   Gearing adjustment

The objective of this adjustment is to bring back into the profit and loss account some of the benefits to the shareholders from the company's borrowings. It is a well-known adage that it pays to borrow at times of inflation. A company borrows a sum of money today, say £100,000, and pays the capital sum back in say two years' time. The purchasing power of the £100,000 it pays out in two years' time will be much less than the sum it receives today; it is paying back less in real terms. The shareholders might well have gained from this transaction; the problem is how to measure the gain. The gearing adjustment was the most controversial aspect of SSAP 16.

It was explained in the 'Guidance notes' why some adjustment was felt necessary:

> The fixed assets and the working capital commonly will have been financed in part by borrowing. Where such borrowing is fixed in monetary amount, any liability to repay remains unaltered, even when price changes affect the operating assets of the business financed by it. If prices rise, the value to the business of assets exceeds the borrowing that has financed them. The excess (less interest payable on the borrowing) in effect accrues to the shareholders, and is realised as the assets are used or sold in the ordinary course of business. The existence of borrowing during a period of rising prices thus provides a benefit to shareholders which offsets, to a greater or lesser extent, the cost of servicing the borrowing and conversely when prices decline.

So far so good. Controversy centred on how a company was to calculate the gearing adjustment and how it introduced it into the accounts.

The cost of sales adjustment, the monetary working capital adjustment, the depreciation adjustment, and any gains or loss on sales of assets have been calculated, and the sum of these is to be used to adjust the historical cost profit to arrive at the current cost operating profit. But, it can be argued, no account has been taken of the existence of borrowing in arriving at current cost operating profit. To illustrate this point with the cost of sales adjustment, it is true that the replacement cost of stock consumed will most likely be higher at times of inflation than the cost of the stock when purchased, but if part of the funds to purchase the stock came from borrowing, then the increase in cost can be partly offset by the gain on the funds borrowed to purchase the stock. The sum of the cost of sales adjustment, the working capital adjustment, the depreciation adjustment, and gains or losses on asset sales should therefore 'be abated by a further adjustment, the "gearing adjustment" in the proportion that finance by borrowing bears to the sum of this plus the shareholders interest'. A gearing ratio for the company is therefore determined, and this gearing ratio times the current cost adjustment is credited to the profit and loss account. If the company does not have net borrowings, or if the net borrowings are negative, no gearing adjustment is needed. If by any chance prices should fall, the gearing adjustment would be a debit to the profit and loss account.

The method of arriving at a gearing adjustment recommended in SSAP 16 is quite easy to calculate. However, there are many critics of the approach, and this has been recognized by the ASC. A company can use the recommended method in its current cost account, and show in the notes to the accounts an alternative method preferred by the directors. Alternatively, a gearing adjustment arrived at by a different method can be shown in the current cost accounts, with the recommended method in the notes. It must be remembered that the directors of the company have an overriding responsibility to ensure that the accounts show a true and fair view.

The method advocated by SSAP 16 will now be illustrated. The gearing proportion is the ratio of net borrowings to the average net operating assets over the year, calculated at their current cost values. The first step in calculating this ratio is to ascertain the average net borrowings (L). This consists of all liabilities and provisions fixed in monetary terms (including convertible debentures and deferred tax, but excluding proposed dividends) except any already included in the monetary working capital adjustment or those that are in substance equity capital less all current assets, except those already included in the cost of sales adjustment or the monetary working capital adjustment.

The second step is to ascertain shareholders' interests. It is emphasized that these figures need to be obtained from the current cost balance sheet, not the historical cost balance sheet. The shareholders' interests therefore take into account the current cost values for fixed assets and stock. The shareholders' interest includes the share capital, all the reserves, including the current cost reserve, the proposed dividends, the preference shares and any minority interests. To arrive at this figure for shareholders' current cost interests (S), it is advisable to construct the asset side of the current cost balance sheet and then to deduct from this asset figure all the liabilities, both current and long-term, and provisions, for example deferred tax.

It is possible that a goodwill figure appears in the current cost balance sheet. SSAP 16 did not specify whether or not goodwill should be included as an asset when calculating shareholders' interests. In the 'Guidance notes', which are non-mandatory, the goodwill was included in arriving at the net asset figure.

The third and final step is to calculate the gearing proportion, which is $L/(L+S)$, and to multiply the sum of the current cost adjustments by this proportion. This gives the gearing adjustment which is to be credited to the profit and loss account and debited to the current cost reserve.

The technique will be illustrated using the Comus example. The first step is to calculate the net borrowings of Comus Ltd, which are as follows:

	As at 31/12/X8	As at 31/12/X9
	£	£
Loan	7,000	8,000
Overdraft	3,000	6,000
Taxation	8,000	9,000
	18,000	23,000
less Cash	6,000	5,000
	12,000	18,000

Average net borrowing over the year (L) came to £15,000. The average figure can be used unless there is evidence that this is misrepresentative of the position over the year. All other items of current assets and current liabilities, i.e. those not allowed for in the gearing adjustment, have already been adjusted through the cost of sales adjustment and the monetary working capital adjustment.

To arrive at the figures representing the shareholders' interests at the beginning and end of the year, it is necessary to formulate the asset side of the balance sheet, taking into account the adjusted current cost figures. This is shown as at 31 December 19X9. The current cost values of fixed assets and stock were calculated earlier in the chapter.

	£	£
Fixed assets	38,400	
less Depreciation	13,200	
		25,200
Stock		14,209
Debtors		6,000
Cash		5,000
		50,409

On the other side of the balance sheet, the liabilities are:

	£
Loan	8,000
Creditors	5,000
Overdraft	6,000
Taxation	9,000
	28,000

With the total of the shareholders' interests plus liabilities needing to equal £50,409, it means the shareholders' funds (S) must equal £22,409.

It is now possible to calculate the gearing adjustment. The formula to be used is $L/(L+S)$; substituting to obtain the average ratio, we have

$$\frac{L19X8 + L19X9}{(L+S)19X8 + (L+S)19X9}.$$

The formula gives an approximate average for the year of the percentage of the total funds obtained from debt. The shareholders' funds in current cost terms at 31 December 19X8 consist of the £5,000 share capital and the £10,000 reserves appearing in the historic cost balance sheet, plus the £3,700 fixed assets revaluation and the £255 inventory revaluation. These last two amounts were calculated earlier in the chapter. The total shareholders' interest as at 31 December 19X8 therefore equalled £18,955.

Substituting in the equation, we have

$$\frac{12,000 + 18,000}{12,000 + 18,955 + 18,000 + 22,409} = 42\%.$$

The gearing adjustment to appear in the profit and loss account and the balance sheet is 42 per cent of the current cost adjustment; that is, 42 per cent of £5,402 = £2,269.

13.4.6 Current cost profit and loss account

All the information is now available to construct the current cost profit and loss account for Comus:

Current cost profit and loss account for year ending 31 December 19X9

	£	£
Historic cost profit		30,000
less Depreciation		7,500
		22,500
Current cost adjustments		
COSA	1,677	
MWCA	225	
Depreciation	1,300	
Loss on sale	2,200	
		5,402
Current cost operating profit		17,098
less Interest		1,000
		16,098
less Tax		10,750
		5,348
Gearing adjustment (42% of £5,402)		2,269
Current cost profit		7,617
Dividends paid		8,750
Retained (over distributed) for year		(1,133)

It is permitted to combine the interest paid figure and the gearing adjustment in the published accounts. As can be seen, in this Comus example an historical cost profit available for distribution of £10,750 becomes a current cost profit available for distribution of £7,617. With the dividends paid being £8,750, it means that Comus is distributing more in the year than it has earned.

SSAP 16 discussed the amount that can be 'prudently' distributed as dividends. The distribution policy of a company depends on a number of factors:

[profits], capital expenditure plans, changes in the volume of working capital, the effect on funding requirements of changes in production methods and efficiency, liquidity, and new financing arrangements. The current cost profit attributable to shareholders should not be assumed to measure the amount that can prudently be distributed. Although the impact of price changes on the shareholders' interest in the net operating assets has been allowed for, the other factors still need to be considered. Even if the effect of such factors is neutral, a full distribution of the current cost profit attributable to shareholders may make it necessary to arrange additional finance (equal to the gearing adjustment) to avoid an erosion of the operating capability of the business. However, an increase in the value to the business of the assets may provide increased cover for such financing.

13.4.7 Current cost reserve

Frequent reference has been made in this chapter to the current cost reserve account. This may at first sight appear to be a strange account; it gives the impression of being used as a home for one-half of a number of adjustments, when the double-entry principle must be upheld but it is not obvious where one-half of the entry should go. SSAP 16 admitted that the interpretation of the amounts in this account can be complex.

The size of the reserve depends on the impact of price changes on the net operating assets, on the policies adopted in preparing the historical cost accounts, and on when precisely the business prepares its first set of current cost accounts. The items included in the account are, where appropriate:

(a) unrealised revaluation surpluses on fixed assets, stock and investments; and
(b) realised amounts equal to the cumulative net total of the current cost adjustment; that is:
    (i)   the depreciation adjustment (and any adjustments on the disposal of fixed assets);
    (ii) the two working capital adjustments; and
    (iii) the gearing adjustment.[17]

The current cost reserve of Comus Ltd as at 31 December 19X9 is made up of the following items:

Revaluation surplus reflecting price changes

	£	£	£
Fixed assets			
Balance at 1/1/X9		3,700	
Gross increase	6,400		
Depreciation	(1,400)	5,000	
			8,700
Stock			
Balance at 1/1/X9		255	
Change during year		(46)	
			209
			8,909
Profit and loss account adjustments			
Cost of sales		1,677	
MWCA		225	
Gearing		(2,269)	
			(367)
			8,542

The balance on the account at the beginning of the year was £3,955, reflecting the revaluation surplus on the fixed assets and stock.

The depreciation of £1,400 debited to this current cost reserve comprises the two elements of backlog depreciation, the amounts of £800 and £600. The actual current cost depreciation adjustment of £1,300 discussed earlier does not appear in this reserve account. As can be seen from the journal entries summarizing the movements in the fixed asset account, the depreciation adjustment was debited to the current profit and loss account.

This balance of £8,542 on the current cost reserve at the end of 19X9 can be divided between the realized element and the unrealized. 'The realised element represents the net cumulative total of the current cost adjustments which have been passed through the profit and loss account. Thus it represents the difference between historical and current cost profits since current cost accounts were first prepared.'[18] It should be noted that this definition of 'realized' differs from the normal usage of the word: it does not mean that cash has been realized.

In the Comus example, 19X9 was the first year in which current cost accounts were prepared, and so the net cumulative total of the current cost adjustments is £3,133 (this being the adjustment of £5,402 less the gearing adjustment of £2,269). This is the difference between the historical and current cost profits. In later years the realized element of the current cost reserve would be the cumulative net annual adjustments. The unrealized element of the current cost reserve is the balance of £5,409.

A presentation of the current cost reserve, which is sometimes suggested, shows the movement on reserves divided between the realized and unrealized for the separate items. With the Comus example this would be:

	Realized £	Unrealized £	£
Opening balance—unrealized			3,955
Current year			
Fixed assets	3,500	1,500	
Inventory		(46)	
Cost of sales adjustment	1,677		
MWCA	225		
Gearing adjustment	(2,269)		
	3,133	1,454	
			4,587
Closing balance			8,542

The £3,500 realized element of fixed assets consists of the inflation-adjusted loss on sale of £2,200 and the extra annual depreciation charge of £1,300.

All revaluation surpluses or deficits need to be transferred to the current cost reserve.

13.4.8 Current cost balance sheet

Once the size of the current cost reserve has been determined, it is possible to complete the current cost balance sheet. Such a balance sheet for Comus is shown below. The closing revenue reserve is the balance from the previous year's current cost balance sheet adjusted by the year's current cost profit or loss. The revenue reserve at the end of the following year, 19X0, would be £8,867, plus or minus the 19X0 profit or loss. It is only in the first year that current cost accounts are prepared that the opening revenue reserve is the same as the reserve in the balance sheet prepared on historical cost principles. The current cost value of fixed assets was calculated in Section 13.4.3.

A business has a choice of whether to calculate its current cost depreciation charge on the value to the business of the fixed assets at the end of the year or on the average for the year. The choice it makes can have a significant impact on the current cost profits reported for a year. In the Comus example, it should be noted that the depreciation charge was based on the average value of the fixed assets for the year. The gross current cost at 1 January 19X9, after the disposal of the asset, was £32,000. There is a 20 per cent rise in price during 19X9 and, for the sake of simplicity, this is assumed to indicate that it was 10 per cent over the first six months. The current cost value at 1 July 19X9 is therefore £35,200, which is assumed to be the average for the year. The current cost depreciation based on this figure is £8,800, and it is this amount that is charged to the profit and loss account for the year. A charge of £800 has to be made to the current cost reserves to reflect the effect of the price change from the mid-year to year-end on the depreciation. This additional charge, it should be noted, is debited to the current cost reserve and not to the profit and loss account.

Current cost balance sheet—Comus Ltd

31/12/X8				31/12/X9
£		£		£
	Fixed assets	38,400		
	less Depreciation	13,200		
16,200				25,200
12,255	Stock			14,209
6,500	Debtors			6,000
6,000	Cash			5,000
40,955				50,409
	Share capital and reserves			
5,000	Share capital	5,000		
3,955	Current cost reserve	8,542		
10,000	Revenue reserves			
	Opening	£10,000		
	less Over-distribution	1,133	8,867	
18,955				22,409
7,000	Loan			8,000
4,000	Creditors			5,000
3,000	Overdraft			6,000
8,000	Taxation			9,000
40,955				50,409

13.4.9 Group accounts

Current cost group accounts could also be prepared in accordance with the principles already discussed. It is recognized that it may not be possible or practical for all foreign subsidiaries to prepare such accounts, and in such situations 'the directors of the parent company should make the best possible estimates of the figures required'.[19]

Foreign currencies
The accounts of an overseas subsidiary and/or associated company should normally be prepared following current cost accounting principles, in the currency of the country, and then should be translated into sterling. The issue of whether to translate foreign currencies in accounts prepared on an historical cost basis according to the closing rate method or the temporal method has been discussed in Chapter 12. This is a not a problem with current cost accounting because foreign currency assets and liabilities are to be stated at their value to the business. This means the value to the business at the balance sheet date, which means using the closing rate. As was pointed out in the 'Guidance notes', using the temporal method will in fact give the same answer as using the closing rate method, as the relevant dates will be the balance sheet dates. If the year-end rate of

exchange has been distorted by short-term movements, then, as with historical-cost-based accounts, it may be more appropriate to use a more meaningful rate that occurred close to the year-end.

Items appearing in the profit and loss account can be translated at either the closing rate of exchange or the average rate for the year. Translation differences arising on consolidation are usually similar to price changes and should be debited or credited to reserves, rather than being taken to the profit and loss account.

Monetary working capital adjustments and gearing adjustments

The monetary working capital adjustment should be calculated on a company-by-company basis, and then aggregated to obtain the total adjustment for the group. On occasion, the monetary working capital of two or more companies in a group may be affected by inter-company debt which arises through normal trading transactions. This will be treated as borrowing (creditors) by the receiving company, and as lending (debtors) by the other company, and will affect the size of the monetary working capital adjustments for the companies involved. It is not long-term debt, but debt through normal trading, and so is part of the monetary working capital adjustment. Such inter-company trading will affect the adjustments of the individual companies. 'Care should be taken that no material distortion arises in group terms due to the use of different indices.'[20] This could happen with different price movements in the countries concerned and with variations in exchange rates between sterling and the currency of the countries of the companies involved. Care must be taken to ensure that the aggregated monetary working capital adjustment is not distorted by such movements.

Problems arise when it comes to the gearing adjustment. The simplest form of gearing adjustment, and the one that will in most cases be used, is to calculate one such adjustment for the whole group, based only on external borrowing by the companies in the group and after all inter-company loans have been eliminated. One argument in favour of such an adjustment, based on the figures in the consolidated balance sheet, is that the gearing ratio for an individual subsidiary may 'not mirror the external group financing arrangements'.[21] A particular foreign subsidiary may have a relatively high level of borrowing because the parent company wishes to finance a high proportion of the local assets with inter-company borrowing and local debt. The group, however, once inter-company borrowing is eliminated, may have a low level of gearing. Therefore, preparing a gearing adjustment for the group, based on aggregating the individual adjustment for each company in the group, may not be meaningful from the overall company point of view. This is the argument for a single adjustment based on consolidated figures, with the minority interests included as part of the figure for shareholders' interests.

However, it may not be possible to use a single overall adjustment where there are material minority interests in an individual subsidiary. These minorities might benefit from the subsidiary's high level of gearing, and this should be taken into account when calculating their interest in the business. The gearing adjustment for certain subsidiaries may need to be calculated separately, and the proportionate share of the minority interests obtained.

13.5   Developments subsequent to SSAP 16

In 1980, when SSAP 16 was issued, inflation was at the abnormally high rate of around 20 per cent per annum. The standard was generally regarded as an important development in the subject of accounting, although it always had its critics. It was the result of a decade of debate on how to develop a technique that would more accurately reflect financial performance during periods of rising prices than the traditional historical cost accounting approach. The standard required listed and large non-listed companies to publish mandatory current cost information.

By 1983 there was still inflation in the UK, but it was now at the rate of 5 per cent per annum. Although still mandatory, many companies were disregarding the standard. Reporting in 1983, the working party set up to monitor the experience of using SSAP 16 found little support for the standard.

By then, alternative methods of reporting the effects of changing prices were being suggested. A more flexible approach was proposed by critics of the current cost method. In 1984 the ASC published a compromise proposal, ED 35.[22] This remained loyal to the current cost method, with the information to be given in the main accounts, either as a note or as part of full current cost accounts. The idea of supplementary current cost accounts was abandoned. The ASC repeated the view that compliance was essential to the presentation of a true and fair view. Auditors were concerned with whether or not, under SSAP 16 and the proposals in ED 35, they should give a qualification in the audit report to companies who did not produce current cost information. In fact, ED 35 was rejected by the professional bodies comprising the Consultative Committee of Accounting Bodies (CCAB), whose support is needed for the introduction of a standard.

The *Survey of UK Published Accounts*, based on the financial reports of 300 industrial and commercial companies, has shown the extent of the disillusionment with current cost accounting.[23] The percentage of companies issuing reports during the year to 30 June 1984 and providing current cost statements in line with the recommendations of SSAP 16 was 59 per cent; a year later only 26 per cent were providing such information, and a year after that, of reports issued during the year to 30 June 1986, the survey revealed that only 4 per cent of companies were producing such statements.[24]

The recommendations of ED 35 had little impact. Reporting in the year up to 30 June 1984, 39 per cent of companies provided no current cost information; in the year up to 30 June 1985, 66 per cent provided no such information; in the year to 30 June 1986 the figure was 94 per cent.

In June 1985 SSAP 16 was made non-mandatory, although at the time there was not complete harmony between the views of professional bodies. The CACA did not think SSAP 16 should be withdrawn until a replacement was provided, believing that an imperfect standard was to be preferred to no standard at all. The other bodies in the CCAB wanted the standard withdrawn in the interests of 'freeing the way' for innovation and the development of appropriate methods of disclosure.

13.5.1 The ASC handbook

The standard was subsequently withdrawn, but to provide 'useful guidance to those who wish to prepare use or audit information on the effects of changing prices', the ASC issued a handbook in 1986 entitled *Accounting for the Effects of Changing Prices*.

Based on a decade's experience of searching for a satisfactory solution', the ASC considered it

most appropriate for companies to disclose information about the current year's result and financial position on the basis of:

● current cost asset valuation, using
● either the opening or financial capital maintenance concept and
● the nominal pound as the unit of measurement.

In addition, the ASC considers it appropriate for companies that publish five or ten-year historical summaries to restate in units of current purchasing power certain figures which are either adjusted for the effects of specific changing prices (such as adjusted earnings) or require no adjustment (such as turnover and dividends).

The importance of capital maintenance concepts for profit measurement were discussed in Chapter 1. The handbook provides an explanation of how the ASC interprets the operating and financial capital maintenance concepts. Operating capital is taken to be

> the productive capital of the company's assets in terms of the volume of goods and services capable of being produced (the volume concept of operating capital).
>
> Profit under the operating capital maintenance concept depends upon the effects of specific price changes on the operating capital, that is the net operating assets of the business.

The operating capital maintenance concept can be regarded as a form of physical capital maintenance based on output capacity and is the approach utilized in SSAP 16 and current cost accounting.

Maintenance of a company's financial capital is commonly seen in terms of shareholders' funds. In money terms, this would provide the foundation for historical cost accounting. When taking account of price change, the concept is viewed in real terms. A practical application of this is current purchasing power accounting, and the handbook describes how a system could utilize current cost asset values:

(a) calculate the shareholders' funds at the beginning of the period based on current cost asset values;
(b) restate that amount in terms of pounds of the reporting date (by adjusting (a) by the relevant change in a general index such as the RPI); and
(c) compare (b) with shareholders' funds at the end of the year based on current cost asset values.

The presidents of the five leading accountancy bodies endorsed the view of ASC that, 'where a company's results and financial position are materially affected by changing prices, historical cost accounts alone are insufficient, and that information on the effects of changing prices is important for an appreciation of the company's results and financial position'.[25] They supported the continuing work on the subject by the ASC. The key word in the above statement is 'materially'.

Companies do not seem to share the ASC commitment to the importance of providing financial information on the effects of changing prices. Presumably, they believe that the results are not materially affected. By 1987 it was difficult to find a set of accounts that made any reference to the effects of inflation. Even companies that had once been enthusiastic supporters of providing inflation-adjusted figures had abandoned the practice.

In his statement in the accounts for the year ended 31 March 1986, the chairman of Pilkington expressed regret that British industry had not adopted current cost accounting (CCA). He explained that the presentation of Pilkington results in CCA terms 'places the group at a considerable disadvantage when compared with those of other UK companies who almost universally adopt the historical cost basis'. From 1 April 1986, therefore, the group's tangible assets would be given only in historical cost terms, and from that date depreciation would be based on these historical cost figures. The chairman pointed out, however, that the group would take account of inflation and obsolescence on its tangible assets in the group's internal management accounts. In its accounts to 31 March 1987, Pilkington made no reference at all to inflation accounting.[26]

The withdrawal of the standard, and the issue of a handbook with recommendations that have had little impact, show that the ASC is in a very weak position. In the face of non-compliance, there is little that it can do. In February 1986 the ASC admitted that the level of resistance from companies was such that achieving even a modest level of minimum disclosure was beyond the profession alone.

But in 1985 the Minister for Corporate and Consumer Affairs had expressed the view that he was not in favour of statutory support for inflation-adjusted accounts. He indicated that the government supported the need to show the effect of changing prices in financial accounts, but believed that the responsibility for this lay with the profession within the framework of company law. To act on this, of course, means interpreting what is meant by accounts showing a 'true and fair' view.

At the time when the private sector companies were showing their dislike of inflation-adjusted accounts, and the accounting profession was showing its inability to force companies to adopt unpopular standards, the public sector was revealing a different picture. In 1986 the Treasury published a report, *Accounting for Economic Costs and Changing Prices* (the Byatt Report),[27] which argued strongly that the principles of current cost accounting apply equally to the private sector and to the nationalized industries and the rest of the public sector. This report backed current cost accounting as a proper base. It pointed out that, even with the comparatively modest rate of inflation of 5 per cent per annum, prices are doubled every 14 years. The effect of this on assets with long lives is considerable. The report states that 'the measurement errors involved in estimating the cost of using resources in current prices pales into insignificance compared with those involved in ignoring the effect of changing prices in spite of the extra degree of judgement involved'.

In fact, no decision was made that all public sector companies should implement the recommendations of the Byatt Report. Nationalized industries are set targets, some of which are expressed in inflation terms while others are not. British Gas before privatization was given statutory targets in current cost profit terms; the Electricity Council, the Regional Water Authorities and the Civil Aviation Authority are given current cost targets.[28] In contrast, British Coal and British Steel were given targets in historical cost terms.

The effect of moving from one basis to the other can be seen from an analysis of the 1985–86 accounts of these last two enterprises. In historical cost terms, British Coal broke even, but after the appropriate current cost adjustments it would have shown a loss of £381 million. British Steel showed an historical cost profit of £38 million, but after current cost adjustments would have shown a loss of £37 million.

British Gas, in its annual report for the year ending 31 March 1987, was still providing current cost accounts—not only a profit and loss account and balance sheet, but also a five-year financial summary in current cost terms. Whether or not the impact of changing prices on such an organization is 'material' can be judged from the fact that, for the year 1986–87, the historical cost profit before taxation was £1,244 million, whereas the current cost profit before taxation was £1,005 million,[29] and the respective returns on average capital employed were 18.5 and 5.8 per cent.

13.6 Legal position

There is no requirement under the Companies Act 1985 that when following the historical cost rules fixed assets must be revalued. Under these rules the balance sheet must show for each item the amount stated at cost at the beginning and end of the financial year, with the effect on that item of any acquisitions, disposals or transfers.

There is a requirement in the Act, however, relating to the revaluation of stocks, even when adopting the historical cost approach. Stocks and work in progress should of course be stated in the balance sheet in accordance with the familiar valuation rule of the lower of cost and net realizable value. However, the 4th schedule of the Act (27(3)–27(5)) states that, if there is a material difference between the value of stocks as included in the accounts and the value of stocks at replacement cost or most recent purchase or production cost, the amount of the difference must be stated in a note to the accounts.

This concern with the difference between historical cost and replacement cost is precisely the point of the cost of sales adjustment in current cost accounting. Although companies have ceased to provide current cost information, it is interesting to observe how they have responded to the requirement of the Companies Act to disclose 'material differences' in stock valuation.

The two groups of assets that give rise to most valuation problems at times of changing prices are tangible assets and stocks. The Companies Act 1985 lays down several principles and rules that must be followed. These rules are of two types: those relating to the historical cost approach and those relating to 'alternative accounting'. The latter apply if the main historical accounts incorporate either certain asset revaluations or current cost accounting. These alternative rules allow for the revaluation of fixed assets, with the requirement that any profit or loss arising on the revaluation be separately disclosed in a revaluation reserve. Such an amount can be transferred to the profit and loss account when the asset is sold and the profit realised.

The 4th schedule of the Act states that, under the alternative rules, tangible fixed assets should be valued at current cost on the date of last valuation. It also states that under the alternative rules stocks should be valued at current cost. However, a company does not have to adopt these alternative rules incorporating either current cost or revaluation: it can prepare its accounts following the historical cost convention.

The *Survey of Published Accounts 1985–86* reveals that compliance with the disclosure requirement has been rather mixed. 'Some companies state that there is no material difference between cost and replacement cost, whilst many others are silent on the subject which implies that there is no material difference.'[30]

There are of course some companies that do give details of the difference. Whether a difference is material depends of course on the opinions of the directors of the company and its auditors. Whitbread and Company, in its 1987 group accounts, shows in the balance sheet that the value of its stocks is £179 million, but reveals in a note that the estimated replacement cost is £185.6 million. This difference is less than 5 per cent, and it is doubtful if most companies would disclose a difference of its magnitude.

What of fixed asset revaluation? At times of even 5 per cent annual inflation, the replacement cost of fixed assets can rise at a significant rate. Of course, not all asset prices change at the same rate, and some can move in the opposite direction to changes in the general price level. As mentioned, companies are not required by the Companies Act to revalue their assets. What happens in practice? The 1986–87 *Survey of Published Accounts* reports that 'most of the companies examined incorporated an element of fixed asset revaluation, principally in connection with freehold and long leasehold land and buildings'. It goes on to say, however that only a few companies indicated that plant and machinery had also been revalued. Such revaluations of plant and machinery were invariable some years ago and the values concerned were relatively small. 'The valuation dates of the non-property assets tended to be about the time of SSAP 16's introduction [1980] and this might be the explanation for their inclusion.'

It is perhaps surprising that during the period 1980–86 there was little appreciation in asset values that was regarded as significant. Perhaps with low rates of inflation the rate of decline in value on plant and machinery through wear and tear exceeds the rate of increase through changes in purchasing power.

13.7 Hyperinflation and consolidation

Although the reduction in inflation rate in the UK to below 5 per cent has taken much of the impetus out of efforts to establish price level accounting for companies operating in Britain, a number of countries continued to face high inflation. The effects of the loss of purchasing power of money will substantially distort accounts prepared in the currencies of such countries. Even after translation, the balance sheets and profit and loss accounts of subsidiaries stated in the currency of a country suffering hyperinflation are inappropriate to be combined with parent companies' accounts produced in a more stable currency for consolidation purposes.

The IASC has given consideration to this matter and has made an effort to ensure that, despite the effective withdrawal in the UK of an inflation accounting standard, there is a recognition that some economies continue to experience hyperinflation, and this must be recognized when relevant. In December 1987 it issued a draft E 31, 'Financial Reporting in Hyperinflationary Economies'.[31] This recommends that a current purchasing power (CPP) approach be adopted when inflation is sufficiently high. It suggests that unadjusted balance sheets and profits and loss accounts should not be disclosed but restated. Balance sheet restatement would involve applying a general price index to all non-monetary items from the date of acquisition. E 31 suggest that assets purchased under arrangements of interest-free deferred payments should treat the date of payment as the date of acquisition for this purpose.

Where the original date of establishing historical cost is not available, the approach can be implemented in the first period by obtaining professional assessments of values. Revalued amounts would be adjusted by the increase in index from the date of such revaluation. The draft acknowledges that, if a restated amount resulting from application of a general index exceeds the amount recoverable from its future use including eventual disposal, its value should be reduced.

In restating owners' equity on the first occasion, contributed capital can be adjusted by the change in index from the date of contribution. The opening reserves become the balancing item in the opening balance sheet after the restatement of non-monetary asssets.

The draft recommends that the income statement requires restatement to apply to each item, including turnover. A gain or loss on holding monetary items will be included. Even where accounts have been produced in current cost terms, if they have been subjected to hyperinflation, indexation will have to be applied to the income statement to adjust the measurement date from the average date of transactions to expression in terms of the currency at the year end. Current cost balance sheets will not require indexation as they will already be stated at year-end prices.

Although it is recommended that corresponding figures be restated, the treatment of the statement of changes in financial position does not involve indexation. The draft advocates providing a statement in terms of cash or cash equivalent which should be expressed in money amounts representing the money movements that took place.

The major relevance for UK companies preparing accounts in sterling will be when dealing with investment in foreign companies. The equity method of accounting for investment was discussed in Chapter 9. When equity methods are employed for an investee company in a hyperinflationary economy, and in particular in the consolidating entries for a subsidiary, it will be necessary to restate the profit and loss and balance sheet statements before translating. Translation would then be carried out using the closing rate method. (See Chapter 12 for an explanation.)

The draft provides a list of characteristics of hyperinflation in terms of five features of the economic environment, which can be summarized as follows.
(a) Wealth is held in nonmonetary assets or in stable foreign currencies, cash balances being converted for as little as only a few days.
(b) Prices may be quoted in terms of stable foreign currencies.
(c) Credit trading includes allowances for interest or loss of purchasing power even for short periods.
(d) Interest rates, wages and prices are linked to a price index.
(e) The cumulative inflation rate approaches or exceeds 100 per cent in three years.

It would seem that disenchantment with price level accounting in the UK does not enable the subject to be closed. Revaluation of assets is widespread; the 1986–87 *Survey of Published Accounts* indicated that over 20 per cent of 300 major companies revalued operating properties.[32] (This excludes any revaluation of investment property.) Hyperinflationary economies cannot be ignored. Even when inflation is only 6 per cent, by the end of a ten-year life, asset depreciation would need to have been increased by 80 per cent to allow for general price change. The issues are sufficiently complex and fundamental to the understanding of income measurement that accountants need to give the subject some attention if they are to contribute to the development of their profession.

Notes

1. See, for example, H. W. Sweeney, *Stabilized Accounting*, Harper, New York, 1936, republished by Holt, Rhinehart and Winston, New York, 1964.
2. There is a brief consideration given to cash flow accounting in *The Report of the Inflation Accounting Committee* (the Sandilands Report), Cmnd 6445, HMSO, 1975. See T. A. Lee, 'Cash flow accounting and corporate financial reporting', and G. H. Lawson, 'The cash flow performance of UK companies: case studies in cash flow accounting', both in M. Bromwich and A. G. Hopwood (eds), *Essays in British Accounting Research*, Pitman, London, 1981.
3. This perceptive description was developed by Professor W. T. Baxter in his *Accounting Values and Inflation*, McGraw-Hill, Maidenhead, 1975, which provides coverage of the subject matter of this chapter, with particular attention not only to the time-lag error but also to asset values and depreciation.
4. SSAP 16, 'Current Cost Accounting', and 'Guidance Notes to SSAP 16', ASC, 1980.
5. R. J. Chambers, *Accounting Evaluation and Economic Behaviour*, ch. 10, Prentice-Hall, Englewood Cliffs, NJ, 1966.
6. E. O. Edwards and P. W. Bell, *The Theory and Measurement of Business Income*, University of California Press 1960.
7. The foundations for this approach were laid by Professor J. C. Bonbright in his *Valuation of Property*, reprinted by Michie in 1965, originally published by McGraw-Hill in 1937. It has been given support and been developed by Professor W. T. Baxter (see Baxter, *Accounting Values*). See also H. C. Edey, 'Deprival value and financial accounting', in H. C. Edey and B. S. Yamey (eds), *Debits, Credits, Finance and Profits*, Sweet and Maxwell, London, 1974.
8. 'Guidance Notes to SSAP 16', para. 32.
9. Ibid., para. 40 ED 18, 'Current Cost Accounting', ASC, 1976.
10. The Sandilands Report.
11. Ibid.
12. Hyde Guidelines, 'Inflation Accounting—An Interim Recommendation by the Accounting Standards Committee', ASC, 1976.
13. ED 24, 'Current Cost Accounting', ASC, 1979.
14. Department of Industry, *Price Index Numbers for Current Cost Accounting*, published three times a year, HMSO; Department of Industry, *Business Monitor*, published monthly, HMSO; Department of Industry, 'Current Cost Accounting—Guide to Price Indices for Overseas Countries', HMSO.
15. Economists Intelligence Unit, *Price Indices*, published quarterly.
16. SSAP 16, para. 13.
17. Ibid., para. 24.
18. 'Guidance Notes to SSAP 16', Appendix (v), illustrative note to current cost accounts.
19. Ibid., para. 122.
20. Ibid., para. 141.
21. Ibid., para. 142.
22. ED 35: 'Accounting for the Effects of Changing Prices', ASC, 1984.
23. D. J. Tonkin and L. C. L. Skerratt (eds), *Financial Reporting 1984–85: A Survey of UK Published Accounts*, ICAEW, 1984.
24. D. J. Tonkin and L. C. L. Skerratt (eds), *Financial Reporting 1986–87: A Survey of UK Published Accounts*, ICAEW, 1987.

25. *Accounting for the Effects of Changing Prices: A Handbook*, ASC, 1986.
26. Pilkington plc Annual Report, 1987.
27. *Accounting for Economic Costs and Changing Prices* (the Byatt Report), HMSO, London, 1986.
28. See 'Nationalised Industries 1986', CIPFA, London, 1987.
29. British Gas Annual Report, 1987; D. J. Tonkin and L. C. L. Skerratt (eds), *Financial Reporting 1987–88: A Survey of UK Published Accounts*, ICAEW, 1988.
30. *Financial Reporting 1985–86: A Survey of UK Published Accounts*, ICAEW, 1986.
31. E 31: 'Financial Reporting in Hyperinflationary Economies', IASC, December 1987.
32. Tonkin and Skerratt, *Financial Reporting 1986–87*.

Further reading

Lemke, K. W. and P. P. Powers, 'The gearing adjustment: an empirical study', *Accounting and Business Research*, Winter 1986.

Peasnell, K. V., L. C. L. Skerratt and C. W. R. Ward, 'The share price impact of UK CCA disclosures', *Accounting and Business Research*, Winter 1987.

Tweedie, D. P. and G. Whittington, *Capital Maintenance Concepts: The Choice*, Accounting Standards Committee, 1985.

Tweedie, D. P. and G. Whittington, *The Debate on Inflation Accounting*, Cambridge University Press, 1984.

Whittington, G., *Inflation Accounting: An Introduction to the Debate*, Cambridge University Press, 1983.

Questions

1. (a) Briefly describe the current value exit model of income measurement and asset valuation (also known as realisable value accounting). (10 marks)
   (b) What are said to be the advantages of the current value exit model? (10 marks)
   (20 marks)
   ACCA, 2.8, RFA, June 1987

2. In 1985, SSAP 16: *Current cost accounting* (1980) ceased to have mandatory status in the UK/Ireland.
   Required:
   (a) Appraise the weaknesses of SSAP 16 which led to its non-acceptance by a considerable part of the business and financial community in the UK/Ireland. (15 marks)
   (b) Analyse the conceptual weaknesses of the gearing adjustment in SSAP 16, and consider alternative methods of computing it. (10 marks)
   (You may refer to any relevant exposure drafts or other statements of the Accounting Standards Committee.) **(25 marks)**
   ACCA, 3.1, AFA, December 1985

3. (a) Explain the 'value to the business' concept in relation to income and value measurement. (8 marks)
   (b) There are several schools of thought on current value accounting: some argue for current entry values; some argue for current exit values; and some argue that it is possible to combine both in one statement. To what extent do you consider that a financial statement containing both entry and exit values (a mixed value statement) can be regarded as a theoretically sound method of current value accounting? (12 marks)
   (20 marks)

4. Three suggested alternatives to historical cost accounting are:
   (1) current purchasing power accounting,
   (2) current cost accounting, and
   (3) 'economic', or present value, accounting.

Required:

(a) Indicate the basis on which each of the three methods values the shareholders' equity of a company as at the end of a financial year. (9 marks)

(b) Evaluate critically the three methods of computation of annual profit, and retained earnings for the year, as shown by each of the three methods mentioned in (a) above. (16 marks)

(25 marks)

ACCA, 3.1, AFA, June 1986

5. Shown below is the profit and loss account which has been produced for Flyford plc for the year ended 31st December 1986, based on the historic cost convention:

	£'000s	£'000s
Sales		869
Cost of goods sold	703	
Depreciation	45	
Interest paid	45	
Other costs	10	803
		66
Taxation		22
		44
Extraordinary items		10
		34
Dividends		7
Retained earnings		27

You are given the following additional information relating to the situation of the company:

(i)   Depreciation of £45,000 has been charged in the profit and loss account. This is made up as follows:

| Plant & machinery | £34,800 | (cost £174,000 at 20%) |
| Motor vehicles | £10,200 | (cost £40,800 at 25%) |

The current replacement costs of these fixed assets are:

| Plant & machinery | £222,200 |
| Motor vehicles | £ 72,000 |

(ii)

	31 December 1985	31 December 1986
Debtors	£34,400	£37,400
Creditors	£26,400	£22,600
Cash	£20,000	£35,000

(iii) The opening stock of £44,000 was purchased on average on 30 November 1985 and the closing stock of £48,200 was purchased on average on 30 November 1986. The price index relevant to the company's stock is as follows:

30 Nov. 1985	100
31 Dec. 1985	108
30 June 1986	120
30 Nov. 1986	127
31 Dec. 1986	130

(iv) The debtors and creditors date, on average, from one month before the respective year-end. The same index numbers apply as for stock. Sales and purchases took place evenly through the year.

(v)   The company has an average gearing (loans less cash balance) equal to 25% of the average equity capital (calculated on a current cost basis).

(vi) The tax of £22,000 was payable on 31 March 1987.

(vii) The 'extraordinary item' refers to redundancy payments that were made on 30 June 1986 upon the closure of a factory.

(viii) The company issued loan stock on 30 June 1983 for £100,000.

(ix) The fixed assets were all purchased on 30 June 1983.

(x)   The retail price index relevant to the transactions of the company was:

30 June 1983	140
30 Nov. 1985	165
31 Dec. 1985	170
30 June 1986	180
30 Nov. 1986	190
31 Dec. 1986	195

You are required to:

(a) prepare the current cost profit and loss account for Flyford plc in accordance with SSAP 16, making appropriate assumptions;   (8 marks)

(b) prepare the profit and loss account according to the current purchasing power convention;
                                                                                              (8 marks)

(c) write a report explaining to the directors of the company the meaning of the three different profit figures, giving guidance as to the relative strengths and weaknesses of the different approaches.
                                                                                              (9 marks)
                                                                                          (25 marks)

6. You are given the following information about Darley plc. It has three items of plant and machinery which were purchased at the dates shown below:

	Cost
1/1/80	£100,000
1/7/84	£100,000
1/1/86	£100,000

The RPI and the index relating to the particular class of assets are as below:

	RPI	Asset index
1/1/80	160	100
1/7/84	200	120
1/1/86	225	125
31/12/86	240	130

The life of the assets is 10 years, and each asset is being depreciated over its life on a straight-line basis.

The Company has a policy of employing an equal amount of borrowed funds to equity funds.

The directors of the company have decided that in their financial accounts for the year ending 31 December 1986 they wish to make allowance for the effects of inflation.

You are required to:
Give your advice on the following points:

(a) The position likely to be adopted by the auditors with regard to disclosing inflation-adjusted figures in the annual accounts;   (4 marks)

(b) What would be the net value of the plant and machinery appearing in the balance sheet as at 31/12/85 and 31/12/86 if the operating capital maintenance concept is adopted?   (7 marks)

(c) Should any allowance be made in the accounts for the effects of gearing, and if so what consequence would this have?   (4 marks)

(d) The asset purchased on 1/7/84 is one whose technology is considered by the directors to be out of date and would not be replaced with a similar asset. The machine which undertakes the same task but uses the latest technology, currently costs £150,000. The maximum output of the new machine is twice that of the present one but if acquired it would not be expected to operate at more than 75% of capacity. What value should be included in current cost accounts?   (6 marks)

(e) The machine purchased on 1/1/80 is producing a product which will soon be discontinued. When this machine comes to the end of its life it will not be replaced. What are the implications of this for current cost accounting?   (4 marks)
                                                                                          (25 marks)

14. Earnings per share

The amount of earnings per share is a valuable guide to the performance of quoted companies. A company expanding as a result of new issues of shares may be able to report rising profits, but unless earnings are growing faster than the number of shares, earnings per share will not increase. The disclosure of earnings per share in the financial statements is necessary only when the company is one with a quotation on a recognized stock exchange for any class of its equity.

Earnings per share is defined as:

> the profit in pence attributable to each equity share, based on the consolidated profit of the period after tax and after deducting minority interests and preference dividends, but before taking into account extraordinary items, divided by the number of equity shares in issue and ranking for dividend in respect of the period.[1]

The definition emphasizes that it is the number of shares, not the value of them, that is to be used as a divisor, and when there have been no changes in this number during the year the calculations are not complex. When there have been changes in the number of shares, the appropriate adjustments must be made to obtain a weighted average for the number of shares appropriate to the funds used in obtaining the earnings for the period. Whenever corresponding figures for an earlier period are included, they must be adjusted to make them as comparable as possible to avoid creating a misleading impression. The possibility of more shares being issued on the exercise of rights existing at the end of the period is, when significant, allowed for by the calculation of a fully diluted earnings per share.

A standard, SSAP 3, which was issued in February 1972 and amended in 1974, indicates very precisely the procedures to be followed in this calculation. The necessity for a standard on the subject arose because of the increasing importance being placed on earnings by the Stock Exchange and the investment community. It is a necessary input in the calculation of the price/earnings (P/E) ratio of a company which is used in evaluating shares. However, it should be remembered that the price used in the ratio is the current one and that normally the earnings are historical.

14.1 Basic earnings per share

At its simplest, the calculation of earnings per share merely requires the appropriate profit to be divided by the number of ordinary shares. This amount is known as the 'basic' earnings per share. The standard requires that the amount of the earnings per share for the period under review and the corresponding previous period be shown in the profit and loss account. Also required to be disclosed are the basis of calculation, the amount of the earnings and the number of equity shares used in the calculation.

The calculation is based on the profits after tax, which under the imputation system is to include all tax. Where materially different (and materiality in this context is not specified), a calculation should also be made on the 'nil distribution' basis. This means that any irrecoverable advance corporation tax and any unrelieved overseas tax arising from the payment or proposed payment of dividends is to be excluded from the tax charge, so that the charge is that which would have arisen if no dividends had been paid.

The *Financial Times* calculates and discloses the P/E ratio for companies included in its share information service as follows:

Financial Times Thursday 2 July 1987
INDUSTRIALS

High	*Low*	*Stock*	*Price*	*+ or −*	*Div. net*	*C'vr*	*Y'ld Gr's*	*P/E*
430	238	London Intnl. 10p	321	+15	5.4		2.3	
97	$71\frac{1}{2}$	Lon. & Nthn. Grp.	97	...	5.15	0.7	7.3	(36.4)
319	230	Low & Bonar 50p	274	+5	5.35	3.1	2.7	13.3

The notes show that the 'P/E's are calculated on the "net" distribution basis, earnings per share being computed on profit after taxation and unrelieved ACT where applicable; bracketed figures indicate 10 per cent or more difference if calculated on "nil" distribution'; the P/E ratio for the London & Northern Group receives this special treatment.

14.2 Changes in share capital

The next situation to be considered is when the issued ordinary share capital has not remained the same for the whole of the period covered by the profit and loss account. There are two changes that often arise: a scrip issue and an issue of new shares for cash. The latter may be one to the market or one restricted to existing shareholders, i.e. a rights issue.

The purpose of the calculation is to show the earnings available per ordinary share. After a scrip issue the average number of shares is not always appropriate as a divisor. It is the number of ordinary shares in issue at the end of the period that is usually used. The corresponding figures for all earlier periods should be similarly adjusted by using the number of shares in issue after the scrip issue as the divisor.

A different calculation is necessary if the issue is for cash. In this circumstance the attempt must be made to reflect the fact that the company has had the use of the money for only part of the year. If the issue is made at full market price (rare in the UK), it is necessary to apportion the earnings over the average equity share capital. This should be done on a time basis unless there are good reasons for using a different basis. If the issue were at full market value, the weighted average number of shares would be used. There is an implied assumption that the issue for cash at the full market price will not, by itself, reduce the rate of earnings on the assets of the company. Whether the resulting employment of that cash will increase earnings by the appropriate amount is another matter.

If the issue is made at less than the market price (usually a rights issue to existing shareholders), the adustment is more complex. It is necessary to reflect the hybrid nature of the issue, which can be considered partly a scrip issue and partly an issue at full market price.

14.3 Fully diluted earnings per share

In the circumstances listed below, the standard requires, in addition to the basic earnings per share, the calculation and disclosure of the fully diluted earnings per share:

(a) where the company has issued a separate class of equity shares which do not rank for any dividend in the period under review, but which will do so in the future;

(b) where the company has issued debentures or loan stock (or preference shares) convertible into equity shares of the company;

(c) where the company has granted options or issued warrants to subscribe for equity shares of the company.

In each case,

(i) the basis of calculation of fully diluted earnings per share should be disclosed;

(ii) the fully diluted earnings per share need not be given unless the dilution is material. Dilution amounting to 5 percent or more of the basic earnings per share is regarded as material for this purpose;

(iii) fully diluted earnings per share for the corresponding previous period should not be shown unless the assumptions on which it was based still apply;

(iv) equal prominence should be given to basic and fully diluted earnings per share wherever both are disclosed.[2]

The intention is to show the earnings per share if all potential shares had been issued. This potential increase may arise from deferred shares, convertible loan stock, preference shares, warrants, options, partly paid shares not ranking for dividend until fully paid, options to trustees of employee pension, save-as-you-earn schemes, etc.

14.3.1   Deferred equity

When a company has a class of equity shares, e.g. deferred ordinary, which do not rank for dividend during the period under review but will be entitled to dividends in the future, the earnings per share should be calculated on the assumption that this class did rank for dividends from the beginning of the period under review. If there are 2 million ordinary shares in issue throughout the year and 1 million deferred ordinary shares which could be converted into ordinary shares on a one-for-one basis in 1989, the divisor in the calculation of fully diluted earnings per share should be 3 million shares.

The calculation may not be so straightforward when the rights attached to the deferred shares are complex. A quoted company (Pentos Ltd) had an issued share capital of £5,378,000 which included £1,597,000 in deferred ordinary shares of 20p each. One of the notes included in the annual report states:

> The deferred ordinary shares of 20p each are not entitled to receive any dividend for any period ending on or before 31st December 1988. On 1st January 1989 each deferred ordinary share will be sub-divided into two ordinary shares of 10p each, which will rank *pari passu* with the ordinary shares in issue, except for the right to dividends in respect of the year to 31st December 1988 or prior periods.
>
> On a distribution of surplus assets, the deferred ordinary shares participation rights are expressed as a percentage of ordinary shareholders' rights, being equal to them in 1979 (100%), increasing to 110% in 1980 and by a further 10% each year until conversion on 1st January 1989.

In the accounts of this company to 31 December 1979, it was stated that the calculation of the fully diluted earnings per share was based on several assumptions. That relating to the deferred shares states: 'one deferred ordinary share equals one ordinary share, being the same basis as that which would have been applicable on a distribution of surplus assets at the balance sheet date'. By the time the accounts for 1984 were published, the basis of inclusion of the deferred shares in the calculation had changed to: 'one deferred share equals two ordinary shares'. The note describing the rights of the deferred shares was similar to before and reflected that the right in a distribution of assets had now risen to 150 per cent. Presumably the recognition of one-deferred-equals-two-ordinary accepted the use of the the maximum possible dilution.

14.3.2   Convertible loan stock

Where a company has convertible loan stock in issue at any time during the year, the divisor should be adjusted to include the maximum number of shares that could have been issued on conversion, assuming it took place at the beginning of the period under review (or on the date of issue if later). The standard states that the earnings should be adjusted by adding back the assumed saving of interest on the stock so converted, net of corporation tax. An example will illustrate this calculation.

Trading results for year to 31 December 1987

	£
Profit before interest and tax	756,000
Interest on 10% convertible unsecured loan stock	200,000
Profit before tax	556,000
Corporation tax	286,000
Profit after tax	270,000

Capital structure

This consists of issued share capital of £1,000,000 in ordinary shares of 50p, and £2,000,000 convertible unsecured loan stock issued on 1 June 1978 convertible into ordinary shares of 50p on the following terms for £1,000 of stock:

On 31 December 1995 600 shares
1996 600 shares
1997 500 shares

Calculation of earnings per share

Basic earnings per share: 270,000 ÷ 2,000,000 =			13.5p
Fully diluted earnings per share		£	
Earnings as above		270,000	
add Interest	£200,000		
less Tax at 35%	70,000		
		130,000	
Adjusted earnings		400,000	
Shares in issue		2,000,000	
Maximum that could arise following conversion (£2,000,000 ÷ £1,000 × 600)		1,200,000	
Adjusted number		3,200,000	
Fully diluted earnings per share: £400,000 ÷ 3,200,000 =			12.5p

There would have been a corresponding calculation in respect of 1986. Given the purpose of calculating the fully diluted earnings per share, the adjustment relating to the number of shares must be the maximum possible. The example reflected that there had been no conversion during the year. When partial or full conversion occurs, the calculations will need to determine the weighted average.

14.3.3 Options

Despite the prevalence of option schemes, they do not always lead to the publication of a diluted earnings per share. There is the materiality aspect, defined as 5 per cent or more of the basic figure, to be considered. Britoil plc is one company which specifically mentioned options under the Savings Related Option Scheme and the Share Option Scheme, and stated that their inclusion in the earnings per share calculation would have no significant effect.

When new money is to be raised by the exercise of the right, the standard requires the assumption that the proceeds had been invested in $2\frac{1}{2}$ per cent consolidated stock.

The presentation of a fully diluted earnings-per-share figure is particularly necessary where the capital structure or commercial arrangements are such that the benefits of future growth will not accrue entirely pro rata to the existing shareholders. Deferred shares are one example; arrangements to issue additional shares to the vendors if profits from a recent acquisition exceed a given level are another.

The calculation of the dilution effect must reflect the extra equity that may be issued in the future based on the situation at the year-end. The benefits available to holders of convertibles, options, warrants, etc. will be adjusted to reflect rights and scrip issues.

If at 1 January holders of convertible loan stock are entitled to 100 shares for every £1000 and there is a scrip issue to ordinary shareholders on 1 July at the rate of one new share for every two held at that date, then the rights of the holders of the convertible loan stock should be amended. To protect their original benefit, the terms of conversion should be changed so that the 100 shares are increased by the amount of the scrip issue, an extra 50 shares (one for two), so that now the holder of £1000 of convertible loan stock could convert into 150 ordinary shares. This latter quantity will be included in the calculation at the end of the year.

14.4   Associated and subsidiary companies

The earnings of associated and subsidiary companies after charging related tax will have been included in the earnings numerator. The earnings of these companies may be subjected to similar dilution, and, if material, the earnings should be excluded and replaced by the fully diluted equivalent. These circumstances will probably be rare but the possibility needs to be considered where the interests in associated or subsidiary companies are a significant proportion of total earnings.

14.5   Current cost accounts

When a current cost profit and loss account is published,the current cost earnings per share should be calculated and disclosed on a basis similar to that described earlier. Although current practice rarely includes this information, when disclosed it is usually found in the current cost part of the annual report and is frequently lower than the earnings per share based on historical cost accounts. One published annual report showed:

	1981	1980
Earnings per share per historical cost accounts	28.6p	27.5p
Earnings per share per current cost accounts	18.6p	19.3p

Not merely are the current cost earnings per share lower, but the change from 1980 is in the opposite direction. It is unusual to find the earnings per share calculated on these two bases disclosed on the same page, but several companies recognize that shareholders are given a clearer picture if the presentation enables them to make this comparison easily.

14.6 Developments

The discretion allowed to companies with respect to deferred tax following SSAP 15 (see Chapter 7) has encouraged some commentators[3] to suggest that earnings per share before tax may be a useful statistic, certainly when making comparison of companies having a different policy on deferral. An alternative aid to comparability when the company has a below-normal tax charge is to show, as some do, the earnings per share on the basis of full provision for deferred tax.

There is also the possibility (as recommended) that, in due course, the five- or ten-year summary of results produced by many companies will be adjusted to reflect the decline in the purchasing power of the pound sterling. Already there is the obligation to make the figures as comparable as possible when there have been changes in capital during the periods covered by the summary, and earnings per share is one of the frequently included items.

Legal and General Group plc, in its ten-year Financial Review, include earnings per share, after adjustment for capitalization issue, as follows:

	1977	1978	1979	1980	1981	1982	1983	1984	1985	1986
As reported (p)	3.28	3.42	3.55	4.77	6.54	7.53	9.40	9.76	7.86	14.85
RPI adjusted to 1986 prices (p)	6.96	6.70	6.13	6.98	8.56	9.07	10.2	10.71	8.13	14.85

Both bases show the great improvement between 1985 and 1986, but the adjusted basis shows the decline, in purchasing power terms, that was reported in the late 1970s and mid-1980s.

Reference has already been made to the ratio that relates the past earnings to the current quoted market price to produce a P/E ratio. When changes are proposed, e.g. acquisition of a new company, the documents will sometimes refer to the perspective earnings per share and the P/E ratio.

Where assets per share are a significant component of the assessment of company performance, it may be useful to calculate and publish the appropriate value per share. Some investment companies do this, and a few also calculate a fully diluted asset value. Clearly, if dilution is a possibility, the estimated effect should be shown to shareholders.

The standard requires, and normal practice accepts, that the dilution calculation be made by reference to historical earnings. It should be remembered that dilution will arise only if it is in the interest of those who hold options, conversion rights, etc., to exercise them. This will usually depend on a growth in earnings. The *Investors Chronicle* commented that Queen's Moat Houses 'is not very keen on this calculation because it argues that the preference shares cannot be converted until 1988, by which time its earnings will have risen'.[4] The fact remains that, because of the possibility of an increase in shares through the exercising of existing rights, the earnings per share applicable to the present ordinary shareholders may be reduced.

As a result of the distinction between extraordinary and exceptional items, and the difficulty in obtaining consistency, one company, at least, published earnings per share excluding exceptional items. (Remember that extraordinary items are excluded from the calculation by the standard.)

> The directors are of the opinion that it is more meaningful for earnings per share to be calculated before both exceptional and extraordinary items, and accordingly it is on this basis that earnings per share are shown on the consolidated profit and loss account. However, in order to comply with SSAP 3, which requires that earnings per share are stated after exceptional but before extraordinary items, both bases are shown below.[5]

Various earnings per share calculations are then shown in detail. The final effect is:

	Excluding exceptional items		In accordance with SSAP 3	
	1986	1985	1986	1985
Basic (p)	49.5	26.4	54.6	26.8
Fully diluted (p)	45.0	22.4	49.4	22.7

Another company, Britoil plc, moved in the opposite direction. The consolidated profit and loss account included:

	1986	1985
Earnings (loss) per share (p):		
pre-extraordinary items	6.56	50.31
post-extraordinary items	(3.35)	50.31

14.7   Worked example

Consider the following data. The summarized profit and loss and appropriation accounts for Kues plc, which trades entirely in the UK, for the two years ended 31 December 19X1, are as follows:

	19X0		19X1	
	£	£	£	£
Profit before tax		1,008,000		1,315,000
Tax at 35%		352,800		460,250
Profit after tax		655,200		854,750
Dividends				
Preference			67,500	
Ordinary paid	100,000		120,000	
proposed	300,000	400,000	375,000	562,500
Retained profit		255,200		292,250

No unrelieved advanced corporation tax is included in the tax charge. The share capital in issue at 1 January 19X0 was 5,000,000 ordinary shares of 25p each.

On 1 July 19X0 Kues made a bonus issue on the basis of one new ordinary share for every five held.

On 1 April 19X1 £900,000 of 10 per cent convertible £1 preference shares were issued at a premium of 20p. The terms of conversion for every £100 of preference shares were as follows:

Conversion in June 19X7	200 ordinary 25p shares
June 19X8	190 ordinary 25p shares
June 19X9	180 ordinary 25p shares

On 1 August 19X1 Kues announced a rights issue. The basis was one for four at 64p exercisable

on 1 September 19X1. At the close of trading on 31 August, the share-price-cum-rights was 84p and the issue was taken up by all eligible shareholders.

The steps given below calculate the basic and fully diluted earnings per share in accordance with SSAP 3 for 19X1, together with comparative figure(s).

(a) Summarize the history of the ordinary (equity) share capital

		Number of shares	
		Actual (millions)	Actual and potential (millions)
19X0	1 January	5.0	5.0
	1 July—1-for-5 bonus	1.0	1.0
19X1	1 January	6.0	6.0
	1 April—convertible prefs	—	1.8
	1 September—1-for-4 rights	1.5	1.59*
		7.5	9.39

*The rights issue on 1/9/X1 of 1 for 4 at a price of 64p when the market price was 84p includes a bonus element:

Original	4	shares	@	84p each gives a value of	336p
Rights	1	share	@	64p increases the value by	64p
After	5	shares		have a value of	400p

i.e., the theoretical ex-rights price is 80p each.

Before the rights issue, the preference share conversion rights (per £100) were worth a maximum of 200 ordinary shares @ 84p each (i.e. £168). If the preference shareholders are to be given protection for the effects of the rights issue, since the theoretical market price falls to 80p, the corresponding number of shares into which the preference shares could be converted must be increased to £168÷80p= 210. As a result, the maximum number of ordinary shares that might have to be issued is £900,000÷£100 × 210=1,890,000 which, therefore, includes an extra 90,000 arising from the rights issue.

Observe that, since conversion into 210 new shares corresponds to the 200 old shares, the rights issue produces the equivalent of a scrip issue of 10 for 200 or 1 for 20 combined with a new issue of 4 for 21 at the market price.

(b) Calculate the weighted average number of shares in issue
For basic earnings per share for 19X1, the rights issue adjustment factor (from share prices) is 84p÷80p=21/20=1.05. The weighted average number of shares is then

6 million × 1.05	× 8/12=	4.2 million
7.5 million	× 4/12=	2.5 million
		6.7 million

Since the only change in the shares in issue in 19X0 resulted from a bonus issue, the number of shares at the end of the year would be used in calculating the earnings per share (e.p.s.) for that year. However, for comparative purposes, this must be adjusted by the bonus element of the rights issue in the later year, i.e. 6 million × 1.05=6.3 million.

(c) Calculate earnings and basic earnings per share

For 19X1, earnings available for ordinary shareholders are

$$£854,750 - £67,650 = £787,250.$$

The basic e.p.s. is

$$£787,250 \div 6,700,000 = 11.75p \text{ per share.}$$

The basic e.p.s. for 19X0 as calculated at the end of 19X0 is

$$£655,200 \div 6,000,000 = 13.10p \text{ per share.}$$

Adjusting this for bonus element of the rights issue gives the comparative basic e.p.s

$$13.10p \times 1.05 = 12.48p.$$

This may be calculated directly as

$$£655,200 \div 6,300,000 = 12.48p.$$

(d) Allow for any potential dilution from convertibles

Both the earnings and the number of shares must be adjusted. Earnings will reflect the change (an increase) in the amount available to the ordinary shareholders. As the convertibles are preference shares, there is no saving of interest (which may have produced an increase in tax), but the preference dividend will not be paid, so that earnings available are £854,750. The number of shares will increase as a result of the potential conversion. The issue of convertible preference shares for cash took place part-way through the year, so the weighted average approach is appropriate. Once again, the bonus element of the rights issue will be applied throughout the life of the shares:

Weighted average number of ordinary shares already in issue	6,700,000
Convertibles from 1 April: 1.89 million × 9/12	1,417,500
	8,117,500

Fully diluted earnings per share for 19X1 are

$$£854,750 \div 8,117,500 = 10.53p \text{ per share.}$$

Since the diluting effect from 11.75 to 10.53 is more than 5 per cent, it would be regarded as material and disclosed. No comparative fully diluted e.p.s. figure would be calculated because the assumptions on which the 19X1 figure is based do not apply.

14.8 Summary

The calculation of basic earnings per ordinary share to provide a useful statistic is not difficult. If there have been changes, or if there are potential changes in the share capital, the calculations become more difficult arithmetically, but there is no need to change the conceptual basis. As the explanatory note to the standard states, 'Outstanding among the matters of interest to shareholders in quoted companies are earnings per share, dividends per share and the trend of these two figures over a number of years.' Accountants should ensure that these are provided in as meaningful a manner as is possible.

Notes

1. SSAP 3, 'Earnings per Share', ASC, 1972, amended 1974.
2. Ibid., para. 12.
3. M. Gibbs and K. Percy, 'The new standard on deferred tax—implications for earnings per share', *Phillips & Drew Research*, 2 November 1978.
4. *Investors Chronicle*, 23 August 1985, p. 68.
5. Williams Holdings plc, Annual Report and Accounts, 1986.

Further reading

Accounting Principles Board Opinion, no. 15: 'Earnings per Share', AICPA.
Accounting Standards Committee, SSAP 3, 'Earnings per Share', 1972, amended 1974.
Beaver, William, *Financial Reporting: An Accounting Revolution*, Chs. 3 and 4, Prentice-Hall, Englewood Cliffs, NJ, 1981.
Board, J. L. G. and Walker, M. 'Information content of SSAP 16 earnings changes', *Accounting and Business Reseach*, Winter 1985.
Gibbs, Martin and Keith Percy, 'The New Standard on Deferred Tax—Implications for Earnings per Share', *Phillips & Drew Research*, 2 November 1978.
Society of Investment Analysts, 'The new definition of earnings per share under current cost accounting', *Investment Analyst*, January 1981.

Questions

1. Drummond House plc are required to redeem £5.6m 9% debentures at par in July 1988. In order to raise the funds, two schemes are being considered as alternatives for implementation on 1 July 1988.

   The first scheme is to make a 1-for-4 rights issue at 80p per share.

   The second is to issue at £1.40 per unit 4 million units each containing one £1, $7\frac{1}{2}$% convertible stock plus 1 warrant for an ordinary share. The conversion terms are as follows:
   Each £100 of loan stock in July 1988 90 ordinary 50p shares
   or in July 1999 95 ordinary 50p shares
   or in July 2000 100 ordinary 50p shares
   and the warrants may be exercised at the date of conversion, the consideration being $62\frac{1}{2}$p share.

   Based on current prices, the forecast share price on 30 June 1988 is 90p per share and the price of $2\frac{1}{2}$% Consolidated Stock on the same day is 31.25p xd. The directors are anticipating profit before tax for the year ending 31 December 1988 to be £7.5 million under the first scheme. A corporation tax rate of 35% may be assumed.

   The company reported earnings per share of 15.3p for the year to 31 December 1987 based on the 28 million 50p shares currently in issue.

   You are required:
   (a) to compute the earnings per share figures which would be disclosed under each of the alternative schemes assuming the forecasts given above are realized;   (14 marks)
   (b) to explain the treatment given to the rights issue in your calculation.   (6 marks)
                                                                                                                 (20 marks)

2. A summary of the profit and loss account for Browning plc for the most recent two financial years was drawn up in February 1987 and showed the following:

	Year ended	
	31/12/85	*31/12/86*
	£'000s	*£'000s*
Operating profit (see note I)	610	720
less Interest	10	20
Profit before tax	600	700
Tax at 40%	240	280
	360	420
less Unrelieved ACT	—	20
Net profit after tax	360	400

Notes

I.   Operating profit for 1986 is calculated after deducting the following charges shown before tax:
  (i)   loss from bad debt on bankruptcy of customer on 30/9/86   £25,000
  (ii) costs of closure of one of its divisions during June 1986   £50,000
  (iii) loss from fire at warehouse on 3 January 1987   £80,000

II. On 30 June 1985, Browning had issued £200,000 10% debentures convertible into ordinary shares during 1995 on the basis of 150 50p shares for every £100 debentures.

III. On 2 April 1986 Browning made a fully subscribed 1-for-4 rights issue at 60p. The share price at the close of trading on 1 April 1986 had been 75p cum rights at which date 3 million shares of 50p were in issue.

IV. The position of debenture holders was protected from any effects of dilution from the issue.

You are required to

(a) Calculate the earnings per share figures for 1986 together with comparative figure(s) in accordance with SSAP 3.   (20 marks)

(b) Explain the purpose of the adjustment made in your calculation in respect of each of the notes I, to IV.
                                                                                (5 marks)
                                                                            (25 marks)

3. The directors of Dantes plc have supplied you with summarised profit and loss account information for the years ended 30 September 1987 and 1986 as follows:

	30 September 1987	*30 September 1986*
	£'000s	*£'000s*
Profit before tax	1,747	1,492
Taxation	(523)	(395)
Profit after tax	1,224	1,097
Minority interests	(87)	(57)
Dividends—ordinary	(100)	(100)
—preference	(35)	—
	1,002	940

The figure of profit after taxation for the year ended 30 September 1987 supplied to you is after charging extraordinary items of £279,000 net of taxation.

The earnings per share for the year ended 30 September 1986 were disclosed as 10.40p, there having been no changes in the number of shares in issue during that year.

On 1 January 1987 the company had a 1-for-4 rights issue at 60p per share which was fully subscribed. The price at the close of trading on 31 December 1986 was 84p, and 10,000,000 50p ordinary shares were in issue at that date.

On 1 July 1987, in order to raise funds for additional working capital, the company issued a package of units each comprising one £1 7% convertible cumulative preference share plus one warrant for one ordinary share. The issue realised a total of £2.4 million with the preference shares being issued at a premium of 20p. The conversion terms were as follows:

£100 nominal of preference shares in June 1997   110 ordinary 50p shares
                                   or in June 1998   120 ordinary 50p shares
                                   or in June 1999   130 ordinary 50p shares

and one warrant for one ordinary share with the consideration being 60p at the date on which the holder exercises his conversion rights.

The dividend on the preference shares is declared annually on 30 June. The price of $2\frac{1}{2}\%$ consolidated stock at 30 June 1987 was 27 xd.

Assume a corporation tax rate of 35% and that there is no unrelieved ACT or overseas tax.

Requirements
(a) Calculate the basic earnings per share for the year ended 30 September 1987 and restate the basic earnings per share for the year ended 30 September 1986.   (6 marks)
(b) Calculate the fully diluted earnings per share for the year ended 3 September 1987.   (6 marks)
(c) Discuss the usefulness and limitations of published earnings per share figures.   (6 marks)
                                                                                    (18 marks)
                                                          ICAEW, PE II, FA II, December 1987

4. You act in the capacity of financial adviser to a number of companies. One of them, Fig plc, whose managing director is not familiar with finance, has asked you to explain some financial terms which he does not understand and has also asked you to assist him in obtaining certain information. An extract of the letter received from the managing director of Fig plc is as follows:

"I should be grateful if you would briefly explain the following matters:

(1) For ordinary shares quoted in the *Financial Times*, the following particulars:

			Dividend		Yield	
Company	Price	+ or −	net	Cover	gross	P/E
x	x	x	x	x	x	x

(2) This extract from the quotations page of the *Financial Times*:
'Price/earnings ratios are calculated on "net" distribution basis . . . ; bracketed figures indicate 10 per cent or more difference if calculated on "nil" distribution. Covers are based on "maximum" distribution.'

In addition, could you please inform me where I might obtain the following information:
(a) daily share prices for any share quoted on the Stock Exchange, London.
(b) recent dividends and rights issues of UK listed companies.
(c) copies of the financial statements of my competitors, which include both public and private companies in the UK."

Requirement
Draft a letter in reply.   (17 marks)
                                                          ICAEW, PE II, FA II, December 1985

15. Supplementary reports

The profit and loss account and balance sheet, for so long the standard outputs of the double-entry bookkeeping process, are an integral part of that process. In the 1970s, however, there was a demand for additional statements. A statement of the source and application of funds is already required by SSAP 10, and such documents as the 'Corporate Report'[1] and the Green Paper on the reform of company law[2] have suggested many others. These statements are not part of the double-entry system but 'merely' rearrange, emphasize or select particular items. It is argued that they cater for some of the rights of non-shareholders and for the less financially aware shareholders for information. From the wide variety of statements requested by these documents, five have been selected, and consideration is given in the following pages to the statements of source and application of funds, statement of added value, report for employees, simplified reports and segmental reporting. There is also a section on interim reports.

There does not seem to be much enthusiasm by directors to disclose more than is required by statute, standard or stock exchange requirements, although this may change with the economic environment. Topics such as human resource accounting and social accounting are not being discussed or published as frequently as in the late 1970s, and requests for additional information are not common now.

15.1 Statements of source and application of funds

'From the beginning [1902] US Steel has included a Statement of source and application of funds',[3] but in 1980 it was still possible for an auditor to request that the need to produce a statement of this kind should be withdrawn.[4]

The earlier statements were titled 'Summary of financial transactions', and this is as accurate a description as the current one. The old title and the present one imply, in a general sense, a summary of transactions which reflects a particular selection and presentation of cash transactions and some other financial transactions which do not involve cash, but do reflect 'funds', or perhaps more accurately 'resources'.

Reseach by Kafer and Zimmerman[5] provides evidence that the statements were for a number of years used internally by the firms but not necessarily included in the annual report, and even when included were not necessarily audited. In 1971 the APB issued Opinion no. 19, which recommended that a statement of changes in financial position be included in annual reports. This activity was followed in the UK, though a few years later. The ASC issued ED 13 in June 1974 which, after discussion and modification, became SSAP 10 in July 1975 and required a statement to be provided for accounting periods beginning on or after 1 January 1976. However, it is not yet a legal requirement, although it has been included in various proposals for future company law.

Even before it became a requirement under SSAP 10, many companies had produced a statement, and since the required date virtually all quoted companies have produced one. The Old Court Currency fund, registered in the Channel Islands, included the following accounting policy in its 1987 Annual Report:

Statement of Source and Application of Funds
A statement of source and application of funds, as required by International Accounting Standard No. 7, is not included in these accounts. In the opinion of the directors, such a statement has little relevance to this Company.

15.1.1   Scope of the statement

Various authors have considered the definitions of the word 'funds'. Common usage has from time to time expressed a preference for 'net current assets', but the most comprehensive statements reflect changes in all the balance sheet accounts during the period covered by the statement, including the acquisition of assets in exchange for new shares. There is also the 'fund theory of accounting' favoured by public utilities or local authorities, but this need not be considered here. Current commercial practice usually interprets it as a comprehensive statement of 'the sources from which funds have flowed into the company and the way in which they have been used'.[6]

Having decided that the statement will be comprehensive, there is still considerable choice as to which format will be used. There are at least four options:

(a) a 'gross' statement, which lists sources and uses (or applications) separately, adding up to the same total;
(b) a 'net' statement, in which related items are offset;
(c) a narrative single-column statement, leading to an explanation of the change in net working capital, net current assets or net liquid assets;
(d) a narrative single-column statement, leading to an explanation of the change in cash, or borrowing.

Even the gross statement involves a large amount of netting, which takes place through the use of 'profit' rather than 'sales revenue and expenses of activities'. Apart from this, the standard expresses a preference for 'gross' figures, e.g. the disclosure of all sales and purchases of fixed assets, or the disclosure of the proceeds of sales of fixed assets and not merely the profit.

There is a requirement in SSAP 10 to show payments rather than accruals for one particular use; dividends and most presentations treat taxation in a similar manner. But this recognition that it is the actual payments that are significant (see also Chapter 8) does not extend to payments for purchases, which are not on a cash flow basis but are adjusted by creditors, and similarly with revenue receipts, which are adjusted by debtors.

Most statements also distinguish between sources and uses of a recurring nature (i.e. flows from operation) and those that are non-recurring, e.g. capital transactions.

Initially, net liquid funds or working capital formats were the preferred form of presentation, but there is now a movement towards using 'external financing' as the definition of funds, although the former formats are still in the majority.

	1983/4	1984/5	1985/6	1986/7
% of top 300 companies using:				
Net liquid funds	40	31	31	33
Working capital	26	27	24	29
Net borrowing	19	20	21	25
External financing	2	11	12	2*
All; i.e. sources = applications	13	11	12	11
	100	100	100	100

*As the survey says, this movement is difficult to explain. It may be that liquidity matters are not considered so important now.

15.1.2   Presentation

There is no prescribed format, and companies should be encouraged to use the one that best presents their own particular circumstances.

Example 15.1

This example, which illustrates the financing requirement, was issued by Redland plc for the year ended 29 March 1986. It clearly shows the external financing required by the group, and a similar format was used in the following year when a further £276.9 million of financing was required.

Group source and use of funds for year ended 29 March 1986

	1985/6	1984/5
	£m	£m
Source of funds		
Profit before taxation	112.8	108.2
Depreciation	28.4	29.7
Pension and employee participation provisions	1.4	1.9
Sale of assets	2.8	4.4
Total source of funds	145.4	144.2
Use of funds		
Capital expenditure	62.9	43.1
Increase in working capital (note 17)	7.1	1.8
Profits of associates in excess of dividends received	15.2	14.9
Cash cost of extraordinary items	—	5.9
Taxes paid	30.8	20.7
Dividends paid to Redland plc shareholders	23.3	20.6
Dividends paid to minority shareholders	6.4	4.5
Total use of funds	145.7	111.5
Flow of funds		
Net cash flow before acquisitions	(0.3)	32.7
Net acquisitions: purchases less sales of companies, including associates	(29.0)	(38.9)
Net flow of funds	(29.3)	(6.2)
Financing		
Shares issued	0.9	11.7
Increase (decrease) in net borrowings	28.4	(5.5)
	29.3	6.2

Note 17: Group source and use of funds

The statement shown above has been produced by consolidating the statements of individual group companies. Figures for overseas companies have been translated at average rates of exchange. The change in working capital can be reconciled with the group balance sheet as follows:

	Stocks	Debtors	Creditors	Total
	£m	£m	£m	£m
Balance at 30 March 1985	104.7	156.8	(147.0)	114.5
Foreign currency adjustments	(0.9)	(4.6)	—	(5.5)
Net acquisitions and other	(1.8)	(4.7)	1.2	(5.3)
	102.0	147.5	(145.8)	103.7
Net increase shown in source and use of funds	3.4	0.3	3.4	7.1
Balance at 29 March 1986	105.4	147.8	(142.4)	110.8

15.1.3 Preparation of the statement

The usual method of preparing the statement is to compare the balance sheets at the beginning and end of the period, and incorporate the appropriate additional items that are necessary to show 'gross' amounts rather than net ones. Where group accounts are concerned, the statement can be prepared from the consolidated balance sheet and profit and loss account or by consolidating the separate statements prepared by the individual companies. As the statement should be useful to management, each company or significant grouping should have prepared its own statement.

As an example, consider the following question set by the Irish Institute:

The Statement of Standard Accounting Practice No. 10 entitled 'Statements of Source and Application of Funds' requires the audited accounts of all enterprises with a turnover or gross income in excess of £25,000 per annum to include a statement of source and application of funds both for the period under review and for the corresponding previous period.

The annual accounts of Green Ltd for the year ended 30th April, 1977 are set out below....

You are required to—

prepare from the accounts provided a statement of source and application of funds for the year ended 30th April, 1977, in the form recommended in SSAP No. 10 (insofar as the information provided in the accounts will permit);

Green Ltd
Balance Sheet as on 30 April 1977

	1977 £'000s	1976 £'000s
Share capital (see note 2)		
Redeemable preference shares of £1 each	—	20
Ordinary shares of £1 each fully paid	840	700
Undistributed profits	259	71
Loans and debentures	416	555
Trade creditors	583	563
Dividends proposed	42	28
Taxation	44	12
	2,184	1,949
Fixed assets (see note 1)	491	643
Stocks and work-in-progress	893	688
Trade debtors	793	608
Cash balances	7	10
	2,184	1,949

Profit and Loss Account for the Year Ended 30 April 1977

	£'000s	1977 £'000	£'000	1976 £'000
Turnover		2,930		1,563
less:				
Directors' emoluments	70		70	
Auditors' remuneration	6		5	
Interest on loans and debentures	39		46	
Depreciation	6		5	
Other operating expenses	2,724		1,431	
		2,845		1,557
Net trading profit		85		6
Profit on sale of fixed assets		205		—
		290		6
Taxation		40		2
		250		4
Balance brought forward		71		95
		321		99
Transfer to capital redemption reserve	20		—	
Proposed dividend	42		28	
		62		28
Balance carried forward		259		71

Notes

(1) Fixed assets   £'000s
    (i) Freehold property
        At cost 30 April 1976   455
        At valuation 30 April 1977   340
        Properties, which originally cost £235,000, were sold during the year for £425,000.

	Cost £'000s	Depreciation £'000s
(ii) Plant and equipment		
On 30 April 1976	282	94
Additions at cost	53	
Disposals (realising £99,000)	(109)	(25)
Provision for the year		6
On 30 April 1977	226	75

(2) Share capital
No shares had been issued in exchange for cash or other assets during the year.

(ICA Ireland, PE II 4, Summer 1977)

Possible solution

Green Ltd
Statement of source and application of funds for the year ended 30 April 1977

	1977	1976
	£'000s	£'000s
Funds from operations		
Profit for year before depreciation	91	—
Funds from other sources		
Sales of fixed assets	524	—
Total inflow of funds	615	—
Application of funds		
Dividend paid	28	—
Tax paid	8	—
Purchase of fixed assets	53	—
Redemption of preference shares	20	—
Repayment of loan	139	—
	248	—
Net increase in funds	367	—
Changes in working capital		
Increase in stocks and work in progress	205	—
Increase in debtors	185	—
Increase in creditors	(20)	—
Decrease in cash	(3)	—
	367	—

Working sheet

Account	Opening £'000s	Closing £'000s	Change* £'000s	Note	Adjustment £'000s	Statement £'000s
Share capital						
Preference	20	—	(20)			(20)
Ordinary	700	840	140	(2)	(140)	—
Capital reserves				(1)	(120)	—
				(2)	140	
				(3)	(20)	
Undistributed profits	71	259	188	(3)	(188)	—
Profit for year						
before depreciation				(3)	85	91
				(4)	6	
Loans	555	416	(139)			(139)
Trade creditors	563	583	20			20
Dividends proposed	28	42	14	(3)	(42)	—
				(6)	28	
Dividends paid				(6)	(28)	(28)
Taxation	12	44	32	(3)	(40)	—
				(5)	8	
Tax paid				(5)	(8)	(8)
	1,949	2,184	235			
Fixed assets	643	491	152	(1)	120	—
				(4a)	(235)	
				(4b)	53	
				(4c)	(6)	
				(4d)	(84)	
Purchases				(4b)	(53)	(53)
Sales proceeds				(3)	205	
				(4a)	235	
				(4d)	84	524
Stocks and work						
in process	688	893	(205)			(205)
Trade debtors	608	793	(185)			(185)
Cash balances	10	7	3			3
	1,949	2,184	235		0	0

*Increase or (decrease) as the effect on cash balance.

The opening and closing balance sheets are listed, including the description of the additional items that will appear in the statement. The change is calculated but cannot always be incorporated in the statement without further adjustment.

The adjustment column incorporates the entries needed to convert the changes in balance sheet items to the 'movement in funds'. These reflect the double entry rules and are referenced to the working notes.

Working notes
1. Freehold property: from the data it can be seen that property which cost £220,0000 has been revalued at £340,000 to give a surplus of £120,000; but this £120,000 is not a new source of funds, nor does it represent additional expenditure on the asset.
2. Some transactions are not shown—what might they be?

	£
Capital redemption reserve fund	20,000
Revaluation of freehold property	120,000
A total of	140,000
Which has been used for a bonus issue of ordinary shares	140,000

None of these transactions involves a movement of funds, but they all need to be included in the adjustments.
3. Analysis of increase in undistributed profits, i.e. following back through the profit and loss account to net trading profit. The change in undistributed profits (£188) reflects all the profit and loss account transactions, in particular operating profits and profit on sale of fixed assets. These have to be separated by the adjusting entries:

	£	£
(a) Capital redemption reserve	20	
(b) Change in year	188	
(c) Profit before depreciation		85
(d) Proposed dividends	42	
(e) Taxation liability	40	
(f) Profit on sales of fixed assets		205
	290	290

4. Other fixed assets transactions have to be incorporated to show the purchases and proceeds of sales:
    (a) elimination of cost (£235) of property sold;
    (b) separate identification of purchases (£53);
    (c) elimination of depreciation provision to provide 'profit before depreciation';
    (d) elimination of cost (£109), depreciation (£25), i.e. net (£84) in respect of plant and equipment sold.
5. Taxation creditor adjusted to tax paid.
6. Dividend proposed adjusted to dividend paid.

When preparing this statement from the records of a company or group, the actual details that have been calculated above would normally be available by direct inspection.

15 1.4   Other considerations

There are few technical problems in the preparation of the statement. Subsidiary companies will be treated in the same way as in the group accounts, which currently means including the whole of the profit, assets and liabilities of the subsidiary. Dividends paid to minority shareholders are an application; the whole of the amounts retained by partially owned subsidiaries would remain in the statement, reflecting the UK view that the group accounts should show the complete transactions of all members of the group.

Associated companies should also be treated in a manner consistent with that in the traditional statements; i.e., the whole of the investor company's proportionate share of earnings should be included as a source, with the amount retained by the associates shown as a further investment, i.e. as a use. Some statements merely include the dividends received, but this is inconsistent with the treatment required in the profit and loss account under SSAP 2.

It has already been seen that changes in exchange rates can be very significant in explaining the changes between the amounts shown for a particular item at different balance sheet dates. Another event which will produce a similar effect is the acquisition or the disposal of a subsidiary. The explanatory note to the standard states that any purchases or disposals of subsidiary companies should be reflected either (a) as separate items, or (b) by showing the effect on separate assets and liabilities. In either case, it will generally be necessary to summarize the effects of the acquisition or disposal by way of a footnote. This explanation will enable the reader to see the effect caused by this particular event, and will isolate it from those caused by the normal business activities.

15.1.5 Summary

The presentation of this statement has generally been welcomed by users. Some have referred to it as the most useful standard that the ASC has issued. Others, however, merely see it as extra work, and there are still many organizations who produce it only because they are required to do so by the standard.

15.2 Added value

The added value statement shows, first, the difference between the sales of an organization and the raw materials and services purchased from outside the organization. Second, it shows how this added value has been shared among those, including employees, who have contributed to its production. It is a rearrangement of figures included in the profit and loss account.

However, the current financial environment has not encouraged companies to produce this statement on a voluntary basis. The annual Survey of UK Published Accounts[7] has not included a discussion of it since 1983/84, i.e. for companies reporting in 1982/83. In that year, only 21 per cent of the 300 companies analysed produced a statement, compared with 26 and 29 per cent in the preceding years.

15.2.1 Advantages and disadvantages

The advantages of a statement of the distribution of added value compared with a profit and loss account are as follows.
(a) The emphasis is on all members of the 'team', employees, government, lenders and shareholders, who are involved in adding value.
(b) 'Profits' is an unpopular word; added value, it is hoped, will be more popular.
(c) It helps towards a productivity scheme.
(d) The employee participates in added value, but not in profit.
(e) The amount of the government interest is more clearly shown.
(f) The amount by which the resources of the company increase, which includes the depreciation charge, is shown.
(g) It may be a more appropriate measure of size.

There are, however, some disadvantages as well.

(a) The meaning is not the same as the economists' 'added value', or as that used for value added taxation. Perhaps calling these statements 'added value' will avoid confusion with the latter meaning.

(b) The team in a wider sense also include suppliers of goods and services, but they do not participate in added value.

(c) Profit needs to be explained and justified—not swept under the carpet.

(d) Added value as generally disclosed, will be increased if fixed assets are bought rather than rented, and if employees are engaged rather than using subcontractors.

(e) While a classification by recipients is useful (to the recipients!), many have found the normal functional one (i.e. the profit and loss account) also useful.

But are both the profit and loss account and an added value statement needed? Because statements have to serve several purposes, the answer is probably 'yes'—that is, unless the profit and loss account can be reorganized to provide both types of information. Alternatively, it could be a political or public relations decision that the particular organization is going to emphasize profit or added value. Profit measures the wealth accrued to shareholders after all other resources have been paid. Added value measures the wealth accrued by the efforts of shareholders, lenders, workers and the government, i.e. the difference between sales and bought-in goods and services (apart from those specifically mentioned). The definition used above is the UK one—others, e.g. West Germany, have included a depreciation charge before calculating added value. Morley[8] distinguishes between a report that discloses how the whole of the sales revenue has been distributed and one that deals with added value, i.e. with sales minus bought-in goods and services.

15.2.2 Data requirements and presentation

A balancing statement, in which the distribution of added value to the various beneficiaries equals the total added value produced by the organization during the period, has a natural appeal to the double-entry background of most accountants, and is the usual form that is used. It will be noticed in the examples that follow that there are no 'new' figures. The usual ones have been rearranged and presented in what is hoped is a more understandable format.

In this format there are a few definitional and presentational problems—bought-out items, sales taxes, depreciation, non-trading credits, associated companies, and minority interests. Sales is not considered as a problem as, although the use of the statement in macro-economics, where added value in production is used, would be increased if production rather than sales were reported, there is little likelihood of a move away from sales in accounting statements. Sales taxes should be treated as they are already dealt with in the accounts—with VAT excluded, but customs and excise duties included in turnover. But what happens to the duties? Are they deducted as an individual part of payments for goods and services? Clearly not. Are they shown as part of government taxes? Possibly. It is clear that they can be significant and should be separately disclosed, but there is no consistency in the present reporting practice.

Theory (and Morely[9]) suggests that all taxes related to bought-in goods and services should be included as part of the cost of the services. PAYE deducted from the employee and paid by the employer to Inland Revenue should be included with employees' remuneration, and only corporation tax and similar taxes on company income remain to be shown as the government share of added value. It is to be expected that biased presentation will include PAYE and other taxes collected on behalf of the govenment wherever the producer of the statement thinks it will best portray his message to show the government's share of added value as high as possible.

Renshall *et al.* argue that 'added value intended for financial information purposes should be distinguished from the presentation of statements of distribution of added value intended for social accounting'.[10]

Is depreciation a bought-in cost or part of retention? When treated as a bought-in cost, the statement is usually called a 'net' statement, in contrast to the 'gross' added value. The major argument for the gross presentation is that it avoids the subjectivity of deciding upon the depreciation policy. The disadvantage is that, if depreciation is excluded, the gross added value is shown without any charge being made for the use of the plant and machinery and other fixed assets. Practice, which does not always mean that it is theoretically the correct treatment, follows the 'Corporate Report' in using a gross statement; for example, the *Survey of Published Accounts* for 1980 shows that, out of the 300 companies (of whom less than one-third included this statement in their annual report), the most popular approach was 'gross'. This approach has remained the most popular, although the number of companies in the sample including an added value statement had fallen from 84 in 1978/9 to 64 in 1982/3:[11]

	1978/9	1979/0	1980/1	1981/2	1982/3
Calculation of added value: per cent using basis					
Gross of depreciation	82	83	82	83	80
Net of depreciation	6	13	10	10	9
Other	12	4	8	7	11
Total statements	84	90	88	77	64

Non-trading items (and extraordinary/exceptional items, investment income, etc.) are those that complicate the traditional profit and loss account. If they are material, they should appear on the added value statement, so that it reconciles with the audited profit and loss account. This will inevitably make it a more complicated statement, but there is a conflict between clarity, or ease of understanding, and comprehensiveness. When the added value statement is additional to the profit and loss account, perhaps simplicity should be given priority. Is the income from associated companies merely a special case of non-trading income? Certainly, in relation to productivity schemes or a statement with which employees can identify, its inclusion as a separate item will not be relevant unless it is very large.

Minority interests raise a greater matter of principle. While the consolidated accounts are prepared on the basis of including the whole of the activities of the companies in the group, the distribution to minority shareholders must be included with other dividends and their share of retentions included as part of the retentions of the group. Unfortunately, current practice is not so settled, as the following extract from the Gray and Maunders work[12] illustrates.

Minority dividend and retentions	
Shown aggregated	37
Shown partly as distribution partly as retention	12

15.2.3   Statement preparation and presentation

Following the presentation of financial statements in one of the prescribed forms, all the information required is now available from the normal financial statements. It merely requires the selection of the appropriate figures to be incorporated into a pro forma value added statement.

Grand Metropolitan is one of the companies that continues to present a value added statement. The most controversial aspect is that turnover, as in the main financial statements, is defined to exclude VAT and inter-company sales but to include duty on beer, wines and spirits together with rents and royalties receivable.

Based on the published presentation, which is in the form of a multi-coloured block diagram, the pattern over the years shows the following:

	30 September	
	1985	1986
	%	%
Source of value added		
Purchases from suppliers		
of goods and services	55.6	53.7
Value added	44.4	46.3
Turnover	100.0	100.0
Disposal of value added		
Government taxes,		
duties, levies and rates	36.8	38.0
Employees gross pay and		
pensions	42.4	42.0
Interest, dividends and minorities	7.6	7.8
Retained for investment		
in the group	13.2	12.2
	100.0	100.0

Certainly between 1986 and 1985 this shows a clear relationship between the increase in the percentage of added value taken by the government and the reduced percentage retained for investment.

The statement was not covered by the auditor's report. The minority interest appears to include the whole amount attributable to them, not merely the dividends paid out to the minority shareholders; but the item is not significant for this group in these years.

15.3 Simplified reports

The term 'simplified reports' can have at least two meanings: first, a selection from a complex report which provides the salient matter of that report, and second, reports not subject to the same regulations that govern large quoted companies.

It is suggested[13] that individuals do not see the similarity in principle between the content of their own financial statements and those of companies because of the complexity of the latter; hence the need for simplified statements, i.e. statements that can be understood by the recipients, who cannot understand the present ones. Empirical work[14] indicates that most shareholders have difficulty in reading and understanding the annual reports issued to them. The remedies for this are virtually unlimited, and only a few of them are the traditional province of accountants.

The first requirements of the annual report is to satisfy the law. If the law requires so much information to be disclosed, then the accountant cannot be criticized for providing it. If the law were changed so that only 'highlights', or relatively few matters, had to be disclosed to shareholders, then simpler statements would be possible. The corporate report requires information that is relevant, understandable, reliable and comparable, and Hammill[15] states that it should be neutral, complete, timely, objective, consistent and verifiable. Some of these requirements must await the clearer expression of users' needs, and it is most likely that there will be a requirement of 'different statements for different purposes'. There is no reason why these should not be 'simple', rather than complex.

The recent privatization programme provided previously nationalized companies with a large number of shareholders, in many cases first-time shareholders. British Gas plc, on page 1 of its annual report and accounts for the year ended 31 March 1987, makes a special attempt to encourage the shareholder to take an interest. The narrative is reproduced below, together with one example of the more customary 'Highlights of the year'.

YOUR COMPANY

This is our first report to you, as a shareholder in British Gas plc. Its aim is to tell you something about us and what we have been doing over the past year.

Energy is our business—we supply more than half the energy used in British homes and about a third of the energy used by British industry and commerce, apart from fuel for transport. We have more than 17 million customers and, with some three million shareholders, we have one of the largest share registers in the world. So British Gas is a big business, however you measure it.

Most of our profit—and your dividend—comes from selling gas to customers. Our fundamental objective is to provide a safe and reliable gas supply, at a competitive price. We also offer a broad range of services to customers and sell gas appliances through a network of nearly 800 showrooms.

This report describes the achievements of your company during the last financial year; we hope that you will find it interesting and informative. If you are a customer as well as a shareholder, you may have an extra interest in finding out how we keep you supplied with gas and what other services are available.

HIGHLIGHTS OF THE YEAR

	1987	1986
Turnover	£7,610m	£7,687m
Current cost profit before taxation	£1,062m	£ 782m
Current cost profit for the year (after taxation)	£ 575m	£ 402m
Current cost earnings per share	13.9p	—
Dividends per share	4.0p	—
Total funds generated	£1,509m	£1,292m
Capital expenditure	£ 363m	£ 571m

British Gas has chosen to use a current cost basis, but in this context the important aspects are the 'profit before taxation', 'profit after taxation' and 'earnings per share'. The 1986 figures per share were not relevant, owing to the change in capital structure that took place during the year.

Many company reports have contained a 'highlights' page (often in the front of the report), where only a few, but presumably the most important, items from the annual accounts are presented. The Annual Surveys of Published Accounts have shown a great increase in the number of those companies included in the sample of 300 that have produced 'highlights' or a similar summary statement:

	1969/70	1979/80	1981/82
No. of companies presenting 'highlights'	69	210	213

There was clear agreement on the most important items, as over 190 companies in 1981/82 included turnover, profit (various definitions), earnings per share and dividends per share. Over the years, more companies have included dividends per share, presumably reflecting the perceived interest of shareholders in this particular statistic.

Without moving to a consideration of the 'statistical summary', there are other items that are regularly included in 'highlights' statements. These include capital employed (129 companies), assets per share (92), dividend cover (50) and return on capital employed (47). It is to be expected that there would be a great variety, as it is the particular items that a particular company considers important that will be included.

It is perhaps a sign of change that small companies are allowed to file with the Registrar of Companies a balance sheet with very much less detail than that which has to be circulated to shareholders. Neither a profit and loss account nor a statement of source and application of funds is required. This simplification was probably justified, as it is normally creditors who use the filed information, and they are more interested in the asset and liability situation than in the profit and loss account as an indication of the security to support any loan that they might be considering. Full statements are still required for the shareholders. The use of audio-visual presentations is also clearly designed to improve communications with shareholders by another method. It may not lead to simpler statements, but if an understanding of the financial situation is improved the statements will appear to be simpler.

Section 255 of the Companies Act 1985 states that, when a company publishes abridged accounts, those accounts must be accompanied by a statement that indicates:

(a) that the abridged accounts are not full financial statements;
(b) whether or not the full financial statements have been delivered to the Registrar of Companies;
(c) whether or not the auditors have reported on the full financial statements;
(d) whether or not the auditors' report was qualified.

15.4   Reports for employees

Reasons for producing a report for employees are many and include the following.

(a) The existing annual report is designed for the shareholder, not the employee; but the latter, or his representative, is entitled to information under the Trade Union and Labour Relations Act 1974 and other legislative measures, in particular 'to assist in collective bargaining'.
(b) European influences on accounting and worker participation, in Germany in particular, increase the need to provide better information to works' councils and other groups of employees.
(c) The 'Corporate Report' considered that those who had 'reasonable rights to information concerning the reporting entity' included the employee group.
(d) Such a report will help to stifle rumours.
(e) It will help to improve public relations.
(f) It will help to improve industrial relations.

Most of these reasons reflect the widening responsibilities of directors and management and the need for better communication. Some, including Hilton,[16] would say that it is not an accountant's problem, or, more strongly, that the accountant is the last person to be in involved in preparing the report. However, it would be unwise for the accountant to abrogate his responsibilities in this area. It has also been suggested that there is nothing worth communicating about accounting until there is an agreed basic principle of measuring profit, and taking account of inflation.[17]

Even with SSAP 16 in operation, there was little enthusiasm from employees to recognize 'real' profits, and it has to be agreed that in the present circumstances those profits based on the basic historical cost convention offer the best opportunity of employee acceptance.

There is little doubt that accountants should be involved in the preparation of a report to employees, and there are four key areas that deserve consideration:

(a) What are the objectives? Why is an employee report being produced?

(b) What form of report—special, house journal? How frequently?
(c) Whose responsability—a communication expert (most unlikely to be the accountant) or an ex-accountant?
(d) What should it contain?

15.4.1   What should be included?

There are three basic concepts:[18]
(a) An employees' report should contain at least what is sent to shareholders, together with more specific employee-related information. 'The employee wants to know that his job is safe, orders are still coming in, reasonable prospects for a pay increase.' 'He wants local information'— his world, his factory, his workmates, his product, his future.
(b) It should include whatever the employees want, though this may cause some concern to management.
(c) It should adopt a business planning approach. Some use the main purpose of an employees' report as a contribution to the improvement of industrial performance. This purpose abandons the idea that information is or should be presented objectively, and the report to employees becomes an aid in the attainment of the business objectives.
There are extensive lists of what might be useful, including a notable one produced by the CBI.[19]

15.5   Interim accounts

An article in *Accountancy* in 1979[20] concluded that the preparation of the interim report had been ignored. It has not received much attention over the last few years, and the FASB discussion memorandum[21] indicates that there are several important unanswered questions. It is a requirement of the listing agreement[22] that companies are 'to prepare a half-yearly or interim report which must be sent to the holders of securities or inserted as a paid advertisement in two leading daily newspapers not later than four months after the end of the period to which it relates.[9] The minimum information required to be included is: net turnover; profit or loss; taxation; minority interests; extraordinary items; profit (or loss) attributable to shareholders; rates of dividend and amount; earnings per share; comparative figures: It is acknowledged that the figures are unaudited, but is recommended that steps should be taken by the directors to ensure that the accounting policies applied to interim figures are consistent with those applied to annual accounts.

Interim statements are prima facie not considered to be abridged accounts as they relate to only a three-, six- or nine-month period and not a full year. When the interim statement contains figures for a full year, then it may be considered an abridged account and will require the appropriate statement (see above).

15.5.1   Purposes

This requirement, though limited to the profit and loss account, provides a reason for the quoted company to prepare interim statements. It says nothing precise about how the usual policies applied to annual accounts should be applied to interim statements. The objectives are not clearly stated, but the FASB offers several:[23]
● as an estimate of earnings for the current year;

- as an estimate for forecasts generally;
- to help identify turning points;
- to evaluate managerial performance;
- as a supplement to the annual report.

The document also emphasizes that there are two basic views of reporting for interim periods: the intergral view and the discrete view.

The integral view accepts that the full year is the primary reporting period and that, if in doubt, estimated annual expenses should be related to parts of a year in proportion to an activity base (e.g. sales or production). Some of its characteristics are reasonably constant operating profit margins, and the use of annual estimates of revenue and expenses.

In the discrete view, each period (of whatever length) is treated as a complete accounting period. The accounting policies are exactly the same as in the annual accounts. In practice, most companies use both views for different types of expense, but there is the need for greater comparability. Depreciation is one example of an expense which on the straight-line basis is calculated for a year, but is often apportioned to months on an activity basis. Maintenance, particularly for major items, is often equalized over a year for purposes of internal reporting, so that at the end of the first half-year there could be a substantial balance which would be carried forward to the second half, where in many cases a balance would not be carried forward to the following year. This discrete view would seem to be the one expected by the Stock Exchange, and the view that follows from the implementation of an accounting system which provides valuable information on a regular basis. Why should the identification of slow moving stock, or slow paying debtors, be an 'annual accounts' exercise? They should be part of the regular routine, and the results of any decisions regarding valuation should be incorporated immediately. The idea of 'year-end' adjustments encourages the suggestion that, when the result is known, adjustments can be considered.

The concept of matching revenues and expenses takes on a different scale as the accounting period shortens. What may be acceptable as 'not material' in relation to a year can become significant in relation to quarterly or even half-yearly figures.

15.5.2 Content of interim reports

What could be disclosed? The Stock Exchange requirements relate to the profit and loss account items only, and it is noticeable that very few interim statements include balance sheets or statements of source and application of funds. The *Survey of UK Published Accounts* for 1979/80 examined a sample of 100 interim reports and found four with balance sheets and two with statements of source and application. Disclosure increased significantly in 1980/81 to 10 and 2 but dropped back slightly in 1981/82 to 9 and 2.[24] During the liquidity crisis a balance sheet would have been of great value, and it was surprising that it did not become standard practice or requirement. Banks and insurance companies have published half-yearly statements of assets and liabilities since the mid-nineteenth century, but for other activities it is unusual.

A non-statistical sample has suggested that interim reports are becoming longer; one, Britoil plc, issues 'The six months in brief'—necessary as the report is eight pages of A5 size. Balance sheets seem to appear more frequently than one in ten cases, and many include comments on future prospects.

The BOC Group also published an eight-page report for the six months to 31 March 1987. It consisted of a chairman's statement, group results unaudited, segmental information and a condensed balance sheet.

Group Results, Unaudited

	Six months to 31 March 1987 £m	*Six months to 31 March 1986 £m*
Turnover, including related companies	1,127.1	1,147.7
less: Turnover of related companies	191.9	196.5
Turnover	935.2	951.2
Operating costs	(799.4)	(837.5)
	135.8	113.7
Share of profits of related companies	8.8	9.0
Operating profit	144.6	122.7
Interest	(24.9)	(30.6)
Profit on ordinary activities before tax	119.7	92.1
Tax (note 1)	(34.3)	(30.4)
Profit on ordinary activities after tax	85.4	61.7
Minority interests	(8.5)	(7.4)
Earnings	76.9	53.3
Extraordinary items	(2.8)	—
Earnings per share, net basis fully diluted (note 2)	16.74p	11.95p

Notes

1. Overseas tax included in the tax charge amounted to £17.7m (1986, £18.6m) and related companies tax to £1.5m (1986, £1.5m).
2. The number of shares used in the earnings per share calculation was 464.7m (1986, 461.4m).
3. An interim dividend of 5.15p net per share (£23.4m) will be paid on 5 October 1987 to the holders of ordinary shares registered at close of business on 7 August 1987 (last year 4.37p; £19.6m).

Condensed Balance Sheet, Unaudited

	At 31 March 1987 £m	*At 30 Sept 1986 £m*
Employment of capital		
Fixed assets		
Tangible assets	1,192.6	1,241.8
Related companies and other investments	154.4	156.5
Working capital		
Working capital (excluding bank balances and short-term loans)	256.5	232.2
	1,603.5	1,630.5

	At 31 March 1987 £m	At 30 Sept 1986 £m
Capital employed		
Shareholders' capital and		
reserves	967.4	936.9
Minority shareholders' interests	86.4	76.3
Non-current liabilities and		
provisions	78.2	88.3
Net borrowings and finance leases	471.5	529.0
	1,603.5	1,630.5

Note

Financial data for the year to 30 September 1986 has been extracted from the unaudited pro forma financial data published in the annual report for that period. This data abridged and restated the full group accounts on the bases adopted with effect from 1 October 1986 whereby asset revaluations are limited to land and buildings. The 1986 accounts received an unqualified auditors' report and have been delivered to the Registrar of Companies.

The note to the balance sheet is necessary owing to the listing agreement and the change in the basis of accounting.

This example is unusual in that the profit and loss account compares the six months to 31 March 1987 with the six months to 31 March 1986, whereas the balance sheet compares 31 March 1987 with 30 September 1986. Many interim reports would also include the 12 months to 1987, which enables the results for the previous six months to be computed, and the balance sheet at 31 March 1986. The choice will presumably be governed by the possibility of seasonal variations. The objective is to provide a valid set of comparative accounts, and some activities are much more seasonal than others.

There is a clear indication that the interim material is unaudited, and this illustrates the problem that can arise with the choice of a comparative date or period. For the balance sheet, the end of the period is an appropriate date and the corresponding dates a year and half a year ago provide a suitable comparison. Should there have been more detail regarding extraordinary items? The line has to be drawn somewhere, and, in the absence of more comprehensive disclosure requirements, the judgement of the directors must prevail.

Disclosure takes place either by circulation to shareholders or by publication in the press, and, as with the annual report, there is a wide range in the volume and quality of presentation.

15.6 Segmental reporting

This refers to the provision of information about the segments that contribute to the overall results or financial position of an economic entity. The most common examples are turnover analysed into product groups, and/or geographical areas.

It has been argued that segmental information is useful to creditors and investors. 'Financial reports should provide information enabling investors to make judgements about profitability, growth and risk of an enterprise.'[25] Consequently, information relevant to these aspects for the different segments is necessary. Arguments against the disclosure of segment information refer to the difficulty of providing understandable, relevant information, and to the potential commercial security risks associated with the disclosure of detailed information to potential competitors. Particular concern for both reasons may arise in connection with a new segment. Early expenditure is often unprofitable, although there may be great prospects, and early disclosure may alert competitors.

However, the decision to provide segmental information is not the end of the discussion. It provides the reason for considering the related problems of identification of segments for reporting purposes: items that will be disclosed (content); the allocation of common costs, revenues, assets, etc., among segments (measurement); reporting inter-segment transactions; materiality; presentation and audit.

15.6.1   Identification of segments

Segments may be identified by using a standard comprehensive list and requiring entities to show the specified information for each item on the list, or by leaving it to the discretion of management. Whichever method is chosen, there is the question of which basis, or bases, of analysis should be adopted:[26]

(a) organization lines such as divisions, subsidiaries, or

(b) areas of economic activity, e.g.
      i)   the products and types of services;
      (ii) the industries in which the company is active;
      (iii) the markets that are served;
      (iv) the geographical areas in which products are manufactured, sales are made.

Most authorities recognize that organizational lines would be meaningful in this context only if they coincided with areas of economic activity. (Results of subsidiaries are usually on 'file' and may be included in group annual report.) Product classification would require substantial detail unless aggregated, which leads to an industry line of business classification (SIC) and is the basis used by the FASB. Segmentation on a geographical basis is not an alternative. It is a distinct and valuable additional analysis, as geographic risk is different in character from industry risk — reflecting inflation, exchange rates, politics, expropriation.

The Companies Act 1985 (sch. 4, 55 c. 2, 3, 4 & 5) requires the disclosure of turnover analysed by different markets (which has been interpreted to mean a geographical analysis).

15.6.2   Which figures should be analysed?

In regard to profit and loss account information, it is generally accepted that the turnover and profit or loss of each line of business should be reported, the profit or loss being arrived at before taking into account taxation, minority interests and extraordinary items. This definition ignores the different rates of taxation and interests of minorities, and it could be argued that the 'bottom line', i.e. earnings from each line of business, available to ordinary shareholders is what is really required.

From data in the Rio Tinto Zinc accounts it is possible to calculate that, for example, energy provided 36 percent of the profit before tax, but only 29 per cent of the net profit attributable to ordinary shareholders.

It is a Stock Exchange regulation that requires UK quoted companies to produce an analysis of profits.

The complete analysis and disclosure of balance sheet items is usually rejected, but in some cases it will be possible to allocate accurately the fixed assets, stock, debtors and creditors for each line of business, and even if the components are not disclosed separately, some companies do provide 'net capital employed' by segment. It is only in special circumstances that other financial statements, e.g. source and application of funds, added value, employees, are disaggregated.

The most recent information available is from the companies reporting in the years ended 30 June 1983[27] and 1986, when 50 and 57 companies out of the 300 did not disclose any segmental data. The percentage of those 250 or 243 companies who reported particular items is as follows:

	By activity		Geographically	
	1983	1986	1983	1986
Turnover	82	89	76	88
Profit	76	78	53	40
Employees	8	n/a	16	n/a
Net assets	10	n/a	13	n/a
Capital expenditure	7	n/a	6	n/a

15.6.3   Allocation of common costs, revenues and assets

This is no easier for financial reporting purposes than for product costing and could be equally misleading unless the effect of fixed costs is carefully considered. As often, the FASB had proposed clearer instructions, requiring

> the contribution from a line of business to be disclosed at two stages:
> (a) the 'profit or loss contribution', which is defined as 'revenue minus directly traceable costs and expenses', in other words those costs which are incurred directly by, or are otherwise directly identifiable with, only one line of business;
> (b) the 'operating profit or loss', which is the profit or loss contribution as in (a) above minus an allocation of those costs and expenses which, although not directly identifiable to only one line of business, are capable of allocation to a number of lines of business on a reasonable basis.[28]

The statement, however, requires presentation of only operating profit or loss for reportable segments. The main reason for the change seems to have been the difficulty to distinguish between 'directly traceable' and 'allocatable'.

15.6.4   Inter-segment activity

Inter-segment activity provides another opportunity for the disciplines of financial reporting and audit requirements to re-examine the normal managerial accounting procedures for reporting inter-segment transactions. Clearly, from the managerial aspect all sales and purchases are relevant, yet it is a well accepted practice that reported turnover is that outside the group. Unless both are shown, there is the danger that readers will attempt to relate unrelated amounts. The pricing of these transfers may (should!) be at 'marginal cost' to the segment for optimal decision-making, but 'market price' might seem more appropriate for calculating public reporting segment results. It is 'market price' for which preference has been expressed by the international bodies – the United Nations, OECD and IASC.

Materiality in this context means the number of segments to be disclosed. The FASB has some quantified tests, based on 10 per cent. An alternative is managerial discretion as to what is significant, particularly with respect to new or declining segments. Perhaps the criteria for disclosure should also reflect any change in the direction of the activities of the entity.

15.6.5   Presentation

Presentation is a very discretionary area at the moment. There is no UK standard for this topic, and even if there were it is very unlikely that format would be prescribed. There is scope for imaginative illustration, but many companies provide a straightforward listing, although some of them attempt to integrate the different bases of analysis. The FASB requirement is to provide audited information, but it is only since the adoption of EEC rules that there has been a legal requirement for audit in the UK. All the problems discussed in this note will have to be decided with the auditors, and this is probably one further reason for the cautious approach that has been adopted with respect to this topic.

GEC provided an analysis of results by class of business:

Classes of business	Profit £m		Turnover £m		Employees '000s	
	1987	1986	1987	1986	1987	1986
Electronic Systems & Components	198.0	206.1	2,016	1.949	59	58
Telecommunications & Business Systems	93.8	84.2	749	773	19	21
Automation & Control	45.4	47.2	457	444	16	17
Medical Equipment	26.0	22.2	398	420	6	6
Power Generation	49.9	58.3	594	638	14	15
Electrical Equipment	51.3	43.0	723	770	28	29
Consumer Products	34.6	33.4	387	331	10	10
Distribution & Trading	12.4	13.1	202	209	4	4
Other activities	4.4	4.0	105	128	4	5
	515.8	511.5	5,631	5,662	160	165

These figures may be used by shareholders or analysts to help in the assessment of the company. One statistic that is probably widely computed is profit per pound sterling of turnover (or profit/sales percentage, or the turnover needed to produce £1 of profit); another might be profit (or turnover) per employee, or increase in turnover for each class, etc.

15.6.6   Prospects

This topic will continue to be of interest in national and international accounting for several years. The increasing concern of the United Nations with the activities of multinational corporations will ensure that politics as well as accounting will be important influences.

In March 1987, the Accounting Standards Committee received a report from a working party on segmental reporting. There is already an international standard, 'IAS 14', and it is unusual for the UK requirements to be less formalized than the international ones.

Notes

1. Accounting Standards Committee, 'The Corporate Report', ASC, 1975.
2. 'The Community and the Company: Reform of Company Law', Report of a working group of the Labour Party Industrial Policy Sub-committee, London, May 1974; see also 'The Future of Company Reports', Cmnd. 6888, July 1977, and 'Company Accounting and Disclosure', Cmnd. 7654, September 1979.
3. T. A. Lee, 'Company Financial Statements: An Essay in Business History 1830–1950', in T. A. Lee and R. H. Parket (eds), *The Evolution of Company Financial Reporting*, Nelson, London, 1979.
4. 'Letters to the Editor' *Accountants Weekly*, 21 November 1980.

5. K. Kafer, and V. K. Zimmerman, 'Notes on the Evolution of the Statement of Sources and Application of Funds', in Lee and Parker, *Evolution of Company Financial Reporting.*
6. Accounting Standards Committee, SSAP 10, para. 3.
7. L. C. L. Skerratt (ed.), *Financial Accounting: A Survey of UK Published Accounts*, ICAEW, various years.
8. M. Morley, *The Value Added Statement*, Gee, ICAS, 1978.
9. Ibid., p. 52.
10. M. Renshall, R. Allan and K. Nicholson, *Added Value in External Financial Reporting*, ICAEW, 1979.
11. Skerratt, *Survey of UK Published Accounts*, various years.
12. S. J. Gray and K. T. Maunders, *Value Added Reporting: Uses and Measurement*, ACCA, 1980, Table 15. (The book also includes a selected bibliography of 172 items.)
13. A. E. Hammill, *Simplified Financial Statements*, ICAEW, 1979.
14. T. A. Lee and D. P. Tweedie, *The Private Shareholder and the Corporate Report*, ICAEW, 1977.
15. Hammill, *Simplified Financial Statements*, p. ii.
16. A. Hilton, *Employee Reports*, Woodhead Faulkner, London, 1978.
17. Ibid., p. v. (Foreword by Sir Ronald Leach).
18. Ibid., p. 24.
19. *The Provision of Information to Employees*, CBI, 1975.
20. H. Lunt, 'Interim reports—the poor relation?' *Accountancy*, March 1979.
21. Financial Accounting Standards Board, *An Analysis of the Issues Related to Interim Financial Accounting and Reporting*, FASB, May 1978.
22. *Admission of Securities to Listing* (The Yellow Book), Stock Exchange, London, 1984, Section S.Ch. 2.
23. FASB, *Analysis of the Issues*, p. 15.
24. Skerratt, *Survey of UK Published Accounts*, various years.
25. S. C. Gray, in T. A. Lee (ed.) *Developments in Financial Reporting*, Longman, London, 1981; see also C. Emmanuel, in *Research Conference Accountancy*, September 1987.
26. ICAEW (Coopers & Lybrand), 'Analysed Reporting—A Background Study', ICAEW, 1977.
27. C. R. Emmanuel in L. C. L. Skerratt (ed.), *Financial Reporting, 1983–1984: A Survey of UK Published Accounts*, ICAEW, 1984; and D. J. Tonkin, in ibid., 1986–87, ICAEW, 1987.
28. Exposure draft and FAS 14: 'Financial Reporting for Segments of a Business Enterprise', FASB, 1976.

Further reading

Statements of source and application of funds
Arnett, H. E., *Proposed Fund Statement for Managers and Investors*, National Association of Accountants, 1979.
Bowen, R. M., D. Burgstahler and L. Daley, 'The incremental information content of accrual versus cash flows', *Accounting Review*, October 1987.
Knox, R. W., *Statements of Source and Application of Funds—A Practical Guide to SSAP 10*, ICAEW, London, 1977.
Lee, T. A. and R. H. Parker (eds), *The Evolution of Company Financial Reporting*, Nelson, London, 1979.
Woolf, E., 'Does ED 13 really stand up to scrutiny?' *Accountancy*, October 1974.

Added value statements

Certified Accountant, 'Value in value added?', *Certified Accountant*, April 1986.

Cox, B, 'Added value and "The Corporate Report"', *Management Accounting*, April 1976.

Gray, S. J. and K. T. Maunders, *Value Added Reporting: Uses and Measurement*, Association of Certified Accountants, 1980. (Includes a selected bibliography of 172 items.)

Morley, M. F., *The Value Added Statement*, Gee, ICAS, 1978.

Morrell, J., 'A way to improve', *Certified Accountant*, May 1986.

Renshall, M., R. Allan and K. Nicholson, *Added Value in External Financial Reporting*, ICAEW, 1979.

Rutherford, B. A., 'Published statements of value added: a survey of three years' experience', *Accounting and Business Research*, Winter 1980.

Skerratt, L. C. L. (ed.), *Financial Reporting: A Survey of UK Published Accounts*, 1979–80.

Simplified statements

Hamill, A. E., *Simplified Financial Statements*, ICAEW, 1979.

Employee reports

CBI, *The Provision of Information to Employees*, 1975.

Goodlad, J. B., *Disclosure of Financial Information to Employees*, ICMA, 1976.

Hilton, Anthony, *Employee Reports*, Woodhead Faulkner, London, 1978.

Hussey, R., *Who Reads Employee Reports?*, Touche Ross, London, 1979.

Marsh, A. and R. Hussey, *Disclosure to Unions—How the Law is Working*, Touche Ross, London, 1979.

Wilkinson, W. Roderick, 'Telling employees the "facts"', *Management Accounting*, November 1980.

Interim reports

American Institute of Certified Public Accountants, Accounting Principles Board no. 28: 'Interim Financial Reporting', AICPA, New York, 1973.

Courtis, J. K., 'Interim reporting issues and uncertainty reduction', *British Accounting Review*, April 1987.

European Federation of Financial Analysts Societies, 'Standards for Interim Information', Second Report of the Corporate Information Committee, Fédération Européene des Associations d'Analystes Financiers, August 1972.

Financial Accounting Standards Board, 'An Analysis of the Issues related to Interim Financial Accounting and Reporting', FASB, May 1978.

Lunt, M. H. C., 'The Role of Interim Accounts and Preliminary Announcements in Financial Reporting in the UK', ICAEW, 1982.

Schiff, M., 'Accounting Reporting Problems—Interim Financial Statements', Financial Executives Institute, 1978.

Segmental reporting

Emmanuel, C. R. and Garrod, N., 'On the segment identification issue', *Accounting and Business Research*, Summer 1987.

General

Lee, T. A. (ed.), *Developments in Financial Reporting*, Philip Allan, Oxford, 1981.

Questions

1. Explain why it is desirable that financial statements should be more easily understood by the shareholder, and how this could be achieved.
2. Describe the purpose of a statement of source and application of funds.
3. Describe and explain the alternative presentations which have been used in published statements of source and application of funds in respect of:
   (a) dividends,
   (b) taxation,
   (c) dividend paid to minority shareholders,
   (d) dividend from associated company,
   (e) profit on sale of plant.
4. Some statements of source and application of funds explain the change in bank balance and others the change in working capital. Discuss the significance of this different presentation.
5. The added value statement is said to be more popular with employees. Explain why this may be true.
6. Why should the company wish to explain financial matters to its employees? Discuss alternative methods which could help to achieve this objective.
7. Distinguish between 'a report for employees' and 'an employment report'. List the usual components of each type of report.
8. Describe the purpose of an interim statement.
9. Explain the difference between the integral view of interim accounts and the discrete view.
10. Should information about segments of a business enterprise be included in financial statements? Why or why not?
11. What approach should be taken in specifying segments to be reported externally?
12. What segment information relating to the results of opertions (income statement) should be reported?
13. What segment information relating to the financial position of an enterprise (balance sheet) should be reported?
14. What segment information relating to the statement of changes in financial position should be reported?
15. What disclosures are necessary in addition to segment information relating to the income statement, balance sheet and statement of changes in financial position?
16. To which business enterprises should a requirement for reporting segment information be applicable?
17. How should segment information be presented?
18. Under what circumstances should previously reported segment information which is presented in the current period for comparative purposes be retroactively restated?
19. To what extent should segment informtion be included in interim financial reports?
20. How important is an agreement on materiality to a requirement for the inclusion of segment information in financial statements to be acceptable? Why or why not?
21. Manvers Ltd includes with its financial statements each year a statement of value added. The draft value added statement for the year ended 31 May 1986 is as follows:

	£	£
Revenue from sales		204,052
Bought in materials and services		146,928
Value added by the company		57,124
applied to:		
The benefit of employees		
Salaries	16,468	
Deductions for income tax and national insurance	3,352	
	13,116	
Pension schemes	2,810	
Employees' profit sharing schemes	525	
Welfare and staff amenities	806	
		17,257

	£	£
Central and local government		
Value added tax	30,608	
Corporation tax	985	
Local rates	325	
Tax etc. deducted from salaries and loan interest	3,832	
		35,750
The providers of capital		
Interest on loan capital	1,600	
Income tax deducted	480	
	1,120	
Interest on bank overdrafts	250	
Dividends to shareholders of the company	500	
		1,870
The replacement of assets and the expansion of the business		
Depreciation	1,835	
Retained profits	412	
		2,247
		57,124

Discussion among the board of directors on the draft figures has revealed a wide variation of opinion on the usefulness of the value added statement to the readers of the accounts.

Some board members say that the added value statement is confusing as it is only a redrafting of the results which are shown in the profit and loss account which gives all the information necessary. Another view is that the statement of changes in financial position is far more important and this should be given in place of the value added statement.

Required

(a) A report to the directors showing the advantages of the value added statement comparing it with the profit and loss account and the source and application of funds statement. Your report should deal specifically with the points raised in discussion by the directors. (18 marks)

(b) Construct a profit and loss account from the information given. (8 marks)

(c) Calculate the operating profit for use in a statement of changes in financial position. (4 marks)

(30 marks)

ACCA, 2.9, AAP 2, June 1986

22. The form and content of published accounts are constantly under discussion to make them more understandable. "The Corporate Report", issued as a discussion paper by the Accounting Standards Steering Committee in August 1975, stated:

"Understandability does not necessarily mean simplicity, or that information must be presented in elementary terms, for that may not be consistent with the proper description of complex economic activities. It does mean that judgement needs to be applied in holding the balance between the need to ensure that all material matters are disclosed and the need to avoid confusing users by the provision of too much detail. Understandability calls for the provision, in the clearest possible form, of all the information which the reasonably instructed reader can make use of and the parallel presentation of the main features for the use of the less sophisticated."

Your client in the motor industry wishes to improve communcation with his employees and has sent you as financial adviser the following information for the year ended 30th June 1986:

Sales (£m)	Total	UK	USA	Europe	Other
Motorcycles	1,450	725	275	385	65
Cars	1,325	520	280	20	505
Vans	490	410	25	35	20
Commercial	235	105	130	—	—
	3,500	1,760	710	440	590

Trading profit (£m)	Total	UK	USA	Europe	Other
Motorcycles	110	55	10	20	25
Cars	65	25	15	10	15
Vans	35	12	8	15	—
Commercial	30	8	22	—	—
	240	100	55	45	40

Other information Year ended 30 June	Shares	Dividend	Profit after tax	Retail price index	Market share
1982	3.0 m	10p	£4 m	390	2%
1983	3.5 m	10p	£10 m	437	3%
1984	3.75 m	12p	£28 m	472	5%
1985	3.75 m	12p	£35 m	495	6%
1986	4.0 m	13p	£75 m	510	9%

Requirements

(a) Briefly describe some of the main methods by which accounting information can be presented in a simplified manner suitable for employees and general readers. Your answer should include an illustration of two of these methods using the information above. (10 marks)

(b) Discuss the trends, advantages and disadvantages of recent attempts to improve the understandability of published accounting reports for the 'less sophisticated reader". (8 marks)

(18 marks)

ICAEW, PEII, FAII, December 1986.

23. Snoweagles Ltd is a private company and operates in the soft fruit industry. It has the following summarised statistics for the three accounting periods ended 31 March 1984, 1981/82 being its first accounting period:

	1981/82 (9 months)	1982/83 (Year)	1983/84 (Year)
Employees	43	45	48
	£	£	£
Turnover	1,200,000	1,500,000	1,350,000
Gross assets	800,000	600,000	750,000
Creditors and provisions	140,000	110,000	120,000

In addition, for the year ended 31 March 1985, the following details are available:

Turnover	£1,450,000
Employees:	
Directors	7
Other full time employees	40
Part time employees (each worked 26 weeks of the year)	10
Gross assets	£680,000
Creditors and provisions	£115,000

Requirements

(a) State concisely the provisions for determining whether small or medium sized companies may or may not submit modified accounts under the Companies Act 1981 (now part of the Companies Act 1985). (4 marks)

(b) Demonstrate whether Snoweagles Ltd can file modified accounts in any of the four accounting periods ended 31 March 1985. (6 marks)

(c) Briefly identify the information which can be omitted from the modified accounts of a medium sized company and the information which needs to be included in the modified accounts of a small company. (7 marks)

(17 marks)

ICAEW, PEII, FAII, December 1985

16. Special-purpose transactions

16.1 Introduction

Whereas the issue of inflation accounting was the 'hot' topic of the 1970s and early 1980s, one that was controversial and caused the ASC many headaches, off-the-balance-sheet financing, took its place in the late 1980s. One of the main reasons for introducing accounting standards was to help eliminate some of the creative accounting techniques that existed; and the development of off-the-balance-sheet financing was the most creative accounting technique of all. With this form of finance, a company simply may not disclose a financial transaction in its annual accounts. This causes particular problems to the users of companies' financial reports, to the banks as creators of imaginative financing schemes, but all the more so in that the banks in their own accounts may not record all the financial commitments with which they could be concerned. It is also a problem to accountants preparing the accounts of companies that have benefited from this form of finance.

Some of these problems arise because the special-purpose transactions and the new financial instruments have not yet been faced up to in the accounting literature or by the accounting professional bodies. The financial transactions and instruments are new and different to those that have been previously encountered by accountants; some are designed to take advantage of the lack of accounting rules or the conflicts in existing rules.

In this chapter a number of special-purpose transactions will be considered. It must be remembered, however, that the subjects of finance and accounting are continually changing. In financial circles new and imaginative schemes are continually being created. In the UK and the USA, the accounting standard-setting committees have been asked to look at special-purpose transactions that have resulted in off-the-balance-sheet situations. Leasing was once one of the major off-the-balance-sheet techniques, but there is now a standard on the subject which has reduced the opportunities for the non-disclosure or limited disclosure of such financing deals. A special transaction that is off the balance sheet in one period need not be so in another period.

In case it is thought that the problem is of minor importance, it should be remembered that, with one type of financial transaction alone—the interest rate swap—the outstanding debts in the USA at the end of 1987 amounted to $400 billion, grown from zero in 1982. This is a financial transaction that seeks to transfer market risk, yet its existence might not be shown at all, either in the accounts of the companies that are undertaking the borrowing or in the accounts of the banks that bring the companies together and act as intermediaries and possibly provide guarantees.

There has been a tremendous increase in the variety of financial instruments and special-purpose transactions since 1982. The financial instruments are given intriguing names and anagrams, such as 'blue-eyed bonds', 'bulldogs', 'CATS', 'collar options', 'DARTS', 'death-backed bonds', 'down-under bonds', 'equity kicker CDs', 'grizzles', 'junk bonds', 'partial ceiling options', 'SPLITS', 'stripped coupon mortgage pass-through certificates' and 'wedding warrants'. Although they all sound interesting, from an accounting point of view they are worrying; they can mean that balance sheets do not disclose the true position.

It must be remembered that nobody is forcing the parties involved to enter into these transactions: they do so presumably because it is in their financial interests. From an accounting point of view, off-balance-sheet financing distorts gearing ratios and return-on-capital-employed ratios. Once such schemes are entered into, the borrowings of a company are disguised and users of the company's accounts may be misled.

The accounting profession has for some time been considering the matter. A technical release (TR 603) issued in December 1985 by the ICAEW gave guidance on the subject and expressed the opinion that substance should triumph over form in situations of window-dressing and off-balance-sheet financing. It is argued that assets and liabilities should be brought together on the balance sheet if this is necessary to give a true and fair view, whether or not the information involved is specifically required by legislation. The Department of Trade and Industry backed this interim guidance given by the profession on the subject.

The preliminary considerations of the ASC on this topic resulted in support for four basic principles. The first is that of global consolidation, which means the consolidation of all entities that are effectively controlled, whatever their main activities. The second is a reiteration of the fact that accounting for transactions should be in accordance with their substance, not their legal form. The third relates to the point that no amount of disclosure in the notes can make up for a distorted balance sheet, and the fourth stipulates that accounting effects should be consistent with economic effects.

Many lawyers, however, were not happy with the guidance that had been given. The Law Society's Standing Committee on Company Law issued a memorandum on the subject, pointing out that in their view the Companies Act 1981, incorporated in the 1985 Act, weakened the 'true and fair view' requirement. They believe that the detailed requirements of the Act cannot be modified simply because the accounts would not otherwise show a true and fair view. Following this argument, if the provision of additional information by way of note is sufficient to give a true and fair view, then it will not be necessary, in the opinion of the legal profession, to show the transaction on the face of the balance sheet. It is only where a note is not sufficient that the law should be overridden with the need to disclose the information on the face of the balance sheet.

In March 1988 the ASC issued an exposure draft (ED 42) on the subject. There are at least three novel aspects about this draft, which is entitled 'Accounting for Special Purpose Transactions'. One is that the ASC has attempted to lay down general principles that should be applied to all special-purpose transactions. It makes recommendations on the rules that are applicable and should be applied to all off-balance-sheet type transactions and financial instruments. It does this rather than attempting to prescribe the accounting treatment for each specific type of special-purpose transaction that at present exists and may be created in the future.

The exposure draft does, however, give a number of examples demonstrating how the general principles would be applied in specific circumstances. These examples are only meant to be illustrative, as the actual circumstances of transaction may well differ from one situation to another. The important thing is for the accountant to deal with every transaction according to the recommended principle.

It is the principles recommended that constitute the second novel aspect of the draft. 'The accounting treatment of a transaction should fairly reflect its commercial effect.' 'It is analysis of the commercial effects flowing from the form of special purpose transaction that will lead to an understanding of their substance.' In other words, it is the substance of the transaction that is to be reported.

The draft points out that this does not imply that 'accounting measurements should necessarily portray economic values such as current costs or discounted cash flows'. Measurement should 'not necessarily' be based on economic values. One special-purpose transaction is leasing. As explained above, this does mean valuing the leasing obligation in terms of economic values, that is, future cash outflows. On the other hand, an employee's service contract, which is an executory contract, commits an employer to make payments over the length of the contract, but the present value of the future payments is not recorded as a liability in the balance sheet.

The proposal is not, therefore, to adopt in all situations the economic concept of true income or true value for measurement for accounting purposes. The statement makes the point that, with special-purpose transactions, the economic value concept need not necessarily be applied. This might appear to give a certain degree of freedom in deciding when it should and should not be applied. The draft admits that the principles outlined 'are not sufficient in themselves to determine whether an item should be recognised in the financial statements and how it should be measured'.

The principles need to be applied 'in conjunction with recognition and measurement criteria found in other standards, company law and generally accepted accounting practice'. The principles in the exposure draft are not therefore to be seen as an overall conceptual framework; they are not to be seen as altering the standards already being applied in other situations which may have been based on different concepts of measurement.

The statement does not change general recognition and measurement principles. It should, however, result in 'additional items being recognised in financial statements, since it requires the application of general principles and specific rules to be based on a searching analysis of the commercial effect of transactions'. It should result in additional assets and liabilities being recognized. That is what it is designed to achieve: to reduce the incidence of off-the-balance-sheet financing.

The third novel aspect of the draft is in its definitions of an asset and liability. An asset should be recognized in financial statements if, as a result of past transactions and events, an enterprise will receive and control economic benefits. The important point is that it is not so much the physical asset that is being recognized as the economic benefits that are expected to accrue from it. The benefits must of course be capable of reasonably reliable measurement. (This is an important concept, which if accepted as an overall concept in accounting would mean that other accounting standards need to change, for example those dealing with goodwill and merger accounting.) A number of parties might have an interest in the benefits; the important issue from the point of view of recognizing the asset in the financial accounts is who controls the benefits. As we have discussed with leasing, one test of who controls the asset is who carries the risks.

'The existence or otherwise of the assets have to be determined by reference to the rights and obligations (including rights and obligations taking effect in the future) resulting from the transaction as a whole and which exists at the balance sheet date.' For example, if a company engages in a transaction with another company and legally the title to an asset is transferred, but if the prospects of future benefit, the exposure to inherent risks and the control that is exercisable over the asset are not affected to any significant degree, then it is to be regarded as a refinancing arrangement, and the asset remains in the balance sheet of the controlling company. Such a situation can arise when a manufacturer supplies goods to a dealer 'on consignment', whereby the dealer can return the goods without incurring a loss. Control implies the ability to obtain future benefits or to restrict others' access to them. It may take a variety of forms; and does not have to imply legal control.

The same accounting concept can be applied to liabilities. A liability is defined in the draft as 'present obligations of a particular enterprise entailing probably future sacrifices of economic benefits by transferring assets or providing services to other entities in the future'. The term 'present obligations' embraces legal liabilities, but is wider in scope. It includes commitments that may be inferred from its dealings or its general business policies. The event giving rise to the obligation must have already taken place, although the obligation may result in a legal liability only on the happening of some future event. For example, deferred tax represents the future sacrifice of economic benefits, the legal liability for which will arise only on the raising of a tax assessment. A provision for warranty claims involves a future sacrifice, but as at a balance sheet date there is no legal liability.

The draft draws attention to the fact that it is a generally accepted accounting principle, as well as a requirement of company law, that amounts representing assets should not be set off against amounts representing liabilities.

The draft is a brave attempt at dealing with a complicated problem. The accountant is seeking to produce statements that give a true and fair view of the state of affairs of an enterprise. It is the commercial effects of a transaction that should be reported, as only then will it give the user of the accounts an understanding of the substance of the transaction. Financiers and bankers have produced financing schemes that, from a strictly legal point of view, do not need to be reported in financial statements; they are often deliberately designed for this purpose, to hide the true substance of a transaction. The exposure draft suggests an approach which, if followed, will lead to 'truer and fairer' financial statements, certainly to statements more meaningful to users. 'If a special purpose transaction has the same commercial effects as a straightforward transaction, the principles of the standard should be applied to determine whether the two should be accounted for in the same manner.'

Whether the ASC is successful in having the approach proposed in the standard adopted depends on a number of factors. It is only an exposure draft; there is opposition to this approach, so it might not result in a standard. Even if it does, there is a certain amount of interpretation required for each individual transaction, and undoubtedly there will be situations when the principles are not applied.

We will now consider some of the special-purpose transactions that have been seen in the past as being off the balance sheet, or where the status has been unclear.

16.2 Controlled non-subsidiary companies

In exceptional circumstances, the Companies Act 1985 and SSAP 14 recognize that subsidiaries need not be consolidated in group accounts. The situations in which non-consolidation of a controlled non-subsidiary is referred to as 'off the balance sheet' are different from those situations that are recognized in company law for non-inclusion. The latter situations are discussed in the consolidation chapter (Chapter 11) and include cases where inclusion would be of no real value, would cause delays, or where the business of the subsidiary is very different from that of the holding company. What is referred to as a non-subsidiary subsidiary, or a controlled non-subsidiary, is different. This is a special company which is in reality controlled by a parent company, but which does not meet the legal definition of a subsidiary, so that its accounts do not have to be consolidated in the group accounts. It is a non-subsidiary of a reporting enterprise, which, although 'not fulfilling the Companies Act definition of a subsidiary, is directly or indirectly controlled by and a source of benefits or risks for the reporting enterprise or its subsidiaries that are in substance no different from those that would arise were the vehicle a subsidiary'.

Control is the key concept. It means more than significant influence or powerful economic pressure. Direct control means that the enterprise controls the benefits itself. Indirect control means control of the enterprise that controls the benefits directly. It is this latter situation that occurs with controlled non-subsidiaries. Usually they are established by arrangements precisely determined to give them that control. An example of this occurs when a non-subsidiary is formed with two forms of equity capital, ordinary shares and preference shares. An equal amount of both shares is issued, the (non-) holding company taking up all the ordinary shares and a bank all the preference shares. One of the conditions which determines that a company is a subsidiary has thereby been avoided: the (non-) holding company does not own more than 50 per cent of the equity capital. In the UK we tend to use legalistic notions of ownership rather than an approach based on economic control or effective control.

The other factor that has to be considered when deciding what is and what is not a subsidiary is the composition of the board of directors. Does the holding company (or non-holding company) control the composition of the board? The key question is does the holding company 'control the composition', not does it control the majority of the votes on the board. The Articles of Association of the 'subsidiary' can be drawn up to state that the holders of the preference shares have the right to appoint a number of directors equal to those appointed by the equity shareholders. The Articles can also state that any loan stock issued carries with it a right to place a director on the board. If the (non-) holding company takes up the loan stock, it can therefore appoint one extra director and have control of the board. But it is the articles that control the composition of the board, not the (non-) holding company.

Having now set up a non-subsidiary, it can be used to raise finance through borrowing which does not have to be disclosed in the group accounts. The non-subsidiary is treated in the holding 'parent' company accounts as an associate company. This 'associate company' can raise cash and distribute it through the group. The parent company can 'sell' assets to the invisible 'subsidiary', which can be used as security for the loans. All of these transactions will misrepresent the true gearing position of the group.

As mentioned at the beginning of this section, there are recognized reasons why some subsidiaries are not consolidated. The most common reason for not consolidating on a line-by-line basis is when the business activity of the subsidiary is so dissimiliar from the main activity of the group that it is judged that consolidation would mislead. An example of this occurs in the accounts of Marks and Spencer, where a subsidiary of the group is responsible for the charge card operation that provides credit to the customers. This subsidiary is a banking type of operation, funded separately from the rest of the group. The subsidiary is not consolidated in the group's balance sheet, but the assets and liabilities are shown as a single item, 'Net assets of financial activities'. A note to the accounts discloses details of the accounts of the subsidiary. The annual report gives details of the company's accounting policies. When describing the policies relating to consolidation, the following point is made 'in order to reflect the different nature of the financial activities and so present fairly the groups state of affairs, the assets and liabilities of such activities are shown as a net investment in the group balance sheet and are analysed separately in note...'

This is not what is being referred to as a special-purpose transaction. It is not hiding the existence of the subsidiary and its reasons for non-consolidation. A number of retailing companies elect not to consolidate their financial subsidiaries and associates.

Attitudes do change, however, and even the practice of non-consolidation of a subsidiary on the grounds of dissimilar activity became subject to criticism. With the increasing interest and criticism of off-the-balance-sheet financing, all exclusions have come under scrutiny. In 1987 the Burton Group were criticised for not consolidating the accounts of their finance house activities. Their credit card operations were either 46 or 50 per cent owned and were not therefore legally subsidiaries. It was claimed, however, that the Burton Group have full management control over these associates; they were in fact controlled non-subsidiaries.

The effect of consolidating these activities in 1987 would have been dramatic. The assets of the group's financial activities were in the region of £500 million, with debts of £400 million. The financial gearing of the group was reported as 41 per cent, but the inclusion of loans of the off-balance-sheet companies would push this level of gearing above 50 per cent. There was however a powerful argument for not including many of these loans, in that there is no right of recourse against the Burton Group in case of non-payment by the associated companies.

The dividing line between the non-consolidation of what is legally recognized as a subsidiary and the non-consolidation of a controlled non-subsidiary has become blurred. There are those who now advocate that the rules be changed. In 1987 the International Accounting Standards Committee published an exposure draft on 'Consolidated Financial Statements and Accounting for Investments in Subsidiaries' (E 30), which proposes that non-consolidation on the ground of dissimiliar business activities no longer be allowed. The accounts of all enterprises controlled by the parent would then need to be consolidated. There are only two minor grounds for exclusion, where control is temporary or impaired.

In the USA the FASB issued a rule in 1987 which forces companies to include all majority-owned subsidiaries in their consolidated accounts. They are not therefore being allowed to exclude because of differences in the type of activities. In addition to its significant impact on UK companies with US subsidiaries, the rule also indicated the direction in which legislation in the UK might be moving.

In the UK the exposure draft on 'Special Purpose Transactions', issued in 1988, addresses the problem of controlled non-subsidiaries. It points out that such subsidiaries are, from the point of view of commercial effect, similar in substance to legally defined subsidiaries. In order to provide a true and fair view, therefore, they need to be treated in the same way in the financial accounts. The draft recommends that, when controlled non-subsidiaries are included in consolidated accounts, it should be made clear that entities from outside the legally defined group have been included, and the reason for and effect of their inclusion should be explained.

If the 'presumption' that a controlled non-subsidiary is, from the point of view of commercial effect, similar in substance to a subsidiary can be rebutted, then information on that 'non-subsidiary' still needs to be provided. This could take the form of similar disclosure to that required by non-consolidated subsidiaries under the provision of the Companies Act 1985, or else the accounts of the controlled non-subsidiary could be presented 'alongside or with equal prominence to the statutory accounts'.

Legal advice was obtained by the ASC with respect to their recommendations contained in the exposure draft. The legal requirements will change from 1990, when the Companies Act will have to be amended to implement the EEC 7th Directive on company law. The basis of consolidation will change and will probably require the consolidation of all subsidiaries. Consolidation will be based on the principles of power of control rather than the percentage of shares owned. Controlled non-subsidiaries could well continue to exist, but they should not result in off-the-balance-sheet situations if the recommendations in the exposure draft are acted upon. Even if the draft is not successful in its efforts to eliminate this form of off-balance-sheet financing, the requirements of the new Companies Act should achieve this result.

16.2.1   Redeemable preference shares

There is another way in which a genuine subsidiary or controlled non-subsidiary can be used to window-dress a set of accounts. Finance can be raised for use within the group without disclosing the true nature of the fact by the issue of redeemable preference shares. It is the subsidiary that issues such shares, which carry a dividend equal to the current market rates of interest. A bank purchases the shares, receiving a level of dividend similar to the interest it would receive on a loan.

These preference shares will be shown as such in the subsidiary's own accounts, but not in the consolidated accounts. That is, if the subsidiary is consolidated in the group accounts, the preference shares will appear as part of minority interest—as equity shares issued by the group, but not held by the holding company. Few people analysing accounts bother to look at the individual accounts of subsidiaries, relying instead on the group accounts. If it is a controlled non-subsidiary making the issue, the question of consolidation does not arise until the concepts introduced in the exposure draft are accepted. The subsidiary can pass the funds thus raised around the group to provide finance wherever it is needed. The transaction is in reality more similar to a loan than an issue of risk-bearing equity capital. The funds will be repaid to the bank at an agreed date, and the finance charge is similar in amount to the appropriate interest payments. If, however, the funds had been raised by the subsidiary as a loan, then it would have needed to have appeared as such on the face of the consolidated accounts. For window-dressing purposes, there can be advantages in having it tucked away as a 'minority interest' in the group accounts.

16.3   Financial arrangements with regard to non-monetary assets

One example of a financial arrangement concerning non-monetary assets relates to the sale of stock. Let us take a company that operates a distillery, a business in which it is normal to carry high levels of stock, in the form of maturing whisky. It is usual practice for the company to borrow to finance the stock, but it is approaching its borrowing limits set by its Articles of Association. A scheme can be devised whereby a merchant bank purchases the unmatured whisky, giving the distiller the option to purchase it back when it reaches maturity at a price that represents the original sale price plus interest over the period the merchant bank 'owns' the whisky. The whisky never, of course, leaves the distiller's premises, even though for a time it is legally owned by the bank.

It can be argued that this is a genuine transaction. The distillery company has sold the whisky, and may or may not buy it back. The appropriate treatment depends on the particular circumstances of the case. In many such deals the repurchase price to the distiller is predetermined. It represents the sale price plus a holding and interest charge and is expected to be below the value of the whisky at the time of repurchase, so the distiller is almost certain to wish to buy it back. In form, the whisky has been sold and so, following normal accounting rules, it need not appear as stock in the accounts of the distiller. No interest charge need appear in the distiller's accounts during the period the whisky is maturing, and certainly no loan has been received from the merchant bank. When the whisky has matured and is bought back from the bank and sold, the profit margin to the distiller will have been reduced by the finance charge and holding charge paid to the merchant bank. Although in form the distillers have not received a loan, it can be argued that in substance they have. The 'loan' has been secured by the whisky stock. It is off-the-balance-sheet financing. The distiller has the free use of the funds obtained from the merchant bank during the period of the deal.

The exposure draft recommends that in these circumstances the transaction should be treated as a special financing arrangement. This means that an annual holding charge and an interest charge should be shown in the profit and loss accounts. The asset would be shown in the balance sheet of the distillers, increasing in value each year by the charges made to the profit and loss account. The cash received from the merchant bank would be shown as a loan received.

In contrast, the sale of stock at the current spot market price, with an agreement to repurchase in the future at the then spot market price, is not a special financial arrangement. This is because the manufacturer, with the sale, has relinquished control over the amount of the net future cash flows. In these circumstances the transaction should be treated as a sale and later as a repurchase.

A similar situation to this artificial sale is the 'assignment of work in progress'. A construction company may be engaged in a large contract that will take many years to complete. As with the distillers, there is the danger that large amounts of money can be tied up in stocks, in this case in work in progress. In this situation the company can agree to assign irrevocably all the amounts that it will receive during the period of the construction contract to a bank. In return, the bank will agree to make periodic payments to the construction company. The construction company now knows with certainty what cash it will receive from the bank and when, rather than being faced with an uncertain cash flow stream to be received from the purchaser, which depends on stages of completion, with possible payment delays through disputes and time lags. With this arrangement the construction company can receive cash in advance of payments it will have to make, whereas payments from the purchaser for work in progress produce cash only when the costs have been incurred. Again, this is in substance a company receiving a loan, but in form it is the sale of stock. At the completion of the contract the construction company receives final payment, and repays the bank for the advances it has received, plus, of course, a financing charge. It has been treated as off-the-balance-sheet financing, but could be seen as a special financial arrangement.

In this situation some reference to the transaction will need to appear in the accounts. The bank could well require a performance bond from the construction company, guaranteeing that the work will be completed. This is in a way the security for the 'loan'. The existence of such a bond means that a contingent liability has been created, and this will at least need to be disclosed by way of a note in the accounts of the construction company.

Another transaction that can result in a special financial arrangement arises with goods on consignment. If the goods are supplied by the manufacturer to a dealer on a sale-or-return basis, with the dealer not incurring any significant charge, the dealer is not taking any risk. It is the manufacturer who is carrying the risk. The exposure draft in this case recommends that the goods appear as stock in the balance sheet of the manufacturer rather than in the balance sheet of the dealer. Which party carries the risk in this situation is regarded as more important than which party receives the possible future benefits.

If, on the other hand, the dealer is obliged at some time to purchase the goods, then it is the dealer who carries the risk, and who should record the goods as stock.

16.4 Financial arrangements with regard to monetary items

One of the biggest problems with off-the balance-sheet financing is to decide whether or not a possible liability should be shown as a contingent liability. In the case of the discounting of bills of exchange, it is generally accepted that a contingent liability exists. Company S sells to company P. Company P signs a bill of exchange, promising to pay the value of the invoice in three months. Company S presents this bill of exchange at a bank and receives an advance for the sum involved less a financing charge. If all goes well, company P pays the amount involved in three months' time and the money is passed on to the bank, in settlement of the advance plus the finance charge.

During the three months between the discounting of the bill and the payment by company P, there is a contingent liability for company S. In most cases, companies receiving the advance from the bank would disclose such liability, usually stating the amounts of money involved. This however, is not the only possible treatment. De La Rue, in their 1985 accounts, stated:

> There are contingent liabilities arising in the ordinary course of business relating principally to discounted bills, bonds outstanding, claims involving products manufactured by the Group and certain indemnities entered into, but in the opinion of the Directors adequate provision has been made for any losses which might fall on the Group.

The Beecham Group reported in the notes to their 1986 accounts that among the contingent liabilities of the group were £13.7 million, 'mainly in respect of bills discounted and bank guarantees for which no provision is considered necessary'.

16.4.1   Factoring of debts

Special financing arrangements can arise with the factoring of debts. A company, ABC, sells its sales invoices to a factoring company. The factor pays money to ABC Company. What happens if the purchaser of the goods fails to pay? Who loses, the factoring company or the selling company? If the factor has accepted the bad debt risk, then there is no reason for the transaction to be mentioned in the financial statement of ABC: the factor has no recourse. However, if the factor does have recourse, if the factor does not carry the risk, then ABC Company has a contingent liability and the amount of the possible liability should be disclosed in the notes to the accounts.

Provision should also be made in the accounts for bad debts. If the reporting company had not used a factor, it would have had to make such provisions; its risks are just the same with a factor with recourse. In substance, the bad debt position is the same.

16.4.2   Defeasance

This is a technique that has been adopted by some companies whereby, in order to satisfy a liability, a matching asset is transferred to an irrevocable trust. The claim of the party against the company is limited to the asset transferred. Both the asset and the debt can be removed from the balance sheet of the company setting up the arrangement if the assets are placed in an irrevocable trust. This type of transaction is more common in the USA than in the UK.

16.4.3   Sale of debtors (receivables)

If a company, say a financial institution, is able to sell some of its debtors to another company, then clearly the transaction is a sale; the debtors figure in the balance sheet will be reduced, the cash figure increased. As mentioned above, the trouble arises in respect of a sale with a right of recourse. If the purchaser of the debts can come back to the seller in the case where the debtor does not pay, then the seller of the debts has a contingent liability, and has to be concerned about possible bad debts.

For example, suppose a building society sells to a third party £50 million of mortgages it has issued. It would have received the repayment of the mortgages over time, but by selling them now it turns the future receivables into cash. With the increase in securitization in financial markets, building societies have been doing just that. The building society continues to manage the mortgages, and to handle the collections, but it passes on the amounts received plus the agreed rate of interest to the buyer of the mortgages. The building society sometimes continues to carry the risk of non-payment on the mortgages; the buyer of the mortgages has recourse. How is the sale of the mortgages to be accounted for? How is the outstanding risk accounted for? In the USA, according to FASB 77 ('Reporting by Transferors for Transfers of Receivables with Recourse'), the mortgages can be removed from the balance sheet, with recognition of the relevant gain or loss in the accounts. This is despite the fact that there may be 100% recourse in the case of bad debts to the seller—in the above example, to the building society making the transfer.

An example of such an arrangement in the UK is that of the National Home Loans Corporation (NHLC). In 1987 they had sold a £50 million bundle of mortgages as marketable securities. A good business reason for such an action is to enable the financial institution to increase its funds available for lending purposes. In this case the corporation argued that to show these securities as a liability in its accounts would be misleading, as the holders of the securities have no right of recourse against the NHLC if the mortgages turn out to be bad debts. One problem that arises is that often the assets, in this case the mortgages, are sold to a controlled non-subsidiary company, which in turn sells the bundle of mortgages a marketable security. The right of recourse is against the non-subsidiary, not against the 'parent' company.

A similar situation can arise with a manufacturing company. In the USA, General Motors Finance subsidiary put together a package of $4 billion of loans it had made to customers to enable them to purchase cars, and sold these in the market; it created a security out of its loans receivable. The purchaser of the security passed cash to General Motors Finance subsidiary, and in return received a stream of payments over time from those who obtained their cars by borrowing from the finance subsidiary.

The key question in these situations is whether the benefits and related risks remain with the seller of the receivables or with the purchaser. If significant risks remain with the seller—the company that packaged the receivables to sell—then the receivables should remain as an asset in that company's balance sheet. The funds received result in a debit to cash and a credit to a liability account. The resulting presentation shows both the receivables due and the liability resulting from the cash received from the sale.

16.5 Interest rate and currency swaps

In 1987 a group of individuals from financial institutions in the USA were invited by the National Center of Financial Services to identify the major unresolved accounting issues that affected them. Of the ten issues they identified, one was the fact that different types of financial institutions account differently for similar financial instruments. Another issue was the problem of sales versus financing arrangements. For example, transactions involving financial instruments can sometimes be structured in such a way that they constitute sales, removal from the balance sheet and immediate recognition of any gain or loss; on other occasions the transaction can be so structured that it is not a sale and so recognition of a gain or loss is delayed. A third issue was off-balance-sheet assets and liabilities. Other issues included economic consequences; for example, if you change the way the financial institutions report, it will change the type of finance they make available.

The same accounting issues require resolution in financial institutions in the UK. They constitute a major problem, one that seriously affects the usefulness of the accounts of financial institutions.

In 1987 it was estimated by a firm of stockbrokers that the off-the-balance-sheet financing by the major UK banks amounted to £200 million. Of this, the amount disclosed as contingent liabilities amounted to only £20 million, one-tenth of the total. The rest of the transactions were not being disclosed.

What type of transactions do banks and other financial institutions now become involved in that mean that their balance sheets do not indicate their possible commitment and consequently their true risk position? In the USA, banks are required to disclose more information about their activities than is the case in the UK, so by examining the accounts of US banks we can see the types of transactions engaged in that are creating contingent liabilities. The US banks, in the notes to their accounts, reveal foreign exchange instruments as the largest type of off-balance-sheet arrangement leading to contingent liabilities, followed by interest rate swaps, currency swaps and stand-by letters of credit. The situation is probably the same in the UK, although as mentioned there is little disclosure.

Although this book is not primarily involved with the peculiarities of the accounts of financial institutions in general and banks in particular, it is thought worthwhile briefly to mention the accounting problems that arise from interest rate and currency swaps.

16.5.1   Interest rate swaps

Interest rate swaps have increased in popularity over recent years. In its simplest form one party, say company C, which has borrowed funds at a fixed interest rate, gets together with another party, say company D, which has borrowed at a floating rate, and the two agree to service each other's loan. In effect, company C finishes up paying a floating rate of interest and company D a fixed rate. In its simplest form the transaction is conducted in just one currency. Both companies, referred to as 'counterparties', will show the loans in their balance sheets; what is not so clear is whether they will both disclose their true interest rate commitments.

The arrangement becomes more complicated from an accounting point of view when a bank becomes involved. A bank may act as a broker bringing the two companies together, or act as a principal. In the latter case the bank is lending its own funds to a company with one type of interest arrangement and borrowing from the other company with the other type of interest payment.

There is no accounting standard relating to interest rate swaps. The disclosure required is not clear. When the bank acts as a principal, can it offset the two transactions, or should it disclose them both? When a bank acts as a broker, it may be exposing itself to a credit risk, in that one of the counterparties may fail to meet its interest rate obligations. The actual accounting treatment varies among companies and financial institutions.

The Institute of Chartered Accountants in England and Wales issued a technical release (TR 677) at the end of 1987 on the subject of 'Accounting for Complex Capital Issues'. One of the examples of such 'complex' issues that is discussed is interest rate swaps. It recommends that

> There should be full disclosure of the arrangement in the notes to the financial statements, so that the true commercial effect on the whole transaction, including any possible risk of exposure in the event of the failure of the swap party, is clearly explained.

Whether companies adopt such a policy remains to be seen.

16.5.2   Currency swaps

Closely linked to interest rate swaps are currency swaps. This is a transaction in which at a particular date two counterparties exchanged specific amounts of two different currencies, and then repay these currencies over time according to predetermined arrangements which reflect the interest payments and possibly the amortization of the principal. There is an alternative form of currency swap, in which one party sells to the other party one currency against another with an agreement to reverse the transaction at a future date. In this type of transaction, only the principal amounts are exchanged at the initial and maturity dates, with no exchange of interest in the interim.

16.6   Options

A company might become involved in the purchase and sale of options for a number of reasons. Two of the main reasons will be covered in this section; to allow the company to transfer risk to another party, and to issue options to purchase shares in the company itself.

A company might face risk, with regard to unexpected movements over time in interest rates, in foreign currency exchange rates and in the price of raw materials. The company may be expecting to receive payments in the future, or to have to make payments in the future, and may be concerned that unfavourable movements will adversely effect its profitability. The company can find a speculator who, for a price, will be willing to accept some of the risk; the speculator will 'write' an option. The company will be willing to 'hedge' by purchasing the option from the speculator, the writer of the option.

The company purchases the option for a premium, and this allows it to buy or sell the items that are the subject of the contract at specified prices during specified periods of time. The company can wait until the time for a decision and then decide whether it wishes to exercise the option or not; it is not required to do so. Alternatively, in many cases the company can in fact trade the option at any time before the expiration date. Traded option markets have developed in both the USA and the UK. In London the Stock Exchange and LIFFE offer opportunities to trade options. We are concerned here with the appropriate accounting treatment.

The basic principle that can be followed is that for purchased options the premium should be recorded as an asset. For the writer of the option, that is for the speculator, the premium should be reflected as a liability. The gross amount that may have to be delivered (if the buyer decides to exercise the option) does not need to be reported in the balance sheet.

There were no standards on the treatment of options as at the end of 1988, but both the ICAEW and the AICPA in the USA have issued papers in which the subject is discussed. A major accounting issue is whether or not realized and unrealized gains and losses resulting from the change in market values of the options being held should be taken to the current profit and loss account. One treatment is to defer such gains and losses. The recommended treatment in the USA is, with most options, to recognize such amounts in the current income statements, except where they meet the criteria for what is called 'hedge accounting'. In this case, specified assets or liabilities need to be identified as being hedged so that the appropriate time can be determined by which the gains and losses must be recognized.

As a straightforward example of the 'hedge accounting' treatment of an option, let us assume that a UK company borrows $1 million on 1 January. The spot rate of exchange at that time is $1.50 = £1. The company is worried that if the pound becomes weaker it will have to repay more than the £666,666 it is expecting. The company buys a 'call option', entitling it to buy $1 million with a 30 September expiration date at a strike price of $1.40. The strike price is the price specified in the contract at which the holder of the option (the company) can buy the dollars from the writer of the option. The price of the option is £0.02 per dollar, which is a total of £20,000. Let us say the value of the pound does fall, which means that the market value of the option will rise. The end of the accounting year is 30 June, when the option price is £0.05 per dollar and the spot exchange rate is $1.42 to the pound.

The company does not have an offsetting dollar-denominated asset, so the dollars borrowed expose the company to risk. The company follows US accounting practice and regards the option as a hedge on the loan. The value of the loan shown in the accounts is at market value, and the unrealized gain on the option will be applied to reduce the foreign currency loss on the loan.

The entries would be:

1 Jan.	Dr.	Cash	£666,666	
		Loan		£666,666
	Dr	Option held	20,000	
		Cash		20,000

This records the loan converted into sterling and the taking out of the option.

30 June	Dr	Foreign exchange loss	£37,559	
		Loan		£37,559

to increase the reported amount of the dollar loan

	Dr	Options held	£30,000	
		Foreign exchange loss		£30,000

to record the increase in the option value

As a result of this accounting treatment, the foreign exchange loss is only £7,559. The same treatment would apply if the option had been sold on 30 June: it is the same offsetting of the exchange loss, whether the gain in the option is realized or not. The additional entry if the option was sold would be:

30 June	Dr	Cash	£50,000	
		Option held		£50,000

being the value of the option

The above is quite a basic example. In the USA with some such transactions the amount of the premium paid for the option is divided for accounting purposes between a time value and an intrinsic value, the latter being the difference between the current strike price and the market price of the subject of the option. The time value is the difference between the price paid for the option and the intrinsic value. The accounting treatment of the parts of the premium differs.

Moving on now to the share option, let us take as an example a company that is the writer of an option. It sells the option to a holder, an investor, and receives a premium. The ICAEW in its technical release on 'Complex Capital Issues' refers to this type of financial instrument. Let us say that the company sells options to purchase its shares for £3 in three years' time, and receives 20 pence for each option sold. The recommended treatment is that the proceeds should be treated as a capital receipt. If eventually the option is exercised, the proceeds from the option sale should be treated as part of the proceeds of the issue of share. If the option is allowed to lapse, then the proceeds from the earlier sale of the options may be released from capital and treated as income.

16.7 Deep discount bonds

In 1982 the Chancellor of the Exchequer announced that companies would be allowed to issue zero coupon bonds and deep discount bonds. Such issues have become quite popular. The main feature is that either no interest is paid each year on the bond, or the interest rate paid is well below the current market level of interest rates. The reason an investor would wish to buy such a security is because it is issued at a price well below the value at which the bond will eventually be redeemed; it is issued at a 'deep' discount. The investor is substituting annual income for a large capital gain at the time of redemption.

From an accounting point of view, there are two problems. One is how much should be charged to the profit and loss account each year: is it simply the interest paid, or should it include some element of the discount which is in substance a rolled up interest charge? The second problem is the value at which the bond should be shown in the balance sheet.

The alternative accounting techniques will be illustrated by means of an example. If the discount is to be charged to the profit and loss account each year, the annual charge can be calculated using the straight-line basis or the actuarial basis. The first approach gives a constant charge each year, the latter a constant rate based on the amount of the loan outstanding each year. Let us say that a company issues a zero coupon bond, repayable in five years' time at par. The issue price is £500, the par value £1,000. On a straight-line basis, the annual charge to profit and loss account for the discount would be £100. To calculate the charge on an actuarial basis, it is necessary to determine the rate of interest implicit in the bond. What is needed is an interest rate (i) that allows £500 to accumulate to £1,000 at the end of five years:

$$500 = \frac{1,000}{(1+i)^5}$$

The use of either a calculator or compound interest tables shows that the rate (i) is approximately 15 per cent. The annual profit and loss charge for the discount can then be calculated:

Year	Amount invested at beginning of year	15% interest charge to P & L account	Amount invested at end of year
1	500	75	575
2	575	87	662
3	662	100	762
4	762	114	876
5	876	134	1000

The guidance given by the profession is that the discount on the bonds should usually be charged to the profit and loss account over the period to maturity. This is recognizing that the discount given is effectively part or all of the cost of borrowing; it is similar to interest payable.

The above treatment recognizes the substance of the transaction. It has to be pointed out, however, that Section 130 of the Companies Act 1985 allows for the discount on issue to be written off against the share premium account. It can be argued that this write-off at the time of issue of the total discount does not give a 'true and fair' view. It is another case of substance over form. Indeed, the ICAEW technical release on 'Complex Capital Issues' states that the direct write-off of the discount to the share premium account does not show a true and fair view of the cost of the debenture. However, in each year 'an amount equivalent to that part of the discount charged as interest for the period in the P & L account may be transferred from share premium account to revenue reserves.' This is just a transfer from one reserve to another. The technical guidance is that the annual write-down of the discount should be taken to the profit and loss account.

Having decided what the annual charge to the profit and loss account should be, we now have to consider the appropriate liability to be shown in the balance sheet. In our example, should the gross liability of £1,000 be shown throughout the five years, or just the net amount? At the end of year 3, it could be argued that the net liability under the straight-line method is £800; the £500 originally received, plus the £300 that has seen set aside out of profits to pay the bondholders the interest that has accrued.

The recommended treatment is that the gross liability be shown, with the unamortized discount shown as an asset as permitted by Schedule 4 of the 1985 Act. There might seem some logic in deducting the unamortized discount from the gross liability to show the net liability, but this is allowed by Schedule 4 of the Companies Act only for loans issued under special terms. The Act requires the company either to show the 'asset' separately on the face of the balance sheet, or to disclose it in notes to the financial statement.

The accounting entries for the first two years, adopting the actuarial basis, would be:

Jan 1 19X0	Dr	Cash	£500	
		Discount on bonds	500	
	Cr	Bond issued		£1,000
Dec 31 19X0	Dr	P & L a/c: discount written off	75	
	Cr	Discount on bonds		75
Dec 31 19X1	Dr	P & L a/c: discount written off	87	
	Cr	Discount on bonds		87

The balance sheet at the end of 19X1 would show a liability of £1,000 and an asset, 'Discount on bonds', representing the discount not written off, of £338. The net liability is £662 (the £500 plus the accrued interest).

The recommended treatment, if the permission given under the Companies Act to write the discount off against the share premium account is followed, is not to debit the share premium account with £500 all in one go. Rather, each year the discount should be debited to the profit and loss account (as above) and then an equivalent amount should be transferred from the share premium account to the revenue reserves:

| Dec 31 19X0 | Dr | Share premium a/c | £75 | |
| | Cr | Revenue reserves | | £75 |

There are special tax rules applying to deep discounted bonds. Basically, a company can obtain tax relief in each accounting period on the discount that accrues to that period.

The recommendations in the UK with regard to the accounting treatment of deep discounted bonds and zero coupon bonds were issued only in 1987. Prior to that, companies recorded the existence of such bonds in a variety of ways. For example, Redland plc, in their 1987 accounts, give details of their loans and bank overdrafts in notes to their accounts. They disclose that a subsidiary has issued '£60 million zero coupon notes 1992'. This £60 million par value is included in the balance sheet but is valued at only £35.3 million. A note explains that these notes are 'guaranteed by Redland plc and are stated at the issue price plus accrued interest from the date of issue'. The figure stated is the net liability.

16.8 Convertible bonds

A variation on the deep discounted bond is a bond issued at a low coupon rate which is convertible into equity shares from a date in the future. Such convertible bonds have been issued by such well-known companies as Burtons, Asda and Lonrho.

In 1987 Burton issued a £110 million convertible Eurobond with the option to convert into 35 million shares in 1992. The interest rate payable on the bond, $4\frac{3}{4}$ per cent, was well below the market rates at the time.

The attraction of such securities depends on the terms of the conversion. If the shares to be received are worth much more than the price paid for the bond, the investor is receiving for a period of five years the below-market rates of interest in exchange for a gain at the time of the conversion, similar to a deep discount. Alternatively, the terms of the bond may be such that they pay interest rates just below market rates during the life of the bond, with the prospect of a small capital gain when the bond is exchanged for equity shares. A variation offered with some convertible bonds is that, if the holder opts not to convert, it is possible to receive instead an increase in interest rates paid on the bond back-dated to the time of issue.

The technical release on the subject recommends that, if the discount on conversion is not 'material', it is acceptable just to charge the interest actually paid each year to the profit and loss account. A note in the financial statement can explain the rights attached to the bond issue.

The problem arises when there is a deep discount on conversion. The technical release recommends that 'an adjustment may need to be made to charge a fair interest cost in the profit and loss account and to treat the difference (between the fair interest cost and the actual interest cost) as a payment received for an option'. The technical release reasonably argues that this treatment is necessary in order to give a true and fair view.

When the rights to conversion can be varied, and the bondholder is offered the opportunity to take higher interest payments instead of converting to equity, the technical release recommends that the potential interest that may have to be paid be charged each year. The difference between the actual interest paid each year and the interest that will need to be paid if the bondholder elects to take the higher interest payments can be set aside as an accrual. If the bondholder converts to equity, this accrued interest can be waived.

The treatment referred to in the technical release is not mandatory; it is only a recommendation. Many companies have chosen to ignore it. They enter in the balance sheet the nominal value of the loan, and debit the profit and loss account with the actual interest paid. They justify such treatment on the grounds that the shares that may have to be issued in the future are not definite liabilities. The bondholders have an option; the share conversion may never be exercised. A note in the financial statement can 'explain the terms of the bond issue. It is up to the users of accounts to examine the footnote carefully.'

16.9 Conclusions

Off-balance-sheet financing arrangements and details of any of the hundred or more financial instruments with which a company may be involved must be disclosed in financial statements. The accounting standard-setting bodies are working to achieve this result. What needs to be disclosed to the users of financial accounts are (a) the credit risks involved; (b) the maturity transformation; (c) the interest rate information; (d) the appropriate market values and (e) any special-purpose companies that have been set up to avoid consolidation. It is only if such information is available that the user can obtain a true and fair view of the state of affairs of a business, including a financial institution such as a bank.

With regard to credit risk, it is necessary to disclose
(a) the maximum credit risk and probable credit loss of each class of financial instrument that bears credit risk;
(b) the concentration of credit risk with individual parties if the maximum risk with a party exceeds more than a certain percentage of equity;
(c) the concentration of credit risk in groups engaged in similar business activities.

With regard to maturity information, that is the future cash receipts and payments position, what is needed is
(a) the amounts of future cash receipts or payments that a business is contractually committed to, showing the class of financial instrument, and the future time periods of the cash flows;
(b) if significant, the commitments in currencies other than the reporting currency.

With regard to interest rates, it should be necessary to show the contractual terms for the different classes of financial instruments, giving the effective interest rates and the principal amounts of the instruments that have been repriced. It would be desirable to know the market value of each class of financial asset and liability. If quoted market prices are not available, a surrogate should be used to estimate the value of the financial instrument.

The above is a list of the type of information that *should* be available. Unfortunately, it is not available, and the accounting profession seems to be in a weak position in trying to enforce greater disclosure. It took ten years to obtain a standard on leasing. In the UK at the end of 1987 there was no standard or even statement of recommended practice from the ASC. The ICAEW had issued a technical release covering some of the issues, but this only makes recommendations. Further proposals from the ASC were released in 1988.

It should be appreciated that many of the financial instruments that have been developed are deliberately designed so that the true position does not have to be disclosed in financial accounts. It makes it very difficult to argue, when such off-balance-sheet positions exist, that the accounts show a true and fair view. This should be a worry to the accounting profession. Unfortunately, the legal position can be in conflict with the 'true and fair' philosophy.

Further reading

Accountancy, 'Off-balance-sheet finance: the beginning of the end', *Accountancy,* January 1986.

Accounting Standards Committee, ED 42, 'Accounting for Special Purpose Transactions', ASC, 1988.

American Institute of Certified Public Accountants, 'Accounting for Options', AICPA, 1985.

Andersen, Arthur, 'Accounting for Interest Rate Futures', Arthur Andersen & Co., Chicago, 1985.

Andersen, Arthur, 'Accounting for Options', Arthur Andersen & Co., Chicago, 1986.

Brindle, I., 'Off-balance-sheet financing', in L. C. L. Skerratt and D. J. Tonkin (eds), *Financial Reporting 1985–86; A survey of UK Published Accounts*, ICAEW, 1986.

Financial Accounting Standards Board, SFAS 12, 'Accounting for Certain Marketable Securities', FASB, 1975.

Financial Accounting Standards Board, SFAS 80, 'Accounting for Futures Contracts', FASB, 1984.

Institute of Chartered Accountants in England and Wales, TR 603, 'Accounting for Complex Capital Issues', ICAEW, 1986.

International Accounting Standards Committee, E 30, 'Consolidated Financial Statements and Accounting for Investments and Subsidiaries', IASC, 1987.

Livnat, J. and A. C. Sondhi, 'Finance subsidiaries: their formation and consolidation', *Journal of Business Finance and Accounting*, Spring 1986.

Rutherford, B. A., 'The true and fair view doctrine: a search for explication', *Journal of Business Finance and Accounting*, Winter 1985.

Sprouse, R. T., 'Commentary on financial reporting', *Accounting Horizons*, September 1987.

Stewart, J. E. and B. S. Neuhausen, 'Financial instruments and transactions: the CPA's newest challenge', *Journal of Accountancy*, August 1986.

Tweedie, D. P. and J. Kellas, 'Off-balance-sheet financing', *Accountancy*, April 1987.

Questions

1. 'Off-the-balance-sheet' financing and financial instruments became a major item in the work programme of the ASC only in 1987. It has resulted in an exposure draft on 'Special Purpose Transactions' (ED 42).
    You are required to answer the following:
    (a) How have 'off-balance-sheet' financing schemes been used to alter the impression given in group accounts?   (6 marks)
    (b) Give three examples of 'new' methods of raising finance that have led to accounting problems in the financial reports.   (6 marks)

(c) Discuss what you consider to be the major issues and obstacles in the resolution of these problem areas. (13 marks)

(25 marks)

2. In large and complex groups of companies, there are often difficulties in deciding how to treat certain companies when preparing the consolidated financial statements for the year.

   Required:
   (a) State the treatments, required by legislation and by UK/Irish accounting standards, of subsidiaries which are unsuitable for inclusion in the consolidated accounts. (17 marks)
   (b) Comment on the validity of each of the treatments so required. (8 marks)

(25 marks)

ACCA, 3·1, AFA, June 1987

17. Corporate change

Over the years, companies change; they can grow by internal growth, through merger or through the acquisition of other companies. During growth, particularly from a small owner-managed organization to a public company, a prospectus will probably be issued. Part of the required information will be a report from the accountants providing the information specified by the Companies Acts and the Stock Exchange.

In some circumstances a company may include a profit forecast in its published statements. These circumstances are not very common at the moment, but many users of accounts have expressed a wish for more frequent forecasts, so this may become more common in the future.

Sometimes a reorganization of a company becomes necessary, and this may involve a reconstruction of its capital structure.

In all these fields there are statutory or commercial rules which prescribe the actual accounting recording of the economic changes. It is to the determination of these changes and the assessment of the alternatives that many accountants direct their skills. The bare rules are well known, their application to each particular case represents an opportunity to use some of the highest skills of the profession.

As with most business activity, taxation matters cannot be ignored in practice. If less than the customary reference is made to them in this chapter, it is because the immediate concern is with accounting matters, not because taxation is considered unimportant.

17.1 Profit forecasts

No self-respecting management would attempt to manage any organization without producing forecasts, sometimes called 'budgets' or 'plans'. It is possible, and in some circumstances desirable, to distinguish between these terms, but in this context a profit forecast is defined as

> any published estimate of financial results made:
> (a) in advance of completion of financial statements up to publication standard for any expired accounting period;
> (b) for a current (or unexpired) accounting period;
> (c) for a future accounting period.
> The definition extends to include other statements which are not expressed in terms of figures; e.g., 'profits would be somewhat higher than last year'.[1]

Forecasts may be made at any time and for a variety of purposes. It is those that are made under the regulations of the Stock Exchange or the City Code that require a report by an accountant. The regulations require reporting accountants

> (a) to examine and report upon the accounting policies and calculations for the profit forecasts;
> (b) to satisfy themselves that the profit forecasts, so far as the accounting policies and calculations are concerned, have been properly compiled on the footing of the assumptions made.[2]

The forecast and the assumptions on which it is based are the sole responsibility of the directors. The accountants have no responsibility for the assumptions made, although they should not allow an assumption to be published which appears to them to be unrealistic (or one to be omitted which appears to them to be important) without commenting on it in their report.[3] Once again, the accountants will be involved in practice to a larger extent than they would acknowledge publicly. The City Code practice note includes two possibly significant sentences:

> Although the accountants have no responsibility for the assumptions, they will as a result of their review be in a position to advise the company on what assumptions should be listed in the circular and the way in which they should be described. The financial advisors and accountants obviously have substantial influence on the information given in a circular about assumptions.[4]

The Code gives no guidance as to what is meant by the phrase 'assumptions including the commercial assumptions upon which the directors have based their forecast', but the rules do provide examples:

(a) The company's present management and accounting policies will not be changed. [For a company being acquired.]
(b) Interest rates and the bases and rates of taxation, both direct and indirect, will not change materially.
(c) There will be no material change in international exchange rates or import duties and regulations.
(d) Percentage of time lost on building sites, due to adverse weather conditions, will be average for the time of the year.
(e) Turnover for the year will be £1m on the basis that sales will continue in line with levels and trends experienced to date, adjusted for normal seasonal factors; a reduction of £100,000 in turnover would result in a reduction of aproximately £10,000 in the profit forecast.
(f) Beer sales will increase in line with the trend established in the previous year, which corresponds to the national average rate of increase.
(g) An increase of about 10% in subscriptions will be achieved as a result of increases in the prices of certain journals and an increase in the number of subscribers.
(h) Trading results will not be affected by industrial disputes in the company's factories or in those of its principal suppliers.
(i) The current national dock strike will not last longer than six weeks.
(j) The new factory at Inverness will be in full production by the end of the first quarter. A delay of one month would cause the profit forecast to be reduced by £5,000.
(k) Increases in labour costs will be restricted to those recently agreed with the trade unions.
(l) Increases in the level of manufacturing costs for the remainder of the year will be kept within the margin of 2% allowed for in the estimates.
(m) The conversion rights attaching to all the convertible loan stock will be exercised on the next conversion date.[5]

It can be seen that some are more explicit and quantified than others. The guiding rule should be that 'the reader should be able to understand their implications and so be helped in forming a judgement as to the reasonableness of the forecasts and to the main uncertainties attaching to it'.

17.1.1 Practical procedure

The reporting accountant's work falls into three main sections:
1. preliminary considerations, the usual ones for any engagement, purpose, scope and time;
2. review of profit forecast;
3. report.
    The review will require consideration by the accountant of:
1. the nature and background of the company's business;
2. the accounting policies normally followed by the company; it would be a cause for enquiry if they had been changed recently;

3. the assumptions on which the forecast is based; these may be economic and commercial factors relating to industry generally or the specific company;
4. the procedures followed by the company for preparing the profit forecast, including:

   (a) whether the profit forecast under review is based on forecasts regularly prepared for the purpose of management, or whether it has been separately and specifically prepared for the immediate purpose;
   (b) where profit forecasts are regularly prepared for management purposes, the degree of accuracy and reliability previously achieved, and the frequency and thoroughness with which estimates are revised;
   (c) whether the profit forecast under review represents the management's best estimate of results which they reasonably believe can and will be achieved as distinct from targets which the management have set as desirable;
   (d) the extent to which profit forecast results for expired periods are supported by reliable interim accounts;
   (e) the details of the procedures followed to generate the profit forecast and the extent to which it is built up from detailed profit forecasts of activity and cash flow;
   (f) the extent to which profits are derived from activities having a proved and consistent trend and those of a more irregular, volatile or unproved nature;
   (g) how the profit forecast takes account of any material extraordinary items and prior-year adjustments, their nature, and how they are presented;
   (h) whether adequate provision is made for foreseeable losses and contingencies and how the profit forecast takes account of factors which may cause it to be subject to a high degree of risk, or which may invalidate the assumptions (see Practice Note 4);
   (i) whether working capital appears adequate for requirements; normally this would require the availability of properly prepared cash-flow forecasts; and where short-term or long-term finance is to be relied on, whether the necessary arrangements have been made and confirmed;
   (j) the arithmetical accuracy of the profit forecast and the supporting information and whether forecast balance sheets and sources and applications of funds statements have been prepared—these help to highlight arithmetical inaccuracies and inconsistent assumptions.[6]

All of these are important, but it is being increasingly recognized that managerial purposes require continuously updated forecasts, so that item (b) above will be increasingly relevant.

17.1.2   Future developments

While the results of the past have a role to play, most users of published financial statements would like to receive a more quantified estimate of the future than is customarily made available. However, there has been an understandable reluctance by management to publish one. 'The failure of a profit forecast is not prima facie evidence of negligence since there is usually a substantial element of uncertainty how events will turn out.'[7]

The review of early forecasts[8] does not indicate any insuperable problems. The discipline of providing a quantified forecast which would subsequently be compared with the achieved results together with reasons for variations would ensure that management follow appropriate procedures. Some would argue that such forecasts are already produced for internal management and that it is the reluctance to provide information for competitors that prevents publication.

17.2   Accountants' report in prospectus

A prospectus in the case where listing is sought for a company, no part of whose capital is already listed, 'should include an accountant's report with respect to the company and its subsidiaries on profits and losses, balance sheets and certain other matters'.[9] The basic contents of the report are those items that are customarily disclosed in the normal financial statements of a company, including

(a) profit and loss statements (normally for each of the preceding five years);
(b) balance sheets at the end of each of the five immediately preceding accounting periods reported upon;
(c) statements of source and applications of funds for each period reported upon;
(d) the accounting policies followed; and
(e) any other matters which appear to be relevant for the purposes of the report.

17.2.1   Current reports

Current reports are much more complex, reflecting the more complex world of finance, regulation and reporting requirements that now influence accounting. The major requirements currently include

(a) five years' balance sheets, profit and loss accounts and statements of source and applications of funds;
(b) more information regarding accounting policies;
(c) disclosure of investments and proposed investments, including methods of financing.

17.2.2   Adjustments

Reports are prepared 'after making such adjustments as we consider necessary'. The statement of adjustments signed by the reporting accountants, setting out the adjustments made by them and giving the reasons therefore, is available for public inspection. 'The accountant's report is necessarily confined to past results. . . . It may therefore be necessary, in order that the trend of past profits may be fairly presented having regard to the purposes of the prospectus, either to make appropriate comments thereon or to adjust the figures.'[10]

The circumstances in which adjustments are usually required arise from

(a) new information;
(b) material sources of revenue or categories of expenditure which are not expected to recur;
(c) material change in accounting principles applied in the accounts.

Particular examples of new information are actual contract prices where provisional ones were used originally, deferred repairs, and bad or doubtful debts. Where material, the correct credit or charge for each year should reflect the new information. Changes in sources of income arising from the acquisition of a business by means of an issue of share or loan capital may require an adjustment to include the profits in respect of the years prior to acquisition,[11] although a similar adjustment would not be necessary if it were acquired out of existing or internally generated resources; similarly with disposal of businesses or sections thereof. Appendix 2 of the ICAEW's 'Prospectuses and the Reporting Accountant' provides examples of changes in group structure that might be the cause of adjustments.[12]

There may have been changes in commercial agreement, e.g. for directors' remuneration, and if material, an indication of the difference should be given. Adjustments should be made in respect of any items that affect the profit and loss account but have not been dealt with through that account. Although significant in 1953 (before accounting standards), this should be less likely now. The major adjustments may be due to changes in accounting policies and principles which have been fairly frequent following the accounting standards programme, e.g. stock valuation and research and development following the implementation of the accounting standards that have been issued, usually three or four each year. The appropriate standards for the report will normally be those relevant to the last financial period reported upon, and wherever possible appropriate adjustments should be made to show the results of all periods in accordance with such standards.

It is not surprising that fixed assets recorded at historic cost caused many adjustments. Guidance on this subject was first issued in 1949.[13] This was concerned with the misleading impression that could be obtained if the fixed assets were revalued to reflect their current value without drawing attention to the correspondingly increased depreciation charges that would be necessary in the future. This was in the days before the disclosure of the accounting policies used in the annual report, and it was recommended that, 'If material to the presentation of the figures, the amounts charged for depreciation in the years under review should be stated in the report.'[14]

17.2.3   Summary

The prospectus is required under statutory regulations; the Companies Act 1985 states the information required. Much of it concerns general information relating to share capital, directors, auditors and promoters, as well as to the report by the accountant which has been discussed above.

17.3   Changes in capital structure

A reconstruction could mean almost any change in the capital structure of a company. There is a legal distinction made in the Companies Act 1985 between a capital reduction achieved under s. 135 by means of a special resolution subsequently confirmed by the Court and a reconstruction whereby a liquidator has power (s. 582) to accept shares in another company (often a new one) as consideration for sale of the property of the old company. Both are considered in the following sections.

Other changes in capital structure include the redemption of preference shares, the forfeiture of shares and the conversion of loan stock or preference shares into ordinary shares. The guiding factor in these redemptions and conversions is that the creditors of the company are not placed in a worse position regarding their security. This is achieved by requiring capitalization of distributable profits unless additional share capital is received to match the monies paid out for the redemption.

The entries following conversion of other securities into ordinary shares are 'Dr Old security'; 'Cr Ordinary share's'; 'Cr Share premium'. If the new ordinary shares are valued at their current market value, the share premium could be substantial and in excess of the nominal value of the securities being converted. This would produce a profit, but it is more likely that the share premium account will merely be credited with the difference between the nominal values of the respective securities.

17.3.1   Capital reduction

Reduction of capital is a relatively rare event and one that gives rise to relatively straightforward accounting entries. the preparation of the scheme usually requires much negotiation and the approval of the Court, which will consider the protection of the rights of creditors; an equitable sharing of the loss among various classes of shareholders must also be obtained.

The necessity for a scheme usually arises when the issued capital is not represented by available assets owing to trading losses, or catastrophic change affecting the value of fixed assets. The accounting entries are needed to reduce the capital, reserve and appropriate asset accounts. These changes will be reflected in a new account, called a 'capital reduction account', in which the entries will balance out.

17.3.2   Purchase of own shares

This is a form of capital reduction, but one that usually takes place for one or two major reasons. The company may have cash available for investment and consider the purchase of its own quoted shares, or a private company shareholder may wish to sell and the company and other shareholders agree that the company should purchase the shares. The Companies Act 1981 provided the original permission, and the current legislation is included in the 1985 Act, s. 162–181.

The first requirement for a company to purchase its own shares is that its articles of association must give it this power. There must also be approval by the shareholders for a general power to buy in the market or specific approval for an off-market purchase. Own shares purchased by a UK company must be cancelled; there is no provision for them to be held for subsequent resale, as there is in the USA.

GEC was one of the first UK quoted companies to obtain and use this power. In the accounts for the year ended 31 March 1985 the Directors' Report gave a summary of the transactions in which 73, 254, 067 shares of 5p each (nominal value £3,662,703) where purchased for £156,484,159. The accounting entries were:

Dr	Profit and loss distributable reserve	£156.5m	
Cr	Cash		£156.5m
Dr	Share capital ordinary shares	3.7m	
Cr	Capital redemption reserve		3.7m

17.3.3   Reconstruction

The accounting entries in this case will be similar to those used for sale of a business to a new company and those used in a capital reduction. Consider the following situation.

Over the past few years, N.M. Ltd, which trades in a highly competitive market, has suffered heavy and increasing losses due to inefficient production methods. A new chief executive has recently been appointed who considers that the company could trade profitably provided that additions to plant are made at a cost of £100,000 and that additional working capital of £48,500 is obtained. Projections based on unit costs at various levels of output indicate that N.M. Ltd will, following the investment programme proposed, become a competitive manufacturer in the market, and it is estimated that a small profit of £17,000 before taxation will be earned in the first year of operation of the new plant, followed by a steady build-up of profitability as the plant becomes fully operational. The company's bankers are sympathetic to the proposals but are unwilling to increase their facilities to N.M. Ltd until further finance has been raised by an appropriate reconstruction of capital.

Additional information:

1.   Summarised balance sheet of N.M. Ltd, as at 31st March 19X8

	£'000s	£'000s
Fixed assets:		
Property at valuation on 31 March 19X8		142
Plant and equipment, at net book value		284
		426
Goodwill		183
Current assets:		
Stock and work-in-progress	350	
Debtors	495	
	845	
less: Current liabilities:		
Bank overdraft (unsecured)	278	
Creditors	510	
	788	
		57
		666

Financed by:
Share capital, authorised, issued and fully paid:

	£'000s	£'000s
5% (actual) non-cum. preference shares of £1 each		269
Ordinary shares of £1 each		538
		807
Reserves:		
Capital	33	
Revenue (debit balance)	(174)	
		(141)
		666

2. The estimated going concern value of the plant and equipment is £189,000.
3. On liquidation –
   (a) preference shareholders do not have priority as to capital; no dividend has been paid on these shares for the past four years; and
   (b) it is estimated that shareholders would receive 30p in the £1.
4. Expenses of reconstruction are estimated at £5,000.

(Based on ICA Scotland, Part II, Paper 2)

One scheme of reconstruction that has been proposed (and there are several alternatives) is that the existing preference and ordinary shareholders should share in the loss pro rata to their shareholdings and subscribe for new ordinary shares, again on a pro rata basis, at par, in the proportion of one new share for every 5.38 shares held originally. The journal entries to record these matters would be

		£'000s	£'000s
Dr	Capital reserve	33	
Cr	Reconstruction account		33
	(being elimination of this reserve)		
Dr	Reconstruction account	95	
Cr	Plant and machinery		95
	(being the reduction of the net book value to the estimated going concern value at this date)		
Dr	Reconstruction account	183	
Cr	Goodwill		183
	(being the elimination of goodwill which in the described circumstances is unlikely to exist)		
Dr	Reconstruction account	174	
Cr	Revenue reserve		174
	(being elimination of adverse balance at this date)		
Dr	Reconstruction account	5	
Cr	Cash		5
	(being payment of expenses)		
Dr	Preference shares	141	
	Ordinary shares	283	
Cr	Reconstruction account		424
	(being sharing of the loss among the preference and ordinary shareholders)		

Note 1 Nothing was said about the value of debtors and stock and work in progress, so it has not been written down. In most practical situations both would be examined with care to ensure that

they were worth the stated amounts. If any reduction were found to be necessary, that would be transferred to the reconstruction account and would increase the amount to be written off the share capital.

Note 2   The total loss of £(95 + 183 + 174 + 5 − 33),000 totalling £424,000 is borne proportionately by the preference and ordinary shareholders, but note the very poor preferential terms 'enjoyed' by the preference shareholders—no priority as to capital and non-cumulative dividends.

$$424 \times 269/807 = 141,333, \text{ leaving } 127,667, \text{ say } 141,000 \text{ and } 128,000$$
$$424 \times 538/807 = 282,667, \text{ leaving } 255,333, \text{ say } 283,000 \text{ and } 255,000$$

The appropriate legal resolutions would be necessary to restore the authorized share capital.

Dr	Cash	150	
Cr	Ordinary shares		150
	(being the issue of ordinary shares to provide new finance for additions to plant £100,000 and increased working capital of say £50,000)		

The new balance sheet would be

	£'000s	£'000s
Fixed assets		
Property at valuation on 31 March 19X8		142
Plant and equipment at valuation 31 March 19X8		189
		331
Current assets		
Stock and work in progress	350	
Debtors	495	
Cash	145	
	990	
less Current liabilities		
Bank overdraft (unsecured)	278	
Creditors, include	510	
	788	
		202
		533
Financed by:		
Share capital		
Issued and fully paid shares of £1 each		
5% non-cumulative preference	128	
Ordinary shares	405	
		533

The ledger accounts can be prepared by the reader to confirm the balances. There is nothing unusual about them.

If a new company had been formed to take over the assets and the liabilities of the old one, there would have been a realization account in the old company's book, and the usual entries for the acquisition and starting up of a new business in the books of the new company.

It is customary during the negotiation stage to show, for the various groups of creditors, shareholders and debenture holders (where appropriate), the extent of the losses being borne by each group. Usually ordinary shares have to be offered to the other groups as compensation for their giving up or deferring an existing right to interest or immediate payment.

Notes

1. 'Accountants' Reports on Profit Forecasts', ICAEW, 1978, para. 1 (originally as S. 23, now 3.918, in ICAEW Members Handbook).
2. Ibid., para. 14.
3. 'City Code', practice note no. 7, para. 5.
4. Ibid., para. 5.
5. Ibid., para. 15.
6. 'Accountants' Reports on Profit Forecasts', para. 27.
7. A. Johnson, *The City Takeover Code*, Oxford University Press, 1980, p. 113.
8. S. Dev, 'Problems in interpreting prospectus profit forecasts', *Accounting and Business Research*, Spring 1973.
9. 'Prospectuses and the Reporting Accountant', ICAEW, 1986 (3.142 in ICAEW Members Handbook or 7.4.12 in CACA Handbook).
10. 'Accountants' Reports for Prospectuses: Adjustments and Other Matters', ICAEW, 1953, para. 2 (originally N. 16 but now 3.914 in ICAEW Members Handbook).
11. Ibid., para. 25.
12. 'Prospectuses and the Reporting Accountant', paras. 73 to 76.
13. 'Accountants' Reports for Prospectuses: Fixed Assests and Depreciation', ICAEW, 1949.
14. Ibid., para. 9.

Further reading

Admission of Securities to Listing (The Yellow Book), Stock Exchange, London, 1984.

'Accountants' Reports on Profit Forecasts', ICAEW, 1978 (originally as S. 23, now 3.918 in ICAEW Members Handbook).

'Accountants' Reports on Prospectuses: Adjustments and Other Matters', ICAEW, 1953 (originally as N. 16, now 3.914 in ICAEW Members Handbook, withdrawn January 1987).

'The City Code on Take-overs and Mergers', Council for the Securities Industry, 1985 (available from The Secretary, Issuing House Association, Granite House, 101 Cannon Street, London EC4N 5BA).

Gee, P., 'Stock Exchange documents: the reporting accountant's role', *Accountancy*, July 1979.

McDonald, B. C., 'Capital reconstructions: are they really necessary?', *Accounting and Finance*, May 1980.

Published Profit Forecasts: Current Practices in Canada, the United Kingdom and the United States, Accountants International Study Group, 1974.

'Prospectuses and the Reporting Accountant', ICAEW, 1986 3.412 in ICAEW Members Handbook and 7.4.12 in CACA Handbook.

Westwick, C. (ed.), 'Profit forecasts: how they are made, reviewed and used', Gower, Farnborough, 1982.

Questions

1. Define a prospectus. State the usual contents to be found therein.
2. Describe the normal contents of an accountant's report included in a prospectus. What is the purpose of the report?
3. Why should an accountant be required to report on a profit forecast?
4. Current trends in relation to disclosure of a greater amount of information relating to public companies often result in the publication of figures relating to future as well as past performance.

   You are required to–
   (a) distinguish briefly between the following:
       (i)   profit target,
       (ii) profit forecast,
       (iii) profit budget;   (6 marks)
   (b) discuss the factors which may be expected to affect the reliability of a profit forecast;   (10 marks)
   (c) state briefly how it would be possible to indicate, for the benefit of the users of profit forecasts, the expected degree of accuracy of such forecasts.   (6 marks)
                                                                              (22 marks)
                                                        ICA Ireland, PE II, 4, Summer 1976

5. (a) Set out below are the summarised balance sheets of A plc and B Ltd at 30 June 1985.

	A £'000s	B £'000s
Capital and reserves		
Called up share capital		
£1 ordinary shares	300	300
Share premium account	60	60
Profit and loss account	160	20
	520	380
Net assets	520	380

On 1 July 1985 A plc and B Ltd each purchased 50,000 of their own ordinary shares as follows:
A plc purchased its own shares at 150p each. The shares were originally issued at a premium of 20p. the redemption was partly financed by the issue at par of 5,000 10% redeemable preference shares of £1 each.
B Ltd purchased its own shares out of capital at a price of 80p each.

Required:
Prepare the summarized balance sheets of A plc and B Ltd at 1 July 1985 immediately after the above transactions have been affected.   **(7 marks)**
   (b) What advantages are there in allowing companies to purchase their own ordinary shares? (8 marks)
                                                                              (15 marks)
                                                        ACCA, 2.8, RFA, June 1986

6. The summarised balance sheets of three companies at 30 June 1985 were:

	Derby Ltd £'000s	Exeter Ltd £'000s	Falkirk Ltd £'000s
Freehold property	—	345	—
Plant	127	98	86
Stocks and work in progress	756	395	393
Debtors	410	535	387
Bank balance	78	—	136
Creditors	(946)	(568)	(860)
Bank overdraft	—	(497)	—
Shares in Derby Ltd at cost	—	126	—
Shares in Falkirk Ltd at cost	26	34	—
	451	468	142
Capital—Preference	100	—	—
—Ordinary	200	400	100
Profit and Loss account	151	68	42
	451	468	142

Before going public, the beneficial owners of all three companies, Mr and Mrs Wise, wish to reorganise them into a group structure and have decided that they will choose as the parent company the one with the largest value per ordinary share. In implementing such a scheme, the following points are relevant:

(1) The freehold property should be revalued to £400,000.
(2) The plant in Derby Ltd should be written down to £100,000.
(3) The shares held by two of the companies were acquired at par and all shares have a nominal value of £1 each.
(4) The dividends have been paid regularly on the preference shares, which are held by Mrs Wise, and the yield at par is in line with market rates.
(5) Apart from the above, all assets and liabilities are fairly stated and the companies may be considered to be worth their net assets including the revised values with no addition for goodwill.
(6) Once the parent company is identified, it will purchase all the shares it does not already own directly in the other two companies at their net asset value for cash. Mr and Mrs Wise hold all the shares not held within the three companies.
(7) The bankers to the companies have intimated that they will restrict the net group overdraft to £300,000. In the event that further funds are required Mr Wise has agreed to leave such shortfall on loan.

Requirements

(a) Set out concisely, and supported by workings, the steps necessary to implement a scheme of reorganisation to meet the wishes of Mr and Mrs Wise.   (11 marks)
(b) Produce the summarised consolidated balance sheet after the reorganisation.   (10 marks)
                                                                                          (21 marks)

NOTE: Make all calculations to the nearest £'000 and ignore taxation and any costs.

                                                                          ICAEW, PE II, FA II, July 1985

7. Saltaire Ltd is seeking a Stock Exchange quotation. The profit and loss accounts given below are to form the basis of the information to be included in the accountant's report.

	19X1 £000's	19X2 £000's	19X3 £000's	19X4 £000's	19X5 £000's
Turnover	2,350	3,200	4,200	5,700	7,150
Profit before tax	190	310	315	480	540
After charging:					
Depreciation	65	78	160	150	180
Directors' remuneration	90	95	100	110	125
	155	173	260	260	305
After crediting:					
Investment income	40	35	42		
Share of associated company profits	—	—	—	90	100
Total profit before tax	190	310	315	570	640
Corporation tax					
Group	70	180	195	280	300
Associated company	—	—	—	45	50
Profit after tax	120	130	120	245	290

In addition, you are given the following information:

(i) Changes in accounting policy
     – from 1/1/X4 Saltaire's investment in shares, which had produced investment income, was treated as an associated company; the balance on reserves at 1/1/X4 was credited with £140,000, representing retained profits of the associate of £35,000, £50,000 and £55,000 in 19X1, 19X2 and 19X3, respectively
     – from 1/1/X3 depreciation is charged on buildings, £60,000 being charged in 19X3, £40,000 of which represented charges of £20,000 for each of the preceding two years.

(ii) the directors have agreed that an immediate increase of 20% in their own salaries and fees should be effected reflecting their position in the management of a publicly quoted company.

You are required to

(a) prepare a summary of profits for inclusion in the accountant's report for Saltaire Ltd: (16 marks)
(b) explain the need for adjustments to accounts for the purposes of a prospectus, making reference to any adjustment(s) carried out in (a) above.   (11 marks)
                                                                                          (27 marks)

Appendix 1. Abbreviations used for accounting bodies and their pronouncements

AAA	American Accounting Association
ACCA	Chartered Association of Certified Accountants (sometimes abbreviated as CACA)
ACT	Advance Corporation tax
AICPA	American Institute of Certified Public Accountants
AISG	Accountants International Study Group
APB	Accounting Principles Board
ARS	Accounting Research Study
ASC	Accounting Standards Committee
ASSC	Accounting Standards Steering Committee (now known as the Accounting Standards Committee)
CACA	see ACCA
CCAB	Consultative Committee of Accounting Bodies
CICA	Canadian Institute of Chartered Accountants
CIMA	Chartered Institute of Management Accountants (formerly ICMA, Institute of Cost and Management Accountants)
CIPFA	Chartered Institute of Public Finance and Accountancy
E	Exposure Draft (International)
ED	Exposure Draft (UK)
FASB	Financial Accounting Standards Board
IAS	International Accounting Standard
IASC	International Accounting Standards Committee
ICA Ireland	Institute of Chartered Accountants in Ireland
ICAEW	Institute of Chartered Accountants in England and Wales
ICAS	Institute of Chartered Accountants in Scotland
ICMA	Institute of Cost and Management Accountants
SFAS	Statement of Financial Accounting Standard
SORP	Statement of Recommended Practice
SSAP	Statement of Standard Accounting Practice

Appendix 2.   Sources of examination questions

ACCA
   AAP   Advanced Accounting Practice
   AFA   Advanced Financial Accounting
   RFA   Regulatory Framework of Accounting

ICAEW
   FA I   Financial Accounting I
   FA II   Financial Accounting II
   PE II   Professional Examination II

Index